T0354763

THEY
FORSAKE
THEIR
OWN
MERCY

THEY FORSAKE THEIR OWN MERCY

Elvis Cardell Banks

THEY FORSAKE THEIR OWN MERCY

iUniverse books may be ordered through booksellers or by contacting:

iUniverse
1663 Liberty Drive
Bloomington, IN 47403
www.iuniverse.com
1-800-Authors (1-800-288-4677)

ISBN: 978-1-5320-0444-5 (sc)
ISBN: 978-1-5320-0443-8 (e)

Library of Congress Control Number: 2016914721

Print information available on the last page.

iUniverse rev. date: 1/26/2017

Scripture taken from the King James Version of the Bible.

CONTENTS

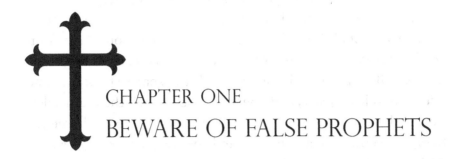

CHAPTER ONE

BEWARE OF FALSE PROPHETS

Jesus Christ, the King of kings, opened the eyes of the blind, healed the sick, raised the dead, and set the captives free. He was in the world, and the world was made by Him. His kingdom, however, was not of this world. In this world, He was despised and rejected of men. The people of the world were wicked, and wicked leaders conspired with their wicked followers to destroy the Holy One.

At the time of Jesus' birth, the Romans had militarily invaded and occupied the Jews' sovereign territory. The Jews had been overtaken by a corrupt power. A Roman officer, King Herod, when told that the King of the Jews had been born, ordered the slaughter of all the Jewish children two years old and under in Bethlehem, and surrounding areas. An astounding number of innocent babies were killed. *(Matthew 2:16-18)* Pontius Pilate, a Roman governor, commanded his men to cut off the head of John the Baptist, a prophet of the Lord. *(Matthew 14:1-10)* Roman leaders were ruthless, evil men.

Jesus was delivered to the Romans to be killed. Herod and Pilate disliked each other. Yet, despite their wicked and depraved hearts, Jesus was such a holy man, until neither could find a reason to kill Him. They laid aside their differences and joined forces in an attempt to save Jesus from death. *(Luke 23:12)* Further, Pilate's wife knew Jesus was an innocent man and admonished her husband not to participate in any evil against Him. *(Matthew 27:19)*

Pilate reminded the Jews that, according to Jewish custom, it was traditional during the Passover to release one man from death. There were several men condemned to die, including some thieves. Pilate presented the Jews with the sharpest contrast: he offered to release Jesus, a divine man who had fed the multitudes, caused the lame to walk, and cast out devils; or he could release Barabbas, a notorious murderer and robber. *(Luke 23:18-19; John 18:40)* Despite Pilate's nudge, Jewish leaders encouraged the people to ask for the release of Barabbas; they demanded that Christ be killed. *(Matthew 27:23)*

What type of satanic leaders could be so cruel and barbaric that they would encourage their followers to save the life of an evil man in order to destroy the life of a holy man? Preachers – men who professed to have been sent by God. *(Matthew 27:20; Matthew 23:2)*

The scribes and Pharisees were the foremost spiritual leaders in Jerusalem. Each Sabbath day, they read the scriptures and professed to teach the word of God. They recounted how Moses delivered the Hebrews out of the bondage of Egypt, and observed that God had prophesied that He was going to raise up another prophet like Moses. They quoted the prophet Isaiah, who foretold that a virgin was going to conceive and bring forth a son, who would be God with the people. Although they had read and taught from the word of God, the spiritual leaders suborned perjury and spearheaded the death of the Son of God.

The Jews lived in spiritual bondage. Jesus saw the misery among the people, had mercy upon them, and came to set them free. However, the scribes and Pharisees believed they were teaching the truth of God and perceived Jesus as a threat to their ministries. They could not deny Jesus' miracles, yet He made statements that sounded like ridiculous lies and performed works that contravened Jewish tradition. For example, Jesus worked on the Sabbath day, which violated the Law of Moses. He told the people to eat His flesh and drink His blood. He observed that He could rebuild a temple in three days, when it had taken others forty-six years to build the temple. Hostility existed between the One who came to save the people, and those who purported to teach the people how to be saved.

Jesus believed in God; the scribes and Pharisees believed in God; yet their beliefs conflicted. Jesus, the new preacher, attacked the integrity of the scribes and Pharisees, the established preachers: "Woe unto you, scribes and Pharisees, hypocrites! for ye are like unto whited sepulchers, which indeed appear beautiful outward, but are within full of dead men's bones, and of all uncleanness." *(Matthew 23:27)* The people loved the scribes and Pharisees, who were perceived as great men of God. Jesus despised the scribes and Pharisees, whom He perceived as devils. The people believed the scribes and Pharisees were saving souls; Jesus knew that the scribes and Pharisees were damning souls.

The scribes and Pharisees traveled widely on missionary trips to encourage the people to turn from Satan to God. Jesus condemned them: "Woe unto you, scribes and Pharisees, hypocrites! for ye compass sea and land to make one proselyte, and when he is made, ye make him twofold more the child of hell than yourselves." *(Matthew 23:15)* Jesus implied that the scribes and Pharisees were so ignorant, until, rather than turning people from Satan to God, their teaching actually strengthened Satan's power over the people.

Nicodemus, a Pharisee, acknowledged Jesus' miracles and admitted Jesus had come from God. He went to see Jesus. During their discussion, Jesus observed, unless a man was born again of the water and of the spirit, he could not enter the Kingdom of God. Nicodemus asked, "How can a man be born when he is old? can he enter the second time into his mother's womb, and be born?" *(John 3:4)* Jesus answered, that which is born of the flesh is flesh, and that which is born of the spirit is spirit. *(John 3:6)*

The prophet Joel had prophesied that God would pour out His spirit upon all flesh. *(Joel 2:28)* The prophet Hosea had prophesied that God would ransom the people from the grave. *(Hosea 13:14)* However, Nicodemus did not understand how a man could be born again. "Nicodemus answered and said unto him, How can these things be? Jesus answered and said unto him, Art thou a *master* of Israel, and knowest not these things?" *(John 3:9-10)* Jesus asked him, are you a *teacher* of the chosen people of God and do not understand the things of God? Those who teach the word of God should understand the things of God.

Nicodemus was sincere in his questioning and truly did not understand Jesus' teaching. Like the other scribes and Pharisees, Nicodemus taught from the scriptures but did not understand the scriptures. They had not been sent by God to teach. Therefore, their teaching was not inspired by the Holy Spirit but was based upon the natural understanding of corrupt men. Since the carnal mind could not discern the things of the spirit, the scribes and Pharisees misinterpreted the words of God and deceived the people.

Jesus observed that the people could not enter the Kingdom of God without being born again. The people had gone into the captivity of sin because of the lack of knowledge, and they would remain in captivity unless someone with knowledge taught them how to escape. If the people remained in captivity, they would be destroyed. Those in captivity did not have masters who had been sent from God. Their masters had been sent by Satan. The preachers—those who taught the people—were ignorant and did not have the knowledge to deliver the people out of captivity. It was not a surprise that the preachers persuaded the people to destroy the Savior and to save the destroyer. As blind leaders, the scribes and Pharisees helped Satan to destroy the people of God.

The false prophets, established leaders in the community, used their influence to persuade their followers to reject Christ. When Pontius Pilate asked the Jews, in accordance with their custom, which prisoner they preferred to be released, the scribes and Pharisees directed the people to ask for the release of Barabbas. Preachers despised Jesus Christ and had Him killed.

The Romans mocked Jesus. They placed a crown of thorns on his head and hung a sign above him that read, "King of the Jews." The battle-tested soldiers mocked the little man who dared to believe that he could set the people free. They did not know that Jesus had not come to deliver the Jews from Roman occupation. Jesus' kingdom was not of this world; His kingdom was spiritual. Jesus' servants were not of this world; His people were spiritual. Jesus' battle was not against natural wickedness; His battle was against spiritual wickedness. Jesus had come to set His people free from sin and deliver them from the power of Satan.

——— **Famous in the Congregation, Men of Renown** ———

If the scribes' and Pharisees' malicious conspiracy against Jesus Christ were the only example of the evil done by false prophets, their mendacity would be of little concern to us. After all, Jesus purposely came into the earth to die for the sins of the people. As a holy man, He would not have committed any act worthy of death. It was, therefore, necessary for Him to be wrongfully put to death. However, the conspiracy against Christ was not the first time that so-called "men of God" led their followers to fight against God.

Egypt was once the most powerful kingdom on earth. The king (Pharaoh) was exalted as a god, and everyone was subject to him. The Egyptians enslaved the Hebrews, the chosen people of God, and kept them in bondage for circa 400 years. At the appointed time, God sent Moses to bring the people out of captivity. An estimated 600,000 men left Egypt, along with an unknown number of women and children. *(Exodus 12:37)* While the scripture does not tell us exactly how many boys left Egypt, it tells us that out of all the Hebrew men and boys that left Egypt, only two—Joshua and Caleb—made it into the Promised Land. *(Deuteronomy 1:34-38)* False teachers persuaded the people to rebel against God—and the Lord destroyed them.

"And they rose up before Moses, with certain of the children of Israel, two hundred and fifty princes of the assembly, famous in the congregation, men of renown: and they gathered themselves against Moses and against Aaron, and said unto them, Ye take too much upon you, seeing all the congregation are holy, every one of them, and the Lord is among them: wherefore then lift ye up yourselves above the congregation of the Lord?" *(Numbers 16:2-3)*

The false teachers in Egypt—spiritual leaders—were men of distinction. To have acquired their fame and renown, the princes had undoubtedly articulated a profound understanding of the slaves' problems and expressed great sensitivity to their burdens. During times of great distress, they had motivated and encouraged the people. Nonetheless, despite all of the false prophets' inspiring homilies and positive platitudes, the Hebrews had remained Egyptian slaves. The false teachers had neither the power nor the knowledge to deliver the people out of bondage.

The envious false teachers wrongly accused Moses of exalting himself above the congregation. In truth, Moses had refused to be called the son of Pharaoh's daughter and abdicated his right to be an Egyptian ruler. He knew the Egyptians were corrupt, refused to go along with their corruption, and had purposed in his heart to deliver the Hebrews out of bondage. He had no desire to rule over anyone. Moses had moved on with his life and did not want to return to Egypt. God sent Moses to Egypt, which was evidenced by the slaves' subsequent deliverance.

The false teachers persisted. They told Moses that all the members of the congregation were holy. In reality, the Egyptians had emasculated the Hebrews, corrupted their minds, and transmuted them into slaves. The slavemasters had taught the Hebrews how to empower Egypt and, by extension, weaken themselves. Slaves who wanted to survive were forced to obey Egyptian commands and labored under heavy burdens. Rather than holy, as the false teachers alleged, the corrupt Hebrews sacrificed their integrity and strengthened their own enemies. If the Lord had been among them, they would not have been slaves.

Later, after the Hebrews made it to the border of the Promised Land, 10 of the 12 men who had gone to spy out the land encouraged the people to return to Egypt. Since the former slaves knew how to survive in the bondage of Egypt, the false teachers were able to persuade the people to return to slavery than to confront the giants in Canaan. In contrast, Joshua and Caleb reported that, with the help of God, the Hebrews were well able to overcome the giants. Most Hebrews, encouraged by false teachers, wanted to stone Joshua and Caleb. The unbelievers did not trust in the Lord and wanted everyone to agree that they should return to Egypt.

The Lord had heard the cry of the children of Israel by reason of their bondage. In His mercy, He had delivered them out of Egypt. The Hebrews' relentless disobedience and desire to return to bondage caused the Lord to turn and fight against them. The Lord destroyed all of the men and boys who had left Egypt, save Joshua and Caleb. *(Numbers 14:1-10; Numbers 26:64-65; Numbers 32:11-12)* False teachers led the children of Israel to forsake their own mercy.

──────────── **The Master is the Teacher** ────────────

Jesus Christ performed many miracles in the earth and provided conclusive evidence that He had come from God. False teachers were able to persuade the people to despise the Son of God. They chose to save the life of a murderer and to crucify the Savior. Moses, a prophet, led the children of Israel out of the bondage of Egypt. False teachers were able to persuade the people to detest and rise up against Moses. They chose to serve as slaves to the Egyptians rather than to reclaim their birthright.

It was not surprising that the Jews in Jerusalem rebelled against Jesus or that the Hebrews in Egypt revolted against Moses. Slavemasters taught slaves how to function as slaves. The corrupt Egyptians, who served false gods, corrupted the minds of their slaves. The entire Hebrew congregation had been slaves. The Hebrew teachers had been taught to be slaves, which is why they thought like slaves. Since they thought like slaves, they lived like slaves. Their followers shared the same slave mentality. Just as Satan blinded the minds of the corrupt scribes and Pharisees, who corrupted the minds of their followers, Pharaoh had corrupted the minds of the Hebrew false teachers, who corrupted the minds of their followers. Hence, the false teachers' message, rather than deliver their followers from the power of their enemies, helped to strengthen the enemies' power over their followers.

In contrast, neither Jesus nor Moses had been raised in slavery. Their liberating thinking did not comport with the slaves' mentality. It was much easier for the people to believe the ignorance of false teachers: Ignorance was all they had ever known. It was much easier for the Hebrews to choose to return to the bondage of Egypt: Slavery was the only life they had ever known. Change required having to confront unknown challenges and fears. Irrespective of Jesus' and Moses' miracles, those who did not have faith in God trusted their own survival skills more than they trusted in the Lord. They preferred to return to Egypt and live as slaves, where, despite the loss of their dignity and integrity, they knew how to survive.

──────────────── **Modern False Prophets** ────────────────

There are billions of people who firmly believe they will spend eternity with God. When individuals die, many families comfort themselves by observing that the person has gone to be with the Lord. Sadly, most individuals will be damned to eternal destruction. Jesus observed that many would say to Him when he returned, Lord, Lord, we have prophesied in your name, and in your name we have cast out devils and done many wonderful works. He will answer, depart from me, ye sinners; I never knew you. *(Matthew 7:23)* False teachers, Satan's messengers, rather than having taught the people how to escape the bondage of sin to serve the Lord, offered lying vanities to the people and deceived them. The false teachers persuaded the people to believe their lies and to ignore the word of God.

Millions of individuals profess to serve the Lord Jesus Christ but remain in the bondage of sin. They believe the corrupt teachings of false prophets who tell them that they are human and cannot live free from sin. "A true witness delivereth souls: but a deceitful witness speaketh lies." *(Proverbs 14:25)* Like the ignorant scribes and Pharisees, these false teachers read the scripture but have no understanding of the scriptures. As a result of their erroneous teachings, their followers—like those who believed the scribes and Pharisees—have unsuspectingly chosen to worship Satan and despise God. Most individuals who profess to be Christians are enemies of Christ.

──────────── **Messengers of the Lord** ────────────

The sins of the people have separated them from God; therefore, God, a spirit, speaks to natural people through natural messengers. From the beginning of time, whenever the Lord wanted to communicate with the people, he would send forth His priests. Similarly, when the people wanted to inquire of the Lord, they would send for the priest. "For the priest's lips should keep knowledge, and they should seek the law at his mouth: for he is the messenger of the Lord of hosts." *(Malachi 2:7)* Priests serve as liaisons between God and His people. For example, Jesus commanded His apostles to go and teach all nations. *(Matthew 28:19)* God commanded Joshua to lead the people into the Promised Land. *(Joshua 1:1-2)* God sends messengers to save the people from their enemies. *(Romans 10:13-15)* Understandably, many people have great confidence in those who profess to have been sent from God.

Satan knows that the most successful con men are those who are most effective in gaining the confidence of the people. Since slaves think like slaves, ignorant false teachers are far more persuasive to ignorant students than teachers who have knowledge. Jesus defeated Satan, yet the Master observed that only a few would enter the gate that leads to eternal life. *(Matthew 7:13-14)* Moses defeated Pharaoh, yet only two males who left Egypt made it into the Promised Land. Neither Satan nor Pharaoh could prevent God from saving the people from their enemies; however, the false prophets could. The false teachers could deceive the people, persuade them to rebel against God, and bewitch the people to destroy themselves. False prophets are God's greatest enemies.

Jesus came to save the people from their sins. *(Matthew 1:21)* The Master did not want the people to be destroyed. Therefore, He warned them to beware of false prophets; they were going to rise up and deceive many. *(Matthew 24:11)* False prophets would convince the people that they had been sent by God and persuade the people to fight against God. False teachers—scribes and Pharisees— persuaded the people to kill the Messsiah. Satan, through the teachings of false prophets, deceived the whole world. *(Revelation 12:9)* "For such are false apostles, deceitful workers, transforming themselves into the apostles of Christ. And no marvel; for Satan himself is transformed into an angel of light." *(2 Corinthians 11:13- 14)* Erudite and eloquent false prophets often appear as ministers of light. According to Jesus Christ, these deceitful workers are going to cause nearly the entire human family to be destroyed. *(Matthew 7:13-15)*

------ **Knowledge is Salvation; Ignorance is Damnation** ------

Through the knowledge of Jesus Christ, sinners will escape the pollution of this world and be sanctified through the truth. *(2 Peter 2:20; John 17:17)* They will be made free from sin. Without the truth, sinners will remain corrupt. Those who reject the knowledge of Jesus Christ will be destroyed. *(Hosea 4:6)* God, holy in all His ways, cannot use corrupt servants. Our salvation or damnation depends upon whether we accept or reject the knowledge of Jesus Christ. To know the truth is to acquire the knowledge of Christ and be saved; to ignore the truth is to remain ignorant of the knowledge of Christ and be destroyed. Satan has sent thousands of false teachers into the world to distort the teachings of Jesus Christ.

Individuals who want to serve the Lord will seek knowledge from their pastors. "And I will give you pastors according to mine heart, which shall feed you with knowledge and understanding." *(Jeremiah 3:15)* Since our knowledge and understanding of God will be based upon what our pastors teach us, if the pastors teach us wrong, our understanding will be wrong. False teaching leads to errors; those who commit errors against the Lord are deceived; and those who are deceived are enemies of God. It was not a coincidence that Saul of Tarsus, a man who was determined to serve God, fought against God. He was a Pharisee and had been deceived. *(Acts 9:5; 1 Timothy 1:13)*

──────── **Where there is No Vision, the People Perish** ────────

"Where there is no vision, the people perish." *(Proverbs 29:18)* Jesus came to save His people from destruction. As the only wise God, He knew who posed danger to the people and consistently condemned the scribes and Pharisees. He warned the people to beware of false prophets and compared such deceivers to wolves in sheep's clothing: Satan used them to lure the sheep away from the shepherd, whereby the wolf would be able to overpower and destroy the helpless sheep. Satan will use false prophets to keep the people separated from the Shepherd of their souls, which will allow him to damn nearly all of God's creation. *(Matthew 7:13-15)*

A vision is only helpful to those who trust the visionary. God presciently saw what would come to pass and warned the people: Satan would use persuasive men and women to convince the people that they were worshipping God when, in fact, the people would be fighting against God. Because deception leads to disobedience, and disobedience leads to destruction, Jesus warned the people to beware of false prophets. Sadly, although Jesus told the people what He saw would come to pass and warned them, the people have ignored the Shepherd's voice. False prophets have deceived nearly the entire world; only a few sheep will be saved.

──────────── **Spiritual Wickedness** ────────────

The apostle Paul told Timothy to flee youthful lust which warred against the soul. Moreover, Paul observed that all that is of the world—the lust of the flesh, the lust of the eyes, and the pride of life—was not of God and was going to be destroyed. Although the flesh is the enemy of the spirit, and the spirit is the enemy of the flesh, Paul did not wrestle against flesh and blood.

Unlike the false prophets, who teach that the people are going to sin because they are human, Paul knew that flesh and blood do not control our behavior. Our minds control our behavior. Those who influence our minds influence our behavior. Ignorance breeds corruption; knowledge precedes redemption. Satan's power resides in sinners' ignorance; therefore, since God sent Paul to turn the Gentiles from darkness to light, from the power of Satan unto God, the apostle wrestled against the rulers of the darkness of this world. *(Ephesians 6:12)* Paul fought against spiritual wickedness— ignorant false teachers who taught lies and kept the people subject to the power of Satan.

Who Hath Believed Our Report?

As human beings, we have been taught practically everything we believe. Our beliefs, even if we do not believe in anything, derive from what we have been taught. The way we live is a reflection of how we think, and how we think is a reflection of what we believe. Our beliefs shape our character. The apostle Paul observed that the people must not have believed in the gospel. Where did he get that idea? They refused to obey God's commandments. "But they have not all obeyed the gospel. For Esaias saith, Lord, who hath believed our report?" *(Romans 10:16)* False teachers deceived the people and caused them to go into captivity. Jesus Christ came and taught the people the truth, which was able to set the people free from sin. Yet the people rejected His teachings and chose to remain in bondage.

The question is still pertinent today: Who believes the word of God? If the people believe, why have they failed to obey the gospel? Paul asked the Galatians, "O foolish, Galatians, who hath bewitched you, that ye should not obey the truth?" *(Galatians 3:1)*

Who taught humans to believe that it was impossible for a

flesh-and-blood being to live a perfect life? Who taught us to believe that we could disobey the commandments of God, yet still enter the Kingdom of God? Who taught us to believe that God loved us unconditionally? Who taught us to believe that our works do not determine whether we are saved or destroyed? Who taught us to believe that once we were saved, we were always saved? Neither the apostles nor the prophets taught such nonsense.

If asked, who is your master, most professed Christians would answer, "God is my master." That cannot be true; Jesus never taught the aforementioned lies. Jesus said anyone who professed to be His disciple and walked in darkness was a liar. Jesus is the light. No one can be a disciple of the Master and be deceived. No one can follow the Master and live in sin. Jesus Christ, who came to set His people free from sin, leads His people in the path of righteousness.

Jesus sent apostles to teach all nations and to admonish the people to obey all that He had commanded them. *(Matthew 28:19-20)* Most contemporary false prophets teach their disciples that they cannot live a perfect life, which is an unspoken way of teaching the people that they are not expected to obey all of God's commandments. Just as the false teachers enticed the children of Israel to rebel against God and return to the bondage of Egypt, modern-day false teachers are tacitly telling the people to reject the knowledge of Jesus Christ and remain in the bondage of sin. If the preachers were messengers of Christ, they would teach the people how to come out of bondage and be made free from sin. It is the priests' responsibility, as God's messengers, to teach the people how to overcome their enemies. It is the pastors' duty to feed the sheep and protect them from the wolves. Unfortunately, false prophets have so deceived the people until professed Christians read the Holy Bible, maintain they have been born again of the Holy Spirit, but believe they cannot live a holy life.

Although I will discuss holiness and perfection in greater details later in the book, I want only to reference here how Satan has used false prophets to keep the people in darkness and subject to his power. In the Old and New Testament, Jesus commanded the people to be perfect. *(Deuteronomy 18:13; Matthews 5:48; James 1:4)* Job was perfect. *(Job 1:1)* Noah was perfect. *(Genesis 6:9)* Daniel was perfect. *(Daniel 6:4)* Not only did the Master tell us, "Be ye therefore perfect, even as your Father which is in heaven is perfect," the scriptures identify men who were perfect. Further, God put apostles, prophets, and others in the church "for the perfecting of the saints," so the holy people could serve their holy God. *(Ephesians 4:12)*

So the question becomes, whose report do the people believe: Do they believe the One who taught that the truth shall make us free? Or those who teach that we cannot be free? Do they believe Jesus who taught to obey all of His commandments? *(Matthew 28:20)* Or do they believe those who teach that, as humans, we are going to sin? Two of the reasons Jesus came into the earth were (1) to bear witness to the truth and (2) to set the captives free. A person who does not believe he can be free from sin does not believe the truth. And that is the purpose of the false prophets: to persuade the people to remain in the bondage of sin.

For example, some false prophets teach that, since the people are saved by grace and not by works, the people do not have to work to be saved. Many false prophets teach that there is nothing people can do to save themselves, lest they should boast. Not only does the scripture tell the people to work out their own salvation, the people are going to be judged according to their works. *(Phillipians 2:12; Revelation 20:12-13; Revelation 22:12)* The whole duty of man is to fear God and keep His commandments. *(Ecclesiastes 12:13)*

Servants are identified by whom they serve. *(Romans 6:16)* Those who serve God *(workers of righteousness)* do the works of Christ and obey God's commandments. Those who serve Satan *(workers of iniquity)* do the works of Satan and disobey God's commandments. Jesus characterized servants as children. *(John 8:34; John 8:39; John 8:44)* He identified the children's father by whom they serve. "Ye do the deeds of your father." Those who serve the Lord are children of God. Those who rebel against God are children of Satan. *(John 8:41-44)* Faith without works is dead, and without faith, it is impossible to please God. *(James 2:17-20; Hebrews 11:6)* Who twisted the scriptures to persuade people that their works did not determine their destiny? False prophets.

―――――――――――――― **I Hate Him** ――――――――――――――

There were two kings: Jehoshaphat, the King of Judah, a God-fearing man *(2 Chronicles 17:1-6)*; and Ahab, the King of Israel, a wicked man. *(1 King 16:30)* Since the children of Judah and the children of Israel descended through the lineage of Abraham, Isaac, and Jacob, they were related.

Israel and Syria had experienced three years of peace. The wicked Ahab, however, was not a man of peace. He wanted to enlarge his kingdom and asked Jehoshaphat to join forces with him to invade Syria. They would unite, defeat the Syrians, and prosper. Jehoshaphat was inclined to help Ahab, but he first sought the word of the Lord. *(2 Chronicles 18:4)* He asked if there were any prophets of the Lord in the land. The prophets of the Lord would communicate with God and convey God's response to the kings.

Ahab called forth his prophets, four hundred men, and asked them to consult with God. The king inquired of the Lord to tell whether Israel should wage war against Syria and prosper, or should the people refrain and preserve the peace. All four hundred prophets agreed: God told them to tell the kings, "Go up; for God will deliver it into the king's hand." *(2 Chronicles 18:5)*

One prophet was particularly enthusiastic. Zedekiah, the son of Chenaanah, made a horn of iron for the king. He prophesied, "Thus saith the Lord, With these thou shalt push Syria until they be consumed. And all the prophets prophesied so, saying, Go up to Ramoth-gilead, and prosper: for the Lord shall deliver it into the hand of the king." *(2 Chronicles 18:10-11)*

As a wise man, Jehoshaphat knew men lied, even those who claimed to have been sent from God. He asked, "Is there not here a prophet of the Lord besides, that we might enquire of him?" *(2 Chronicles 18:6)* Ahab answered, "There is yet one man, by whom we may enquire of the Lord: but I hate him; for he never prophesied good unto me, but always evil." *(2 Chronicles 18:7)* The wicked king hated the prophet who refused to tell him what he wanted to hear.

Four hundred prophets agreed that the Lord had spoken positive words about the king, which had Ahab in a great spirit. Nonetheless, in deference to King Jehoshaphat, Ahab sent an officer to fetch the prophet Micaiah from prison. Before they appeared before the kings, the officer told Micaiah that all of the prophets agreed that God guaranteed Ahab victory over the Syrians. The officer advised, "let thy word therefore, I pray thee, be like one of their's, and speak thou good." *(2 Chronicles 18:12)*

From a natural perspective, Micaiah had many incentives to support the groupthink: he could incur favors from the king, possibly secure his release from prison, and return to his family. But men of God are faithful priests and must tell the truth. Despite the officer's coaxing to go along with the false prophets, Micaiah refused to sacrifice his relationship with God. "And Micaiah said, As the Lord liveth, what the Lord saith unto me, that will I speak." *(1 Kings 22:13-14)* It did not matter if the false prophets thought he was self-righteous. It did not matter if the king hated him. It did not matter if he languished in prison. Micaiah was going to obey God.

Ahab asked Micaiah whether he should wage war against Syria or not. Micaiah answered that the Lord wanted the king to go up and prosper. Ahab became annoyed and told the prophet not to mock him. Micaiah had never spoken well about Ahab; the king did not need or want his satire. The king demanded Micaiah to tell him only what the Lord had said. Micaiah disclosed that the Lord had put a lying spirit in the mouth of all of the king's prophets; the prophets had deceived the king. Ahab was not going to go up to Syria and prosper; he was going to go up to Syria and get killed.

Ahab was insulted and greatly unnerved. Four hundred "prophets of God" had agreed that God was going to bless him. One man, Micaiah, came along and implied that God was going to have him killed. The agitated king ordered Micaiah back to prison and told his servants to afflict him. As he was being led back to prison,

Micaiah warned the people, "Hearken, O people, every one of you." *(1 Kings 22:28)* The prophet wanted the people to pay attention to what was about to happen to the wicked king.

God had mercy upon the wicked king and warned him what would happen if he attacked Syria, but stubborn Ahab was determined to expand his kingdom. He refused to allow the fear of God to prevent him from doing what he wanted. Further, he did not want to display a lack of trust in his four hundred prophets; after all, they had appealed to his vanity and prophesied that God was going to bless him. Conversely, he could not cavalierly dismiss Micaiah's prophecy, because the prophet always told the truth. Ahab took precaution and disguised himself. He intended to go unrecognized into the battle, return home safely, and prove that God blessed him.

Sure enough, Ahab disguised himself and went into battle. The Syrians may not have recognized him, but the Lord did. A certain man shot an arrow, and the Lord guided the arrow to a spot where it was able to strike Ahab. The king cried out to the driver of his chariot that he was wounded; take him out of the battle. Micaiah warned Ahab, but the king disregarded God's warning. The wicked king chose to observe the lying vanities of the false prophets and to forsake his own mercy. He died that day. *(1Kings 22:34-35)*

——— **I Have Hated Them That Regard Lying Vanities** ———

God gave Micaiah a vision of what would come to pass, but the king dismissed what the prophet had seen. Ahab would have saved his life had he believed Micaiah. However, the king ignored the messenger who spoke the truth. He chose to observe the lying vanities of the false prophets and lost his life. In a corrupt world, evil men and women do not want to serve the Lord and will persecute those who uphold integrity. Those who promote corruption and deceive the people have a far superior opportunity to succeed. The psalmist observed, "I have hated them that regard lying vanities: but I trust in the Lord." *(Psalm 31:6)* Most people choose to live in denial and remain slaves to corruption rather than trust in the Lord and transform their lives.

Ahab is an example of the wickedness of man. He did not want to hear the truth, but deliberately chose false prophets who told him what he wanted to hear. Further, it was in the false prophets' self-interest to tell the king what he wanted to hear: they received the king's favor. They had wealth and prominence in the community. According to the false prophets' lying vanities, the Lord was going to deliver Ahab's enemies into his hands. Instead, the Lord delivered Ahab into the hands of his enemies. It is an age-old conundrum: rebellious men and women repeatedly disobey the commandments of God, yet are presumptuous enough to believe false prophets' lying vanities that God loves them unconditionally and will save them from death.

Satan's objective is to broadcast lies and silence truth. In his kingdom, corruption is exalted and righteousness denounced. Jesus was despised and rejected of men; false prophets were esteemed in the community. The psalmist hated those who observed lying vanities; he hated to see them engage in self-delusion and destroy themselves.

--------- **Thou Shalt Surely Die** ---------

The Lord commanded the prophet Jeremiah to go and warn the people that He would destroy them if they refused to turn from their wickedness. "Now it came to pass, when Jeremiah had made an end of speaking all that the Lord had commanded him to speak unto all the people, that the priests and the prophets and all the people took him, saying, Thou shalt surely die." *(Jeremiah 26:8)* Think about that: Men who professed to be priests and prophets of God wanted to kill Jeremiah because the prophet warned the people to obey God.

—————— **We Ought to Give the More Earnest Heed** ——————

Satan manipulated his own mind to rebel against God. He manipulated arguably one-third of the angels in Heaven to rebel against God. He manipulated Eve to rebel against God. He knows how to manipulate the mind. All he needs to succeed are messengers who will communicate his lies and people who do not meditate upon the scriptures to see if the messages comport with God's word. "Jesus answered and said unto them, Ye do err, not knowing the scriptures, nor the power of God." *(Matthew 22:29)*

Jesus sent apostles to turn the people from darkness to light, from the power of Satan to the power of God. The apostles will teach the people how to overcome sin. Satan has sent messengers to keep the people in darkness, which, by extension, will keep the people in the bondage of sin. Since the wages of sin is death, those who remain in bondage will be destroyed. "Therefore we ought to give the more earnest heed to the things which we have heard, lest at any time we should let them slip. For if the word spoken by angels was stedfast, and every transgression and disobedience received a just recompence of reward; how shall we escape, if we neglect so great salvation; which at the first began to be spoken by the Lord, and was confirmed unto us by them that heard him." *(Hebrews 2:1-3)*

Jesus commanded His apostles to teach all nations, and commanded the people to obey all of His commandments. *(Matthew 28:19-20)* Just as the words spoken by angels were stedfast and every transgression and disobedience received a just recompence of reward, those who disobey the commandments of God will be rewarded for their disobedience.

—————— **Ye Are as Graves Which Appear Not** ——————

False prophets are destroying billions and billions of souls, and the people have no idea that they are on their way to destruction. Jesus denoted: "Woe unto you, scribes and Pharisees, hypocrites!

for ye are as graves which appear not, and the men that walk over them are not aware of them." *(Luke 11:44)* Jesus warned the people. Moses warned the people. Jeremiah warned the people. Paul warned the people. Peter warned the people. God sent many servants to warn the people, yet the people refuse to question their pastors' teachings, which is exactly why Satan will deceive them.

False prophets have established churches with names such as truth of god, deliverance, overcome, redeemed, and holiness. They are teaching all types of heresy, and their congregants are shouting and clapping in support of such ignorance. Followers are completely unaware they are headed to eternal destruction. "While they promise them liberty, they themselves are the servants of corruption: for of whom a man is overcome, of the same is he brought in bondage." *(2 Peter 2:19)* Satan has the false prophets working for him to keep the people enslaved.

——————————— **That is Your Opinion** ———————————

A common statement offered to reject God's word is that everyone has his or her own personal opinion and interpretation of the scriptures. The statement itself is an indication of ignorance: there are no private interpretations of the scripture. *(2 Peter 1:20)* The same spirit that moved on the prophets to write the Bible is the same spirit that opens up the understanding of those God sends to teach the Bible. The same spirit that opens up the understanding of those God sends to teach the Bible is the same spirit that resides in those who have been born again of the spirit. All of the people of God should be on one accord. God has either opened individuals' understanding that they might understand the scripture, or they have rejected God's knowledge and are on their way to destruction. *(Hosea 4:6; 2 Corinthians 4:3-4)*

God is not the author of confusion. There is only one Lord, one faith, and one Spirit. When the Spirit of Truth comes, it guides the people into all truth. All of those in the body of Christ are perfectly joined together and of one mind. However, the multitudinous religions, denominations, and beliefs among the people bear witness to widespread false teachings and deception.

———————————— **Among the Few** ————————————

The coming of Christ is upon us. Since the Lord does not want anyone destroyed, He does not want anyone deceived. This book cannot possibly address all of the lies of the false prophets; nonetheless, it will debunk some popular lying vanities and errors that false prophets teach to deceive the people. To avoid repetition, I have chosen to discuss some matters in greater details in more pertinent sections of the book. To promote clarity, I have repeated some matters several times to help readers make connections. It should be obvious that when only a few shall be saved, many have been led away by the error of the wicked. *(2 Peter 3:17)*

As you read through the book, many statements that I propound will go against established religious teachings. Such unorthodoxy should be easy to understand: Wide is the gate that leads to destruction. *(Matthew 7:13-14)* A few will be saved because most have been deceived. In order to serve the Lord, we must be willing to change the ways we think. His ways are not our ways; His thoughts are not our thoughts. His ways are mysterious to us, because all of His ways are holy, and the enemy has corrupted our thinking. The Lord needs servants who are not slaves to their ways of thinking but are willing to learn of His ways. The Lord wants servants who are unwilling to follow the lies of their slavemasters, but who want to learn the truth. Within the pages of this book is wisdom and knowledge that can save your soul from an everlasting fire. "O earth, earth, earth, hear the word of the Lord." *(Jeremiah 22:29)*

CHAPTER TWO

CARNAL MIND

A fter the birth of Christ, Herod was troubled when told that the King of the Jews had been born. He ordered the death of all babies in Bethlehem and around the coasts in the hope of killing the deliverer. *(Matthew 2:16-18)* Years later, the Romans paid Judas to identify the deliverer and arrested Jesus. Once the Romans perceived that Jesus had no intention to deliver Jerusalem from Rome, they tried to release Him. The same Herod who had killed arguably hundreds, if not thousands, of babies in a preemptive attempt to destroy Christ, subsequently advocated to save His life.

The scribes and Pharisees read about the coming of the deliverer and undoubtedly rejoiced in anticipation of His coming. Wise men worshipped the prince and bestowed gifts upon Him. When the Messiah entered into Jerusalem one fateful day, many threw palms in the street and shouted "Hosanna!" in adoration of the entering Savior. A few days later, some of those who had rejoiced upon the Savior's arrival cried out, "Away with him, away with him, crucify him." *(John 19:15)* The scribes and Pharisees instigated the death of the Messiah whom they had preached would come and save the people.

———————— **To the Unknown God** ————————

Athens, Greece, was once widely considered the intellectual capital of the world. It was a city known for its great wise men: Socrates, Plato, Aristotle, et al. The Hippocratic Oath, a standard of medical care many physicians swear to uphold, was named after the Greek doctor Hippocrates. The Pythagorean Theorem, a watershed geometric axiom, was named after a Greek mathematician, Pythagoras. The Greeks were well educated and many of their ideas continue to influence modern thinking. Yet, when the apostle Paul visited Athens, his spirit was stirred in him. He found a city filled with pagan beliefs. The people worshipped all types of gods—a god of this, a god of that, and a god of something else. They did not know who or what to worship. Afraid they might have ignorantly omitted a god, they built a monument to an unknown god. *(Acts 17:23)* The Greeks were intellectually gifted in natural matters but woefully ignorant in spiritual matters. The carnal mind could not comprehend the things of God.

Rome would later become an earthly power, and Roman leaders would become men of great admiration. In the West, the Gregorian calendar is used to mark days, weeks, and months. Named in honor of Pope Gregory XIII, the Bishop of Rome, there is not one day, week or month of the calendar named after any person in the Holy Bible. Many of the names are derived from false gods. For example, the first day of the week, Sunday, is named in honor of the sun. The second day of the week, Monday, honors the moon. Tuesday is named after Tiw, the god of combat. The month of January honors Janus, the Roman god of beginnings. March honors Mars, the Greek god of war. July honors Julius Caesar. August honors Augustus Caesar. The Caesars, of course, were Roman emperors who traveled the word and killed innocent people such as Jesus Christ. The prefix Octo means eight, but October is the tenth month. Deca means ten, but December is the twelfth month. Wise people question everything man says. "Cursed be the man that trusteth in man." *(Jeremiah 17:5)*

─────────────── **Theologians** ───────────────

Many preachers received their training in seminary schools. It makes sense from a natural perspective. Lawyers are trained at law schools. Doctors are trained at medical schools. Thus, it seems practical that a teacher of the gospel should acquire seminary training. Future servants of God should be trained in the service of God.

Many seminary-trained preachers utter theological jargon to impress upon their congregation that they attended school to study the word of God. They explain the origin of biblical words and pontificate on the etymology of certain words and their various meaning in Latin, Greek and Hebrew. These "wells without water" use swelling words and appear as ministers of light. *(2 Peter 2:17-18)* Members of their congregation have confidence in the teaching of such learned scholars. The unsuspecting congregants fail to perceive that seminary schools are of the devil.

The United States, for example, has some of the best educational institutions in the world. At some schools, students may be as demonic as Satan but can acquire a theology degree. If they gain admittance to the school and satisfy the required course of study, institutions would certify them to preach the word of God. We are indeed exhorted to study the scripture to confirm that what we are taught is consistent with the word of God. *(Acts 17:11)* However, theology schools are approved by man-made organizations; apostles and prophets are approved by God.

─────────────── **Pagan Practice** ───────────────

A war took place between the people of God, led by Abijah, and a corrupt spiritual people, led by Jeroboam. Jeroboam's followers were deceived and worshipped false gods. *(2 Chronicles 13:6-7)* God asked Jeroboam and those who followed after him: "Have ye not cast out the priests of the Lord, the sons of Aaron, and the Levites, and have made you priests after the manner of the nations of other lands? so that whosoever cometh to consecrate himself with a young bullock and seven rams, the same may be a priest of them that are no gods." *(2 Chronicles 13:9)* Jeroboam and his followers had departed from the way of God and taken up the ways of the heathens. *(2 Chronicles 13:10)* God did not select Jeroboam's priests. The pagans allowed anyone who was willing to pay a young bullock and seven rams to become a priest. It should not surprise anyone that they worshipped gods made up of golden calves. *(2 Chronicles 13:8)* Pagan teachers taught pagan doctrine, so they all engaged in pagan worship.

Similarly, admission officers at seminary schools do not have the authority to select God's priests. It does not matter how much an individual wants to teach the word of God, only God can select his messenger. "For not he that commendeth himself is approved, but whom the Lord commendeth." *(2 Corinthians 10:18)* If God did not send the preacher, the preacher's message did not come from God.

If the false prophets had been sent from God, they would have the knowledge to set the people free. God told Jeremiah: "I have not sent these prophets, yet they ran: I have not spoken to them, yet they prophesied. But if they had stood in my counsel, and had caused my people to hear my words, then they should have turned them from their evil way, and from the evil of their doings." *(Jeremiah 23:21-22)* Rather than teach the people how to overcome sin, theology-school trained teachers tell the people that there is nothing they can do to save themselves. According to the ignorant teachers, the people are saved by grace, not by work, lest any man should boast. The false teachers quote the word of God, but twist God's words to their own—and those that follow them—destruction. *(2 Peter 3:16)*

—————————— **My Doctrine is His that Sent Me** ——————————

Jesus went into the temple and taught. The Jews were surprised at His knowledge; Jesus never studied at seminary school nor learned from false teachers. "Jesus answered them, and said, My doctrine is not mine, but his that sent me." *(John 7:16)* Jesus did not need seminarians to teach Him; He had the Spirit of God. Those trained in seminary schools teach students about God but are not taught by God. Carnal-minded teachers teach carnal-minded students, who convey carnal-minded doctrines to carnal-minded worshippers. The blind lead the blind. Jeroboam's prophets taught paganism, because Satan sent false teachers to deceive the people. Similarly, most people today worship in vain, because Satan has sent false teachers—many trained in seminary schools—to teach spiritual corruption, which is why few are going to enter into eternal life.

Ahab listened to the false prophets and was destroyed. The people listened to Jeroboam's prophets and were destroyed. *(2 Chronicles 13:15-18)* Those who follow the teachings of theology school graduates are going to be destroyed. "The heads thereof judge for reward, and the priests thereof teach for hire, and the prophets thereof divine for money: yet will they lean upon the Lord, and say, Is not the Lord among us? None evil can come upon us." *(Micah 3:11)* Those who taught the people did not teach them the truth. In fact, they could not teach the truth because they did not know the truth. Their objective was to acquire money, so they taught whatever appealed to the people. The Lord destroyed them. *(Micah 3:12)*

--------- **Then Opened He Their Understanding** ---------

It is absurd that a secular school would confer a degree upon a student and offer him to the people as capable of teaching the sacred word of God. God is spirit. Man is natural. God selects His preachers and opens up their understanding that they might correctly understand and explain the scriptures. "Then opened he their understanding, that they might understand the scriptures." *(Luke 24:45)* If preachers were sent by God, they would not need teachers in secular schools to teach them the scriptures; they would go up to the house of the Lord, where God teaches of His ways, and the people learn to walk in His path. *(Isaiah 2:3)*

God teaches facts. False prophets teach theories, which is one reason there are so many different religious beliefs. Those who support theology schools strengthen the credibility of false teachers. Although there is only one faith, theology schools train students to teach different faiths. *(Ephesians 4:5)* Hence, theology school administrators and teachers have no knowledge of what is the truth themselves. Despite their admitted ignorance of the truth, they certify men and women to teach multiple false doctrines; in other words, they may not know what the truth is, but they know that everything they teach cannot be true. Yet, they certify their students to teach lies to unsuspecting worshippers.

Saul of Tarsus

Saul of Tarsus was a Pharisee, a religious leader, who had been taught by an eminent religious scholar—Gamaliel, a doctor of the law, and also a Pharisee. *(Acts 5:34)* Gamaliel commanded great respect among the people and taught Saul the perfect manner of the law. Saul, a dedicated student and sincere seeker of God, was zealous in upholding the traditions of the Jews. *(Galatians 1:14)* He delivered to prisons both men and women who followed after Christ and stood by and encouraged the people to stone the faithful Stephen. *(Acts 22:4; Acts 8:1-2)* Saul wanted to serve the Lord and attended theology school. As a result of his ignorant teaching, Saul fought against God. *(Acts 9:4; Galatians 1:6-16)*

Gamaliel, Saul's teacher, was a preeminent Hebrew scholar. When the apostles were persecuted for teaching the gospel, Gamaliel had no idea whether they were right or wrong. *(Acts 5:33-40)* He had no idea whether Jesus was a prophet or whether the disciples who had walked with Him were men of God. He did not know because God had not called him to teach. Gamaliel had taught the scriptures, although he did not understand the scriptures. Accordingly, students who learned from him were ignorant. The scribes and Pharisees—and other ignorant teachers—taught errors to their students, who taught errors to their followers. All of them were enemies of God. They caused Jesus to be killed and persecuted the church. *(Acts 9:5)*

When God later moved on Paul to certify his gospel, the enlightened apostle did not return to his theology teacher to confirm his certification. He contacted those whom Jesus had chosen—James, Peter, and John. *(Galatians 2:9; John 1:42)* Jesus opened the apostles' understanding and sent them to teach the people. Those whom Jesus sent understood the scripture and taught the people how to be saved. *(Luke 24:45)* Peter was poorly educated but had the keys to the Kingdom of God. *(Acts 4:13; Matthew 16:17)* Gamaliel had a doctorate in theology but taught errors. Saul of Tarsus had been taught by a religious scholar but was spiritually ignorant. *(1 Timothy 1:13)* Those who were taught in theology school persecuted the church and deceived the people. *(Galatians 1:13)*

Those who seek truth have no interest in the personal philosophies and theories of corrupt men. False prophets have gone to theology school, and, like Jeroboam's deceived priests, teach man-made philosophies. Their carnal minds are unable to understand the divinely inspired word of God. "Beware lest any man spoil you through philosophy and vain deceit, after the tradition of men, after the rudiments of the world, and not after Christ." *(Colossians 2:8)* There are ways that seem right to men but they lead to death. *(Proverbs 14:12)* When it comes to the word of God, sincere people want to know only what the Lord says, and they want those who have been taught by God to teach them.

God's ways are not our ways. His thoughts are not our thoughts. The way men think is contrary to the way God thinks. "For to be carnally minded is death; but to be spiritually minded is life and peace. Because the carnal mind is enmity against God: for it is not subject to the law of God, neither indeed can be." *(Romans 8:6-7)* Men read the scriptures and twist the scripture to their own destruction. *(2 Peter 3:16)* It takes God to open up the scripture for human understanding. *(Luke 24:45)* God does not teach in seminary schools. God does not teach anywhere where lies are taught.

─────────── **Blind Leading the Blind** ───────────

God saw the burden placed upon the children of Israel. He had mercy upon them and delivered them out of the bondage of Egypt; however, the children of Israel listened to the false teachers and chose to forsake God's mercy. They preferred to serve the Egyptians and their pagan gods rather than to reclaim their inheritance. God destroyed practically all of them.

Similarly, God saw the wickedness in the earth and the burden Satan imposed upon the people. The Lord had mercy on the people and came into the earth to set the people free from the bondage of sin. Jesus knew how Satan corrupted us, and He knew how we could overcome corruption. He sent pastors to teach the people and to set them free. Satan sent messengers to distort the word of God. False prophets became famous in the congregation, men of renown. They spoke smooth words, positive words, words of motivation and encouragement. The devil knew that positive words without the power of God were not going to defeat him. Inspiring words without the Spirit of God were not going to set the people free. We need the knowledge and power of Jesus Christ to overcome corruption—and we cannot get them through the teachings of the false prophets. The teachings of the false prophets keep us in darkness, subject to the power of Satan, which is why only a few shall enter into the gate that leads to eternal life.

CHAPTER THREE

PARABLES

The Holy Bible is the infallible word of God. We must believe upon the Lord according to what is written in the scriptures. *(John 7:38)* There is one Lord, yet Satan quoted scriptures to induce Jesus to follow him. *(Ephesian 4:5; Matthew 4:9)* There is one faith, yet there are thousands of preachers who quote the same scriptures and have thousands of different beliefs. There is one baptism, yet some preachers baptize in the name of the Father, Son, and Holy Ghost; some baptize in the name of the Lord Jesus Christ; and some say that baptism is not necessary. There is one spirit, yet billions worship various gods.

As the all-wise God, Jesus never taught the multitude, unless He taught in parables. *(Matthew 13:34)* "Therefore speak I to them in parables: because they seeing see not; and hearing they hear not, neither do they understand." *(Matthew 13:13)* It is critical that you understand this: Jesus never preached one message to the multitude to help them understand the word of God. In fact, the apostles did not understand His message until after He was crucified. *(Luke 24:45)* Every sermon Jesus taught to the multitude was designed to confuse the people. Yet God is not the author of confusion. *(1 Corinthians 14:33)*

-------------------------- **Confound Their Language** ---------------------------

The whole earth was once of one language and of one speech. At a certain place, the people agreed to make bricks and build a tower to heaven. "And the Lord said, Behold, the people is one, and they have all one language; and this they begin to do: and now nothing will be restrained from them, which they have imagined to do. Go to, let us go down, and there confound their language, that they may not understand one another's speech." *(Genesis 11:6-7)*

If the false prophets could completely understand the word of God, all the preachers would have comparable understanding. Sincere souls would be unable to distinguish messengers of God from messengers of Satan. The false prophets would twist the scripture just enough to lead the people wrong. Since the Lord does not want anyone to be lost, His sheep must be able to clearly identify His voice. Thus, God wisely used confusing words and confounded the people's language. His sheep know His voice.

-------------------------- **Moses Stuttered** ---------------------------

The Lord appeared as a burning bush on the mountain, and Moses went to investigate. The Lord spoke to Moses and acknowledged He had heard the cry of the children of Israel by reason of their bondage in Egypt. He told Moses to go and deliver the people out of the hands of Pharaoh. "And Moses said unto the Lord, O my Lord, I am not eloquent, neither heretofore, nor since thou hast spoken unto thy servant: but I am slow of speech, and of a slow tongue." *(Exodus 4:10)*

Many false prophets have read Moses' response and taught their followers that, since Moses was slow of speech and of a slow tongue, the prophet had a speech impediment. Some have taught that Moses stuttered. In the Acts of the Apostles, we read, "And Moses was learned in all the wisdom of the Egyptians, and was mighty in words and in deeds." *(Acts 7:22)* Hence, we have two scriptures that seem to contradict each other. One scripture denotes that Moses was slow of speech and of a slow tongue. Another scripture says that Moses was mighty in words and in deeds. Did Moses stutter or have a speech impediment? Or was he articulate and intelligent?

Moses had been raised from infancy in an Egyptian palace. At the age of 40, he went out among the Hebrews and killed an Egyptian. When he perceived that his murder was known, he fled to Midian. One day, some women went to water their sheep, but shepherds drove them from the well. Moses defended the women and drove away the shepherds. When the women went home earlier than usual, Jethro asked his daughter how they had come home so soon. "And they said, An Egyptian delivered us out of the hand of the shepherds." *(Exodus 2:16-19)* Jethro's daughters characterized Moses as an Egyptian. He had been raised in the Egyptian culture and spoke the Egyptian language. Moses was identified as an Egyptian.

Soon thereafter, Moses married one of Reuel's daughters and dwelled in Midian another 40 years. When God called him out of the burning bush and told him to go speak to the Hebrews, Moses had not lived among the Hebrews for 80 years. His limited interactions with Hebrews did not allow him to speak their language well. Moses' statement that he was not eloquent and of a slow tongue simply implied that, since he was not fluent in the Hebrew tongue, he would have difficulty communicating with the slaves.

God told Moses that Aaron, his brother, spoke well. The Lord would put words in Moses' mouth, and Moses would put words in Aaron's mouth. Moses was mighty in words and learned in all the ways of the Egyptians; God would use him to speak to the Egyptians. Aaron had lived among the slaves his entire life and spoke fluent Hebrew; Moses would use him to communicate to the Hebrews. Ergo, Moses would serve as God's messenger to Pharaoh, and Aaron would serve as Moses' messenger to the Hebrews. *(Exodus 4:12-16)*

Consider: Joseph, a Hebrew, was sold into Egypt and became a member of the Egyptian ruling authority. As an Egyptian ruler,

Joseph spoke Egyptian. Since he had been raised Hebrew, he also understood and spoke Hebrew. When his brothers came to purchase corn, they talked freely among themselves in front of Joseph. They did not expect the insular Egyptian ruler to understand the Hebrew language. Joseph's brothers spoke Hebrew; Joseph spoke Egyptian; and they spoke to each other through an interpreter. *(Genesis 42:23)*

Like Joseph, Moses spoke Egyptian, the language of the ruling authority. Unlike Joseph, who had been raised among the Hebrews and knew the language well, Moses had been raised among the Egyptians. He had not spoken Hebrew since he was a toddler and would struggle to communicate with the Hebrew people. He did not have a speech impediment or a stuttering problem. The false prophets did not understand the scriptures.

────────────── **My Sheep Will Know My Voice** ──────────────

Parables are very effective. God opens the understanding of his messengers. Satan blinds the understanding of his messengers. God uses confusing language to help His people avoid confusion. Those who are sincere will, with the Spirit of God, be able to distinguish between preachers whom God has sent from those Satan has sent. God will open the understanding of His prophets. Parables will confuse the carnal-minded false prophets.

The only way we can be saved is through the teachings of Jesus Christ, whose teachings are recorded in the scriptures. False teachers, like the scribes and Pharisees, teach from the scriptures, yet the Pharisees rejected John. If God had sent the scribes and Pharisees, they would not have fought against John. The scriptures foretold of his coming. *(Isaiah 40:3)* If the scribes and Pharisees had been sent from God, they would have known, like John the Baptist, who Jesus was and not have crucified Him. *(John 1:29; 1 Corinthians 2:8)* Since Satan had blinded them, they lied to have Jesus killed.

Despite their blindness, the scribes and Pharisees—including

Nicodemus, Gamaliel, and Saul—dominated the spiritual culture in Jerusalem. They studied the Law of Moses, taught the word of God, but did not understand the scriptures. Similarly, modern-day false teachers read the scriptures, teach the scriptures, yet do not understand the scriptures. They see but do not understand; they read but do not comprehend. Nonetheless, false teachers dominate contemporary spiritual teaching. Just as the scribes and Pharisees led the people to reject Jesus Christ, false prophets today lead the people to reject His word. *(Matthew 7:13-23)*

——————— No Voice is Without Significance ———————

God does not want any to perish. Since Satan sends wolves in sheep's clothing to lure the sheep away from the shepherd, God has to ensure that those who want to follow him will be able to distinguish the voice of the Master from those who attempt to imitate the Master's voice. "And even things without life giving sound, whether pipe or harp, except they give a distinction in the sounds, how shall it be known what is piped or harped? For if the trumpet give an uncertain sound, who shall prepare himself to the battle? . . . There are, it may be, many kind of voices in the world, and none of them is without signification." *(1 Corinthians 14:7, 8, 10)* Every voice is significant. The people must know the word of God to obey the word of God.

It is critical that people know whether preachers have been sent by God or by Satan. If preachers have been sent by God, they have come to turn the people from the power of Satan to the power of God. If they have been sent by Satan, they have come to keep the people subject to the power of Satan. The only way to know whether a preacher has been sent by God or sent by Satan is whether the preacher understands the word of God. The use of parables is effective in differentiating those who know how to rightfully divide the word of God from those who do not. "The legs of the lame are not equal: so is a parable in the mouth of fools." *(Proverbs 26:7)*

God's words are spirit and are able to restore man to his spiritual state. *(John 6:63)* False teachers interpret the teachings of Christ based upon their natural ways of thinking. Natural thinking will keep the people in their natural state—the bondage of sin. If the people remain in the bondage of sin, they will remain separated from the Spirit of God. Since the wages of sin is death, those who are not reconciled with God will be destroyed. *(Romans 6:23)* Just as Adam sinned against God and died, all souls that sin must die. *(Ezekiel 18:20)* It is imperative that the people know the truth, which will set the people free from sin and sanctify their souls.

Parable: Saul of Tarsus, a zealous Pharisee, was committed to preserving the Law of Moses and persecuted many who followed the teaching of Christ. One day, as he journeyed toward Damascus, Jesus spoke from Heaven and asked, "Saul, Saul, why persecutest thou me?" *(Acts 9:4)* The scripture continued: "And the men which journeyed with him stood speechless, hearing a voice, but seeing no man." *(Acts 9:7)* Saul later observed: "And they that were with me saw indeed the light, and were afraid; but they heard not the voice of him that spake to me." *(Acts 22:9)*

One scripture tells us that the people heard a voice but saw no man; a different scripture says that they saw a light but did not hear a voice. The scriptures do not contradict. When facts show some people that their beliefs are wrong, pride or fear causes them emotional distress. To restore mental comfort, people will take the new information and interpret it in a manner that is consistent with their existing belief system. If they cannot make the new information fit within their existing beliefs, most will simply reject the new information. Psychologists have termed such behavior, "cognitive dissonance." To prevent their minds from being disturbed, those who lack integrity deny reality—they see what they want to see and hear what they want to hear. They reject facts to maintain their beliefs. They are stubborn and resist change.

Saul and those with him did not believe in Jesus Christ, but Saul had integrity. When he heard the voice, Saul was honest and acknowledged the voice. He asked, "Who art thou, Lord?" *(Acts*

9:5) The men who were with him were not honest with themselves. They admitted to seeing the light; after all, the sun does shine; but they refused to admit they had heard a voice. Saul heard the voice and asked a question, and Jesus responded. The men heard Saul talk to Jesus, and heard Jesus talk to Saul. They heard Saul, "but they heard not the voice of him that spake to me." They had to either admit that they were wrong and acknowledge Jesus as Lord or disregard the voice from Heaven. They chose to deny the truth to maintain their false beliefs. On another occasion, the Spirit of God spoke to Jesus. The unbelievers refused to acknowledge the voice of God; they said they heard thunder. *(John 12:29)*

Parable: The scripture tells us, "For God so loved the world, that he gave his only begotten Son." *(John 3:16)* In another place, it tells us, "Love not the world." *(1 John 2:15-17)* In fact, the scripture says if we love the world, we do not love God. Why did God love the world, but tell His people that if they loved the world, they did not love Him? God loved his creation. However, His creation rebelled against Him and chose to exalt Satan above Him. Therefore, the Lord gave the world over to the children of men. *(Psalm 115:16)* God's kingdom is not of this world. Thus, the people of God do not love the world. We exalt spirit above flesh; hence, we sacrifice the life of the flesh in exchange for the life of the spirit. We renounce corruption to inherit incorruption.

Parable: The scripture tells us that in His humiliation, Christ's life was taken from Him. *(Acts 8:33)* Jesus observed that no man took His life. *(John 10:18)* The Romans crucified Christ. They took away His life, but only because He allowed them. He had the power to save His life.

It is impossible for a natural individual to fully comprehend the spiritual words of God. "But the natural man receiveth not the things of the Spirit of God: for they are foolishness unto him: neither can he know them, because they are spiritually discerned." *(1 Corinthians 2:14)* It takes the Spirit of God to understand the Word of God because the Word is God—and God is a spirit. Those who are led of the spirit are able to understand the things of the spirit.

──────── **Do You Understand What You Are Reading?** ────────

The apostle Philip was traveling. The Lord told him to go and meet with an Ethiopian eunuch, who sat in his chariot and read the scriptures. Philip asked the eunuch, "Understandest thou what thou readest? And he said, How can I, except some man should guide me? And he desired Philip that he would come up and sit with him." *(Acts 8:26-40)* No one can pick up the Bible and understand the scriptures, unless God has opened his understanding. The Lord opened His apostles' understanding and commanded them to go and teach all nations. *(Luke 24:45; Matthew 28:19)*

The Bible was written by men who had been sent forth from God. "For the prophecy came not in old time by the will of man: but holy men of God spake as they were moved by the Holy Ghost." *(2 Peter 1:21)* Since the Spirit of God moved on men to write the scriptures, those who have the Spirit of God should have the ability to understand the scripture. "And the spirits of the prophets are subject to the prophets. For God is not the author of confusion, but of peace, as in all churches of the saints." *(1Corinthians 14:32-33)* God's people should not be confused. The word of God should be so plain, until a fool should be able to understand. *(Isaiah 35:8)*

Every scripture is given by the inspiration of God. *(2 Timothy 3:16)* Individuals may disagree on the meaning of scriptures, "Howbeit when he, the Spirit of truth, is come, he will guide you into all truth." *(John 16:13)* Those who walk in the Spirit of God will be corrected. The Spirit of truth enables the people of God to distinguish the voice of the prophets from the voice of the false prophets. *(Mark 4:10-12; 1 Corinthians 2:10-14)* The scriptures are written in a mystery, but it is given to those who have the Spirit of God to understand the mystery. *(Matthew 13:11; Luke 8:10; Mark 4:11; 1 Corinthians 2:7-10)*

Judge Not

Satan does not want false prophets revealed and will move on critics to say, "Judge not, that ye be not judged. For with what judgment ye judge, ye shall be judged." *(Matthew 7:1)* Thus, the devil wants people to believe that it is wrong to judge; after all, Jesus taught the people to judge not. Jesus, when speaking to the multitude, always taught in parables. His words—spiritual—did not mean what the people—natural—thought they meant. Jesus deliberately spoke in parables to confuse those who lacked spiritual understanding. He explained His teachings to His disciples when they were alone. *(Mark 4:34)*

Jesus instructed us to judge. The Master taught us that the false prophets would deceive many and warned us to beware of them. *(Matthew 7:15)* Beware implies there is danger. The Lord wanted us to be on the lookout for wolves in sheep's clothing. The Master taught us to believe not every spirit; false prophets are lying and deceiving the people. *(1 John 4:1)* The Master taught us that false teachers would appear as ministers of righteousness. *(2 Corinthians 11:15)* There would be no reason for the Master to tell us to beware and warn us to be on alert for false teachers if He did not expect us to exercise judgment and question the preachers' doctrine. *(2 John 1:9-11)*

The apostle Paul taught us to judge. "Now I beseech you, brethren, mark them which cause divisions and offences contrary to the doctrine which ye have learned; and avoid them. For they that are such serve not our Lord Jesus Christ, but their own belly; and by good words and fair speeches deceive the hearts of the simple." *(Romans 16:17-18)* Paul admonished the Romans to take notice of the preachers who spoke well but manipulated the people to believe lies. Such charlatans seek tithes and offerings, not the salvation of souls. Similarly, he denounced the Galatians for exercising poor judgment and allowing false teachers to deceive them: "O foolish Galatians, who hath bewitched you, that ye should not obey the truth?" *(Galatians 3:1)*

Judgment is the most important thing an individual needs. "Wisdom is the principal thing; therefore get wisdom: and with all thy getting get understanding." *(Proverbs 4:7)* Our souls are in danger. We are exhorted to get understanding, so that we can save our souls. Those who want to be saved must judge: We must mark them which cause division and offences contrary to the apostles' doctrine. *(Romans 16:17; Acts 2:42)* Wisdom, understanding, and judgment are the principal things we need in our lives.

Example: The scripture tells us that we should not be unequally yoked with unbelievers. *(2 Corinthians 6:14)* We have to judge to determine whether we are unequally yoked. The scripture tells us to train up a child in the way he should go. *(Proverbs 22:6)* How can we train up a child in the way he should go, unless we judge between the right and wrong way to go?

Throughout the scriptures, we are shown the need to judge: Paul said the Galatians were foolish. *(Galatians 3:1)* Jesus gave Peter the keys to the Kingdom of God, and told him that whosoever he loosed on earth would be loosed in heaven, and whosoever he bound on earth would be bound in heaven. *(Matthew 16:19)* Peter had to judge who should be loosed and bound. The prophets were told to cry aloud, spare not, but to lift up their voices as trumpets and show the people their transgressions. *(Isaiah 58:1)* Paul observed that if his gospel was hid, it was hid to them that were lost, in whom the god of this world had blinded the minds of them which believed not. *(2 Corinthians 4:3-4)* David observed, I have not sat with vain persons. *(Psalm 26:4)* Evil communications corrupt good manners. *(1 Corinthians 15:33)* We have to judge whether communication is good or evil. The apostle John observed, "If there come any unto you, and bring not this doctrine, receive him not into your house, neither bid him God speed." *(2 John 1:10)* We have to judge if the doctrine is the apostles' doctrine. Jesus warned us to beware of wolves in sheep clothing. *(Matthew 7:15)* We are required to judge whether the preacher is a wolf or sheep. It is given unto the saints to understand the mystery of God, because they are going to judge the world. *(1 Corinthians 6:2)* "Evil men understand not judgment: but they that seek the Lord understand all things." *(Proverbs 28:5)*

——— **Men of Nineveh Will Rise Up in Judgment** ———

Jonah went to Nineveh and warned the people that the wrath of God was going to come upon them. The people believed God and turned from their wickedness. As a result of their repentance, God spared them from destruction. Jesus observed that the men of Nineveh would rise in judgment and condemn the hypocrites in Jerusalem. *(Matthew 12:41)* Although Jesus was far greater than Jonah, the people of Jerusalem lacked judgment.

Those in Nineveh listened to Jonah. The prophet warned them, the people took heed, and turned from their wickedness. As a result of their good judgment, they were saved from the wrath of God. The people of Jerusalem listened to the false teachings of the scribes and Pharisees. As a result of their poor judgment, they condemned Christ. "For they that dwell at Jerusalem, and their rulers, because they knew him not, nor yet the voices of the prophets which are read every sabbath day, they have fulfilled them in condemning him." *(Acts 13:26-27)*

Let us consider this: Jesus asked Nicodemus, are you a teacher of the people of God, yet you do not understand the things of God? *(John 3:10)* Nicodemus was a Pharisee, one of the men who taught the people in Jerusalem. He was an ignorant teacher. Therefore, those who learned from him were ignorant, which is why Jesus condemned the scribes and Pharisees. The rulers read the scripture every Sabbath day, yet they not only did not know Christ, they condemned Him to death. In judgment, the people who followed the teachings of the scribes and Pharisees are going to be destroyed. They allowed the false teachers to manipulate them to fight against God.

There are preachers today who teach that individuals do not have to be baptized to be saved. As support for their position, they teach that the thief on the cross was not baptized. Therefore, the people disregard Jesus' teaching that a person has to be born again of the water in order to enter the Kingdom of God. *(John 3:5)* Those who are not baptized will be destroyed. There are false prophets who teach that no one can live a perfect life. Jesus told some Jews that if they continued in His words, they were His disciples indeed. "And ye shall know the truth, and the truth shall make you free." *(John 8:32)* The Jews told Jesus that they had never known bondage. "Jesus answered them, Verily, verily, I say unto you, Whosoever committeth sin is the servant of sin." *(John 8:34)* In other words, those who commit sin are corrupt and work for Satan. Those who walk in the truth are free from sin and work for the Lord, which is why Jesus commanded His disciples to be perfect. *(Matthew 5:48)* All of the Lord's ways are perfect. *(Psalm 18:30)* We cannot keep all of His commandments unless we are perfect. *(Matthew 28:20)*

Billions of people have read, "Therefore my people are gone into captivity, because they have no knowledge." *(Isaiah 5:13)* They have also read, "My people are destroyed for lack of knowledge." *(Hosea 4:6)* Moreover, they have read that we can escape the pollution of this world through the knowledge of Jesus Christ. *(2 Peter 2:20)* Yet, the people do not make the connection. Since the people could escape the pollution of this world through the knowledge of Jesus Christ, there is only one way the people could remain in the bondage of sin: "Because thou hast rejected knowledge." *(Hosea 4:6)* The people rejected the teachings of Jesus Christ and believed the lying vanities of the false prophets. They chose to remain in sin and serve Satan than to follow Christ to freedom.

False prophets teach lying vanities and deceive the people, and the people love the false prophets for deceiving them. "The prophets prophesy falsely, and the priests bear rule by their means; and my people love to have it so: and what will ye do in the end thereof?" *(Jeremiah 5:31)* The people walk in darkness because their deeds are evil, yet believe that God will not hold them accountable because their preachers lied. They and the lying false prophets are going to burn in hell. *(Revelation 19:20; Revelation 20:19; Revelation 21:8)*

---------- **I Have Set Before You Life and Death** ----------

God has set life and death before the people. We are encouraged to choose life. Our salvation or damnation is contingent upon how well we exercise judgment. God will tell good and faithful servants (workers of righteousness) to enter into the joy of the Lord. *(Matthew 25:23)* God will tell disobedient servants (workers of iniquity) to depart from Him. *(Luke 13:27)* Servants of God have to judge whether they are obeying or disobeying God. Since priests are messengers, servants of God must judge whether the priests came from God. Satan has sent many priests into the earth. Remember: Ahab had four hundred prophets; God had one.

The apostle Paul told the Galatians they were foolish to have allowed false teachers to cause them to depart from the truth. Paul condemned the Galatians' lack of judgment. False prophets have bewitched many and told them that once they are saved, they are always saved. We are saved through the grace of God: His knowledge and power. If we renounce His grace, we renounce His salvation. *(Hebrews 2:3)*

Those who fail to exercise sound judgment will fall for the seduction of the false prophets. Jonah wrote, "They that observe lying vanities forsake their own mercy." *(Jonah 2:8)* Individuals who allow false prophets to deceive them are headed for destruction. Those who want to be saved must judge whether their pastors' teaching is consistent with the apostles' teachings. *(Acts 2:42)* We have sinned, which should have resulted in our death. The Lord had mercy upon our soul. If we continue to listen to the lies of the false prophets and do not turn from our wickedness, we will forsake our own mercy.

In plain language, what did Jesus mean when He exhorted the people to judge not? There were men who had found a woman in the act of adultery. According to the Law of Moses, the woman was to be stoned. Jesus permitted the men to stone the woman. He told the one without sin to cast the first stone. Of course, since all of them had sinned, none of them stoned her. Jesus, the only one without sin, had the right to stone the woman. He told the woman that He was not going to *condemn* her either.

Jesus, in flesh and blood, came in the form of a servant. He did not come into the world to condemn, but to save. Hence, He saved the woman from her sin. Jesus is the light of the world. He has called the whole earth to come unto Him. Jesus wants to bring us out of darkness and redeem us from Satan's corruption. "For every one that doeth evil hateth the light, neither cometh to the light, lest his deeds should be reproved." *(John 3:20)* Jesus came to redeem us from witchcraft and correct us from error. The next time He comes, He is coming as a judge. At that point, those in sin are going to be condemned and sentenced to death. *(Matthew 16:27-28)*

All humans were born in sin. God was establishing a new covenant with mankind. The Law of Moses was being replaced by the dispensation of grace. It was the time of redemption. Jesus had come to set the people free from the bondage of sin. Jesus did not condemn the woman; He extended mercy to the woman and saved her from death. The Master did not tell the woman that it was okay to sin; He admonished her to "go, and sin no more." *(John 8:11)* Jesus knew if the woman continued to sin, something worse would come. *(John 5:14)* She would be condemned to hell.

Jesus' admonition that we should judge not simply means that we should stop focusing on how others are living and focus on our own lives. If we are disobedient, what gives us the right to believe that we see clearly enough to judge others? We should first cast the beam out of our own eye. *(Matthew 7:5)* It is foolish for people to be focused on how others are living when their own lives are in ruin. We should first solve our own problems. It is okay to recognize when others are wrong. We should pray for them. Just as we need help, we should help them. We should not be ready to condemn them.

God does not want us focused on the sins of others when we are living in sin ourselves. If we are not living right, we are headed for destruction. Hence, before we destroy others for their sins, we need to first save ourselves from sin. Before we try to tell someone else how to live, we need to first live right ourselves. We need to save ourselves before we concern ourselves with saving others. If we cannot see where we need to make corrections in our lives, then we surely do not have the ability to see what others need to do. Jesus cautioned, "Judge not according to appearance, but judge righteous judgment." *(John 7:24)* Jesus told us to judge, but He wants us to judge righteously; most of us do not know enough about others to judge righteous judgment.

Many deceived individuals, like the scribes and Pharisees, judge according to appearance. As a result of their ignorance, they destroy innocent men and women. Deceived individuals condemned Christ, John the Baptist, Stephen, and many others who served God. "But the natural man receiveth not the things of the Spirit of God: for they are foolishness unto him: neither can he know them, because they are spiritually discerned. But he that is spiritual judgeth all things, yet he himself is judged of no man." *(1 Corinthians 2:14-15)* Spiritual people do not condemn others; we are too busy worrying and trembling about our own salvation; however, we can see when others are not living according to the word of God.

When we judge those who profess to be preaching the word of God, we are taking heed to Christ's warning that false prophets will deceive most people. Satan deceived the whole world. False prophets led the people to revolt against Jesus and Moses. It is Satan's desire to lure the sheep from the shepherd, which would allow the wolves to destroy the sheep. The sheep's only hope to save its life is to have the judgment to distinguish its Master's voice from the disguised voice of the wolves. If the sheep exercises poor judgment, it will be killed. False prophets are very cunning and persuasive. If the wolves bewitch us with lying vanities, we will be separated from the shepherd and destroyed.

Children of God do not judge to destroy others. They judge to keep others from destroying them. We are engaged in spiritual warfare, fighting against spiritual wickedness. We cannot believe everyone who says, Lord, Lord. We have to exercise spiritual judgment, lest we will also be led away by the error of the wicked.

——— **God Cannot Lie; His Messengers Do Not Lie** ———

Jesus came into the earth to teach us of His ways, so that we could walk in His path. *(Isaiah 2:2-3)* The Master knew how to overcome sin. He set an example and instructed His apostles to teach us His knowledge. If the disciples (students) learned from the Master (teacher) and implemented His discipline (knowledge) into their lives, they would also overcome sin. The knowledge of Jesus Christ, therefore, is essential to salvation.

Since only the truth of God can sanctify the people, God must ensure that the people know the truth. To prevent the sheep from being manipulated by wolves masquerading as sheep, Jesus used parables to expose the false prophets. "For there must be also heresies among you, that they which are approved may be made manifest among you." *(1 Corinthians 11:19)* An eloquent preacher can use fair speech and his seminary education to deceive many, but the Spirit of truth will reveal to those in the church—those in the Spirit of Jesus Christ—that he is a lying false prophet.

———————— **Worship in Vain** ————————

Many false prophets appear to mean well. The scribes and Pharisees saw Jesus working on the Sabbath day and honestly believed He was disobeying the Law of Moses. The Master observed, "This people draweth nigh unto me with their mouth, and honoureth me with their lips; but their heart is far from me. But in vain they do worship me, teaching for doctrines the commandments of men." *(Matthew 15:8-9)* The scribes and Pharisees may have meant well, but their corruption manifested itself when they suborned lies to kill Jesus.

Many people are paying tithes and offerings, praying for the sick, feeding the hungry, and making other sacrifices. All of it will be in vain. Satan and his false prophets are going into the lake of fire, and those who believe in their lies will be cast into the fire with them. *(Revelation 20:10-15)* I exhort every reader to disregard your personal feelings about your preacher. The scribes and Pharisees were the foremost spiritual leaders in the days that Jesus walked on the earth; they were Jesus' greatest enemies. The men who rose up against Moses were famous in the congregation, men of renown. Spiritual children of Abraham should walk like Abraham: exalt truth above father, mother, children, and yourself. Submit ourselves and acknowledge Jesus as Lord.

---------------------------- **Holy Faith** ----------------------------

Some false prophets correctly teach that people should live holy. After all, without holiness, no one can see God. *(Hebrews 12:14)* There are deceived teachers who preach holiness and lead the people straight to hell. For example, there are false prophets who teach the people that the one faith is the "holy faith." The phrase "holy faith" simply means that God's word is sacred; God's word does not have any errors; we can trust in God's word. The saints could trust in the apostles' teachings. For example, God's name is holy. *(Ezekiel 39:7)* Holy is not God's actual name; holy describes that God's name is sacred. "Hallowed be thy name." *(Matthew 6:9)* At the mention of His name, we can trust in His word. God's name is reverend. *(Psalm 111:9)* His name is worthy to be praised. Reverend is not His actual name.

Messengers of God deliver messages from God. The apostles were sent by God and commanded to teach the people. The apostles' doctrine is the set of instructions that will determine whether the people will live holy or unholy. *(Galatians 1:8; Romans 2:16)* We build ourselves up on our holy faith when we contend for the teaching that was delivered to the saints. *(Jude 1:3)* Jesus sent the apostles to deliver the one faith to the saints—the testimony of Jesus Christ. *(Matthew 28:19)* We overcome sin through the apostles' testimonies. *(Revelation 12:11)* The teaching of the apostles is the holy faith, which is why those who are wise remain steadfast in the apostles' doctrine. *(Romans 10:8; Acts 2:42)*

─────────────── **Choose This Day** ───────────────

If you had been Adam or Eve, would you have obeyed God? Or would you have allowed Satan to beguile you to disobey? If you had been delivered out of Egypt, would you have been like Joshua and Caleb and trusted God? Or would you have allowed the false prophets to entice you to return into the bondage of Egypt? If you had been in Jerusalem, would you have been among the few who followed Christ? Or would you have joined with the scribes and Pharisees to crucify Christ? God has allowed you to be your own witness.

CHAPTER FOUR

SATAN'S KINGDOM

The Kingdom of God is beyond human comprehension. I cannot envision it and will not dare attempt to describe it. Nonetheless, the Lord created angels to serve in His kingdom. The angels were spirits, and their behavior reflected the will of the King. They did not have to work for anything. All they had to do was enjoy their utopian life.

The angels recognized God's superior knowledge, power, and integrity. He was supreme; they were His subjects. In accordance with the kingdom, angels told the truth and promoted trust. They exalted the Lord and humbled themselves. They exercised self-discipline and respected the dignity of others. As spirits, none could die. Thus, angels were blessed with eternal bliss.

But there was one angel not content to live in paradise. Although a prince, he wanted to be king. He wanted to exalt himself and fantasized about being supreme. He imagined himself as the center of attention, the one worthy to be praised. Vanity and pride led him to believe that he should be the Almighty. "How art thou fallen from heaven, O Lucifer, son of the morning! how art thou cut down to the ground, which didst weaken the nations! For thou hast said in thine heart, I will ascend into heaven, I will exalt my throne above the stars of God: I will sit also upon the mount of the congregation, in the sides of the north: I will ascend above the heights of the clouds; I will be like the most High." *(Isaiah 14:12-14)*

Fighting erupted in paradise. Satan fought to gain supreme power but was soundly defeated. Not only did Satan fall victim to his own vainglory, he manipulated arguably one-third of the heavenly host to join in his vanity. *(Revelation 12:4)* "And the great dragon was cast out, that old serpent, called the Devil, and Satan, which deceiveth the whole world: he was cast out into the earth, and his angels were cast out with him." *(Revelation 12:9)* The scripture does not denote what blandishments Satan offered to manipulate other angels to revolt along with him, but their perception was undoubtedly likewise distorted by their own vanity and pride.

Satan and his servants rose up against God in an effort to exalt themselves. Had they prevailed, they would have never had peace: everyone could not be the king. Vanity and pride lead to envy and strife; they would have fought continuously among themselves. A utopian society can only exist if a supreme authority possesses the power, wisdom, and integrity to ensure the ultimate happiness for all. He would have to be God. Furthermore, His subjects would need to have complete trust in Him and exercise perfect obedience—obey all of His commandments.

God cast Satan and his wicked angels down into the earth. *(Revelation 12:12)* The Lord created light and divided the light from the darkness. He created dry land, which he called earth. He gathered the waters together and called them seas. He spoke into existence grass, herbs, and trees. He created the sun and moon and stars. He created species that could fly in the air, swim in the water, and survive upon land. God created the earth with everything needed to be inhabited by men and women. *(Isaiah 45:18)*

The Garden of Eden

The Lord created Adam and Eve, and placed them in an earthly paradise. There were lovely trees, an abundance of fruits, vegetables and animals, and plenty of water. Trees supplied fresh air to breathe. Fruits, vegetables, and meats provided nourishment to maintain strong bodies. Water kept the bodies cleansed and hydrated. The

Lord blessed Adam and Eve far beyond what they needed and gave them dominion over the earth. He gave them only one command: do not eat from the tree of the knowledge of good and evil.

The man and woman, filled with the Spirit of God, walked with God. However, they would soon fall for the witchcraft that has bedeviled many. God is the Creator, yet many in His creation have great difficulty accepting that there are others who are greater than themselves. Those who wrestle with feelings of inadequacy or inferiority are vulnerable to manipulation—and deceivers who can unsuspectingly stroke such individuals' egos and appeal to their vanity have a great opportunity to distort their judgment.

Most Subtle Beast of the Field

Most beasts are true to their character. If they intend to harm you, they will make their threat clear. They will bare their fangs, extend their claws, stare with menace, and make warning sounds. Satan is a different type of beast. He will not let you know that he intends to kill you. He knows that within every creature is the desire for self-preservation. Every creature wants to live according to his own desires. Satan, therefore, will typically flatter and compliment those he intends to destroy. Since God has given every man and woman the freedom to choose life and death, Satan must persuade us—as he enticed Adam and Eve—to destroy ourselves—to forsake our own mercy.

Satan disguises his evil intention with words of empowerment. "Now the serpent was more subtil than any beast of the field which the Lord God had made. And he said unto the woman, Yea, hath God said, Ye shall not eat of every tree of the garden?" *(Genesis 3:1)* The woman answered that she and Adam had been given the right to eat of the fruit of the trees of the garden, but not the fruit of the tree in the midst of the garden. God had said, "Ye shall not eat of it, neither shall ye touch it, lest ye die." *(Genesis 3:3)* Satan lied: "And the serpent said unto the woman, Ye shall not surely die." *(Genesis 3:4)* Then he told her the truth: "For God doth know that in the day ye eat thereof, then your eyes shall be opened, and ye shall be as gods, knowing good and evil." *(Genesis 3:5)*

Adam and Eve had not eaten from the tree because: (1) God said they would die if they ate from the tree. However, if they did not have a reason to fear death, they were willing to disobey God. Satan removed her fear: Ye shall not surely die. (2) They had no incentive. Not only would she not die, Satan assured her, she would become like God. Satan was subtle. He did not encourage Eve to eat. He did not tell her to disobey God. He simply implied that if she ate, she could "sit also among the mount of the congregation" and "be like the most High." The same vanity and pride that distorted Satan's judgment and caused him to self-destruct, the same vanity and pride that distorted the other fallen angels' perception and caused them to self-destruct, was used to disarm Eve. Satan tacitly told Eve that God was a liar; he implied that Eve should trust his words more than God's.

Let me digress to make a comparison: the word of God denotes that God hated Esau, but the false prophets tell the people: God loves you unconditionally. *(Malachi 1:3)* The people read the Holy Bible, listen to the preachers' contradicting statement, yet, they believe the preachers. The foolishness that God loves us unconditionally will be thoroughly debunked, but I reference it here only to underscore how gullible people are. They say that they believe in God, which means that they exalt Him above everyone, yet they believe the words of their preacher more than the word of God. In fact, once they perceive that the preacher has lied, they still believe that he has been sent from God. Incredible!

It should not have mattered that God had placed the man and woman into the earth where Satan had been cast. God had created and placed them in a garden paradise. He had blessed them with dominion over the fish of the sea, fowls of the air, and every creeping thing upon the earth. In contrast, Satan had not created them, placed them in paradise, or empowered them in any way. It should have been clear that, since God had the power to create life, He had the power to destroy life. However, Satan had aroused Eve's desires. She began to imagine herself as a goddess; she fantasized about her possible powers; she envisioned herself exalted. Fantasy had more allure than reality.

During her temptation, Eve did not ask God why she could not eat from the tree. She did not seek His advice or disclose what Satan had told her. Interestingly, God had not offered Adam or Eve any explanation as to why they could not eat from the tree; Satan offered an explanation why she should. Did God want to hide something? Did Satan want Eve to enjoy life more than God?

If God did not want Adam and Eve to eat from one tree out of all the others, one would suspect there had to be something mystical about that tree. Why did the Lord not want them to eat from that tree? What was so significant about that particular tree that, if she and Adam ate from it, they would have to die? She looked at the tree again and allowed her mind to imagine. It was good for food. (Lust of the flesh) It was pleasant to the eyes. (Lust of the eyes) It was to be desired to make one wise. (Pride of life) Everything about the tree had appeal. *(Genesis 3:6)* In fact, the tree was in the middle of the garden. Conspicuous. Unavoidable. Satan's encouragement was "positive." God's discouragement was "negative." Satan "encouraged" Eve and supported her "growth." God "inhibited" Eve and wanted her to "submit." Satan prevailed. Eve took of the tree and did eat. And she offered some to Adam, and he did eat.

Prior to their disobedience, Adam and Eve, created by the spirit, were spiritual beings. They were integrated with God. Since God is eternal, Adam and Eve had eternal life within them. As spiritual beings, their minds were on the things of the spirit; they were naked and unashamed. *(Genesis 2:25)* Satan, however, corrupted Eve's mind and manipulated her to rebel against God. He persuaded her to look at the tree and convinced her that the evil she saw—the lust of the flesh, lust of the eyes, and the pride of life—would elevate her to God's level. After she and Adam ate, they realized that they had been at the highest level; they had been angels of God. The devil had bewitched them and caused them to fall below his level: they had been separated from God and damned to death. Naked and ashamed, they realized the devil had made fools of them. *(Revelation 16:15; Exodus 32:25; 2 Chronicles 28:19; Ezekiel 16:7)*

Adam and Eve were special. They were children of God, filled with the Holy Ghost. They had dominon over all the earth. *(Genesis 1:26)* After they sinned, they were separated from the spirit. They discovered, without God, they were simply weak, flesh-and-blood beings. Their power and dominion were gone. Satan had manipulated them to self-destruct. Note: Eve looked at the tree of the knowledge of good and evil. It was good for food, and it was pleasant to the eyes. *(Genesis 3:6)* However, the other trees were good for food and pleasant to the eyes. *(Genesis 2:9)* Satan told her that the tree of the knowledge of good and evil would give her wisdom to be desired to make one wise, and she thought the wisdom would elevate her.

Satan had told Eve the truth, "For God doth know that in the day ye eat thereof, then your eyes shall be opened, and ye shall be as gods, knowing good and evil." *(Genesis 3:5)* Once Adam and Eve ate, their eyes were opened. They saw the difference between good and evil. God is good and gives life to those who trust Him; Satan is evil and destroys those who trust him. *(Mark 10:18; Roman 7:18)* Adam and Eve paid a terrible price to learn a valuable lesson. The fear of the Lord is the beginning of wisdom. Those who fear God and keep His commandments will live; those who trust in Satan's lying vanities will die.

─────────── **Body without the Spirit is Dead** ───────────

The human body was created to inhabit the earth. Just as the earth is going to pass away, the human body is going to pass away. Only the spirit shall live forever. Thus, when the spirit leaves the body, eternal life is gone from the body. God and His angels reside in Heaven. When Adam and Eve separated from God, the Lord no longer dwelled within humans. Satan and his angels were the only spirits in the earth. Satan, a spiritual being not subject to the laws of nature, became the god of this world. He—and other demon spirits—would rule. Men and women—separated from the Almighty—became subject to demon powers. *(Hebrews 2:14-15)*

───────────────── **Great Sex Life** ─────────────────

There are false prophets who tell the people that God wants them to have a great sex life. They support their position by denoting that Adam and Eve were naked and unashamed. The scripture plainly tells the people that all that is of the world—the lust of the flesh, the lust of the eyes, and the pride of life—is not of the Father. *(1 John 2:16)* Adam and Eve were naked and unashamed because they walked in the Spirit of God. "But ye are not in the flesh, but in the Spirit, if so be that the Spirit of God dwell in you. Now if any man have not the Spirit of Christ, he is none of his." *(Romans 8:9)* Adam and Eve were children of God.

Adam and Eve, filled with the Holy Ghost, were not in the flesh. As spirits, Adam and Eve were unaware of evil. They had obeyed God and only eaten from the allowed trees. When they chose to eat from the tree of the knowledge of good and evil—when they fell for Satan's witchcraft—they became separated from the spirit. They were "none of his"; they had been corrupted and separated from the spirit. Naked and ashamed, they hid from God. As flesh-and blood beings, they perceived that Satan had deceived them. The flesh is the enemy of the spirit, and the spirit is the enemy of the flesh. *(Romans 8:5-8)* An individual who is naked and unashamed is deceived. *(Exodus 32:25)* He has been separated from the Spirit of God, but is too ignorant to realize that Satan has corrupted him to lust after the very flesh that God will destroy.

Jesus told Nicodemus that which is born of the spirit is spirit, and that which is born of the flesh is flesh. God made Adam from the dust. God breathed into Adam, and Adam became a living soul. Adam was human and divine. He had a natural life and a spiritual life. When Adam disobeyed, his spiritual life ended. Since the flesh (natural life) was made only to inhabit the earth (natural world), the body without the spirit died. Adam had lost his soul. Without the spirit, Adam could not live forever. He was driven from the garden, lest he touch the tree of life and live forever. *(Genesis 3:22)*

To not be ashamed of our nakedness is to disregard Adam's foolish decision to separate from the Spirit of God and to lose his soul. As descendants of Adam, we also lost our soul; we were separated from the Spirit of God. As a result of the lust of the flesh, we were conceived in sin. We were born dead—born separated from God and eternal life. Adam and Eve understood it and were ashamed. Their disobedience led all of mankind to its death. Unless we overcome the lust of the flesh and restore our soul, we will be destroyed. False prophets who teach that God wants the people to have a good sex life have been sent by Satan to encourage the people to pleasure the flesh. "This wisdom descendeth not from above, but is earthly, sensual, devilish." *(James 3:15)* Christ taught the people to crucify the flesh. Satan knows that Adam and Eve lusted after the flesh and lost their souls—the Spirit of God. The lust of the flesh is corruption—separation from God—death. *(Romans 8:5-8)*

———— **Christ Came to Destroy the Works of the Devil** ————

Adam and Eve exalted the flesh above the spirit. Their disobedience separated them from God. Since God's kingdom is spiritual, the people must have their spirit restored (born again of the spirit) to enter into God's kingdom. Satan, to discourage the people from attempting to escape the pollution of this world, has imposed harsh burdens upon the people. Accordingly, the world is filled with pain and suffering. However, we can derive pleasure from the flesh to reduce the pain of life. Hence, Satan uses false teachers to encourage people to lust after the flesh. The deceiver knows that they that are after the flesh mind the things of the flesh—and the lust of the flesh is the enemy of God. *(Romans 8:5-7)*

The life of the flesh is in the blood. All of the weaknesses and shortcomings of man have been passed down through the blood.

When we lust after the flesh, we lust after the weaknesses and shortcomings that have corrupted men and women, and separated us from God. Without the grace of God, we are slaves to our own corruption; we are dying in our own blood. Thus, we have been bewitched: we lust after the very corruption that gives Satan power over us. The devil has manipulated us to lust for our own destruction.

Just as false prophets lied to Ahab and pretended God supported his evil, false prophets lie to the people and tell them that God supports their sex life. Satan knows that those who lust after the flesh will not worship the spirit. Lust of the flesh militates against spiritual growth. "So then they that are in the flesh cannot please God." *(Romans 8:8)* Therefore, those who lust after the flesh will rebel against the spirit to please the flesh—like Adam—and lose their soul. Of course, false prophets will not tell the people to exalt lust above God; such witchcraft would be too obvious. The people were conceived in sin. The life of the flesh is the only life they know. They do not require much persuasion to pursue the lust of the flesh. Once people are told that God wants them to enjoy the lust of flesh, the false prophets have removed sinners' motivation to overcome corruption. *(Isaiah 32:6)* Now Satan can twist scriptures to bewitch the people.

For example, if most people believe they are saved by grace and not by works, they will not work to overcome corruption. Those who lust after the flesh will typically commit adultery and fornication. Of course, those who commit fornication and adultery cannot inherit the Kingdom of God. *(1 Corinthians 6:9)* False prophets who tell the people that God wants them to have a great sex life will never directly tell the people that lust of the flesh is not of the Father; Satan is subtle. Remember, he did not tell Eve to eat from the tree. He simply told her that she would not die. False prophets will simply say that Adam and Eve were naked and unashamed. That is true, but Adam and Eve were naked and unashamed because they did not know they were flesh. Until they sinned, Adam and Eve had never had sex. They only became aware of their flesh after they separated from the spirit. God told them to go forth and multiply after He separated from them. Those who walk after the flesh are dead. *(Galatians 5:19-21)*

──────────── **Kill All the Amalekites** ────────────

After the children of Israel exited from Egypt, they passed through occupied territories, where they encountered hostile inhabitants. One group was the Amalekites. The Amalekites were Israel's enemies, and they fought against the people of God generation after generation. To ensure the safety of His people, the Lord prophesied that He would destroy all the Amalekites. *(Exodus 17:14)*

The children of Israel wanted a king to lead them. God selected Saul from the tribe of Benjamin. Not only was Saul from the smallest tribe of Israel, his family was the least of the tribe of Benjamin. *(1 Samuel 9:21)* Saul came from low degree, but he was about to be exalted. The Lord sent the prophet Samuel to anoint Saul as king of Israel.

God had made a covenant with His people: if they would serve Him, He would save them from their enemies. *(Exodus Chapter 24; Joshua Chapter 24)* At the appropriate time, God remembered the evil the Amalekites had done to Israel and sent the prophet to the king. Samuel told Saul to go and destroy Amalek "and utterly destroy all that they have, and spare them not; but slay both man and woman, infant and suckling, ox and sheep, camel and ass." *(1 Samuel 15:3)* God has no mercy for His enemies—not for babies, animals, or anything.

Saul went and destroyed most of the people. However, he spared Agag, the king of the Amalekites, and the best of the sheep, oxen, fatlings, and lambs. God was displeased and sent Samuel back to Saul. When Samuel arrived, the king greeted the prophet, "Blessed be thou of the Lord: I have performed the commandment of the Lord." *(1 Samuel 15:13)* The king had killed most of the Amalekites; he had killed most of the animals; but the Lord had commanded him to kill **all** of them. In failing to do as the Lord commanded, he had disobeyed God, yet Saul completely failed to recognize the seriousness of his disobedience.

According to Saul, the people had only spared the best of the sheep and oxen to sacrifice unto the Lord. In other words, Saul had good intentions. He had been disobedient, but he had not intended to be disloyal. Samuel made it clear to the king that it did not matter what his motivations had been, the Lord had given him a command. When the Lord gives a command, the command has to be performed exactly as the Lord ordered. Obedience to God takes preeminence above everything.

The prophet explained to the king that anytime someone can persuade another to disobey the word of God, the former has manipulated the latter to self-destruct. When we do what we want instead of what God commands, we have exalted our will above the Lord's will. "For rebellion is as the sin of witchcraft, and stubbornness is as iniquity and idolatry. Because thou hast rejected the word of the Lord, he hath also rejected thee from being king." *(1 Samuel 15:23)*

God has all wisdom and knowledge. No one should be foolish enough to believe he has greater knowledge and wisdom than the Almighty. Since Saul chose to reject the word of the Lord, God rejected him as king. Those who reject the word of God will be rejected by God. *(Hosea 4:6)* He is the King in His kingdom. Disobedient servants are not allowed in God's kingdom. They will remain in Satan's kingdom—among the pagan worshippers—which will be set on fire.

If Saul had obeyed the Lord, God's enemies would have been destroyed. While Saul and his men were saving the animals, some Amalekites escaped. Later, after Saul had been wounded by an archer, he attempted but failed to kill himself. *(1 Samuel 31:3-4)* He perceived that he could survive his wounds and asked an Amalekite to kill him. Rather than help Saul, the Amalekite "stood upon him, and slew him." *(2 Samuel 1:9-10)* If Saul had obeyed the commandment of God, he would have lived.

The Amalekites also invaded and burned Ziklag, where they took as hostages the wives and children of King David and his men. *(1 Samuel Chapter 30)* The aggrieved men wanted to stone King David. According to the covenant, it was the Lord's responsibility to save His people from their enemies. The Lord had indeed attempted to save the people from the Amalekites, but Saul had failed to perform His commandments. Although the Lord would give King David the victory and allow him to reclaim the women and children from the enemy, the people of God had greatly suffered because Saul had sinned against God.

Saul's disobedience had far more serious repercussions. As a visionary, the Lord knew that the Amalekites had to be destroyed, or they would continue their attempts to destroy the Jews. In the book of Esther, we learn that King Ahasuerus promoted Haman, an Agagite, "and set his seat above all the princes that were with him." *(Esther 3:1)* Haman was a descendent of Agag, the king of the Amalekites, whom the Lord had ordered Saul to destroy. "And the king said unto Haman, The silver is given to thee, the people also, to do with them as it seemeth good to thee." *(Esther 3:11)* Alas, King Ahasuerus gave an Agagite the authority to do whatever he wanted.

And what did this Amalekite want done? He sent a letter "into all the king's provinces to destroy, to kill, and to cause to perish, all Jews, both young and old, little children and women." *(Esther 3:13)* Saul, the King of Israel, disobeyed the commandment of the Lord. As a result, an enemy of God, who should have been destroyed, had decreed that all of the children of Israel would be destroyed. The Jews, who had made a covenant with God and depended upon Him for their protection, had fallen under the authority of one who was determined to annihilate them. Saul had cried unto the Lord when he lost his kingship, yet, as a result of his sin, millions of innocent people were targeted for destruction.

In fact, if all the Jews had been killed, there would have been no redemption or salvation. "Salvation is of the Jews." *(John 4:22)* Jesus Christ, the Messiah, was going to come through the tribe of Judah. *(Matthew 1:2, 21; Genesis 49:8-10)* If the Jews had been annihilated, Jesus would have never been born. Without a sacrifice to pay for the sins of the people, the entire human family would have been destroyed.

─────────── **Rebellion is as the Sin of Witchcraft** ───────────

Samuel told Saul that "rebellion is as the sin of witchcraft." *(1 Samuel 15:23)* Just as Acts is a short version of the book, "Acts of the Apostles," the word sin is a short version of the phrase "sin of witchcraft." A witch is someone who purports to communicate with spirits. *(Zechariah 10:2; 2 Kings 21:6)* Ergo, those who practice witchcraft communicate with lying spirits. *(Leviticus 19:26; 1 Samuel 15:23; Galatians 5:19-21)* To better understand the concept of witchcraft, the word "craft" means to create something that did not exist. For example, a craftsman is someone who is highly skilled in making something up. Satan is crafty. The devil simply makes up lies to deceive the people. Remember: when confronted with her evil, Eve observed, "The serpent beguiled me." *(Genesis 3:13)* Satan simply made up a lie and "charmed, enchanted, and mesmerized" her. The devil directly contradicted the words of God, yet his lie was so appealing, until Eve chose to believe it and rebel against the Almighty. The sin of witchcraft is when a false spirit entices sinners to rebel against God. Remember: Ahab's prophets had lying spirits in their mouths. They told the king that the Lord guaranteed him victory against the Syrians. God killed him. *(2 Chronicles 18:19-21)*

Satan, a demonic spirit, has sent false prophets into the world. The false prophets have made up enchanting lies to deceive the people: (1) God loves them unconditionally; (2) there is nothing the people can do to get into Heaven; their works will not save them; (3) once they are saved, they are always saved; (4) Christ is their personal savior; (5) Nobody is perfect; etc. Such lying vanities sound wonderful, but they are examples of Satan's witchcraft. God is saying, "I have not sent these prophets, yet they ran: I have not spoken to them, yet they prophesied. But if they had stood in my counsel, and had caused my people to hear my words, then they should have turned them from their evil way, and from the evil of their doings." *(Jeremiah 23:21-22)* Satan has sent his messengers into the world to beguile the people and lead them to believe that they can sin against God and yet not see destruction. Remember: the serpent told Eve: "Ye shall not surely die." *(Genesis 3:4)*

———————————— **Lying Vanity** ————————————

When God issues a command, the command must be performed. Since He is the King of kings, those who disobey Him and undermine His authority must be destroyed. He will not allow the weak and ignorant to subvert His rule. One of the worst lying vanities false prophets have told the people is that their works have no bearing upon whether they are saved or lost. Adam disobeyed one commandment, and lost his soul. He was ashamed at what he had done; nonetheless, God drove him out of the garden. Saul disobeyed one commandment, and lost his kingship. Saul pleaded for forgiveness, and Samuel mourned for Saul. God, however, rejected Saul. Judas betrayed Christ one time. Judas regretted his sin and hanged himself. God damned Judas. Adam, Saul, and Judas—just as the children of Israel who rebelled—died without mercy. *(Hebrews 10:28)*

He who rebels against Jesus Christ is a sinner, an idol worshipper, someone who has chosen to elevate himself above the Almighty. Anyone who has persuaded you that your works do not determine your salvation or damnation has deceived you. The Lord identifies whose servant you are—whose child you are—by whom you choose to obey. If you are a worker of righteousness, you are a child of God. *(John 8:39)* If you are a worker of iniquity, you are a child of Satan. *(John 8:44; Romans 6:16)* An entire chapter has been written to debunk the lie that our works do not get us into Heaven; however, I chose to briefly mention here how Satan uses false prophets to deceive the people. We are not to simply hear the word of God; we are to obey the word of God. Those who hear the word of God and do not obey are like the foolish man who built his house upon the sand: when the wrath of God comes, they will be destroyed. *(Matthew 7:24-27)*

The apostle Paul called the Galatians foolish for allowing false teachers to bewitch them to depart from the truth. The whole duty of man is to fear God and to keep His commandments. Do not believe because Jesus taught forgiveness that God has given humans the freedom to sin. Forgiveness was only extended to those who were ignorant or powerless. Once Jesus came and taught the truth, the people had no cloak for their sins. *(John 15:22)* Those who reject God's word will be destroyed. *(Hosea 4:6)*

Satan's objective is to get people to believe that God will always love them, which is why false prophets tell the people that God loves them unconditionally. If God loves us without conditions, the presumption is that He will not destroy us when we rebel against Him. God loved the children of Israel. When they refused to obey, He destroyed them. Do not believe that God loves you unconditionally. The wages of sin is death. *(Romans 6:23)* If you want to live, keep God's commandments. *(Proverbs 7:2)*

I Have Hated Them

Weak and insecure people often resent those who make them recognize their weakness and insecurity. Ahab detested and incarcerated Micaiah who tried to save the king's life. Paul tried to save the Galatians from witchcraft. Their resistance to correction provoked him to ask, "Am I therefore become your enemy, because I tell you the truth?" *(Galatians 4:16)* Sinners reject the truth and walk in darkness because their deeds—their works—are evil. *(John 3:19)*

It has been observed that those who bite the hands that feed them often lick the boots of those that kick them. Individuals who help others often find that they are hated by those they help. In contrast, those who resent the people who help them will sacrifice to help those who abuse them. Individuals who receive help often feel inadequate and inferior. Rather than be thankful for help, their pride makes them resent the very people that care enough to help them. Their ability to help those who abuse them makes them feel superior. Hence, their vanity and pride entice them to hate those who help them and love those who hurt them.

David observed, "I have hated them that regard lying vanities: but I trust in the Lord." *(Psalm 31:6)* As humans we are weak creatures. Positive thinking inspires, but striking your head against a rock and thinking positive will not break the rock. The rock is stronger than the skull. Rather than be honest with ourselves and trust in the Lord to defeat our more powerful enemies, most people rebel against God and trust in lying vanities.

The corruption of the world is so pervasive, until the madness of men often goes undetected; craziness sounds like truth. For example, a certain singer observed that she did not need a hero. Whether she failed or succeeded, all that mattered was that she lived as she believed. Since she chose to live as she believed, even if she failed, according to her way of thinking, she kept her dignity. After all, the singer concluded, the greatest love of all was to learn to love herself. Such sentiments may sound wise in Satan's kingdom, where failure and misery are common. They do not exist in God's kingdom where there is no misery or failure. No one can fail when she is humble enough to obey the One who has all wisdom and power. There is no dignity in rejecting knowledge and self-destructing.

CHAPTER FIVE
PREDESTINATION

The Lord cast Satan down into the earth. Satan, a master of deception, had convinced arguably one out of every three angels to rise up against their Creator. The Lord created the earth and fixed it whereby it could be inhabited by men and women. He subsequently created Adam and Eve. The Lord told the man and woman not to eat from the tree of the knowledge of good and evil, which would obviously arouse curiosity about the mystical nature of the tree. Then the Lord gave Satan, the artful deceiver, unimpeded access to the woman. Satan used the mysterious nature of the tree to stimulate the imagination of the woman. Unlike the Lord, who offered no explanation as to why Adam and Eve should not eat from the tree, Satan's explanation appealed to Eve's vanity.

Eve looked at the tree. The tree of the knowledge of good and evil was the same as the tree of life. *(Genesis 2:9; Genesis 3:6)* They were both pleasant to the sight and good for food; the only difference was that Eve had fallen for Satan's witchcraft and desired that the tree of the knowledge of good and evil would make her wise. Eve ate from the tree. She offered food to Adam, and he ate. Satan persuaded Eve that rebellion against God would result in her elevation. She rebelled and died.

Without the spirit, they spiritually died. The only life they had was flesh—and the life of the flesh is in our blood. As the father and mother of all the living, their corruption passed down through our bloodline. *(Genesis 3:20; 1 Corinthians 15:22)* We inherited the lust of the flesh, lust of the eyes, and the pride of life. We inherited corruption.

Unlike what the false prophets teach, God does not want us to have a great sex life. Adam and Eve were naked and unashamed because they did not know they were flesh. They had not eaten from the tree of the knowledge of good and evil; therefore, all they knew was good. All they knew was the Spirit of God. They had never had sex; Adam had never known his wife. *(Genesis 4:1)* The human family came about because of Adam's disobedience. We were not created by the Spirit of God. "In Adam all died." *(1 Corinthians 15:22)* We were created through sexual intercourse. Men and women were conceived of the lust of the flesh. "That which is born of the flesh is flesh." *(John 3:6)* The life of the flesh—corruption—is Satan's craftsmanship.

Those who seek to please the flesh—like Adam and Eve—have fallen for Satan's witchcraft. "For all that is in the world, the lust of the flesh, and the lust of the eyes, and the pride of life, is not of the Father, but is of the world." *(1 John 2:16)* Those who walk after the things of the world exalt the life of the flesh above life with God. *(Luke 4:5-8)* The world is for those who exalt the natural above the spiritual, the flesh above the spirit, corruption above integrity. In Satan's kingdom, a natural kingdom, Jesus is despised and rejected of men. *(Isaiah 53:3)* Jesus' kingdom, a spiritual kingdom, is not of this world. *(John 18:36)*

Famine in the Land—Food

God made a promise: if Abraham came out from among the pagans and served Him, He would bless Abraham. Abraham obeyed God, and the Lord drove out the inhabitants of Canaan and gave it to His faithful servant. Abraham bequeathed the land as an inheritance to his heirs. The Lord, however, wanted to see if the seed of Abraham would serve him like the patriarch.

The Lord told Abraham hundreds of years before it came to

pass that his descendants, the Hebrews, would be strangers in a foreign land. They would be afflicted and forced to serve for 400 years. *(Genesis 15:13)* Afterwards, the Lord promised to deliver them out of bondage. If they were obedient, they would inherit the Promised Land. He would be their God, and they would be His people.

In time, Joseph interpreted Pharaoh's dream and told him that a famine was going to take place in Egypt. *(Genesis 41:1-57)* Pharaoh was advised to store up corn. Famine also gripped Canaan; however, no one told the children of Israel to store up food. When famine struck, the Hebrews were without food. To survive, they had to go to Egypt where there was corn. Over time, the Egyptians saw the number of Jews in Egypt and became concerned that the Hebrews could conspire with an enemy to overtake Egypt. They decided to enslave the Hebrews. "Therefore they did set over them taskmasters to afflict them with their burdens. And they built for Pharaoh treasure cities, Pithom and Raamses." *(Exodus 1:11)*

The Hebrews were enslaved by the Egyptians, yet the Hebrews were actually stronger than the Egyptians. *(Psalm 105:24-25)* In fact, the Egyptians deliberately enslaved the Hebrews out of fear that the Hebrews would conspire to overtake them. *(Exodus 1:9-10)* The cruel irony was that Pharaoh provided the slaves with the straws needed to make the bricks to build his treasure cities. The longer the Hebrews worked, the wealthier the Egyptians became. As the Egyptians increased in power, the Hebrews descended into weakness.

"And it came to pass in process of time, that the king of Egypt died: and the children of Israel sighed by reason of the bondage, and they cried, and their cry came up unto God by reason of the bondage. And God heard their groaning, and God remembered his covenant with Abraham, with Isaac, and with Jacob. And God looked upon the children of Israel, and God had respect unto them." *(Exodus 2:23-25)*

God heard the cry of the Hebrews in the bondage of Egypt and had mercy upon them. True to His word, after the days of captivity had been fulfilled, the Lord sent Moses to deliver the Hebrews out of Egypt. When Pharaoh learned that the people expected Moses to deliver them out of Egypt, he ordered that no straws should be supplied to the slaves to make their tally of bricks. Pharaoh lorded over the Hebrews with an iron fist. Egypt was his kingdom, and he dared the Hebrews to believe that anyone had the power to deliver them out of his hand.

After 400 years of bondage, emasculated of dignity and integrity, the Hebrews had resigned themselves to a life of slavery. They had heard about the God of their fathers but had become too disillusioned to believe and were quick to relinquish hope of deliverance. Not having to secure their own straws to make bricks provided Hebrews some relief from their burden. Since Pharaoh made their lives more difficult because Moses came to deliver them, the Hebrews told Moses to leave. They would remain in the bondage of Egypt. *(Exodus Chapter 5)*

─────────── **Famine in the Land -- Knowledge** ───────────

The prophet Amos prophesied that there was going to be famine in the land—not for food or drink, but for the word of the Lord of host. "Behold the days come, saith the Lord God, that I will send a famine in the land, not a famine of bread, nor a thirst for water, but of hearing the words of the Lord." *(Amos 8:11)* The word of God is life, and the people could live if they could hear from God. *(John 6:63)* However, God deliberately caused a famine in the land and starved the people of knowledge. All tables were filled with vomit. The only spiritual food available was the lies of false prophets. With no one to feed them knowledge, the people were taken into the captivity of sin. "Therefore my people are gone into captivity, because they have no knowledge: and their honourable men are famished; and their multitude dried up with thirst." *(Isaiah 5:13)*

Just as God sent famine into Canaan to force Abraham's heritage into Egypt, where they were taken into captivity and forced to serve a false god (Pharaoh), the Lord sent famine of His word into the earth, where His heritage was taken into captivity and forced to serve a false god (Satan). The Lord purposed in the Old Testament, the natural covenant, that His naturally chosen people would go into captivity. He would ultimately deliver them out of captivity to determine who would serve and obey Him. Those who chose to exalt the Lord would inherit the natural Promised Land. Similarly, the Lord purposed in the New Testament, the spiritual covenant, that the people would be taken into spiritual captivity. He would ultimately deliver them out of captivity to determine who would serve and obey Him. Those who exalted the Lord would inherit the spiritual Promised Land.

Recapitulate

The Lord cast Satan, a master manipulator, into the earth. God placed the man and woman in close proximity to Satan. The Lord knew that the mystical nature of the tree would arouse suspicions about the tree, yet He did not offer Adam and Eve any explanation. Further, the Lord gave Satan unfettered access to Eve and made no effort to intervene. He knew that the devil would deceive the woman. The Lord also knew that it was not good for man to be alone. Hence, He knew the man would side with his companion.

Sure enough, Satan deceived Eve, and Adam disobeyed God to remain with Eve. Adam and Eve rebelled against God to pursue what they thought was in their own self-interest. God knew that Adam and Eve would sin, which is why He had rested on the seventh day. He had finished creating the heaven and earth, but His work was not finished. *(Genesis 2:1)* Jesus would come and finish the work. *(John 4:34; John 17:4)*

We also observed that the Lord told Abraham that the children of Israel would serve a strange people. God promised to bring them out of captivity. Sure enough, God sent famine into Canaan and forced the Hebrews to go into Egypt. The Egyptians had saved food, thanks to Joseph's interpretation of the king's dream. In the course of time, the Egyptians overtook the Hebrews and forced them into slavery. After 400 years of bondage, as God had predestined, Moses led the children of Israel out of captivity.

We also observed that the Lord told Amos that He would send famine into the land—not for food or drink, but for the word of the Lord. As a result of spiritual famine, the people would go into the captivity of sin because of the lack of knowledge. Moses had already prophesied that God was going to raise up a prophet like unto him. Whereas Moses came to deliver the natural children of God out of the bondage of Egypt, Jesus Christ would come to deliver the spiritual children of God out of the bondage of sin.

—————————— **Children of Israel** ——————————

Abraham knew that the Lord was God and renounced his natural inheritance from his father to walk with the spirit. The Lord made a covenant with Abraham: if Abraham and his children walked upright before Him, the Lord would bless them. Abraham had one child, Ishmael, who was the child of his maid, an Egyptian named Hagar. However, the Lord did not want His covenant to be based upon the natural order of things. God is a spirit; therefore, His servants must be spiritual.

As a servant of the Lord, Abraham needed a child to perpetuate servants of God. Abraham's wife, Sarah, had been barren from the womb; she had also passed the child-bearing age. It would take the power of God for Sarah to create human life. Abraham was 100 and Sarah 90 years old when their child, Isaac, was conceived. It was not happenstance that God waited until Sarah had passed child-bearing age, nor was it coincidental that Sarah had been barren from the womb—God's children are conceived by faith. "Know ye therefore that they which are of faith, the same are the children of Abraham." *(Galatians 3:7)*

God gets His glory when those who are natural trust in His word. We do not see Him or understand His power, but we believe that He is able to perform what He has promised. *(Romans 4:21)* Ergo, God's children are children of promise. We believe in Him based upon His word, not based upon what we see or understand. If He commands us to be perfect, we believe that we can be perfect. We may not understand how we can be perfect, but we know that He would not have given us a command that we could not obey. Hence, we bring our minds under subjection to the obedience of Christ.

Ishmael, Abraham's first born, having been naturally conceived without divine intervention, did not have a right to inherit the spiritual blessings of God. The spiritual blessings of God do not follow by operation of natural law but by faith in His word. "For if the inheritance be of the law, it is no more of promise: but God gave it to Abraham by promise." *(Galatians 3:18)* Natural people are Adam's and Eve's children. Those who have chosen to disobey God to pursue their natural interest—like Adam and Eve—do not have a right to inherit eternal life. Such individuals have chosen to exalt the weakness of the flesh above the power of the Spirit; they have chosen to promote their own vanity than to give God the glory. The Kingdom of God is comprised of spiritual beings—individuals, like Abraham—who have exalted the spirit above the flesh.

Remember: prior to going into Egypt, the Hebrews lived in Canaan, the land God had given to the patriarch, Abraham, for his faithfulness. The Lord purposely caused a famine in Canaan. The Lord subsequently gave Joseph the ability to interpret dreams, and Joseph interpreted Pharaoh's dream that there would be a bountiful harvest in Egypt followed by years of famine. The Egyptians were warned to store food in preparation for the impending famine. When the famine struck, the Egyptians had food in abundance. Afterward, Joseph became governor and oversaw the distribution of food.

While Egypt had food in abundance, famine also spread throughout Canaan. The Hebrews had no food. The Lord caused famine in Canaan, but He did not give the Hebrews advance notice of the famine. When famine struck, the Hebrews had not sufficiently saved and had to go into Egypt where there was food. Consider: God intentionally separated Joseph, a Hebrew, from the

Hebrews and placed him in Egypt, so that Joseph could warn the Egyptians of the impending famine. God did not allow anyone to warn the Hebrews.

Joseph had dreamed his brothers would one day bow before him. God sent Joseph into Egypt and elevated him. The Lord forced the Hebrews to go into Egypt to acquire food. As the Hebrews remained in Egypt to wait out the famine, the Lord turned the Egyptians' hearts against His own people. "And he increased his people greatly; and made them stronger than their enemies. He turned their heart to hate his people, to deal subtilly with his servants." *(Psalm 105:24-25)* The Lord increased the strength of the Hebrews and made the Egyptians feel threatened. The Lord created the circumstances that caused the Egyptians to enslave His own people. God had prophesied to Abraham what would happen, and He created the conditions that fulfilled His prophecy.

Moses told the children of Israel that God was going to raise up a prophet like unto him. Moses foretold of the coming of Christ. Just as Moses delivered the natural children of Abraham out of the natural bondage of Egypt, Jesus came to deliver the spiritual children of Abraham out of the spiritual bondage of sin. Just as God placed Moses in Pharaoh's natural kingdom, so that Moses could subsequently deliver the people out of natural bondage, God placed Jesus in Satan's kingdom, so that Jesus could subsequently deliver the people out of spiritual bondage. Just as Moses refused to be called the son of Pharaoh's daughter and rejected Pharaoh's kingdom because he was determined to deliver the children of God out of the bondage of Egypt, Jesus refused to become Satan's son and rejected Satan's offer to give Him all the kingdoms of the earth because He was determined to deliver the children of God from the bondage of sin.

God Caused Our Bondage

The scripture makes it very clear that the Lord created the earth, and He created it to be inhabited by men and women. *(Isaiah 45:18)*

The Lord cast Satan down into the earth and knew in advance that the devil would deceive Adam and Eve. *(Revelation 12:9)* Further, the Lord told Abraham centuries before it occurred that the children of Israel would go into captivity, and that He would subsequently deliver them. *(Genesis 15:13-14)* The Lord gave Joseph the power to interpret dreams, and Joseph interpreted the king's dream. *(Genesis 41:1-57)* God blessed Egypt with an abundance of food and warned the king to save; famine would follow. The Lord did not bless the children of Israel with food but caused them to go into Egypt. The Lord turned the Egyptians against His people and had them enslaved. *(Psalm 105:24-25)* Similarly, the Lord sent famine into the earth—not for food or drink, but for the words of the Lord of Host. *(Amos 8:11)* The Lord knew the people, without knowledge, would be deceived. The Lord, therefore, withheld His knowledge and allowed Satan to take the people into the captivity of sin. *(Isaiah 5:13)* God deliberately allowed Satan to deceive the whole world. *(Revelation 12:9)*

Conceived in Sin

We were not born children of God. "That which is born of the flesh is flesh." In Adam all died spiritually. Adam's and Eve's separation from the spirit reduced them to flesh-and-blood beings, which allowed them to be overtaken. Satan, a spirit, became the god of this world. All of Adam's and Eve's children were conceived through lust of the flesh. Since the life of the flesh is in the blood, we were conceived in sin. Through our parents' lust for pleasure of the flesh, we were born corrupted. *(Psalm 51:5)* We were born genetically predisposed to destroy ourselves.

Without the power and knowledge of God, humans served Satan. To survive, they had to subject themselves to Satan's rules. Hence, they had to acquire survival skills that were conducive to living in Satan's kingdom. Not only did the people learn to live according to the flesh, which strengthened Satan's power over them, they passed along their survival strategies to their children.

Thus, parents, who had been forced to rebel against God, taught their own children how to survive in a corrupt world. Over time, people accepted the life of sin as the normal way to live.

When spiritual famine covered the land, all humans were taken into the bondage of sin. The phrase "bondage of sin" implies that sinners were slaves to Satan, because the devil had overtaken them—and they could not escape. In a wicked world, where nations rose against nations, evil abounded. Skin for skin, the people wanted to survive. The only relief Satan offered the people was pleasure of the flesh and vanity in their corruption. Unlike Adam and Eve, who were naked and ashamed, ignorant sinners did not comprehend that they had been bewitched to idolize weak flesh. In their attempts to derive relief from their burdens, sinners worshipped the very corruption that strengthened their enemy's power over them. Hence, sinners, who would have been stronger than Satan had they walked with God, were slaves to Satan because they walked after the flesh. And God orchestrated their captivity.

Just as God foretold Abraham that He would allow the Hebrews to be enslaved but would deliver them from captivity, the Lord allowed the human family to be enslaved but had already purposed that He would deliver them from the power of the grave. *(Hosea 13:14)* Just as the natural children of God, in order to survive, built Pharaoh's treasure cities, the spiritual children of God, in order to survive, built Satan's kingdom. They sacrificed their integrity and chose to serve a false god, who possessed the power of death. Moses delivered the children of Israel out of Egypt in order for them to reclaim their natural birthright. He prophesied that God would raise up a prophet like unto him, who would come and deliver the people out of bondage to reclaim their spiritual birthright.

Will You Serve the Lord?

The Lord did not take the Hebrews through the wilderness to destroy them. As a just God, the Lord simply wanted the people to prove that they would serve Him. The Hebrews had learned the corrupt ways of the Egyptians. The Lord possessed the power to ransom the children of Israel from the grave; He possessed the power to redeem their dignity. Would the people humble themselves, admit to their weakness, and submit to their God? Or would they, despite their weakness, rebel against their Savior? Would they choose to reclaim their inheritance and serve Him? Or would they prefer to serve false gods and rely upon their own survival skills? He wanted the people to witness for themselves.

Similarly, the Lord allowed men and women to be taken into the bondage of sin. Jesus Christ knew the truth: He was Lord. He possessed the power to ransom the people from the grave of sin. He did not have any fear of manifesting Himself in a natural body and coming into the earth to redeem His people. The Spirit of God, even in an earthly temple, had power over Satan and all demons. Satan roamed the earth like a roaring lion, seeking whom he may devour; yet the Lord, the Good Shepherd, had the power to deliver His people out of the mouth of the lion.

King David

David, a man after God's own heart, knew how to protect his sheep. "And David said unto Saul, Thy servant kept his father's sheep, and there came a lion, and a bear, and took a lamb out of the flock: And I went out after him, and smote him, and delivered it out of his mouth: and when he arose against me, I caught him by his beard, and smote him, and slew him." *(1 Samuel 17:34-35)* David, who had knowledge and courage, did not fear wild beasts.

When he visited his brothers on the battlefield, he was insulted by the taunts and mocking of Goliath, who "stood and cried unto the armies of Israel, and said unto them, Why are ye come out to set your battle in array? am not I a Philistine, and ye servants to Saul? choose you a man for you, and let him come down to me. If he be able to fight with me, and to kill me, then will we be your servants: but if I prevail against him, and kill him, then shall ye be our servants, and serve us." *(1 Samuel 17:8-9)*

The Hebrew soldiers feared death and were afraid to fight the uncircumcised Philistine giant. David did not fear Goliath and was prepared to defend God's naturally chosen people. Remember, the children of Israel feared the giants in Canaan and preferred to return into the bondage of Egypt rather than trust the Lord to defeat the giants. Similarly, the children of Israel were afraid to fight against Goliath. David, who trusted in the Lord, had courage and slew the giant.

Just as David slew a lion and delivered the sheep out of its mouth, Jesus came to deliver the sheep out of the mouth of the roaring lion, Satan. Just as David defeated the uncircumcised giant, Goliath, Jesus came into the earth and defeated the uncircumcised giant, Satan. Jesus, in the flesh, was a descendant of King David. God's people do not allow fear to make them bow down to their enemies and worship false gods. We serve Jesus Christ, who defeated the uncircumcised giant, Satan, and trust in the Lord to defeat all of our enemies.

Jesus came into the world and lived free from sin. Despite His flesh-and-blood body, the power that was in Christ was greater than the power that was in the world. The unbelieving spies did not believe they could overcome the giants in Canaan. As a result, they wanted to return to the bondage of Egypt. God destroyed the unbelievers. Joshua and Caleb believed in God and said they were able to overcome the enemies. The Lord gave Joshua and Caleb victory over their enemies and allowed them to inherit the Promised Land.

Jesus has destroyed the power of Satan over the people. False prophets have taught men and women that they cannot overcome sin in Satan's kingdom. The people have been in bondage because of the lack of knowledge, and the ignorant false prophets have continued to teach the people that they must remain in bondage. Thus, the blind false prophets have tacitly taught the people to reject the knowledge of Jesus Christ, which will cause the people to be destroyed. *(Hosea 4:6)* If the people acquired the knowledge of Jesus Christ, the people would walk in His path and escape from the bondage of sin. *(Isaiah 2:2; Revelation 12:11)* Those who believe that Jesus is Lord are well able to overcome the enemy, because God will give them the victory over their enemies. They will overcome and inherit all of the promises of God. *(Revelation 21:7)*

—————————— **Bear Witness to the Truth** ——————————

The Roman soldiers mocked Jesus and laughed at the idea that He purported to be a king, but Jesus did not back down. When asked if He was a king, Jesus answered, "To this end was I born and for this cause came I into the world, that I should bear witness unto the truth." *(John 18:37)* Jesus defeated Satan and demonstrated that He is the King of kings and the Lord of lords. As the Almighty God, He can defeat all other gods and deliver His people from their enemies.

Jesus came to destroy the works of the devil. *(1 John 3:8)* Just as David slew the Philistine giant, Goliath, which prevented the children of Israel from having to work for the pagans, Jesus Christ, the Son of David, slew Satan, the demonic giant, which prevents us from having to work for Satan. He defeated the devil in the devil's kingdom, and taught us how to overcome sin and escape from bondage. Moreover, although the wages of sin is death, He paid the ransom for our release from sin. Ergo, Jesus paid the price for everyone who wanted to come out of the grave of sin. *(1 Corinthians 15:22)*

—————————— **We are Stronger with the Spirit** ——————————

God predestined before the foundation of the world that men and women should live holy. Yet, He deliberately allowed the human family to be overtaken. Thus, although God commanded the people to live holy and to serve Him, He created the conditions for humans to be taken into bondage and corrupted. Let us reflect: Adam and Eve were filled with the Spirit of God and were stronger than Satan, but Satan manipulated the man and woman to exalt themselves above God. Since they chose to rebel against Him, the Lord separated from them. Without the power of the Almighty, Adam and Eve were reduced to mere mortals, flesh-and-blood beings, which gave Satan, a spirit not subject to the physical laws of nature, power over them.

─────────────── **Mightier Than We** ───────────────

The children of Israel inherited Abraham's blessings, but they were unwilling to serve the Lord like Abraham. In fact, after more than 400 years of suffering in Egypt, most of the Hebrews refused to serve the Lord after He delivered them out of bondage. They exalted life as slaves above life with God. Since they did not trust in the Lord to save them from their enemies, they chose to return to the only life they knew. The irony was that the Lord had defeated Pharaoh in Pharaoh's own kingdom, and demonstrated that the Egyptians were frauds. Pharaoh was a false god. The Egyptians were weaker than the Hebrews. "And he said unto his people, behold, the people of the children of Israel are more and mightier than we:" *(Exodus 1:9)* The Egyptians had subjugated the Hebrews out of fear the Hebrews would conspire to overtake them. The Hebrews served as slaves to those who were weaker than themselves.

The Lord had mercy upon them. They had worked for four hundred years without wages. They had served Egypt for free. They did not own anything. As slaves, neither the adults nor their children inherited anything. The Lord purposed to destroy their enemy, redeem them from death, and restore their inheritance. However, they could not inherit the Promised Land. They did not trust God. They placed more trust in their enslavers than in their Savior. "For whatsoever is not of faith is sin." *(Romans 14:23)* They rebelled against the Almighty—although He had destroyed their enemies and delivered them out of bondage. The Hebrews chose to renounce their inheritance, return to Egypt, and serve the false gods that had oppressed and enslaved them. They chose to forsake their own mercy. God destroyed them.

Similarly, just as the children of Israel were mightier than their captors, those in the Spirit of God are stronger than Satan. Alas, unbelievers have chosen to remain separated from the Almighty and continue to serve Satan. Their lack of faith makes them cling to the life of the flesh—the life of corruption—which will require them to remain in the bondage of sin. Accordingly, since corruption cannot inherit incorruption, they must be destroyed.

Satan Trembles

A devil is an individual who disobeys the holy commandments and sins against God. God is good; His ways are perfect. *(Mark 10:18; Psalm 18:30)* Devils are evil; they have chosen to depart from the perfect way. Since God hates sinners, He will cast sinners out of His sight. *(Psalm 5:5)* He will say to workers of iniquity (sinners), depart from me. *(Matthew 7:23)* God, to use a colloquial expression, cannot stand devils (sinners). Jesus went into the countryside and met two individuals who were possessed with devils. When the devils saw Jesus approaching, they became afraid and started to holler. They asked Jesus if He were going to torment them before the appointed time. Since they knew who Jesus was, they knew what Jesus was going to do to them: cast them out of His sight.

They asked the Lord if they could go into the swine. Jesus permitted the devils to go into the swine. The devils came out of the men, went into the swine, and caused the swine to go into the water and destroy themselves. *(Matthew 8:28-32)* When the people in the city heard how Jesus had cast the devils out of the possessed, they asked the Lord to depart from their territory. They were also filled with demon spirits and feared the Lord.

Jesus came to heal all those that have been oppressed by the devil. *(Acts 10:38)* When the people call upon the name of the Lord, Satan gets nervous; Jesus will save those who call upon His name. *(Romans 10:13)* Satan is a fake god, who scares those who are ignorant. The devil has no power over those who know that Jesus is Lord. Like the Egyptians, Satan rules through lies and intimidation. Just as the children of Israel were stronger than the Egyptians, those who are filled with the Spirit of God are stronger than Satan. Just as God delivered the Hebrews out of the bondage of Egypt, where they would no longer be forced to work for their enemies, God came to deliver us out of the bondage of sin, where we would no longer be forced to work for Satan.

God hated to see Pharaoh and Satan abuse His people, yet He wanted His people to see how their separation from Him was death. Obedience to God is life. He will save us from our enemies. Rebellion against God is death. He will allow our enemies to destroy us.

───────── **Came That You Might Have Life** ─────────

Abraham's works demonstrated that he was a man of integrity. He renounced his father's pagan inheritance and refused to serve false gods. He came out from among his family and trusted in the Lord. He obeyed God's commandments and exalted God's wisdom above his own. Abraham knew that the Lord was holy in all his ways and acknowledged the supremacy of the spirit above the flesh. Accordingly, he exalted God and humbled himself.

Most of those who descended from him, however, did not do the works of Abraham. While in Egypt, the children of Israel cried out for mercy from the bondage of Egypt. The Lord heard their cry and sent Moses to deliver them out of bondage. Unlike Abraham, the children of Israel did not trust in the Lord and refused to renounce paganism. They chose to renounce their spiritual inheritance to serve the pagans. They did not trust God to defeat their enemies. They recognized God's superior power and wisdom, but they did not trust in His integrity. Since the children of Israel did not trust in Him, God destroyed them.

Someone observed that no snowflake wants to be held responsible for the damage caused by the avalanche. Although wickedness abounds, most people reject God and refuse to obey His commandments. They love false prophets and do not want to be corrected. Evil men and seducers are waxing worse and worse. The people know that Satan is the god of evil, yet they have chosen to reject God's offer to deliver them from the bondage of sin to partake in Satan's evil. They love the pleasure of the flesh more than they love God. *(2 Timothy 3:4)* They love to display their nudity, flex their muscles, and highlight their power. They are not interested in serving the Lord. They want to promote themselves.

The Lord will soon come and destroy Satan and those who exalt his evil and corruption. The question is: are you humble enough to admit that Jesus is Lord and obey His commandments? Or are you determined to exalt yourself above God? "And I heard another voice from heaven, saying, Come out of her, my people, that ye be not partakers of her sins, and that ye receive not of her plagues." *(Revelation 18:4)*

CHAPTER SIX

WILL THOU BE MADE WHOLE?

A kingdom reflects the will of the king. A king who tolerates defiance encourages rebellion. Those who do not submit to the king openly challenge his rule and undermine his authority. A merciful king sabotages his own throne. Subjects must know that fierce punishment will be executed upon those who defy the king's commands. God had mercy upon the children of Israel when they were in the bondage of Egypt. He was willing to forgive their sins after they came out of captivity, because He had allowed them to be overtaken by their enemies. However, once the Lord defeated their enemies and delivered them out of bondage, the Hebrews had no reason to serve the Egyptians. When the Hebrews voluntarily expressed a desire to return to the bondage of Egypt, God destroyed them without mercy.

Similarly, God cast Satan into the earth and created the human family to inhabit the earth. The Lord sent famine into the earth and deprived the people of His knowledge, which allowed Satan to deceive the entire world. All humans are witnesses to the satanic madness in the earth. We acknowledge our own irrational, self-destructive behavior. Ergo, we admit that Satan has corrupted us with the lust of the flesh and has us dying in our own blood. Jesus Christ came and defeated Satan. The human family has been given the opportunity to exit out of the bondage of sin. Further, the Lord offers forgiveness of sins and redemption from corruption to those who want to walk in integrity. The Lord will not have mercy upon those who reject Him as king and choose to join Satan in rebellion against Him.

During the time of ignorance, God winked. *(Acts 17:30)* He only extended mercy to those who were forced to sin against Him—they could not save themselves. Jesus Christ came with grace and truth. *(John 1:14)* Through His knowledge and power, He overcame sin, and He taught us how to overcome the enemy. Therefore, we have no reason to remain in bondage and serve the enemy. We have no cloak for our sins. *(John 15:22)* Once the Lord demonstrated that He was the Almighty, those who refused to admit that He was Lord of lords and King of kings died without mercy.

─────────── **A Man's Enemies** ───────────

In the Father's house are many mansions. Jesus went to prepare a place for those who are prepared to serve in His Father's house. *(Luke 1:17; John 14:2)* However, sinners hate God; they are enemies of God; and a man's enemies are those of his own house. *(Proverbs 8:36; Colossians 1:21; Matthew 10:36)*

The history of the world is filled with family squabbles and sibling rivalries. Abel offered the Lord a better sacrifice than his brother, Cain; Cain became envious and slew Abel. *(Genesis 4:3-8)* Jacob valued God's blessings; Esau despised God's blessings. Esau voluntarily sold his birthright to Jacob, yet he nonetheless wanted to kill Jacob because Jacob was wise. *(Genesis 27:41)* Joseph's brothers envied him and sold him into slavery. *(Genesis 37:26-28)* God chose Solomon as heir to King David. Solomon's brother, Adonijah, however, schemed to become king and purposed to kill Solomon. *(1 King 1:5; 1 King 1:12)*

Envy leads to strife and corruption. Envy motivated the scribes and Pharisees to fight against Christ. *(Mark 15:10)* Envy caused the famous men in the assembly to rebel against Moses. *(Numbers*

16:12-15) Envy caused Ahab's false prophets to hate Micaiah. *(1 Kings 22:24)* Envy caused the Babylonians to scheme to destroy Daniel. *(Daniel 6:3-4)* Envy caused the brothers of Jephthah, a mighty man of valor, to hate him. *(Judges 11:1)*

The Lord will not allow enemies into His kingdom. Satan allowed his vanity and pride to overtake his judgment. He rose up to fight against God and was cast out of the kingdom. The Lord cast Satan into the earth and allowed the demon to corrupt all men and women. Our God is wise: He allowed Satan, who persuaded perhaps one-third of the heavenly host to rebel against Him, to overtake the whole world. All humans have witnessed the madness in Satan's kingdom. All humans have witnessed Satan's power over them. Those who have integrity will confess Jesus is Lord and bow down before the Almighty. Just as Abraham renounced his father's pagan inheritance to bear witness to the truth, all those who have integrity will admit Jesus is Lord, renounce Satan's witchcraft, overcome corruption, and serve the Lord.

Sin is Evil

Despite the satanic nature of the world, most people refuse to obey God's commandments. Like Satan, most people are determined to do what they want. Although each time a sin is committed, someone suffers evil, sin has nonetheless become acceptable to the people of the world. People complain about the evil in the world, yet they insist on committing evil themselves. Sin undermines cooperation and cultivates exploitation. Sin breeds distrust and abuse. Satan condones and encourages madness in his kingdom; the Lord will not tolerate madness in His.

As the all-wise God, the Lord can only ensure a utopian kingdom if everyone adheres to His instructions. He allowed Satan to capture men and women, and He allowed the human family to see for itself that all acts of sin perpetrate evil against someone else. People are filled with dread because of the wicked and deceitful nature of Satan's kingdom. Jesus cast Satan out of His kingdom. He came and defeated Satan in Satan's own kingdom to demonstrate that the power of God, regardless of the form it takes, has power over Satan. Jesus has allowed everyone to see that He is God. If the people cannot deliver themselves out of Satan's hands, they will surely not deliver themselves out of His. *(Jeremiah 12:5)*

God has given men and women the freedom to choose whether to be like Terah, Abraham's father, who served pagan gods and was destroyed; or to be like Abraham, who served the Lord, and received an inheritance. *(Joshua 24:2-15)* They can be like their father, the devil, and attempt to exalt themselves above the Almighty; or they can be like Christ, who, having found Himself in the form of a servant, became obedient unto the will of the spirit. Everyone has been given the option to choose life or death. *(Deuteronomy 30:15-20)*

The Lord has integrity. He has allowed sinners to witness the wages of sin. Humans who will not submit to their Creator hate their own soul. *(Proverbs 8:36)* Now is the time of God's mercy. He is exhorting everyone to choose life, to turn from their wickedness, to repent of their sins, and to avoid the plague that will be unleashed upon those who refuse to obey His commandments. Those who are so self-willed, until they will defy the wisdom and power of God—and exalt themselves above the Almighty—will forsake His mercy and be destroyed.

His Ways Are Not Our Ways

The Lord's ways are not our ways; His thoughts are not our thoughts. The Lord deliberately created conditions that would cause mankind to be corrupted. Yet the Lord told the people that corruption cannot inherit incorruption. The Lord deliberately placed Adam and Eve in the garden and created conditions that would cause them to sin. Yet God kicked them out of the garden after they sinned. The Lord sent famine into Canaan and forced the people to go into Egypt. The Egyptians corrupted the Hebrews and made the Hebrews serve them. Yet the Lord destroyed the corrupt Hebrews when they would not serve Him. The Lord sent famine into the earth and withheld his knowledge. As a result of their ignorance, the people were taken into the captivity of sin. Yet the Lord told the people that the wages of sin is death. The Lord is wise. He confounds the wisdom of this world with His power.

─────────── **Healeth Thee from Thine Diseases** ───────────

At a certain time in Jerusalem, an angel would visit a pool and trouble the water. Whoever stepped in the water first would be healed. Many powerless individuals, those with an assortment of weaknesses and shortcomings, lay near the pool. A certain man who had suffered from a debilitating condition for 38 years lay by the pool. Jesus asked him, "Wilt thou be made whole?" *(John 5:6)*

From a natural perspective, it would seem that Jesus asked an impertinent question. Jesus knew the man had been there a long time, and it was unlikely the man would have remained by the pool if he did not want to be made whole. Jesus knew that many individuals do not want to be made whole. They may complain about their problems, but they are unwilling to accept the changes necessary to alleviate the problem. For example, the Hebrews cried to God for more than 400 years to be delivered out of the bondage of Egypt. Moses had hardly taken them across the Red Sea before they wanted to return to Egypt.

Jesus knew that the man was sincere and told him to rise, take up his bed, and walk—and immediately the man was made whole. The man had been powerless for 38 years; Jesus healed him instantly. Jesus Christ is a spirit. His power is not subject to the laws of nature, which is why He can perform what humans call miracles. He has the power to restore what has been lost. He has the knowledge to overcome Satan's witchcraft. Jesus is calling men and women of integrity to come unto Him; they will find rest for their souls.

———————— **Thy Faith Hath Made Thee Whole** ————————

As Jesus walked one day, a crowd gathered around Him. "And Jesus said, Who touched me?" *(Luke 8:45)* A woman who had suffered from an issue of blood for twelve years came forward and told Jesus that she had touched Him. When the woman touched him, she was healed immediately. "And he said unto her, Daughter, be of good comfort: thy faith hath made thee whole; go in peace." *(Luke 8:48)* False prophets have taught the people that we cannot be made whole; we cannot be redeemed back to the perfect state in which God created us.

The lame man at the pool and the woman with an issue of blood were sick. Their own bodies worked against them. Through the power of Jesus Christ, they were made whole. All of us were conceived in sin. The life of the flesh is in the blood. Satan corrupted Adam and Eve, and their corruption has been passed down to all flesh. All of us have issues because of the corruption within our blood. Thankfully, through the grace of God, we can be made whole. Jesus came to heal all of us who are possessed of Satan's corruption. *(Matthew 8:16; Matthew 4:24)*

———————————— **Lazarus** ————————————

Mary and Martha sent an urgent message to Jesus that their brother, Lazarus, was deathly sick. They wanted Jesus to come and heal their brother. Jesus received the message, but did not take action to prevent Lazarus from dying. "When Jesus heard that, he said, This sickness is not unto death, but for the glory of God, that the Son of God might be glorified thereby." *(John 11:4)* After waiting two more days, Jesus decided to return to Judea. He told His disciples that Lazarus was asleep, and He wanted to go and awake Lazarus out of His sleep. Although Jesus said Lazarus' sickness was not unto death, Lazarus had died. *(John 11:4-14)*

As Jesus neared Judea, Martha went to meet Jesus. Martha told the Lord that if he had been there, Lazarus would not have died. But, she added, that "even now" she believed God would still do whatever Jesus wanted. Jesus told Martha that her brother would rise again. Martha quickly displayed her carnal mind. She told the Lord that she knew that Lazarus would rise again "in the resurrection at the last day." Although Martha professed to believe that God would do whatever Jesus wanted "even now," when Jesus observed that she would see her brother again, her mind shifted to the resurrection at the last day. Rather than learn from the Master, she tried to teach the Master.

"Jesus said unto her, I am the resurrection, and the life: he that believeth in me, though he were dead, yet shall he live. And whosoever liveth and believeth in me shall never die. Believest thou this?" *(John 11:23-25)* A chastened Martha did not how to answer. She believed in Christ, but her brother was dead, and she expected to die herself one day. Jesus' words did not make sense to her carnal mind. She simply responded, "Yea, Lord: I believe thou art the Christ, the Son of God, which should come into the world." *(John 11:27)*

Jesus commanded the people to remove the stone from Lazarus' grave. Martha displayed her carnal mind again. She told the Lord that Lazarus had probably begun to stink; he had been dead four days. Jesus expressed His exasperation. "Jesus saith unto her, Said I not unto thee, that, if thou wouldest believe, thou shouldest see the glory of God." *(John 11:40)* Martha meant well, yet she offended Christ. She called Him "Lord," yet she again attempted to restrict His action based upon her way of thinking. After they had removed the stone, Jesus cried with a loud voice, Lazarus, come forth. Lazarus, bound hand and feet with graveclothes, came forth. Jesus told them, "Loose him, and let him go." *(John 11:44)*

Jesus waited and allowed Lazarus to die, although Jesus characterized his death as sleep. Jesus used Lazarus to demonstrate God's redeeming power. There are two types of death in the scripture. The first death is characterized as sleep. *(Ephesians 5:14)* God allowed men and women to go into the grave of sin: "in Adam all died." It does not matter how long an individual has been in the bondage of sin, God has the power "even now" to raise us up from the grave of sin. The Lord has told the people, "Come now, and let us reason together, said the Lord: though your sins be as scarlet, they shall be as white as snow; though they be red like crimson, they shall be as wool." *(Isaiah 1:18)* God has the power "even now" to redeem and sanctify sinners.

There are those who went to sleep (sin; first death). When given the opportunity to overcome the grave (redemption), they came out of the bondage of sin to serve the Lord. Such individuals will be resurrected from the grave of sin and redeemed from corruption. Those who went to sleep (sin; first death) but chose to remain in the bondage of sin and rebel against God will die in their sins. (second death). "But the fearful, and unbelieving, and the abominable, and murderers, and whoremongers, and sorcerers, and idolaters, and all liars, shall have their part in the lake which burneth with fire and brimstone: which is the second death." *(Revelation 21:8)* Individuals who rejected the knowledge of Jesus Christ, chose to stay in darkness, and remained corrupt will die in their sins. They will be destroyed.

Jesus allowed Lazarus to die. Lazarus' sickness was unto the first death that God might be glorified. The Father created the world and allowed the human family to be taken into the grave of sin. Jesus came to resurrect the human family from the grave. The Father created the human family; the Son came to redeem it. "I will ransom them from the power of the grave; I will redeem them from death." *(Hosea 13:14)* Satan possesses the power of death, and the people, through fear of death, serve Satan. *(Hebrews 2:14-15)* Jesus, however, has power over death. Jesus has the power to raise all from the grave of sin and to set at liberty all that are bound through fear of death. Lazarus' death was sleep. Those who believe in Jesus Christ may go to sleep, but they will not experience a second death. God will resurrect them—like He resurrected Lazarus—from the grave—from death. In fact, there will come a day in which everyone in the grave will hear Jesus' voice and be resurrected. *(John 5:28-29)*

Please remember, in Adam all died. However, Adam's death

was predestined. God sent famine in the land and hid His word. He allowed the entire world to go into the grave, into darkness. He allowed us to see the madness of those who would substitute their ignorance and weakness above His knowledge and power. All were taken into captivity. His objective was not to leave our souls in hell, but to ransom us from the grave. *(Psalm 49:15; Hosea 13:14)* The cry went out that the people who sat in darkness saw a great light. *(Isaiah 9:2)* Jesus came and put an end to the darkness, the ignorance. The people were encouraged to arise and shine, for their light had come. *(Isaiah 60:1)* The apostle Paul would later command those who were in the grave of sin (those who were asleep), "Awake thou that sleepest, and arise from the dead, and Christ shall give thee light." *(Ephesians 5:14)*

Jesus came with grace and truth: He came with the power to defeat the enemy, and the knowledge to overcome the enemies' corruption. *(John 1:14)* Further, He was willing to forgive our sins and trespasses. "To wit, that God was in Christ, reconciling the world unto himself, not imputing their trespasses unto them; and hath committed unto us the word of reconciliation." *(2 Corinthians 5:19)* He did not impute our trespasses to us, because He had deliberately hidden His word from us and caused us to go into captivity. *(Amos 8:11; Isaiah 5:13)*

—————————————— **Blind From Birth** ——————————————

We were conceived in sin. We were blind from birth. Jesus met a blind man, who had been blind from birth. His disciples asked him, "Master, who did sin, this man, or his parents, that he was born blind? Jesus answered, Neither hath this man sinned, nor his parents: but that the works of God should be made manifest in him." *(John 9:2-3)* God predestined that the man would be born blind that the power of God would be demonstrated. Similarly, God allowed the human family to be taken into the captivity of sin through the lack of knowledge (blind), so that Jesus could open our eyes and turn us from darkness to light, from the power of Satan to

God. *(Acts 26:18)* Those who have the knowledge of Jesus Christ do not walk in darkness, subject to the power of Satan. Jesus has sent His word and healed us. We no longer walk in darkness but walk as the Master walked. The Master has instructed us to, "Let your light so shine before men, that they may see your good works, and glorify your Father which is in heaven." *(Matthew 5:16)* Those who walk with God have been delivered from Satan's witchcraft. They have separated themselves from the corruption of the world and bear witness to God's redeeming power.

―――――― **God Winked at Their Ignorance** ――――――

God saw the people in darkness and smirked at how foolish they were. He allowed men and women to observe their inferior understanding, to perceive their own weakness. He wants us to admit He is Lord, and to obey His commandments. Individuals who take heed to the word of God can cleanse their ways. *(Psalm 119:9)* We can escape the pollution of this world through the knowledge of Jesus Christ. *(2 Peter 2:20)* In Christ, all the human family can be made alive. *(1 Corinthians 15:22)* His word is life. *(John 6:63)* His word will heal us from our sickness and deliver us from destruction. *(Psalm 107:20)*

Jesus waited until Lazarus went to sleep; Jesus waited until Lazarus died. Jesus allowed Adam to die. Jesus allowed the entire human family to die. He sent famine into the world and ensured that all of humanity walked in darkness. However, our sickness was not unto death. It was for the glory of God. The redeemed will forever testify that God had mercy upon our soul and redeemed us from the hands of our enemies. *(Psalm 107:1-2)* God commanded the people, "Awake thou that sleepest, and arise from the dead, and Christ shall give thee light." *(Ephesians 5:14)* Christ came to deliver us out of darkness (ignorance). Jesus called all of the people to come unto Him; He would restore their lives. His word is a lamp unto our feet and a light unto our pathway. *(Psalm 119:105)* The redeemed is able to testify that Jesus taught us how to overcome Satan's witchcraft and resurrected us from the grave of sin.

Isaiah observed that those who sat in darkness saw a great light. "Then spake Jesus again unto them, saying, I am the light of the world: he that followeth me shall not walk in darkness, but shall have the light of life." *(John 8:12)* The Lord is our light and our salvation. *(Psalm 27:1)* If the people believe, they will see the works of God. We will be turned from darkness to light, from the power of Satan unto God. Though we have been separated from God (dead in sin) and headed for destruction, God has the power, "even now," to resurrect our soul. The Lord has the power to set us free from bondage and restore our soul. "Let the redeemed of the Lord say so, whom he hath redeemed from the hand of the enemy." *(Psalm 107:2)* Jesus came and saved us from our sin; He saved us from death. *(Matthew 1:21; Romans 6:23)* He destroyed our last enemy. *(1 Corinthians 15:26)* After the Lord delivered us from the enemy, we obeyed His commandments. *(Luke 1:67-75)* God saw our works; we turned from our wickedness. *(Jonah 3:10)* We were spared the second death. *(Revelation 20:13-15)*

He Restores My Soul

In Adam all died, but we do not have to remain dead. By divine right, we are entitled to two lives—a spiritual life and a natural life. Christ came to make us whole. Christ came to restore our soul, to renew within us a new life. Satan has sent carnal-minded false prophets to persuade the people that God loves sinners, and that sinners will get into Heaven by grace. In other words, false prophets have told the people that, although God cast the father of sin out of Heaven, He will allow the children of sin into Heaven. Adam died because he sinned in the earth, and his sin separated him from God. Those who continue to sin will remain dead; separated from the spirit. God commands those who want to enter into His kingdom to exalt Him in the earth, to do His will in the earth. *(Psalm 46:10; Matthew 6:10)*

Adam and Eve walked in the Holy Ghost. Satan bewitched them to believe that disobedience would lead to a better life. It led to their death. Jesus came to reconcile us with the spirit, to restore our soul. If we are willing to obey, God will give us His spirit and resurrect us from the grave of sin. Through the sin of witchcraft, Satan has us separated from God. As a result of Satan's witchcraft, we lust after decaying human tissue. Hence, we foolishly lust after mortal flesh and renounce the restoration of our immortal soul. Christ came to turn the people from darkness to light; to save us from our sins; to save us from the second death. "This is a faithful saying, and worthy of all acceptation, that Christ Jesus came into the world to save sinners; of whom I am chief." *(1 Timothy 1:15)*

Trust in the Lord

The Lord wants His people to humble themselves and obey His commandments, which promote love, peace, and harmony. "He hath shewed thee, O man, what is good; and what doth the Lord require of thee, but to do justly, and to love mercy, and to walk humbly with thy God?" *(Micah 6:8)* As the all-wise God, the Lord commands His people to show the love of Christ and to separate from the wicked. He has promised an inheritance to those who, like Abraham, will renounce paganism. He wants us to stop worshipping false gods—Satan and ourselves. In all our ways, we should acknowledge the Lord. *(Proverbs 3:6)* He will lead us in the path of righteousness.

The Lord knows that He sent famine into the land and caused the people to be taken captive by the heathens. "I form the light, and create darkness: I make peace, and create evil: I the Lord do all these things." *(Isaiah 45:7)* He had a purpose for His actions. God allowed all humans to witness for themselves whether they would obey or disobey His commandments. At the appropriate time, Jesus came to deliver the people out of captivity. "He sent his word, and healed them, and delivered them from their destructions." *(Psalm 107:20)* Jesus was the word made flesh. *(John 1:14)* He came to bear witness to the truth and to deliver us out of darkness. Those who will obey His commandments will come out of sin "even now." Those who reject His knowledge and remain in sin will be destroyed.

Do not believe the lies of the false prophets who teach that we cannot be perfect. Jesus commanded us to be perfect. *(Matthew 5:48)* He would not have given a command if He did not expect us to keep His command. "The soul that sinneth, it shall die." *(Ezekiel 18:20)* Ergo, if God gives us a command, He will give us what we need to keep the commandment. "Have not I commanded thee? Be strong and of a good courage; be not afraid, neither be thou dismayed: for the Lord thy God is with thee whithersoever thou goest." *(Joshua 1:9)*

Reconciled with God

What does it mean to be made whole? God created Adam and Eve. He breathed into them and they became living souls. The breath of God, His spirit, is our soul. Since Adam and Eve were created by the spirit, they were spiritual beings. They walked in the Spirit of God. Adam and Eve, created by God, did not have any concept of evil. Their minds—spiritual—perceived only what was good.

Since Adam and Eve were obedient, they exalted the will of the Lord. Accordingly, they walked after the things of the spirit. Satan, however, bewitched Eve. Her desire to exalt herself caused her to fall for Satan's deceit. She looked at the tree and experienced lust of the flesh, lust of the eyes, and the pride of life. She chose to disobey God. Rather than ascend above the cloud like the Almighty, she had fallen for Satan's witchcraft and lost her soul—lost her spiritual life. She had ignorantly chosen to separate from the spirit and walk after the flesh. Satan bewitched her to self-destruct. Similarly, Adam allowed his lust of the flesh—his lust for Eve—to cause him to disobey the spirit. Both exalted their will above the will of God. Their lack of integrity caused the Spirit of God to depart from them. They were no longer spirit and human; they were simply human. To be whole is to be integrated with God. To be whole is to be human and divine. Complete. Perfect. The way Adam and Eve were created.

―――――――――― **Walking in Integrity** ――――――――――

There was a man by the name of Job, a perfect man who feared God and shunned evil. The Lord asked Satan if he had considered His servant Job, who walked upright before the Lord. The Lord knew that such statement was a challenge to Satan. It was an affront to Satan, the god of this world, that Job would serve God in his kingdom. According to Satan, there was no need for Job, who had great wealth and a healthy family, to rebel against God. He had a comfortable life. *(Job 1:9-10)* Since God is the Almighty, Satan countered that the Lord had placed a hedge around Job; the devil had not been given a chance to test Job.

The Lord gave Satan consent to challenge Job. Satan destroyed Job's sheep, servants, camels, and sons. In other words, Satan destroyed Job's wealth; Job could no longer appear or feel financially secure. Satan destroyed Job's sons; Job had no boys who would carry on his family's name. Satan destroyed all of the things that elevated Job in the community; Job's honor was obliterated. Yet, despite all of the evil, Job worshipped God.

On another day, the Lord told Satan that Job continued to be a perfect man. God told Satan that, despite the devil's evil, Job had kept his integrity and walked upright before the Lord. Satan admitted that Job had kept the faith. However, the devil knew that he had not employed his most effective weapon—the fear of death. *(Hebrew 2:14-15)* Satan told the Lord that, skin for skin, a man would give everything he had to save his life. *(Job 2:4)* Man would lie, steal, cheat, or do whatever he thought necessary to survive. After all, how does it benefit a dead man to serve the Lord? In other words, according to Satan, Job may admit that the Lord is God; however, he would not sacrifice his life to serve Him.

God granted Satan permission to do what he wanted to Job, only save his life. Satan afflicted Job with sores from the top of his head to the bottom of his feet. It was bad enough that Job had lost his sons and animals; it was bad enough that Job's prestige and position in society had been destroyed; the boils made him look like a man who had incurred the wrath of God. The multitudinous sores confirmed that all of the adversity Job had encountered was not mere coincidence; God had allowed evil to come upon Job. His wife scoffed at him—Job was a fool to serve God, when the evidence indicated that the Almighty had not served him. She told her husband not to suffer the pain and humiliation. As far as the wife was concerned, God had forsaken Job; therefore, Job should forsake God.

Job replied that she talked like a foolish woman. Job knew that God meant supreme. He could not exalt himself above the Lord. He could not consider himself in any way equal to God. Job knew that the Lord was holy in all His ways. Thus, Job made it clear that he did not have the ability to question the works of God. Further, Job understood that it was foolish to expect God to greatly bless him without requiring him to show that he truly loved God. It was suicide for a man to rebel against God, even if God allowed evil to come upon him. Job subordinated his pride, suffered the shame, and blessed the name of the Lord.

The great Job whom many had praised and believed to be an obedient servant of God appeared to have been exposed as a fraud. His friends admonished him that he should stop lying about his self-righteousness and admit to his wrongdoings. *(Job 32:1-2)* There were those who looked upon him with derision, like he was a piece of trash. *(Job 30:1)* Those who envied him finally felt vindicated: Job was no better than the others. But Job despised the shame and kept his integrity. He trusted God and would not rebel against Him.

Satan hit Job with everything that would destroy man—the lust of the flesh, the lust of the eyes, and the pride of life. Although Job was the greatest man in the land, he did not allow the loss of wealth, honor, sons, or the fear of death to make him rebel. Further, a man of his wealth and statue easily attracted female attention. Job guarded his eyes and refused to lust after other women. *(Job 31:1)* Job did not allow his pride to induce him to rebel against God. He suffered the shame and derision. *(Job 30:1)* Job exalted God above all the things of the world—even his own life.

Job was wise. His flesh was going to die. God abideth forever. Job kept his integrity. As long as Job remained integrated with God, Job could never die, because the Spirit of God cannot die. As long as Job remained intergrated with God, Job would be blessed, because everything of God is blessed. Job knew he was not God; therefore, he was pleased to serve the Lord, because the Lord's servants have it far better than those who rebel against Him.

All of us were conceived in sin. We were all born in the grave of sin. It is appointed unto us once to die. "And as it is appointed unto men once to die, but after this the judgment." *(Hebrews 9:27)* It is the judgment that is paramount. Are we going to die a second death? Or will we be in the first resurrection? *(Revelation 20:12-13)* Corruption will be destroyed. Are we going to redeem our soul from the grave of sin and cleanse ourselves for the Master's use? Or are we going to remain in the bondage of sin and damn our own soul?

Skin for Skin

Many false prophets tell the people that Satan has been destroyed. Utterly ridiculous! Satan is the god of this world. The evil and corruption of the world attest to his power. God will chain the devil before there will be peace on earth. *(Revelation 20:2)* It is important that readers understand what gives Satan power over humans. Remember: Satan initially attacked Job's family, wealth, and reputation; nonetheless, Job kept his integrity. However, when God reminded Satan that Job had refused to rebel, Satan made it clear to the Lord that he had not utilized his greatest weapon—the power of death.

The devil knew, "skin for skin, yea, all that a man hath will he give for his life." *(Job 2:4)* Satan suspected that Job, like most humans, exalted survival above integrity. Many people will surrender some of their desires to God; they will obey some commandments. Very few will surrender their entire life; they will not obey all commandments.

Integrity—integration with God—does not mean anything to those who exalt their natural lives over God. Such people, through fear of death, are willing to spend their entire lives in the bondage of sin—separated from God. *(Hebrews 2:14-15)* For example, nearly all the children of Israel demonstrated that they would rather live as slaves in Egypt rather than die in the wilderness. Each time they encountered danger, they recoiled in fear and yearned to return to Egypt. When the spies told them that they could not overcome the giants in the land, they murmured against God. The people agreed that it was better to serve the Egyptians. At least in Egypt, they would remain alive.

Satan, the god of this world, demands rebellion against the Almighty. If the people serve Satan and rebel against God, the devil will "bless" them, just as he offered to "bless" Jesus with all the kingdoms of the earth. It is Satan's kingdom, and, as king, he has the power to "bless" those who exalt him. *(Luke 4:5-7)* If Jesus had served Satan, the devil would not have allowed the Romans to crucify Him. *(Matthew 16:23)* Conversely, the devil will persecute those who reject him to exalt Jesus Christ. *(2 Timothy 3:12)* Satan will attack everything that impacts your ability to live. Followers of Christ may suffer the loss of their job, husbands may abandon them, children may rebel against parents, fathers may disinherit their children, or experience other acts of evil. Those who try to escape from the bondage of sin will suffer persecution. Like Pharaoh, Satan will attempt to overtake anyone who tries to escape from captivity.

It is easy for false prophets to persuade unbelievers that no one can be perfect. Those who do not trust in the Lord are not going to keep their integrity when confronted with the fear of death and obey "all that I have commanded them." *(Matthew 28:20)* They may obey some commandments but not all. Similar to the children of Israel, if the challenges become gigantic, they will retreat to the bondage of sin. Individuals must have faith in God's promises to sacrifice the only life they know.

─────────── **Came to Bear Witness to the Truth** ───────────

The Roman soldiers mocked Jesus and asked if he was a king. Jesus answered, "Thou sayest that I am a king. To this end was I born and for this cause came I into the world, that I should bear witness unto the truth." *(John 18:37)* Jesus' simple answer is perhaps the most comforting and important words ever written, yet almost the entire world will be destroyed because few believed Him.

In the eighth chapter of Mark, we learn that Jesus met some Jews which believed in Him. He told them, "If ye continue in my word, then are ye my disciples indeed; And ye shall know the truth, and truth shall make you free." *(John 8:31-32)* The disciples responded that they were children of Abraham and had never been in bondage. Why, they asked, would Jesus say the truth would make them free? Jesus answered, "Verily, verily, I say unto you, Whosoever committeth sin is the servant of sin." *(John 8:34)* Those Jews had descended from Abraham, but were not children of Abraham. Abraham, a perfect man, was a faithful servant of God. Children of Abraham, obedient and faithful servants, obey God. Disobedient servants are not children of Abraham. Disobedient servants, children of Satan, commit sin. *(John 8:41-44)*

Abraham knew that the pagan gods of his father were not the true God, and refused to worship them. A man of integrity, he exalted the truth. He was a free man. He refused to allow fear of death or separation from family to make him renounce the truth. He knew the Lord was God and walked perfect before Him. He trusted in the Lord to save him from his enemies. His descendants, however, were not children of God. They allowed fear of death to cause them to remain in bondage; they were willing to return to Egypt and serve false gods. They knew that the Lord was God, yet chose to serve Pharaoh. They did not believe in the Lord and trusted not in His salvation. (Psalm 78:22)

The children of Israel knew that Pharaoh was a false god. Nonetheless, they believed that they had a better chance to survive in the bondage of Egypt than they would by serving the Lord. Similarly, most people today believe that they can better enjoy life and survive in this world by serving Satan. They truly believe that Satan offers them a better life than God, although everyone in Satan's kingdom dies. They cannot fathom that everlasting life in the Spirit of Jesus Christ is far preferable than eternal damnation in flames of fire. Or else they do not believe they will suffer any consequence for their disobedience.

Flatter Him with Their Mouth

It has been observed that imitation is the sincerest form of flattery. We emulate those we admire. Those who sin against God imitate Satan—they exalt themselves. Those who worship God with their mouths but Satan with their lives are children of Satan—liars. "Nevertheless they did flatter him with their mouth, and they lied unto him with their tongue." *(Psalm 78:36)* They are stubborn and will not change to please God. They idolize themselves and seek teachers who tell them what they want to hear. *(1 Samuel 15:23; 2 Timothy 4:3)* They gravitate toward false prophets, who use flattering words to corrupt those who do not want to obey God. *(Daniel 11:32)*

The people are so self-deluded, until they think God is flattered by their duplicity. God is not mocked and will judge the people according to their works. *(Galatians 6:7; Revelation 20:12-13)* If Jesus is the Lord of lords and King of kings, His servants should obey Him and repudiate Satan. Hypocrites are not sincere about serving the Lord. Since God means supreme, to exalt our will above His will is to worship ourselves. Christ did the works of God. His disciples do the works of God. Sinners do the works of Satan. His disciples do the works of Satan. *(John 8:31; John 8:41)*

——————— **Save the People from Their Sins** ———————

Jesus denoted that His disciples would know the truth, and truth would make them free. When Jesus was born, an angel told His mother that Jesus would save His people from their sin. *(Matthew 1:21)* Because of its great importance, let me reiterate: Jesus said that He came to bear witness to the truth, and the truth would make the people free. Furthermore, the angel observed that Jesus would save the people from their sins. What does the truth have to do with saving the people from their sins? Why would Jesus characterize people who had never been enslaved as having a need to be set free? How did Jesus' answer that He came to bear witness to the truth address Pilates's question of whether He was a king? What does this have to do with being made whole?

——————— **Flesh is the Only Life They Know** ———————

Satan told the Lord, "Skin for skin, yea, all that a man hath will he give for his life." The children of Israel chose to renounce their spiritual inheritance because they feared death. Slavery was all they had ever known. Despite God's annihilation of the most powerful nation on the face of the earth, they were afraid of the giants in Canaan and preferred to return to Egypt. Men and women have continuously rebelled against God in order to survive. However, those who had integrity trusted in the Lord and refused to separate from God in order to preserve their natural lives. Abraham left his natural family to follow God; he had no idea where he was going or what would happen to him. Job did not know if he would live or die. Jesus came into the earth purposely to shed his blood. Since the life of the flesh is in the blood, Jesus' primary purpose in living was to die. His willingness to consent to death evidenced that He exalted His spiritual life above His natural life—and He exhorted His disciples to be of the same mind. *(Philippians 2:5-8; Revelation 12:11)*

Most people walk after the weakness and corruption of the

flesh. They honor God with their lips. However, to walk with God requires them to trust in Him—and most do not. Since they do not trust in the Lord, they do not obey the Lord. Skin for skin, they are going to do whatever they believe is necessary to preserve the life of the flesh. Since the spirit is the enemy of the flesh, and the flesh is the enemy of the spirit, those who walk after the flesh see the spirit as their enemy. The flesh is the only life they know, and they have no faith in the spirit. Therefore, like the children of Israel, who wanted to stone Joshua and Caleb for expressing faith in God, unbelievers prefer to remain in the bondage of sin.

The Body without the Spirit is Corrupt

Adam and Eve lost their souls; they were separated from God. Without the Spirit of God, the human family quickly descended into corruption and passed the corruption down through the blood from one generation to the next. The people of the world despised and rejected Jesus—and chose Satan as their king. God gave the earth over to the rebellious children of men—those who walk after the flesh. *(Psalm 115:16)* All that is of the world is of Satan. *(1 John 2:16)*

As the god of this world, the devil had the authority to offer Jesus all of the kingdoms of the earth. "All this power will I give thee, and the glory of them: for that is delivered unto me; and to whomsoever I will I give it." *(Luke 4:5-6)* Satan has the power to "bless" and "exalt" those whom he wants. He chooses to "bless" and "exalt" those who promote his kingdom; he sends fiery trials to persecute those who serve the Lord. Just as the children of Israel preferred to live in the bondage of Egypt rather than face death, most humans prefer to live in the bondage of sin rather than face death. How do we know? In order to overcome evil and do what is good, the flesh has to die. *(Romans 7:13)* We have to give up the life of the flesh to serve the Lord—and almost everyone in the world disobeys God.

The fear of death is so powerful until Peter betrayed Jesus three times on the very same night that Judas betrayed Christ once. Men and women are determined to save their natural lives. If they have to choose between risking their natual lives to obey God or sinning against God to save their natural lives, most will betray God. It is for this cause that God has commanded His people to love not the world, nor the things that are in the world. If any man loves the world, the love of God is not in him. *(1 John 2:15)* This is Satan's kingdom. The works of the flesh prevail in Satan's kingdom, and those who exalt flesh reject the Spirit of God.

Fearful Heart

The life of the flesh is in the blood, and the people, in order to live, have chosen to walk after the corruption within their blood rather than to redeem themselves from corruption and restore their souls. They have chosen to renounce their spiritual inheritance to preserve their natural lives. They do not want to hear Joshua, Caleb, or anyone else testify about God's ability to defeat the giants in their lives. Many rebuke others: "Don't preach to me!" They do not want to hear anything about God's saving power.

They want to believe false prophets who say they cannot live holy, although God commanded the people to live holy before the foundation of the world, and without holiness, no one will see the Lord. *(Ephesians 1:4; Hebrews 12:14)* They want to believe false prophets who say that no one can live a perfect life, although Jesus has commanded us to be perfect. *(Matthew 5:48)* God is a spirit, and faith requires confidence in things that are not seen. Men and women may attempt to impress others with expressions of devotion to God, but their lives indicate that they exalt flesh.

It is axiomatic that spiritual growth empowers individuals and cultivates integrity. Conversely, lust of the flesh distorts perception and undermines morality. The spirit transcends the flesh, yet Satan has manipulated the people to reject the transcendental power of the spirit to pursue the emasculating weakness of the flesh. Satan has so deceived and scared the people, until they lust after the very weakness that gives the devil power over them. Satan has so corrupted the people's minds, until they destroy themselves. *(Luke 8:27-35)*

———————————— **People of Integrity** ————————————

The scripture tells us, "Forasmuch then as the children are partakers of flesh and blood, he also himself likewise took part of the same; that through death he might destroy him that had the power of death, that is, the devil; And deliver them who through fear of death were all their lifetime subject to bondage." *(Hebrews 2:14-15)* Jesus set the captives free. Sinners were no longer forced to serve Satan and disobey God. The people could redeem themselves from corruption and restore their souls. They could worship God in spirit and in truth. They could walk in integrity and become integrated with God.

The Lord allowed humans to go into sin and to bear witness to their own frailty. Since He created the conditions for men and women to go into the bondage of sin, God, a spirit, manifested Himself in the flesh and offered up His life as sacrifice for the sins of the people. Jesus set an example for the human family. He shed His blood to demonstrate that He exalted the Spirit of God above the life of the flesh. He showed that the power of God, even inside of a weak, flesh-and-blood body, had power over Satan, the god of this world. Those who confess Jesus as Lord should not allow Satan to scare them and cause them to disobey God. They should not fear the one who can destroy the body; they should fear the one who can destroy the body and cast their souls into hell. They should walk as the Master walked.

Jesus set an example of integrity. In his humiliation, His life was taken from Him, and He opened not His mouth. He knew that the life of the flesh was in the blood. He knew the flesh was the enemy of the spirit, and the spirit was the enemy of the flesh. Further, Jesus had two lives: He had been conceived of the spirit; He was spirit. He had been conceived of the flesh; He was flesh. He was the Son of God; He was the Son of flesh. The life He chose to live reflected what His heart treasured. He obeyed the spirit and crucified the flesh. He trusted in the promises of God and renounced the things of this world.

Since He wanted to save His spiritual life, He had to destroy the enemy—His natural life—which warred against His soul. *(1 Peter 2:11)* Therefore, Jesus was obedient unto death, even the death of the cross. *(Philippians 2:8)* Similarly, His disciples take up their cross and follow Him. They know that the life of the flesh is corrupt, and they are unwilling to remain corrupt. They want a new life, a spiritual life; they want to walk with God. They present their natural bodies as a living sacrifice and consent to the death of corruption.

Created to Live Holy

The Lord required the people before the world was created to live holy. *(Ephesians 1:4)* Just as He allowed the children of Israel to be taken into the bondage of Egypt, He allowed the human family to be taken into the bondage of sin. Just as He drove out the pagans in Canaan to give to the natural descendants of Abraham as an inheritance, He drove out Satan and the other rebellious, self-worshipping angels out of Heaven to give to the spiritual descendants of Abraham as an inheritance. The natural children of Israel could not defeat Pharaoh; God defeated Pharaoh in Pharaoh's kingdom. The natural children of Abraham could not defeat Satan; Jesus defeated Satan in Satan's kingdom. God allowed humans to witness His power and their weakness. Honest people exalt Jesus as Lord and submit to His commands.

God wanted the people to bear witness to the truth. The Egyptians kept the Hebrews in slavery for 400 years, although the Hebrews were stronger than the Egyptians. The fear of death caused the Hebrews to build Pharaoh's kingdom, which reinforced Egypt's power over them. Similarly, Satan has kept the world in the bondage of sin for thousands of years. The people of the world are so afraid, until they renounce the power of their Savior and reinforce the power of their enemy. Unlike Adam and Eve, who were naked and ashamed to have been separated from the power of God Almighty, humans have been bewitched with the pleasure and vanity of the flesh; they worship their own weakness, and lust after their own destruction.

───────── **Thy Will be Done in Earth** ─────────

God will not wait until an individual gets into His kingdom to determine whether the individual will obey His commandments. The Lord will find out on earth who will obey Him. Those who submit their will to God and exalt the Lord in the earth will exalt the Lord in Heaven. Those who disobey God in the earth will disobey God in Heaven. Therefore, anyone who teaches that God loves the sinner and will allow sinners to enter the Kingdom of God is a liar. *(Matthew 5:19-20)* God cast sinners out of Heaven, put them in the earth, and allowed humans to obey God or join forces with His enemies. Those who disobey the Lord will not enter into His kingdom. "Know ye not, that to whom ye yield yourselves servants to obey, his servants ye are to whom ye obey; whether of sin unto death, or of obedience unto righteousness?" *(Romans 6:16)* The wages of sin is death; sinners shall be destroyed.

The children of Israel were overtaken and enslaved in the bondage of Egypt; Jesus delivered them. Lazarus died; Jesus resurrected him. Men and women were corrupted by Satan and enslaved in the bondage of sin; Jesus redeemed them and set them free. Jesus was crucified; Jesus rose again. God has supreme power. Those who confess that Jesus Christ is Lord should not fear death and remain in the bondage of sin. God has shined the light upon us, and awakened us out of sleep. We are no longer in darkness, subject to the power of Satan. We have been enlightened and know that Jesus is Lord. We walk in integrity and serve the Lord.

The earth is going to melt with a fervent heat. Individuals are going to inherit either eternal life or eternal damnation. The

Lord will not countenance rebellion in His kingdom. Those who enter His kingdom must submit to His will and trust in His word. They may not understand; they may not agree; but they will obey. Servants know that all of His ways are holy; thus, we must walk in the way of holiness. *(Isaiah 35:8)* We want to see God in peace. *(Hebrews 12:14)*

Those who will enter the Kingdom of God have ultimate trust in God. Jesus taught them how they were captured and how they could escape. He gave them power over the enemy. Therefore, they exalt the Lord, and are willing to do His will in the earth as His will is done in Heaven. When confronted with adversity, they refuse to serve false gods or to return into captivity. Though the Lord may slay them, they trust in Him. *(Job 13:15)* To reclaim their birthright and inherit eternal life, they keep their integrity and exalt the Lord.

─────── **Ransom Us from the Power of the Grave** ───────

God saved the children of Israel out of the graves of Egypt. However, when they heard there were giants in Canaan, they yearned to return to the graves of Egypt. The fear of death caused them to renounce their own inheritance. They chose to serve as slaves in Egypt until they died rather than live with integrity in the Promised Land. Satan knows that "skin for skin" most people are not going to give up the only life they know to serve Jesus Christ. Most people are going to preserve the flesh—and the corruption inherent in their flesh—before they give up their lives to trust in God. Through the fear of death, most people will remain in the bondage of sin. *(Hebrews 2:14)*

The sting of death is sin. *(1 Corinthians 15:56)* Satan, through the fear of death, forced the people to rebel against God and serve him. The dilemma humans faced was that the wages of sin is death. *(Romans 6:23)* Hence, humans remained in the bondage of sin because they feared death, yet, as a result of sin, they were going to burn in hell. The people needed to come out of captivity to serve the Lord, but Satan possessed the power of death. Hosea foretold that

God would deliver us from the power of the grave: "I will ransom them from the power of the grave; I will redeem them from death." *(Hosea 13:14)* Zechariah exulted when he learned that Christ was going to come: "That we should be saved from our enemies, and from the hand of all that hate us; . . . That he would grant unto us, that we being delivered out of the hand of our enemies might serve him without fear, in holiness and righteousness before him, all the days of our life." *(Luke 1:71-74)*

Thankfully, Jesus came into the earth to destroy him that had the power of death. Those who confess that Jesus is Lord and believe that God raised Him from the dead shall be saved. If we believe God is the Almighty and that He delivered Jesus from death, we believe that He can also deliver us from death. Accordingly, we will not capitulate to fear but will call upon the Lord and be saved. *(Romans 10:13)*

Jesus opened the eyes of the blind, to turn us from the power of Satan unto God. We do not have to fear Satan; Jesus is Lord. Those who want to serve the Lord are able to come out of the grave of sin and restore their soul. He will forgive our sins and sanctify us through our faith in Him. *(Acts 26:18)* "And it shall be said in that day, Lo, this is our God; we have waited for him, and he will save us: this is the Lord; we have waited for him, we will be glad and rejoice in his salvation." *(Isaiah 25:9)*

Recapitulate

Jesus shed His blood to pay for the sins of those who disobeyed God; He ransomed them from the power of the grave. Those who served Satan through fear of death do not have to be afraid anymore. Those who know that Jesus Christ is Lord know that He is Lord over Satan. They will keep their integrity and not bow down to the god of this world. They trust in the Lord and abide safely in the power of His might.

We worship the Lord because we acknowledge the supremacy of God above Satan, and the supremacy of God above ourselves. We recognize the power of Satan over our flesh, yet we acknowledge the power of God over Satan. Since God offers us the Holy Ghost, we consent to the death of the flesh (weakness and corruption) to reclaim our birthright (Spirit of God) and restore our power over the enemy. We give up the life of the flesh—the life of sin—because Jesus has ransomed us from the power of the grave. God has given us a new life—the Holy Ghost—and restored our soul. We gladly give up the life of sin, which had us destroying our own soul, to walk in the Spirit of God, which restored our soul and allowed us to inherit His kingdom. Those who walk with Christ are not in the grave of sin. "Why seek ye the living among the dead?" *(Luke 24:5)* Christ has ransomed us from the grave of sin; we are no longer dead. In Christ, we have been made alive.

The Lord had mercy upon the children of Israel. They had been enslaved by the Egyptians and forced to serve a pagan god. Once the Lord delivered them, they were no longer compelled to serve the Egyptians. They were given the choice to choose life or death. In their desire to save their natural lives, they chose to return to Egypt. Thus, they renounced their spiritual inheritance. They rejected God's commandment and challenged His authority. The Lord destroyed them without mercy.

The Lord has shown mercy upon the human family. He allowed Satan to capture and corrupt us. Jesus came and defeated Satan; He ransomed us from the grave. Death has been defeated. Jesus has promised to save those who call upon His name. Sinners do not have any cloak for our sins. We have been given the choice to come out of the grave of sin or to remain in the grave of sin. Those who relinquish the life of the flesh (forsake their wickedness) and return unto the Lord will restore their soul. Those who seek to save their natural lives (the life of the flesh) and continue to do the works of the flesh will lose their soul. They will forsake their own mercy.

CHAPTER SEVEN
SAVED

God told Abraham to come out from among his family and walk upright before Him. Individuals who did not have faith in the Lord would have remained with their pagan families. Fear of death would have triumphed over dignity and integrity. Abraham trusted God. Therefore, he obeyed God. Some kings attacked Abraham's family; they took Lot, women, and goods. Many individuals would have remained with their pagan families and not have served the Lord purposely because they feared such things would happen. Abraham left his family because he trusted in the Lord to save him—and the Lord gave Abraham victory over his enemies.

To celebrate the victory, Melchizedek, King of Salem, brought forth bread and wine. Abraham, in turn, gave ten percent of all he had to the King. *(Genesis 14:18-20; Hebrews 7:1-3)* God and Abraham had entered into a covenant. Abraham obeyed the Lord and came out from pagan worship. Abraham kept his part of the covenant with God. "And blessed be the most high God, which hath delivered thine enemies into thy hand." *(Genesis 14:20)* God did not allow Abraham's enemies to destroy him or his family. According to His word, the Lord not only saved Abraham from his enemies but delivered Abraham's enemies into his hand.

──────────── **Children of God Are Faithful** ────────────

Those who trust in the Lord are the children of Abraham. "Know ye therefore that they which are of faith, the same are the children of Abraham." *(Galatians 3:7)* Jesus told some Jews that if they continued in His words, they were His disciples indeed. Hence, they would know the truth, and the truth would make them free. They responded that they were the children of Abraham and had never been in bondage. Jesus answered, "Whosoever committeth sin is the servant of sin." *(John 8:34)* Jesus went on to tell them that if they were the children of Abraham, they would do the works of Abraham. *(John 8:39)* Jesus wanted them to know that they were not the children of Abraham (faithful), but they were children of the devil (sinners). *(John 8:44)*

Jesus spoke in parables to those Jews, but here is what the Master told them: the fact that they were descendants of Abraham did not make them children of Abraham. Children are the offsprings of their father. Children do the deeds of their father; their creator. The Lord has integrity and cannot lie. *(Titus 1:2)* His children do not lie. *(Isaiah 63:8)* Satan is the father of lies. *(John 8:44)* Satan's children are liars. God hates liars, and will cast all liars into a lake of fire. *(Psalm 5:5-6; Revelation 21:8)* As a man of integrity, Abraham renounced the corruption of his father and learned the ways of God. He became a child of God. Those Jews committed sin because they had learned the ways of Satan, the father of corruption. Satan was their father. *(John 8:44)* If the people had continued in Jesus' words, the truth would have sanctified them and redeemed them from corruption. They would have become children of God. *(John 1:12)*

The Lord is slow to anger and rich in mercy, but He will destroy the wicked. The Lord understands that we have been corrupted and is patient with His people. He told His disciples if they continued in His word, they would be made free. *(John 8:31-32)* The word of God will build us up and sanctify us through the truth. *(John 17:17)* We have to continue in the apostles' doctrine and move on to perfection. *(Hebrews 6:1)* Hence, sinners will not overcome corruption overnight; however, God is not mocked. We have to earnestly contend for the faith. *(Jude 1:3)* We have to diligently seek after Him. *(Hebrews 11:6)* In other words, we have to be sincere.

Remember: Jesus came and ransomed us from the power of the grave. He can resurrect us "even now." He has called us to come out of the grave. He will remove the stony heart out of our flesh and save us from all uncleanness. *(Ezekiel 36:23-29)* We have a choice: thanks to the death of Jesus Christ, we can follow Christ out of the bondage of sin, walk in the newness of life, and serve the Lord in holiness and righteousness. Or we can remain in the grave of sin, slaves to corruption, and be destroyed along with Satan and other corrupt souls.

———————— **Save the People from Their Sins** ————————

God told the prophet Isaiah to tell those of a fearful heart to be strong; their God was going to come and save them. When their God came, the eyes of the blind were going to be opened, the lame man would leap as a hart, and the ears of the deaf were going to be unstopped. *(Isaiah 35:3-6)* John, while in prison, heard about Jesus and sent some of his disciples to Him. They asked Jesus if He was the one that should come, or should they look for another. Jesus told them to go and tell John that the blind received their sight, the lame man leaped as a hart, and the deaf heard. *(Luke 7:22; Matthew 11:4-5)* Thus, John, knowing the scripture, understood that Jesus was the One who was going to come and save the people. Jesus came to take away the sins of the world. Through death, He would destroy him that had the power of death and deliver the people out of the bondage of sin.

Jesus' answer was the good news that John had wanted to hear. God had sent John to turn the people from Satan to God: "And he shall go before him in the spirit and the power of Elias, to turn the hearts of the fathers to the children, and the disobedient to the wisdom of the just; to make ready a people prepared for the Lord."

(Luke 1:17) Thus, God sent John to baptize the people with the baptism of repentance and to make the people ready to serve the Lord. John's responsibility was to tell men and women to repent of their sins—forsake their wicked ways. The Lord had come to save them from their sins.

Before John was born, an angel of the Lord told Zacharias, the father of John, that his son would pave the way for the coming of the Messiah. Zacharias was filled with joy and blessed the name of the Lord. He thanked God for coming to redeem His people. Zachiarias remembered that the Lord had promised "That we should be **saved** from our enemies, and from the hand of all that hate us . . . that we being delivered out of the hand of our enemies might serve him without fear, in holiness and righteousness before him, all the days of our life." *(Luke 1:71,74,75)*

Zacharias' comment was the good news those who wanted to come out of spiritual Egypt, out of the bondage of sin, had waited to hear. Satan, the enemy of God, had enslaved us in the bondage of sin. Skin for skin, we were so afraid of death, until we sacrificed our life (integrity) to survive. We were the living dead and worked to build Satan's kingdom. The devil corrupted our minds and transmuted us into his demonic children. We adapted to corruption and learned the ways of God's enemies. We exalted the life of the flesh above the commandments of God. "For the wages of sin is death; but the gift of God is eternal life through Jesus Christ our Lord." *(Romans 6:23)* Rather than fear the One who could destroy our bodies and souls (Jesus Christ), we were so fixated on saving our natural lives, until we feared Satan and disobeyed God. We were unsuspectingly damning our own soul.

Jesus Christ, our God, came to deliver the people out of the hands of the enemies, out of the bondage of sin. We no longer, because of fear of death, had to serve the enemy and remain in captivity. We no longer had to do the works of the devil. We could come out of bondage and serve the Lord, without fear, in holiness and righteousness all the days of our life.

─────────────── **Fear of Death** ───────────────

Please remember why Jesus came into the earth:

(1) Jesus came to save the people from their sins. "And she shall bring forth a son, and thou shalt call his name JESUS: for he shall save his people from their sins." *(Matthew 1:21)* The wages of sin is death, and God did not want any to perish. *(John 3:16)*

Why were the people in sin? They wanted to survive and did what they thought was necessary to survive. Since we were conceived in sin, the life of the flesh (life of sin) was the only life we had ever known. Yet, all that is of the world—the lust of the flesh, lust of the eyes, and pride of life—is of the devil. *(1 John 2:16)* They that walk after the flesh and conform to the world live in sin and serve Satan.

Jesus overcame the world. He came to deliver the people out of sin. "Forasmuch then as the children are partakers of flesh and blood, he also himself likewise took part of the same; that through death he might destroy him that had the power of death, that is, the devil; and deliver them who through fear of death were all their lifetime subject to bondage." *(Hebrews 2:14-15)* Jesus came and defeated death. He overcame the grave of sin. Jesus demonstrated that the power of God, despite being housed in a corrupt flesh-and-blood body, was able to overcome the power of Satan. Those who believed in Christ did not have to fear death anymore. Satan could no longer force us to serve him. We did not have to sin against God to survive. Our God had come to save us from the enemy. *(Isaiah 35:4)*

Although the life of the flesh is in the blood, Jesus demonstrated that everyone should exalt the spirit. God has power over Satan; those who walk in the Spirit of God have no need to fear Satan. The spirit cannot die; those who walk in the Spirit of God have no need to fear death. Those who walk with God do not the works of the devil anymore. Just as God raised Jesus out of the grave of sin (death), God has raised all faithful servants out of the grave of sin.

In Adam all died; in Christ all shall be made alive. Satan

defeated Adam and separated the people from God; Christ defeated Satan and reconciled the people back to God. Jesus paid the price to ransom the people from the grave. Satan cannot use the fear of death to intimidate believers to rebel against God anymore. Not only did Jesus live without sin, God raised Him from the grave. Death had no victory over Christ. Death does not have any power over those who walk in the spirit. Satan cannot prevail against the church (the body of Christ), because those who walk in the Spirit of God have been resurrected from the grave of sin and liberated from bondage. Death has no sting to those who walk in the Spirit of God. *(1 Corinthians 15:54-57)* The Spirit of God cannot die; those who have the Spirit of God cannot die. The body without the spirit is already dead. *(James 2:26)* Ergo, those who walk in the light know that Satan uses the fear of death to scare unbelievers to sin against God, when the people are already dead. If the people remain dead (corrupt) and are not born again (redeemed), God will destroy them. *(John 3:5)* Thus, Satan uses the fear of death to keep the people from coming out of the grave of sin, reconciling with God and saving their soul.

Adam and Eve only knew good; they did not know evil. We have to choose between good and evil. We have to either serve the Lord (spirit) or serve Satan (flesh). Those who know Jesus is Lord will not allow Satan to continue to corrupt us with witchcraft (lust of the flesh and pride) or through fear of death. Since we know that Jesus is Lord and the spirit shall live forever, we exalt the spirit above the flesh. We are not afraid of death, because we know that the flesh is corrupt. Therefore, we are not going to preserve the life of the flesh, preserve corruption, which will keep us out of the Kingdom of God. *(1 Corinthians 15:50)* We exalt our soul, and Satan has no power over our soul. Hence, Satan cannot scare us with fear of death because he does not have power over anything that we want to preserve.

(2) Jesus came to bear witness to the truth: He was Lord. The people did not need to fear the one who could take their natural life. Satan, the god of this world, had the power of death of the

flesh. As King of kings and Lord of lords, Jesus had the power to destroy the flesh and the soul. The people needed to fear Him. *(Matthew 10:28)* Those who were wise feared God and kept His commandments. *(Ecclesiastes 12:31)*

Unlike Abraham, the children of Israel did not trust God. The fear of death led them to renounce their natural inheritance to serve the Egyptians. They preferred to serve false gods (the Egyptians) whom the Almighty had already defeated. Similarly, Jesus told the Jews that if Abraham were their father, they would do the works of Abraham—they would not remain among the pagans and worship false gods. They would renounce paganism and obey the Lord. However, because they disobeyed the commandments of God and did the works of Satan, they were children of Satan, the father of corruption.

The natural children of Abraham refused to do the works of Abraham and obey God. In their desire to live, they preferred to live as slaves in Egypt, do the works of Pharaoh, and build his kingdom. In their effort to save their lives, they lost their lives. They rebelled against God, and the Lord destroyed them. In contrast, Abraham's children are children of faith and walk in integrity. They do not serve a false god and rebel against the Almighty. They know the truth: Jesus is Lord. Joshua and Caleb knew God was well able to overcome the enemy and did not allow fear of death to make them rebel against the Almighty. They had confidence in God, who defeated the giants in Canaan and allowed them to inherit the Promised Land.

Just as God defeated Pharaoh in Pharaoh's kingdom to demonstrate that Pharaoh was a false god, Jesus came and defeated Satan in Satan's kingdom to demonstrate that Satan was a false god. We were in captivity because of ignorance. Pharaoh ruled over the Hebrews because they built his treasure cities; hence, they empowered their own slavemasters, who taught the children of Israel, if they wanted to live, how to be good slaves. Not only were we conceived in sin, God hid His word and allowed false teachers to deceive us. We were completely ignorant. Satan ruled over us because we lusted after the very corruption that gave him power over us. Satan offered us the temporary pleasure of the flesh to keep us permanently dependent upon the flesh, which perpetuated our corruption and kept us separated from God. Through the grace of God, we learned the truth: Pharaoh and Satan ruled only because, out of fear, the people of God worked and empowered them. With the power of God, the people of God were actually stronger than their enemies.

Obedient Unto the Cross

Jesus gave Satan unrestricted access to Job; there was no hedge around Job to protect him. Satan could challenge Job, but Satan could not destroy Job. Satan hit Job with everything short of death, but Job did not rebel against God. He trusted in the Lord. God will allow Satan to attack us, but Satan cannot destroy us. The Lord will not allow the devil to put on us more than we can bear. If we have faith, the Lord will save us. We will have to give up the life of sin, the only life we know; however, with the Holy Ghost, we have a new life—a spiritual life. The devil cannot defeat us and take away our spiritual life; he has power only over the flesh. He will attack our natural life, but we will endure the hardship and sacrifice our natural life, because we exalt our spiritual life. We know that if we suffer with Christ, we will reign with Christ. The eternal reward far exceeds the ephemeral sacrifice.

Died Without Mercy

The Lord heard the children of Israel's cry for deliverance and had mercy upon them. Moses delivered the children of Israel out of the bondage of Egypt; they did not have to work for Pharaoh anymore. They did not have to build their enemy's kingdom and strengthen the power of those who destroyed them and their children. The Egyptians subsequently pursued after the Hebrews to recapture them. Although the Lord destroyed the Egyptians, most of the Hebrews trusted not in the Lord and repeatedly murmured against Him. They complained that He had taken them out of Egypt to die in the wilderness. Since most of them renounced their spiritual inheritance and expressed the desire to return into bondage, there was no need for God to have mercy upon them. He destroyed them without mercy.

─────────── **Destroy the Works of the Devil** ───────────

Jesus Christ saw a world filled with wickedness and madness. There was no peace. People were burdened by distrust, betrayal, deceitfulness. Everyone lied, stole, cheated, or engaged in some form of wickedness to survive; they could find no rest for their own soul. Satan had the people working for him and destroying themselves.

Jesus had mercy upon the people. He came and defeated Satan. Through the grace of God, those who wanted to come out of the bondage of sin and serve the Lord could find rest for their soul. They were no longer forced to work for their enemy and sacrifice their integrity. They were no longer forced to destroy themselves. They were free to leave bondage. If the people simply admitted the truth, confessed that Jesus was Lord, and obeyed His commandments, the Lord would save them from their enemies.

─────────── **Saved From Your Enemies** ───────────

Ever since false prophets began to preach the gospel, they have twisted the scripture and deceived the people. *(2 Peter 3:16)* One of the worst errors false prophets have taught is that being saved means that people are going to Heaven. More people would exert greater effort to obey God if they understood that being saved does not mean that they are going to Heaven. God saved the children of Israel out of Egypt and afterward destroyed nearly all of them. *(Jude 1:5)*

(A) To be saved simply means that God has saved (delivered) us from our enemies. When the scripture denotes that Jesus came to save us from our sins, it does not imply that Jesus died for our sins, so we would have the freedom to sin against God. It means that Jesus broke the power of Satan over our lives. As a flesh-and-blood being, Jesus triumphed over the power of Satan; He was Lord. Since Jesus defeated Satan, He had the power and authority to deliver those who wanted to come out of the bondage of sin; He had the power and authority to deliver those who wanted to serve Him. We do not have to work and empower pagans anymore; we know the truth: Jesus is Lord. He is the only God we serve.

(B) To be saved by grace through faith simply means that those who trusted in the Lord refused to rebel against Him. Despite all of the adversity that comes against us, we will keep the faith—and the Lord will deliver us. The Lord is the Almighty God, and through the power of His might, we will overcome our enemies. He defeated the giants in Canaan. He gave David victory over Goliath. He saved Daniel from the mouth of the lion. When the ship was falling apart, when all hope of being saved had been taken away, He saved Paul. Those who trust in the Lord will keep the faith and wait upon Him. They will not lose faith and rebel against the Almighty.

(C) To be saved by grace, through faith, and not by works, because God did not want any flesh to boast simply underscores the weakness of man. The Hebrews worked, but their work built their enemies' treasure cities. Sinners work, but the works of the flesh separate us from God and reinforce Satan's power over us. Our enemies force us to work for them, which strengthens their control over our lives. As slaves, we do not benefit at all from our labor. Yet, out of the fear of death, we have joined forces with the enemies of God. They forced us to serve them rather than the Almighty and made us enemies of our own savior. Alas, we were not saved by our works. Our enemies used our works to make us enslave ourselves. We were too ignorant to realize that the enemies gave us the spiritual straws to build their treasure cities. We were too ignorant to realize that those who wanted us to self-destruct had us lusting after the very flesh that gave them the power to compel us to destroy our souls. We could not boast about our ignorance.

"He delivered me from my strong enemy, and from them that hated me: for they were too strong for me." (2 Samuel 22:18)

———————— **According to His Purpose** ————————

God commanded the people before the foundation of the world to live holy; however, the Lord deliberately allowed men and women to be taken captive and corrupted. The Lord knew that those who attempted to serve Him in Satan's kingdom would suffer persecution. Abraham was robbed. Lot was assaulted. Daniel was placed in the lion's den. Shadrach, Meshach, and Abednego were cast into the fiery furnace. Jesus was killed. Stephen was stoned. John the Baptist was beheaded. Spiritual men and women have suffered great persecution in Satan's kingdom, but those who trusted in the Lord kept their integrity. They knew the Lord was God and refused to serve pagan gods. They exalted spirit above flesh; integrity above corruption; eternal life above eternal damnation.

"If it be so, our God whom we serve is able to deliver us from the burning fiery furnace, and he will deliver us out of thine hand, O king. But if not, be it known unto thee, O king, that we will not serve thy gods, nor worship the golden image which thou hast set up." (Daniel 3:17-18)

———————— **We Trust in the Lord** ————————

As a spirit, Satan, our enemy, has greater power than the whole of mankind. He is too strong for us. This is his kingdom. He has the power of death. Satan will pressure us to conform to the wickedness of the world or suffer persecution. If Jesus does not save us, we will either be forced to serve a pagan god or subjected to death, which is why most individuals remain in the bondage of sin: they fear death.

Many assert that Jesus is Lord, but they do not trust in Him to save them, so they sin against Him. The problem is, either Satan will attempt to destroy us for serving Jesus or Jesus will destroy us for serving Satan. *(Hebrews 2:14-15; Romans 6:23)* Hence, the truth is important. We must fear the Almighty, the One who has the power to take our life and destroy our soul.

We have been commanded to serve the Lord. Since corruption cannot inherit incorruption, justice dictates that we must be given the opportunity to redeem ourselves. After all, we were conceived in sin. We cannot serve the Lord in holiness and righteousness unless we have been redeemed from corruption. The devil will send fiery darts at those who attempt to overcome corruption. He will attempt to intimidate us and compel us to remain in sin. Since the devil is too strong for us, we cannot serve the Lord unless He saves us.

"I cried unto thee; save me, and I shall keep thy testimonies."
(Psalm 119:146)

Jesus will save us. "He delivered me from my strong enemy, and from them which hated me: for they were too strong for me." *(Psalm 18:17; 2 Samuel 22:18)* Satan has the power of death, and most of us have spent our lives in the bondage of sin because of the fear of death. Through the knowledge of Jesus Christ, we know that Jesus is Lord. We are no longer afraid to serve the Lord. We trust in the Lord to save us and deliver us out of the hand of our enemies. Although we walk through the valley of the shadow of death, we fear no evil; the Lord is our Shepherd. He will save us.

"And the Lord shall help them, and deliver them: he shall deliver them from the wicked, and save them, because they trust in him." (Psalm 37:40)

──────── **Confess With Your Mouth the Lord Jesus** ────────

Modern false prophets have persuaded the people that they are saved, although the people remain slaves to sin. If the people were saved, they would have been set free. To be saved means that God has delivered us from the enemy. For example, God saved the Hebrews out of Egypt connotes that the Hebrews were no longer forced to work for the Egyptians; God destroyed the power of the Egyptians over His people and set them free to serve Him. To be saved under the New Testament implies that God has saved us from the enemy; we do not have to work for the enemy, because of the fear of death. Since God is holy in all His ways, He must have servants who are holy. We cannot be holy if our enemy has power over us and forces us to rebel against God. Jesus' victory over Satan destroyed the power of Satan over our lives. He came and set the captives free. We are now free to serve the Lord in holiness and righteousness all the days of our lives. *(Luke 1:67-75)* "But now being made free from sin, and become servants to God, ye have your fruit unto holiness, and the end everlasting life." *(Romans 6:22)*

The people have been taught that, although they are sinners, they are saved. A person cannot be delivered from the enemy and captured by the enemy at the same time. Where God is, there is liberty. *(2 Corinthians 3:17)* Hence, if we are sinners, we have chosen to reject Christ, because Christ has indeed destroyed the power of Satan over our lives and ransomed us from the grave of sin. "He that saith, I know him, and keepeth not his commandments, is a liar, and the truth is not in him." *(1 John 2:4)* Bondage means that our enemy has power over us. We cannot serve the Lord Jesus Christ while enslaved by an enemy of God. We cannot have the power of Almighty God within us and be subject to a false god. Sinners are not saved. God cast sinners out of His sight and allowed their enemies to overtake them. *(Psalm 5:5)* We cannot serve Him and serve His enemy, too. Who we serve illustrates who we exalt as our Lord. *(Romans 6:16)*

According to the false prophets, Jesus died for the sins of the people. Therefore, whosoever confesses with his mouth the Lord Jesus and believes in his heart that God raised Him from the dead shall go to Heaven. That is not what is written in the scripture, and that is not what is meant by the scripture. The scripture says, "That if thou confess with thy mouth the Lord Jesus, and shalt believe in thine heart that God hath raised him from the dead, thou shalt be saved." *(Romans 10:9)* God does not want any to perish. If we trust in Him, He will save us from our enemies. We do not have to fear death. "Fear thou not; for I am with thee: be not dismayed; for I am thy God: I will strengthen thee; yea, I will help thee; yea, I will uphold thee with the right hand of my righteousness." *(Isaiah 41:10)* Our God does not want us to disobey Him and serve false gods out of fear. He wants us to obey and trust in Him. If we confess that Jesus is Lord, we will do what He says. *(Luke 6:46)*

The people were in the bondage of sin because of fear of death. Jesus rose from the grave and demonstrated that He had power over death. The apostle Paul wanted the people to understand that Jesus was Lord: "O death, where is thy sting? O grave, where is thy victory?" *(1 Corinthians 15:55)* The sting of death is sin. *(1 Corintians 15:56)* Jesus ransomed us from the grave of sin. Those who have been redeemed from corruption were buried with Christ; they stopped walking after the pollution in their blood. We buried the life of the flesh (sin) and are free from sin, because we were filled with the Spirit of God and walked in the newness of life. *(Romans 6:4)* We were new creatures, spiritual creatures, created by God. The former life was passed away; all things had become new. *(2 Corinthians 5:17)* We renounced the life of corruption and exercised our right of redemption. We chose to reclaim our birthright and restore our soul.

God saw the corruption in the world and had mercy upon the people. True to His promise, He came and delivered us out of the hands of our enemies. *(Psalm 18:48)* Everyone will be held accountable in the judgment: Those who confessed that Jesus was Lord and served Him were justified. They had only served Satan because their enemies were too strong for them. When Jesus delivered them, they came out of bondage and served the Lord. Those who confessed Jesus was Lord, yet refused to obey God's commandments will be destroyed. They knew Satan was a pagan, a fraud, yet they exalted him above the Almighty. "For by thy words thou shalt be justified, and by thy words thou shalt be condemned." *(Matthew 12:37)*

The false prophets have persuaded the people that because they confess with their mouth the Lord Jesus and say they believe in their heart that God raised Him from the dead, they are saved. When Jesus returns, many will say, Lord, Lord, we have prophesied in thy name, cast out devils, and done many great works. He will tell them to depart from Him; He never knew them. They had confessed Jesus was Lord; they professed to worship God; but they had served Satan. As a result, not only were they not saved from sin; they rejected God's knowledge to remain in sin. If they were saved, they would have been delivered from sin and would have obeyed all of God's commandments. *(Matthew 7:21-23)*

Hell Hath Enlarged Itself

Just as the Lord had mercy upon the children of Israel and delivered them out of the bondage of Egypt, He has shown mercy to us and given us the opportunity to come out of the bondage of sin. However, just as He destroyed the Hebrews who, after having been delivered out of Egypt, chose to return to Egypt to serve pagan gods, the Lord will destroy those who, having been delivered from the power of Satan, chose to remain in sin and serve Satan. God did not want any to perish, but, just as Satan and other rebellious demons were cast out of Heaven and reserved unto fire, those in the earth who rebel against God will join them. There is a wide gate that leads to destruction.

Humble Yourself and Obey

God sent famine into the land and purposely allowed the Egyptians to enslave (overtake) the Hebrews. The Lord later saved (delivered) the Hebrews out of the bondage of Egypt. God sent famine into the land and purposely allowed Satan to overtake the human family. The Lord later saved (delivered) the people out of the bondage of sin. The Lord has sent His word to heal and deliver the people. Do the people want to be made whole and integrated with God? Or do they want to remain corrupted and separated from God?

The Lord wanted the people to see how frail they were. Satan had the power of death, overtook the people, and made them live in the bondage of sin. The devil was too powerful for the people. Jesus put on a weak, flesh-and-blood body and destroyed Satan in Satan's own kingdom. Jesus delivered the people out of the hands of their enemies. If the people could not defeat Satan, they should have enough sense to know that they cannot defeat God.

God hates disobedience. He was willing to forgive the people, because He had deliberately sent famine into the land and refused to teach the people. It was the Lord's will that the people went into captivity. "Therefore my people are gone into captivity, because they have no knowledge: and their honourable men are famished, and their multitude dried up with thirst." *(Isaiah 5:13)* However, once He delivered the people out of captivity, they were commanded to obey Him. "And the times of this ignorance God winked at; but now commandeth all men every where to repent." *(Acts 17:30)*

Remember: Judas Iscariot betrayed Christ one time. He was damned to destruction. Simon Peter betrayed Christ three times on the very same night that Judas betrayed Christ. Simon Peter, however, feared death and betrayed Christ only to save his own life. Once Peter received the Holy Ghost, he did not fear death anymore and gladly suffered persecution. Peter received forgiveness for his sins.

Jesus died for our sins. Those who profess Jesus as Lord and believe He rose from the grave will turn from their wickedness. God shined His light upon us and woke us from sleep. With our eyes opened, we saw Satan's witchcraft and the false prophets' lying vanities. When given the opportunity to come out of the bondage of sin and serve the Lord, we obeyed. We were justified in asking for forgiveness of sin. In our ignorance and weakness, we served Satan. Once we confessed Jesus was Lord, we overcame sin and obeyed His commandments, which confirmed that we are His disciples indeed. Those who refuse to come out of the bondage of sin when given a chance will be condemned. They professed Jesus as Lord, yet refused to submit to Him. Thus, their words bear witness to their idolatry; they exalt false gods above the Almighty.

Make Ready a People

God sent John the Baptist to make ready a people to serve the Lord. The whole duty of man is to fear God and to keep His commandments. *(Ecclesiastes 12:13)* Faithful subjects have to prepare themselves to execute His command. All of His ways are perfect—and He came to teach us of His ways, so that we could walk in His path. We must walk the way Jesus walked. *(Psalm 18:30; 2 Samuel 22:31; Isaiah 2:2-3; 1 John 2:6)*

When Satan observes that we are going to serve the Lord, he will attack us. If we believe that Jesus is Lord, we will not give in to Satan's attacks. Let the enemy put us in the fiery furnace. Let the enemy put us in the lion's den. Our shield of faith will quench the fiery darts of the wicked. We know that our God is the Almighty and will deliver us out of our enemies' hands. He will not allow His servants to be forced to sin against Him.

"For the Lord your God is he that goeth with you, to fight for you against your enemies, to save you." (Deuteronomy 20:4)

───────────── **They Trust in Him** ─────────────

Just as the Lord delivered (saved) Abraham from the hands of his enemies, He will deliver (save) those who trust in Him out of the mouth of the lion, out of the fiery furnace, out of the miry clay, and from all troubles and afflictions. "But the salvation of the righteous is of the Lord: he is their strength in the time of trouble. And the Lord shall help them, and deliver them: he shall deliver them from the wicked, and save them, because they trust in him." *(Psalm 37:39-40)* The Lord did not send His servants to Heaven when He saved them; He kept their wicked enemies from destroying those who exalted Him in the earth.

Remember: the Lord saved the children of Israel out of Egypt and afterward destroyed them. The people did not reach the Promised Land; they did not reclaim their inheritance. "Therefore the Lord heard this, and was wroth: so a fire was kindled against Jacob, and anger also came up against Israel; because they believed not in God, and trusted not in his salvation." *(Psalm 78:21-22)* They refused to trust in the Lord and chose to return into bondage. The Lord saved them (delivered them) out of the hands of their enemies, but the people did not trust in the Lord. As a result of their distrust, they refused to serve Him. The Lord destroyed them.

───────────── **Thou Shalt Save Israel** ─────────────

Gideon complained to an angel that the Lord had forsaken the people and delivered them into the hands of the Midianites. "And Gideon said unto him, Oh my Lord, if the Lord be with us, why then is all this befallen us? and where be all his miracles which our fathers told us of, saying, Did not the Lord bring us up from Egypt? but now the Lord hath forsaken us, and **delivered** us into the hands of the Midianites." *(Judges 6:13)* Many people have heard about God's saving power, yet they have doubt whether He will deliver them from the hands of their enemies. Accordingly, out of fear, they disobey God and give in to the enemy.

The Lord told Gideon that Gideon would save Israel from the Midianites. "And he said unto him, oh my Lord, wherewith shall I **save** Israel? . . . and the Lord said unto him, Surely I will be with thee, and thou shalt smite the Midianites as one man." *(Judges 6:15-16)* The Lord made it clear that He had not forsaken His people and **delivered** them into the hands of the Midianites. Gideon would **save** them; Gideon would **deliver** them from the hands of the Midianites. "And the Lord looked upon him, and said, Go in this thy might, and thou shalt **save** Israel from the hand of the Midianites: have not I sent thee?" *(Judges 6:14)* God did not deliver the Hebrews into the hands of the Midianites; God delivered them out of the hands of the Midianites. God saved Israel from the hands of their enemies.

When God saved Israel out of the hands of the Midianites, Israel did not go to Heaven. "God saved Israel" simply meant God fought for His people and refused to allow their enemies to prevail against His people; He delivered them from death.

Scarlet Thread

Joshua was leading the children of Israel to their inheritance—the Promised Land of milk and honey God had promised to Abraham's descendants. The man of God sent two spies to Jericho to secretly collect information on their enemies' activities. Men of Jericho had heard about the children of Israel and were fearful because they knew God had destroyed the Egyptians. Some people in Jericho learned that Hebrew spies were in the home of Rahab, a harlot. They went to her house and demanded she put forth the spies.

Rahab was among her own people. Irrespective, she hid the spies and told them that she knew that God would give the Hebrews victory. In exchange for her sacrifice, she asked that when God gave them the victory, the Hebrews would spare her life and the life of her family. The spies agreed. They gave her a scarlet thread and told her to hang the thread in the window. The scarlet thread indicated the house where a sacrifice had been made to the Lord. When the destroyers came to the city, the scarlet thread would be the sign to pass over that house and save the inhabitants from death. *(Joshua Chapter 2)*

Similarly, when God prepared to destroy Egypt, He commanded the children of Israel to kill an unblemished lamb. They were to take the blood of the lamb and place it around the door. After they placed the blood around the door, they were to cook and eat the lamb meat. When the destroying angel passed through Egypt, the angel of death passed over those who had the blood around their door. Those under the blood were saved from destruction. *(Exodus Chapter 12)* The sacrifice allowed God to break the power of Egypt over the slaves and to destroy the works of the Egyptians. His people did not have to work as slaves any more. They were set free to leave Egypt. When the Egyptians pursued after the exiting children of Israel, God saved His people and destroyed the Egyptians in the sea. "And Israel saw that great work which the Lord did upon the Egyptians: and the people feared the Lord, and believed the Lord, and his servant Moses." *(Exodus 14:30)*

"My times are in thy hand: deliver me from the hand of mine enemies, and from them that persecute me. Make thy face to shine upon thy servant: save me for thy mercies' sake." *(Psalm 31:16)*

——————— **Saved by Grace through Faith** ———————

There are many individuals who profess faith in God, yet their faith is based upon what they can see and understand. Faith in God is not based upon what you can see. Faith is based upon trusting in His word. Jesus deliberately waited until Lazarus died to demonstrate His power to restore life. He did not have to wait until the resurrection to redeem Lazarus from death; He had the power right then to resurrect Lazarus. "Jesus saith unto her, Said I not unto thee, that, if thou wouldest believe, thou shouldest see the glory of God?" *(John 11:40)* The critical issue was whether Mary and Martha believed in the power of the Almighty. If they believed, they would see the works of God.

Many of us have suffered affliction and persecution. We have been wronged. Our enemies have pounced on our weakness and rejoiced over our fall. Those who trusted in the Lord, however, did not draw back into perdition. We waited on the Lord to redeem us. Jesus came to a blind man. "And his disciples asked him, saying, Master, who did sin, this man, or his parents, that he was born blind? Jesus answered, Neither hath this man sinned, nor his parents: but that the works of God should be made manifest in him." *(John 9:2-3)* The Lord allows humans to experience adversity to assess whether they will trust in Him or rebel against Him. If we trust in Him, we will see the works of God manifested in our lives.

Sickness Not Unto Death

If the Lord had been there, Lazarus would not have died. Jesus observed that Lazarus sickness was "not unto death"—although Lazarus died. Adam and Eve would not have fallen for Satan's tricks, if the Lord had been there. The Lord purposely allowed the man and woman to fall into Satan's hands. As a result of Adam's disobedience, all of the human family died. Our sickness, however, was not unto death. It was not the Lord's will for any of His people to perish. The Lord has the power to ransom the dead from the grave of sin and to restore our life. The Lord has the power to save us from destruction. The Lord will fight for us and save us from sin. He will not allow our enemies to put more on us than we can bear and make us serve them. He will make a way of escape to keep His people from being overtaken. *(1 Corinthians 10:13)*

Jesus is the resurrection. No one who walks with Jesus can be in the grave of sin. The Spirit cannot die, and those who have the Spirit of God—those who have the Spirit of Christ—should never be found among the dead. *(John 11:25; Luke 24:5)* When Christ was on the cross, the Spirit of God came out to allow the flesh to die; the body could not die as long as it housed the eternal Spirit of God. The body of Christ died. When the Spirit of God went back into the body, the body came up out of the grave. The flesh-and-blood body did not come back to life; the blood had been shed. Jesus raised His temple out of the grave. We (the church) comprised the temple that rose from the grave; we were lively stones. *(1 Peter 2:5)* Like Christ, those who shed their blood and stopped walking after Satan's witchcraft were born again. God came into our souls and resurrected us from the grave of sin. With the Spirit of Christ, we had power over our enemies and overcame them. We were no longer subject to the enemies; our enemies were subject to us. We were liberated from sin through the power of Jesus Christ.

Even Now

False prophets have convinced the people that, because they are walking in the flesh, they cannot live a perfect life. Thus, it is assumed that sinners will obey God once they enter Heaven. Of course, the ignorant false teachers can only teach what they know or understand. It is imperative for believers to understand that God told Adam that if he ate from the tree of the knowledge of good and evil, he would die. If Adam and Eve had eaten only from the tree of life (learned only the ways of God), they would have lived forever. Adam, however, ate from the tree of the knowledge of good and evil; he learned Satan's corrupt ways. God, holy in all His ways, separated from evil. Adam did not physically die immediately; His soul died. The Spirit of God departed from him. Those who are in the grave of sin are separated from the Spirit of God. Unless they overcome corruption and are resurrected from the grave of sin, they cannot inherit eternal life. *(John 3:5; Revelation 21:7; 1 Corinthians 15:50)*

The truth is, God wants His will done in the earth as it is in Heaven. *(Matthew 6:10)* God wants to be exalted in the earth. *(Psalm 46:10)* Only those who do His will in the earth are going to be given the opportunity to do His will in Heaven. The good and faithful servant will enter into the joy of the Lord. *(Matthew 25:23)*

God has the power "even now" to resurrect sinners from death. Isaiah prophesied that our God was going to come and save the people. *(Isaiah 35:4)* Matthew made it plain that Jesus came to save the people from their sins. *(Matthew 1:21)* Isaiah made it plain that a virgin was going to conceive and bear a son, whose name would be Immanuel. *(Isaiah 7:14)* Jesus was God with us. *(Matthew 1:23)* The Good News was that we did not have to live in sin anymore; we did not have to remain dead, separated from God. Jesus is the resurrection. He is not a God of the dead, but a God of the living. He came to ransom us from the grave of sin and to restore our soul.

——————— Thou Shalt Serve No Other God ———————

It is important to understand that it does not matter how far an individual has fallen, the arms of the Lord are not too short that He cannot save. *(Isaiah 59:1)* It does not matter what muck a person has gotten stuck into, the Lord has the power to bring him out of the miry clay. *(Psalm 40:2)* It does not matter if your life has been taken away; the Lord has the power to restore life. Do we want to be redeemed? Do we want to be made whole? Will we obey?

——————— Save the People from Their Sins ———————

Jesus came to bless us, to save us. He defeated Satan. There is no need for the people to remain in iniquity. We can let go of the fear of death and trust God to save us. He is a God that cannot lie and is holy in all His works. He will perform what He has promised. We can turn from our sins and obey God: "unto you first God, having raised up his Son Jesus, sent him to bless you, in turning away every one of you from his iniquities." *(Acts 3:26)* Jesus came to save us from our sins.

God allowed us to see how Satan had us polluted in our own blood. *(Ezekiel 16:6)* We lusted after the very corruption that kept us weak and in bondage. Further, not only did Adam and Eve pass down lust of the flesh and vanity through the blood, Satan used the false prophets to bewitch us with lies. Ergo, just as Pharoah gave straws to the children of Israel for them to make bricks to build his treasure cities, Satan offers us pleasure to keep us lusting after corrupted flesh. The weakness of the flesh gives Satan power over us. Just as the 250 famous men in the congregation, men of renown, persuaded the people to return to Egypt and rebel against Moses, Satan has sent false prophets to deceive us and lead us to believe that God sacrificed Jesus, so we can remain in sin and continue to rebel against Him.

Saved by Grace through Faith

We are saved by grace through faith. Abraham's faith that God would keep His promise was the decisive factor that made him leave his doomed family. Paul's faith that God would keep His promise was the decisive factor that made him stay aboard a disintegrating ship. *(Acts 27:6-44)* If Jesus is indeed our Lord, we will trust Him and come out from among the wickedness of the world, serve the Lord in holiness and righteousness, and save our souls from destruction.

Saved -- Delivered

Saved does not mean we are going to Heaven. To be saved means that God has delivered us out of the bondage of sin. God has delivered us out of the hands of our enemies. Since the wages of sin is death, Jesus has saved us from death. Remember: we went into captivity because of the lack of knowledge. When we went into captivity, hell enlarged itself and opened her mouth without measure. *(Isaiah 5:13-14)* If we want to escape from captivity and not burn in hell, we need the knowledge of Jesus Christ. *(2 Peter 2:20)* We must obey God's commandments and continue steadfastly in the apostles' doctrine. Enemies will attack on the way to the Promised Land, but our God is well able to overcome them. If we do not trust in the Lord and attempt to save our lives by rebelling against God, like the children of Israel, we will be destroyed.

Serve Only the Lord

We are witnesses to the madness and corruption in the earth. The Lord has allowed us to see that He has supreme wisdom, knowledge, and power. We are to serve Him. We are to obey His commandments. Satan, through the fear of death, has the people in the bondage of sin. The Lord came to destroy the works of the devil. We are not to serve Satan and work to destroy ourselves. The Lord heard our cry and sent His word to heal us from our sickness. His knowledge will bring us out of the bondage of sin. However, if we reject His knowledge and choose to remain in bondage, when the Lord destroys Satan, He will also destroy those who chose to serve Satan.

Please remember, Jesus observed that the people of Nineveh would rise up in judgment and condemn those in Jerusalem. The people of Nineveh believed Jonah and turned from their wickedness. Those in Jerusalem believed the teachings of the scribes and Pharisees, men who were ignorant about the things of God. As a result of their leaders' deception, the people fought against God and were destroyed. Those who will escape the wrath of God will be saved by the truth. (John 17:17) When given the chance to come out of captivity, they acquired the knowledge of Jesus Christ and came out of bondage.

Additional Edifying Scriptures:

"And Saul said unto the Kenites, Go, depart, get you down from among the Amalekites, lest I destroy you with them: for ye shewed kindness to all the children of Israel, when they came up out of Egypt. So the Kenites departed from among the Amalekites." (1 Samuel 15:6)

"Then the king commanded, and they brought Daniel, and cast him into the den of lions. Now the king spake and said unto Daniel, Thy God whom thou servest continually, he will deliver thee." (Daniel 6:16)

"The rest said, Let be, let us see whether Elias will come to save him." (Matthew 27:49)

"This poor man cried, and the Lord heard him, and saved him out of all his troubles." (Psalm 34:6)

"And if any man hear my words, and believe not, I judge him not: for I came not to judge the world, but to save the world." (John 12:47)

"And when the morning arose, then the angels hastened Lot, saying arise, take thy wife, and thy two daughters, which are here; lest thou be consumed in the iniquity of the city. And while he lingered, the two men laid hold upon his hand, and upon the hand of his wife, and upon the hand of his two daughters; the Lord being merciful unto him: and they brought him forth, and set him without the city. . . Behold now, thy servant hath found grace in thy sight, and thou hast magnified thy mercy, which thou has shewed unto me in saving my life." (Genesis 19: 15, 16,19)

"If it had not been the Lord who was on our side, now may Israel say; if it had not been the Lord who was on our side, when men rose up against us: then they had swallowed us up quick, when their wrath was kindled against us." (Psalm 124:1-3)

"And Moses said unto the people, Fear ye not, stand still, and see the salvation of the Lord, which he will shew to you to day." (Exodus 14:13)

"And Samuel called the people together unto the Lord to Mizpeh; and said unto the children of Israel, Thus saith the Lord God of Israel, I brought up Israel out of Egypt, and delivered you out of the hand of the Egyptians, and out of the hand of all kingdoms, and of them that oppressed you: And ye have this day rejected your God, who himself saved you out of all your adversities and your tribulations." (1 Samuel 10:17-19)

"Though an host should encamp against me, my heart shall not fear: though war should rise against me, in this will I be confident." (Psalms 27:3)

"Yea, though I walk through the valley of the shadow of death, I will fear no evil: for thou art with me; thy rod and thy staff they comfort me." (Psalms 23:4)

CHAPTER EIGHT

INHERITANCE

A s believers, our paramount objective is not simply to be saved. God saved the children of Israel out of Egypt and afterwards destroyed them. *(Jude 1:5)* God saved many that were ultimately destroyed. *(Isaiah 42:24; Psalm 106:41-42; Nehemiah 9:26-37)* Dogs went back to their vomit. *(Proverbs 26:11)* Sows went back to wallowing in the mire. *(2 Peter 2:22)* We do not simply want to be saved from the enemy. We want to inherit eternal life.

God is a spirit; His kingdom is not of this natural world. We have to be changed from flesh to spirit, from mortal into immortality, to inherit His kingdom. We have to be born again of the spirit and redeemed back to the way God created us. Adam and Eve rebelled against God and died. Through the grace of God, we can overcome corruption and redeem our soul from death. We renounce Satan— the god of this world—and serve the Lord Jesus Christ. We bear witness that Jesus is Lord and exalt the Spirit of God above the life of our flesh.

Before He ever formed man, God predestined that He would allow humans to be taken into the captivity of sin. The people experienced for themselves the difference between God and Satan. God empowers; Satan weakens. God requires His people to love one another and walk in integrity. Satan requires his people to engage in wickedness and betrayal. The people have a clear choice: they can exalt Jesus as Lord and obey His commandments, or they can exalt witchcraft and rebel against God. *(Deuteronomy 30:15-20)*

As a just God, Jesus is obligated to allow the people to decide for themselves whether they will obey or disobey His commandments; the people have to be given the right to save or destroy themselves. Although natural human beings are not children of God (Jesus was God's only begotten child), they are natural descendants of Adam and Eve—who were created by God. Accordingly, those who descended from Adam and Eve are the heritage of the Lord and have the right to be reconciled with the Father. *(Psalm 127:3)*

Since the Lord worked and created the human family, He has the first right to our service. *(2 Timothy 2:6)* Although the people rebelled against Him, the Lord has the right to redeem His creation. Moreover, children have a right to inherit from their father. Just as Abraham renounced his pagan father's inheritance to acquire God's inheritance, all humans have the right to renounce our pagan father's inheritance (eternal destruction) to acquire God's inheritance (eternal life).

Further, just as God drove the seven nations out of Canaan and replaced them with the natural children of Abraham, God cast Satan and other disobedient servants out of His kingdom and will replace them with faithful servants. *(Acts 13:17-19)* The Lord demands obedient servants and will reward all people according to their works. *(Revelation 22:12)* Ergo, as a God holy in all His works, the Lord gives everyone the freedom to choose whom they will serve: those who want to serve the Lord have the right to serve the Lord; those who want to serve Satan have the right to serve Satan.

Adam caused us to lose our birthright—the right to inherit the Kingdom of God. Jesus paid the ransom to redeem our birthright. "So Hanameel mine uncle's son came to me in the court of the prison according to the word of the Lord, and said unto me, Buy my field, I pray thee, that is in Anathoth, which is in the country of Benjamin: for the right of inheritance is thine, and the redemption is thine; buy it for thyself. Then I knew that this was the word of the Lord." *(Jeremiah 32:8)* Jesus purchased our right of inheritance with His own blood. *(Acts 20:28)*

Jesus Christ, conceived of the spirit, descended naturally from Abraham, Isaac, and Jacob, which gave Him the right to redeem the Hebrews' inheritance. Additionally, as a natural descendant of King David, Jesus also had the blood of the Moabite woman, Ruth, a Gentile, which gave Him the right to redeem the Gentiles as well. *(Matthew 1:5)* Jesus, the God of all flesh, had the right to redeem all of humanity. *(Jeremiah 32:27)* Those who choose, like Abraham, to renounce paganism and exalt the Lord can inherit from the Father. Those in the bondage of sin, however, cannot be heirs with Christ. *(Galatians 4:30)* They renounced their inheritance to remain in the bondage of sin and serve another god. They wanted to inherit from their natural father, Satan; they chose to inherit death.

Abraham's seed – Chosen People

As the eldest son of his father, Terah, Abraham had the right to inherit from his father. Sadly, his father served pagan gods. Abraham had integrity. God told Abraham to come out from among his country, his kindred, and his father's house; He would bless him. "So Abram departed, as the Lord had spoken unto him." *(Genesis 12:4)* Abraham obeyed God and renounced the right to his father's inheritance.

As a man, it was no doubt a difficult task for Abraham. He assuredly loved his father and mother; he loved the rest of his people; and he knew the land where he was born and raised. Further, there were no laws in the land; and where there was no law, there was no transgression. People could rob and kill each other with impunity. In renouncing his father's inheritance to serve the true God, Abraham renounced his father's false gods, wealth, and protection. When the Lord told him to come out from among his family, Abraham obeyed. Although he did not know where he was going, he trusted in the Lord. His obedience to God demonstrated that he trusted God to do better for him than he could do for himself.

The Lord found Abraham faithful. Abraham put the love of God above the love of his mother and father, his people, his son, and his own life. God kept His promise and blessed Abraham. Abraham's children, as heirs, had a right to inherit the Promised Land. Alas, when the children were tested to see whether they would serve the Lord, they failed.

Abraham had faith in the Lord and renounced his father's natural inheritance to follow God to an unknown location. His heirs, in contrast, renounced their spiritual inheritance to return to bondage. The Lord gave them the opportunity to reclaim their spiritual inheritance, but they did not trust God. As a result of the fear of death, they chose to renounce their spiritual inheritance to remain slaves to their enemies. As slaves, they did not inherit anything. They consented to allow the Egyptians to destroy them and their children.

Enter the Kingdom of God

Our paramount objective is to enter the Kingdom of God. "And when he was gone forth into the way, there came one running, and kneeled to him, and asked him, Good Master, what shall I do that I may **inherit eternal life?**" *(Mark 10:17)* Jesus told the man to sell everything he had and give it to the poor; the man would have treasure in Heaven. The man was grieved because he was very wealthy. Jesus observed, "It is easier for a camel to go through the eye of a needle, than for a rich man to **enter into the kingdom of God.**" *(Mark 10:25)* Jesus, the Good Master, was the preeminent teacher. He made it clear that inheriting eternal life is the same as entering the Kingdom of God. Understand the difference: To be saved is to be delivered from the enemy—we do not want to serve Satan; we want to serve the Lord. God saved us from death and allowed us to escape when our enemy tried to force us to serve him. To inherit the Kingdom of God is to renounce the enemy's corruption and sanctify ourselves for the Master's use. A person who has chosen to reject the knowledge and power of God to live in sin is not saved. Despite his words to the contrary, he does not want to be delivered from the enemy but has chosen to serve the enemy. Those who exalt Satan as their god and choose to remain corrupt cannot inherit the Kingdom of the Most High.

Prodigal Son

The scribes and Pharisees criticized Jesus for eating with sinners. In response to their criticism, Jesus spoke a parable: A man had two sons. The younger son told his father that he wanted his inheritance now. After receiving his portion, the son left and went into a far country where he wasted his money in a sinful lifestyle. Afterwards, there was famine in the land, and the son had no food. He went and joined himself to a citizen in the country, and the citizen sent the son into the field to feed swine. The son's hunger was so great, until he was prepared to get down on the ground and eat with the swine.

However, the son humbled himself. He recognized that he was the son of a wealthy man. In his ignorance, he had rebelled against his father, only to realize later what a fool he had been. The boy decided to return home. When the son neared the house, the father saw him coming and had great compassion upon him. He kissed his son, allowed the son to clean himself up, and fed the child; "for this my son was dead, and is alive again; he was lost, and is found. And they began to be merry." *(Luke 15:11-32)* The prodigal son had lost his soul; he was dead. He had defiled himself with the pollution of this world. Thankfully, he humbled himself and returned to the father, who redeemed him from the grave and restored his life.

We live in Satan's kingdom. Like the prodigal son, most people want their inheritance now. We were born in sin. The life of the flesh is the only life we know. We have been indoctrinated with all of the world's ignorance and internalized all of Satan's corruption. Our lives are filled with pollution and uncleanness, and we engage in all manner of wickedness. Many will eat any type of slop to survive. The Lord wants us to humble ourselves and admit that we deserve better than to live like savage beasts.

God, our Creator (Father) wants His creation (son) to renounce Satan's slop (riotous living) and return home (reconciled with the Father). He will give us an inheritance at the proper time. Eyes have not seen nor has it entered into the hearts of men what God has in store for those who love Him. The ultimate objective is for us to recognize that we can trust Him, and we need to demonstrate that He can trust us. We must obey.

"But which of you, having a servant plowing or feeding cattle, will say unto him by and by, when he is come from the field, Go and sit down to meat? And will not rather say unto him, Make ready wherewith I may sup, and gird thyself, and serve me, till I have eaten and drunken; and afterward thou shalt eat and drink? Doth he thank that servant because he did the things that were commanded him? I trow not. So likewise ye, when ye shall have done all those things which are commanded you, say, We are unprofitable servants: we have done that which was our duty to do." *(Luke 17:7-10)*

Now is the time to show the Lord that you will obey His commandments. Now is the time to acknowledge that the Lord is God; it is He that has made us and not we ourselves. *(Psalms 100:3)* Satan wants us to exalt ourselves above the Lord. We must renounce Satan's witchcraft, reject the false prophets' lying vanities, and humble ourselves before the Lord. We must return unto the Father, who is willing to redeem us from corruption and restore our soul.

——— You Have No Right, You Have No Portion ———

Fornication and adultery are rampant in the earth. The word of God explicitly tells the people that no fornicator or adulterer will inherit the Kingdom of God. *(1 Corinthians 6:9)* Deception and deceitfulness are widespread. The scripture instructs us that God hates liars, and all liars shall have their part in the lake that burns with fire and brimstone. *(Psalms 5:6; Revelation 21:8)* The scripture denotes that without holiness, no one will see God. *(Hebrew 12:14)* Yet many professed Christians believe they can disobey the commandments of God and inherit the Kingdom of God.

If the Spirit of God is the Almighty, why are we walking after Satan's witchcraft? If we exalt Jesus as Lord, why are we disobeying His commandments? If the spirit is supreme, why do we lust after the things of the flesh and reject the things of the spirit? If Jesus' kingdom is not of this world, why are professed Christians walking after the things of the world? God will not allow us into His kingdom, if we have rejected Him to serve Satan.

Those who want to serve the Lord and inherit His kingdom must be redeemed. *(Revelation 3:21)* To be redeemed from corruption, a man needs to know how he became corrupt and how he had been kept in corruption. He needs knowledge. As we learned from Samson, an enemy can only defeat a stronger opponent if he can neutralize his opponent's superior power.

Satan separated man from his power source—God—and reduced man to flesh-and-blood. The devil imposed harsh conditions and heavy burdens upon man. Man's grief and pain were so great, until he capitulated to the devil's will. The corrupt demon bewitched man to serve him, and man was compelled to perform the work of the Satan or suffer death. Over time, man repeated the work, until it became a habit, which ultimately shaped his character. Through repetition, man became inured to corruption and assimilated the ways of Satan. Corrupted parents, in order to save their children from death, taught their children the ways of corruption. Ultimately, all that remained were corrupt souls.

Let me express it another way: men and women want to survive. Many corrupt souls have invaded other countries, enslaved other people, raped, robbed, and engaged in all manner of oppression. In order to survive oppression, the oppressed had to submit to the will of their oppressors. The oppressed learn the ways of oppression and assimilated the ways of their captors. Many joined with their oppressors, lest they were annihilated—and they taught their ways to their children.

Unlike a slave, who has given up hope, a captive yearns to regain his freedom. A captive has the desire to escape and, if given the opportunity, will escape. Jesus came to set the captives free. *(Luke 4:18)* The scripture teaches us that we can escape the pollution of this world through the knowledge of Jesus Christ. *(2 Peter 2:20)* Although famine caused the people to go into captivity, Jesus assured those who hungered and thirsted after righteousness that they would be filled. *(Matthew 5:6)* "Yea, if thou criest after knowledge, and liftest up thy voice for understanding; if thou seekest her as silver, and searchest for her as for hid treasures; then shalt thou understand the fear of the Lord, and find the knowledge of God. For the Lord giveth wisdom: out of his mouth cometh knowledge and understanding." *(Proverbs 2:3-6)*

The Lord finished the heaven and the earth in six days. *(Genesis 2:-1-2)* The Lord rested on the seventh day. The Lord had not finished His work; He had simply finished creating everything necessary to accomplish His purpose: He wanted to prove who had the integrity to admit that He was Lord and exalt Him above themselves. The Lord forced humans into captivity and allowed them to recognize their weakness and ignorance. Honest men and women are willing to exalt the Lord above themselves. They know that they will either obey God and live or disobey God and die. Those who exalt Jesus as Lord will keep His commandments and live. Those who exalt themselves above Jesus—like Satan and Adam—will die.

The Father finished creating the Heaven and earth. According to His purpose, the human family was separated from the spirit and taken into captivity by the enemy. The Son came to finish the Father's work. *(John 4:34; John 17:4)* Jesus came and taught us how to overcome the enemy. Further, He shed His blood that the people might receive remission of their sins. Those who repent (turn from their wickedness) and are baptized into the death of Jesus Christ (renounce the corruption of the flesh) will be forgiven of their sins and allowed to inherit eternal life. *(Acts 2:38)*

—————————— **Walk by Faith** ——————————

God called Abraham out from among the pagans, and Abraham went out with no idea where he was going. He nonetheless went out because he had faith in God. The Lord promised to bless and give him an inheritance. Abraham trusted God and repudiated the paganism of his family to inherit the blessings of God. The Lord blessed Abraham and saved him from his enemies. Abraham's father, Terah, served pagan gods. He and the rest of those who served pagan gods were on the other side of the flood; they were destroyed. *(Joshua Chapter 24)*

Children of Abraham repudiate the things of the world—we give up the only life we have known and refuse to serve pagan gods. Like Abraham, we walk by faith and trust in our God to save us from our enemies. "By faith Abraham, when he was called to go out into a place which he should after receive for an inheritance, obeyed; and he went out, not knowing whither he went." *(Hebrews 11:8)* We are not like the children of Israel, who were willing to serve pagan gods to save their natural lives. Consider: if Abraham had remained with his family and inherited from his father, he would have been subsequently destroyed along with his father. Ergo, he would have inherited destruction. *(Joshua 24:2-3)* Similarly, those who have chosen to receive their inheritance in Satan's kingdom and conform to the world will ineluctably discover that they have inherited eternal destruction. *(1 Corinthians 15:50)*

In Adam all died. In Christ all shall be made alive. We can continue to walk after the flesh and remain dead in sin. Or we can renounce Satan's witchcraft and overcome the corruption within us. God has promised that, if we serve Him, we shall inherit eternal life. We do not know what eternal life with God shall be like; however, we walk by faith and not by sight. We know that the Lord is the true God, the everlasting God, and the holy God. We know His utopian kingdom shall transcend Satan's madness. Accordingly, we want to redeem ourselves from corruption and inherit eternal life.

―――――――― **Additional Edifying Scriptures:** ――――――――

"Are they not all ministering spirits, sent forth to minister for them who shall be heirs of salvation?" (Hebrews 1:14)

"Behold, what manner of love the Father hath bestowed upon us, that we should be called the sons of God: therefore the world knoweth us not, because it knew him not. Beloved, now are we the sons of God, and it doth not yet appear what we shall be be: but we know that, when he shall appear, we shall be like him; for we shall see him as he is. And every man hath this hope in him purifieth himself, even as he is pure." (1 John 3:1-3)

"For this ye know, that no whoremonger, nor unclean person, nor covetous man, who is an idolater, hath any inheritance in the kingdom of Christ and of God. Let no man deceive you with vain words: for because of these things cometh the wrath of God upon the children of disobedience. Be not ye therefore partakers with them." (Ephesians 5:5-7)

"Now this I say, brethren, that flesh and blood cannot inherit the kingdom of God; neither doth corruption inherit incorruption." (1 Corinthians 15:50)

"He that overcometh shall inherit all things; and I will be his God, and he shall be my son." (Revelation 21:7)

"Now the works of the flesh are manifest, which are these; adultery, fornication, uncleanness, lasciviousness, idolatry, witchcraft, hatred, variance, emulations, wrath, strife, seditions, heresies, envying, murder, drunkenness, revellings, and such like: of the which I tell you before . . . that they which do such things shall not inherit the kingdom of God." (Galatians 5:19-21)

"And if ye be Christ's, then are ye Abraham's seed, and heirs according to the promise." (Galatians 3:29)

"And now, brethren, I commend you to God, and to the word of his grace, which is able to build you up, and to give you an inheritance among all them which are sanctified." (Acts 20:32)

"Knowing that of the Lord ye shall receive the reward of the inheritance: for ye serve the Lord Christ." (Colossians 3:24)

"For as many as are led by the Spirit of God, they are the sons of God. . . The Spirit itself beareth witness with our spirit, that we are the children of God: And if children, then heirs; heirs of God, and joint-heirs with Christ; if so be that we suffer with him, that we may be also glorified together." (Romans 8:14,16,17)

"And now, brethren, I commend you to God, and to the word of his grace, which is able to build you up, and to give you an inheritance among all of them which are sanctified." (Acts 20:32)

"To open their eyes, and to turn them from darkness to light, and from the power of Satan unto God, that they may receive forgiveness of sins, and inheritance among them which are sanctified by faith that is in me." (Acts 26:18)

"Then shall the King say unto them on his right hand, Come, ye blessed of my Father, inherit the kingdom prepared for you from the foundation of the world." (Matthew 25:34)

"For if the inheritance be of the law, it is no more of promise: but God gave it to Abraham by promise." (Galatians 3:18)

"Nevertheless what saith the scripture? Cast out the bondwoman and her son: For the son of the bondwoman shall not be heir with the son of the freewoman." (Galatians 4:30)

"In whom also we have obtained an inheritance, being predestinated according to the purpose of him who worketh all things after the counsel of his own will: That we should be to the praise of his glory, who first trusted in Christ." (Ephesians 1:11-12)

"Giving thanks unto the Father, which hath made us meet to be partakers of the inheritance of the saints in light: who hath delivered us from the power of darkness, and hath translated us into the kingdom of his dear Son:" (Colossians 1:12-13)

"To an inheritance incorruptible, and undefiled, and that fadeth not away, reserved in heaven for you, who are kept by the power of God through faith unto salvation ready to be revealed in the last time." (1 Peter 1:4-5)

CHAPTER NINE

COVENANT BY SACRIFICE

Jesus Christ came to bear witness to the truth: He is the King of kings and Lord of lords. He has the power and knowledge to deliver the people out of the bondage of sin, and it is His good pleasure to allow us to inherit His Kingdom. But, in order to receive the inheritance, we must renounce our natural inheritance (life of the flesh). We cannot pretend that we worship God when our sinful lifestyle (corruption) requires us to separate from God. Those who walk after the flesh exalt Satan's witchcraft over Christ's redemption. Those who want to inherit eternal life must demonstrate that we exalt the spirit above the flesh.

Honest men and women admit that wickedness should not exist, and it only exists because sinners disobey God to follow after Satan's witchcraft. Unredeemed sinners have embraced wickedness as a way of life. Those who want to inherit eternal life must exalt integrity above corruption. In their hunger and thirst for righteousness, those who love God will renounce Satan's witchcraft and overcome their corruption. Ergo, they change their lives to reflect the will of God.

All have sinned and fallen short of the glory of God. We lie. We commit fornication or adultery. We may not do everything wrong, but, unless we have overcome, we engage in some form of corruption. If we are honest, we admit that we have contributed to the distrust and madness in the earth. We may not have intentionally committed evil, but, in our ignorance, we committed evil. In disobeying the commandments of God, we collaborated with Satan and fought against God. We resisted the fact that Satan controlled our lives. Ultimately, we had to admit that we did not control our lives. We had no dignity or integrity. As much as we wanted to believe that we were free, we had to admit that we were slaves to fear. We were afraid of death. In our effort to survive, Satan made us renounce integrity and become slaves to sin. In fact, the devil sent false prophets to persuade the people that they could not overcome sin. To inherit the Kingdom is to acknowledge that Satan has corrupted us, and he is too strong for us. Believers know, though, that Jesus is Lord. All power has been given to Jesus; therefore, we will not remain corrupt. We will bear witness to the truth and exalt Jesus as Lord.

If we had been in Heaven, we would like to believe that we would have remained faithful to God. Yet, we now recognize that, when we walk after the things of the world, we have joined Satan in his fight against God. We have fallen for the same witchcraft—lying vanities—that Satan used to deceive Eve. We have fallen for the same witchcraft that Satan used to deceive himself and the other fallen angels. We have chosen to exalt ourselves above the Almighty. The Lord allowed Satan to overtake us to demonstrate our inferiority; the Lord defeated Satan to demonstrate His superiority.

Everything that hath breath should praise the Lord. Satan is a demonic spirit. Consider all of the evil in the world: slavery, rape, murder, etc. If Satan were the Almighty God, he could easily create a hell and torture innocent souls. He has no integrity or dignity. He does whatever he deems necessary to achieve his objective; that is the nature of evil. Sinners are those who will do—right or wrong—whatever they want to do. They do not base their action on holiness or unholiness. Their action is based upon self-will, whatever they deem is necessary to achieve their goal, which will inevitably conflict with the will of others.

Please remember that Satan rebelled against God and was

cast out of the Kingdom of God. The devil manipulated Adam and Eve to rebel against God, and the Lord drove the man and woman out of the garden. There can be no paradise where is there is corruption. Envy, strife, distrust, wickedness—there can never be peace and joy where there is a struggle for power. God has allowed everyone to witness His preeminence. The Lord, who is holy in all His ways, has given everyone the right to choose whom they will serve. Although the Lord does not want anyone to be destroyed, He will allow all humans to decide for themselves whether they are saved or damned.

Satan has imposed harsh burdens upon his subjects—and corrupted the entire world. War, violence, deception, and distrust are rampant in the earth. Peace does not exist anywhere. Jesus has offered the people rest for their souls. Those who obey the Lord have His word that He will save them from their enemies. We can serve God without fear in holiness and righteousness.

Honest people are not too proud to admit that Jesus is Lord. Unlike us, whom Satan has kept in bondage through ignorance and weakness, Jesus demonstrated His superior power and destroyed the works of Satan. Jesus' ability to walk free of sin did not reside exclusively in the fact that He possessed the power of the Almighty. Many damned souls, including Satan, once possessed the Spirit of God. Jesus also possessed superior knowledge. The children of Israel were in bondage for 400 years. Moses, learned in all the ways of the Egyptians, possessed knowledge that the Egyptian slaves did not. When Moses needed to save his life, he had the knowledge to quickly escape from Egypt. Jesus possessed knowledge that sinners did not; He walked free of sin and did not capitulate to Satan's witchcraft. And He revealed to the apostles how sinners could overcome Satan: "And they overcame him by the blood of the Lamb, and by the word of their testimony; and they loved not their lives unto the death." *(Revelation 12:11)* Those who want to overcome sin will take heed to the knowledge of Jesus Christ—the apostles' doctrine. *(Acts 2:42; 1 Timothy 4:16)*

Sin Separates and Destroys

There can only be one King in the Kingdom of God. When we sin against the Almighty, we refuse to submit to His rule. The Lord cannot serve another god; therefore, those who exalt themselves against the Almighty must be separated from Him. To damn our souls to hell, Satan needs us to sin against God. Like Adam and Eve, once we sin against God, we become separated from God. As a spirit, Satan has greater power than flesh-and-blood mortals. As the god of this world, Satan has the power of death. Individuals who do not capitulate to his will face death. If we refuse to surrender to Satan, the devil can cause us to lose our jobs, family, and reputation in the community. Satan can unleash all of the evils that he brought upon Job to bear upon those who refuse to serve him. Weak, flesh-and-blood creatures have no power to defeat the god of this world. Satan rules the flesh according to his will. *(2 Timothy 2:26)*

Without the delivering power of God, humans would never overcome corruption. Satan's ability to manipulate humans to lust after the flesh means that the people, like Eve, have been beguiled into destroying their own soul. Their willingness to disobey the Spirit of God to please the lust of the flesh indicates that they have been deceived. Satan has corrupted our minds to pursue the things of the world, which separates us from the spirit. Our minds are so fixated on the lust of the flesh and vanity, until we refuse to redeem our lost soul.

The earth is Satan's kingdom. The people of the world, those who have chosen to pattern themselves after their king, are his subjects. When the Lord destroys the earth, all natural elements are going to melt with fervent heat. The flesh is going to pass away. Wicked spirits, however, are not going to be dissolved. Unredeemed souls are going to be tormented throughout eternity. The Lord will not have mercy upon false gods. Mercy shall be accorded those who humbled themselves and overcame corruption; they shall inherit the Kingdom of God. *(Revelation 12:10-11)*

———————————— **How to Overcome Sin** ————————————

(A) Blood of the Lamb: Jesus died that we might receive the remission of sin. Jesus did not fear death. He knew that the power and glory belonged to the spirit. Those who worshipped the flesh were ignorant and deceived individuals. Satan had bewitched those who lusted after the flesh to exalt ignorance and destroy themselves. Jesus volunteered to sacrifice His natural life. He exalted the eternal life of the spirit over the ephemeral life of the flesh. He exalted the power of God over the weakness of man. He sacrified His life, so that those who were humble enough to admit they had been deceived could be ransomed from the grave and redeemed from corruption.

(B) And by the word of their testimony: Jesus opened the apostles' understanding and commanded them to teach His disciples how to overcome Satan's witchcraft. The apostles taught the people how Satan corrupted them. We were conceived in sin—the lust of the flesh, lust of the eyes, and the pride of life are in our blood. We lust after the witchcraft that Satan used to deceive Eve. We lust after the flesh that caused Adam to disobey God.

(C) And they loved not their lives unto the death: Through the apostles' teaching, we also learned that Satan used fear of death to intimidate us to remain in bondage. Those who wanted to serve the Lord were confronted with death, if we tried to escape. For example, since the life of the flesh is in the blood, those who attempt to change their lives will invariably encounter death. We have to hate our own lives (life of corruption) to serve the Lord. In order to overcome corruption, the people must overcome the fear of death; the people must be willing to crucify the only life they know—the life of sin—to walk with God. Since sinners do not walk in the newness of life (we were born in sin), they cannot inherit the Kingdom of God—they have not been redeemed from corruption. *(1 Corinthians 15:50)*

The apostles taught us that Jesus is Lord, and, with the Spirit of Jesus Christ, we do not have to be subject to Satan. With the Spirit of Jesus Christ, Satan—and all demons—are subject to us. Thus, since we know that the life of the flesh is corrupt, we are not going to allow the fear of death to make us remain corrupt. We renounce Satan's kingdom and crucify the flesh. We exalt the Spirit of God above the lust of the flesh. We cast down imaginations and bring into captivity every thing that exalts itself unto the obedience of Christ. *(2 Corinthians 10:5)* Although sin works death in us by that which is good, we consent to death. The flesh will ultimately die anyway. The spirit is life, and we want to inherit eternal life.

———————————— **Now is the Day of Salvation** ————————————

Jesus had mercy upon the people. He shed His blood and paid the price to ransom the people from the grave. He loved the people so much, until He deliberately allowed them to see the difference between good and evil. Satan wants to destroy the people, and the people have done nothing to hurt Satan. Jesus gave His life to save the people, although the people had rebelled against Him. Jesus opened the understanding of His disciples and commanded them to teach the people. After the people were taught the gospel, they had the choice whether to exalt the will of the Lord above themselves or to exalt themselves above the will of the Lord. They could apply the word of God, overcome Satan's witchcraft, and redeem themselves from corruption. Or they could reject the word of God, remain in the bondage of sin, and destroy their own soul.

God sent famine into Canaan. As a result, the children of Israel left their spiritual inheritance and relocated to Egypt to save their natural lives. In the course of time, the Egyptians overtook the Hebrews and placed them in bondage. The irony was, the Hebrews were stronger than the Egyptians. *(Psalm 105:24)* It was only out of fear of the Hebrews that the Egyptians enslaved them. *(Exodus 1:7-11)* Hence, the weaker Egyptians ruled over the stronger Hebrews. The people did not know the origin of their own enslavement. In their attempt to survive, the children of Israel surrendered to their slave masters, who taught them how to survive as slaves. The slaves, to save their children from death, taught them how to work as good slaves. Thus, the Hebrews, despite having greater strength than the Egyptians, empowered their enemies to keep them as slaves for 400 years.

Similarly, God sent famine into the earth—not for food or drink, but for the words of the Lord of host. As a result of the people's lack of knowledge, Satan conquered and placed them in the captivity of sin. The irony was, if the people had known, they could have walked with the Spirit of God and been stronger than Satan. It was only out of fear of death (Satan had the power of death) that people rebelled against God. Their sins separated them from the spirit—their power source—which allowed Satan to keep them subject to him. If the people had walked with God, Satan would have been subject to them—and they would have had no need to fear.

But the prophesy went out that a Messiah would come and ransom the people from the power of the grave. *(Hosea 13:14)* Those who believed Jesus was Lord did not have to fear the power of death. *(Hebrews 2:14-15)* The Romans laughed at the King of the Jews; however, the carnal-minded Romans did not realize that Jesus was doing the will of God. Jesus did not fear death. In His humiliation, His life was taken from Him, and He opened not His mouth. Jesus' natural death saved many natual people from dying in their sins and allowed them to resurrect their spiritual lives. Ergo, unlike unbelievers, Jesus did not sin against God to save His natural life. *(Job 2:4; Luke 22:42)* Jesus kept His integrity and sacrificed His natural life. He knew the Spirit of God was supreme and did not allow fear of death to make Him disobey. He was obedient unto death, even the death of the cross. Similarly, His disciples refuse to worship a false god to save their natural lives. They love not their natural lives, even unto death. *(Philippians 2:8; Revelation 12:11)*

-------------------- **Not My Will, But Thine, Be Done** --------------------

A disciple is a student. If we obey Jesus' instructions, we are His disciples indeed. We will know the truth, and the truth will make us free. *(John 8:31-32)* The life of the flesh (corruption) is in the blood. Without the shedding of blood, there could be no remission of sin. Jesus shed His blood that we might receive the forgiveness of sin. We have to repent of our sins (turn from wickedness) and be baptized (crucify the corruption within us) to receive the forgiveness of sin. *(Acts 2:38)* Thus, those who are Christ's disciples take up their cross and follow Him. *(Matthew 16:24)* We shed our blood, too. We deny the lust, corruption, and evil inherent within our blood and offer up our bodies as a living sacrifice, which is only reasonable. We renounce the corruption of Satan to become integrated with God. We renounce our natural inheritance (eternal damnation) to redeem our inheritance from God (eternal life).

-------------------- **Tree of the Knowledge of Good and Evil** --------------------

Satan and other rebellious angels fought against God. They attempted to exalt themselves above the Almighty; they were defeated and cast out of Heaven. Adam and Eve exalted their will above the will of the Lord; they were cast out of the garden. Those who attempt to exalt themselves above God refuse to submit to His authority. Accordingly, those who cannot admit that God has more wisdom and power—and submit to His will—cannot abide in His kingdom. Humans rebel against God because they fear death, yet they cannot get into the Kingdom of God because they rebel against God, which, of course, is Satan's objective—to keep the people in fear. Others rebel because of their vanity and pride, which is why Satan sends false prophets to teach lying vanities. Satan wants the people to believe, like he persuaded Eve, that they can disobey the commandments of God and not die. *(Genesis 3:3-4)*

God created man out of the dust of the earth. Man was natural.

God breathed into man, and man became a living soul. Thus, man was also spiritual. That which was born of the flesh was flesh. That which was born of the spirit was spirit. Man was natural and spiritual. In the garden, every tree was good for food. God permitted man to eat from every tree of life in the midst of the garden; however, man was commanded not to eat from the tree of the knowledge of good and evil. *(Genesis 2:8-9; Genesis 16:17)* The tree of life represented the knowledge of good; eternal life. The tree of the knowledge of good and evil represented the knowledge of life and death.

As long as Adam and Eve ate from the tree of life, they walked in the Spirit of God and knew only good. Once they ate from the tree of the knowledge of good and evil, their eyes were immediately opened. They knew about the spirit and the flesh; they knew about good and evil. When they meditated on good, they meditated on the word of God. When they meditated on evil, they meditated on the word of Satan. When they rebelled against God and saw the evil that had come upon them, they perceived that the devil had made a fool of them and caused them to destroy their own souls. They were naked and ashamed. God cast Adam and Eve out of the garden. If they had touched the tree of life, evil would have lived forever. *(Genesis 3:22-24)*

Satan corrupted the human family and manipulated men and women to exalt their ignorance and weakness above the knowledge and power of God. The Lord subsequently sent famine into the earth—famine for His knowledge. He did not allow the human family to know the goodness of the Lord, but allowed the people to know evil. All of the people were corrupted. All were filthy. "There is none that doeth good, no, not one." *(Psalm 14:3)* The world was filled with corruption and death. The Lord allowed men and women to decide if they were so determined to exalt themselves above Him, until they were willing to destroy themselves.

--------- **Where Will Hungry Souls Eat** ---------

False prophets do not have meat. They profess to be teaching the people, but, like the ignorant scribes and Pharisees, are ignorant themselves. "For when for the time ye ought to be teachers, ye have need that one teach you again which be the first principles of the oracles of God; and are become such as have need of milk, and not of strong meat. For every one that useth milk is unskillful in the word of righteousness: for he is a babe. But strong meat belongeth to them that are of full age, even those who by reason of use have their senses exercised to discern both good and evil." *(Hebrews 5:12:14)* False prophets are blind leaders of the blind; they cannot see through Satan's witchcraft and are unable to lead the people out of the bondage of sin.

The human family is engaged in spiritual warfare. The people are being destroyed because of the lack of knowledge. The false prophets are teaching the people, yet the evidence shows that the people lack knowledge. Like helpless babies, the false prophets are unskillful in the word of God and have kept the people subject to the power of Satan. For example, they have taught the people that they cannot be perfect, which is an unspoken way of teaching that the people must sin. Since sin is witchcraft, Satan uses false prophets to bewitch the people to destroy their own souls. The false prophets have also taught the people that God loves them unconditionally, which is an unspoken way of saying that God will love the people even if they remain corrupt. Jesus made it plain that except a man was born again of the water and spirit, he could not enter the Kingdom of God. Jesus hates workers of iniquity and will destroy them. *(Psalm 5:5; Matthew 7:23)* Satan, through the false prophets, has bewitched the people with lying vanities; therefore, most people think God loves them, when the truth is God is about to open a wide gate and cast nearly the entire world into a bottomless pit. *(Matthew 7:13; Revelation 20:3)*

——————————— **Do Not Eat the King's Meat** ———————————

God allowed King Nebuchadnezzar to overtake Jerusalem. *(Daniel 1:1-2)* The king subsequently took some of the Hebrews back to Babylon. Nebuchadnezzar told the teacher of his eunuchs that he should bring some of the Hebrews into the palace and teach them the pagan's language and knowledge. The king agreed to provide meat and wine to the Hebrews. After three years of having been taught by the Chaldeans, the king presumed that the Hebrews would be ready to serve him. *(Daniel 1:5)*

Daniel and some of the other Hebrews did not want to defile themselves by eating the king's meat or drinking the king's wine. *(Daniel 1:8)* The Hebrew boys did not want to be fed Babylonian knowledge; they did not want to be taught paganism. Of course, the prince of the eunuchs did not want to disobey the king's command and incur the king's wrath.

Daniel reached an agreement with the prince. The Hebrews would refain from eating the king's meat. After ten days, the eunuch would compare the faces of the Hebrews who did not eat the king's meat with those who ate the king's meat. After ten days, the faces of the Hebrew boys who had not eaten the king's meat appeared much healthier than those who had eaten. "Who is as the wise man? and who knoweth the interpretation of a thing? a man's wisdom maketh his face to shine, and the boldness of his face shall be changed." *(Ecclesiastes 8:1)* Daniel did not need to eat the king's meat for three years to be of service to the king. God had given the four Hebrew boys ten times more knowledge and skill than the others in the kingdom. *(Daniel 1:20)*

Daniel did not want the king's meat; he did not want to be defiled. The Lord fed Daniel, and gave him understanding in all visions and dreams. "I have even heard of thee, that the spirit of the gods is in thee, and that light and understanding and excellent wisdom is found in thee." *(Daniel 5:14)* The king made Daniel ruler over the whole province of Babylon. *(Daniel 2:48)*

I Have Meat

The Lord sent famine of His word into the earth. As a result, the people went into captivity. *(Amos 8:11; Isaiah 5:13)* If we wanted to survive, we had to eat what our enemies fed us. Our enemies corrupted us and taught us how to serve them; hence, we were forced to sacrifice our integrity to save our lives. In order to live, we had to give up our life. We were dying in our own blood. Our enemies made us corrupt our own soul.

Mercifully, God sent His word and healed us, and delivered us from destruction. *(Psalm 107:20)* Jesus Christ was the word made flesh. *(John 1:14)* His flesh was meat indeed. *(John 6:55)* Jesus came into the earth and ended the famine for the hearing of the word. Zacharias, a faithful priest, testified that Jesus had come to save us from our enemies and deliver us out of their hands. The famine had ended. Jesus came to teach the people and deliver us out of captivity. We did not have to fear our enemies anymore, but were free to serve the Lord in holiness and righteousness all the days of our lives. *(Luke 1:67-75)*

Jesus taught the people how to overcome Satan's witchcraft. Those who want to acquire knowledge and learn doctrine have to get away from being babies, drinking milk. Spiritual adults need meat to become strong in the Lord and in the power of His might. "For all tables are full of vomit and filthiness, so that there is no place clean. Whom shall he teach knowledge? and whom shall he make to understand doctrine? them that are weaned from the milk, and drawn from the breasts." *(Isaiah 28:8-9)* Jesus had meat; He had work to finish. *(John 4:32-34)* He came to redeem the people from corruption and to ransom them from the grave. *(Hosea 13:14)* He came to teach us of His ways, so that we could walk in His path. *(Isaiah 2:2-3)* Taste the Lord and see that He is good. *(Psalm 34:8)*

God is a spirit, and the spirit is life. The body without the spirit is dead. Therefore, those who walk in the Spirit of God (integrated) cannot die and will inherit eternal life. Those who do not walk in the Spirit of God (separated) are already dead and will be tormented throughout eternity. Since all humans were born of the lust of the flesh (corruption), those who want to inherit eternal life must be born again of the spirit. (redeemed from corruption) In order for us to walk in the Spirit of God, we have to overcome the pollution of this world. "If a man therefore purge himself from these, he shall be a vessel unto honour, sanctified, and meet for the master's use, and prepared unto every good work." *(2 Timothy 2:21)* Jesus went to prepare a place for us in His Father's house; however, we must be prepared to serve the Lord. *(Luke 1:17)*

--------------------- **Meat of Eternal Life** ---------------------

As a result of famine, the Hebrews went into Egypt, where they were overtaken and enslaved. When the Lord prepared to deliver the children of Israel out of Egypt, He commanded the people to take an unblemished male lamb. They were commanded to kill the lamb, take its blood and place it around the door of the house. They thereafter ate the meat with unleavened bread and bitter herbs. When the death angel came into Egypt and saw the blood upon the door posts, it knew to pass over that house. *(Exodus Chapter 12)* The Lord sent the death angel to deliver His people out of the bondage of Egypt and to destroy the works of the Egyptians. The Hebrews were no longer forced to serve pagan gods but were free to leave bondage.

As the children of Israel journeyed from bondage to reclaim their inheritance, God gave them food and drink for their journey. "And did all eat the same spiritual meat; and did all drink the same spiritual drink: for they drank of that spiritual Rock that followed them: and that Rock was Christ." *(1 Corinthians 10:2-3)* The people ate the spiritual meat and drank the spiritual drink of Jesus Christ.

Just as the natural children of Abraham had remained in the bondage of Egypt because they feared Pharaoh would destroy them, the spiritual children of Abraham had remained in the bondage of sin because they feared Satan would destroy them. Moses led the natural children of Abraham out of the bondage of Egypt and fed them with the meat and drink of Jesus Christ. Afterwards, Jesus came into the earth and told the people that those who hungered and thirsted after righteousness would be filled. Those who love the Lord do not want to eat the vomit from Satan's table and remain corrupt. They want to eat from the Lord's table and be delivered.

--- **Eat of My Flesh** ---

As a result of famine, the people were taken into the bondage of sin. Satan overtook and corrupted them. False prophets offered only polluted vomit—ignorance—which strengthened Satan's power and corruption. Jesus came to set the people free. How was the Messiah going to fill those who hungered and thirsted for righteousness? *(Matthew 5:6)* "Whoso eateth my flesh, and drinketh my blood, hath eternal life; and I will raise him up at the last day. For my flesh is meat indeed, and my blood is drink indeed." *(John 6:54-55)*

The famine has ended. The people do not have to eat from tables filled with vomit and remain in captivity. Those who hunger for righteousness will dine at the Master's table and consume His knowledge. Those who want to acquire knowledge and learn doctrine will eat the flesh of Jesus Christ. He will teach us how to overcome the enemy and escape the pollution of this world.

Jesus told His disciples that His meat was to do the will of Him that sent Him, and to finish His work. *(John 4:34)* God finished the Heaven and earth, and rested from His work. *(Genesis 2:1-2)* If God had finished His work during creation, what work did Jesus have to finish? God created the earth to be inhabited by men and women. He finished creating the conditions to implement His purpose, but He did not finish all the work that was required to complete His purpose. As a spirit, God could create human beings. However, as a spirit, God could not redeem human being from sin. Remission of sin required the shedding of blood, and God, as a spirit, had no blood.

Yet, as a just God, He could not destroy the human family

for sinning against Him, when He created the conditions that caused them to sin. He had to give the people a chance to prove themselves. Therefore, the Lord would need a natural body to offer blood as sacrifice for the sins of the people. Moreover, since He had sent famine into the land and allowed the people to go into bondage because of ignorance, He had to deliver those who wanted to come out of bondage. *(Isaiah 2:2-3)*

Afterwards, since Jesus had to go away to allow the Holy Ghost to come, He commanded Peter to feed His sheep, to feed his lamb. *(John 21:15-17)* He commanded the apostles to teach all nations. Just as the children of Israel ate from the same spiritual meat and drank of the same spiritual drink, those who wanted to be delivered from the bondage of sin would eat of the same spiritual meat that the children of Israel ate from. Both the spiritual meat and the spiritual drink was Christ. *(1 Corinthians 10:1-4)*

The apostle Paul observed, "And I, brethren, could not speak unto you as unto spiritual, but as unto carnal, even as unto babes in Christ. I have fed you with milk, and not with meat: for hitherto ye were not able to bear it, neither yet now are ye able. For ye are yet carnal." *(1 Corinthians 3:1-3)* Paul knew that the people were carnal minded and were not ready to understand the whole truth. The false prophets had fed the people ignorant vomit, which is why the enemy was able to keep the people in captivity and destroy them. The people did not know Christ; they were none of His. Those who wanted to inherit the Kingdom of God had to walk in the spirit. They needed to eat the spiritual meat and drink the spiritual drink that delivered the children of Israel out of Egypt; they needed the knowledge of Jesus Christ.

——— Those Who Sat in Darkness Saw a Great Light ———

The life of a disciple reflects the teaching of his master. Jesus is the light. *(John 8:12)* Those who walk with Jesus walk in the light. *(1 John 1:5-7)* Moses' face shone when he stood in the presence of God. *(Exodus 34:29-30)* With the Spirit of God, Daniel had light, understanding, and excellent wisdom. *(Daniel 5:11)* Jesus opened His disciples' understanding. *(Luke 24:45)* God sent the apostle Paul to turn the Gentiles from darkness to light. *(Acts 26:18)* The people of God walk in the light. *(Ephesians 5:8)* Those who have the knowledge of God are enlightened. "Make thy face to shine upon thy servant; and teach me thy statutes." *(Psalm 119:135)* "The people that walked in darkness have seen a great light: they that dwell in the land of the shadow of death, unto them hath the light shined." *(Isaiah 9:2)* God has told those in the grave of sin, "Arise, shine; for thy light is come, and the glory of the Lord is risen upon thee." *(Isaiah 60:1)*

Daniel did not want to eat the king's meat and defile himself. People of integrity do not want to eat Satan's teaching and defile themselves. We do not have to eat false prophets' vomit and remain in the bondage of sin. This is not our kingdom, and Satan is not our king. Those who serve the Lord have the knowledge of Jesus Christ. "I have more understanding than all my teachers: for thy testimonies are my meditation." *(Psalm 119:99)* The apostles had the testimony of Jesus Christ and knew how to overcome the enemy. *(Revelation 12:11)* Jesus told Peter to feed His lamb, feed His sheep. He told Paul to turn the Gentiles from darkness to light. He commanded His apostles to teach all nations. The apostles' doctrine is food for our soul. The Master taught the apostles, and the apostles taught the people. *(Matthew 28:19)* The Master (teacher) has given disciples (students) perfect discipline (knowledge). No one can follow Christ and walk in darkness; no one can sin unless he rejects the Master's knowledge and fails to follow His instructions. The Master taught us how to exercise self-control.

Through the knowledge of Jesus Christ, we are no longer subject to the power of Satan. We will overcome sin and walk in the power of God. *(Revelation 12:11)* Although Satan sent false prophets to tell the people lies to keep them under his power, God's sheep do not fall for the witchcraft. Jesus taught us how to escape. *(2 Peter 2:20)*

---------- **Drink of My Blood** ----------

God is holy in all His ways, and He needs holy servants. The Good Master is able to effectively communicate knowledge to students to ensure their understanding. Jesus overcame the world, and He came to teach His disciples how to overcome the world. *(John 16:33)* "He that saith he abideth in him ought himself also so to walk, even as he walked." *(1 John 2:6)* "He that saith, I know him, and keepeth not his commandments, is a liar, and the truth is not in him." *(1 John 2:4)* Jesus knew that men and women could live holy, but He had to first turn the people away from the false prophets. Jesus inveighed against the scribes and Pharisees, because the false prophets blinded the minds of the people. If the people learned the truth, they would be set free from sin and save their souls from destruction.

A disciple follows the teaching of his master. Jesus was in all points tempted like we, yet He did not sin. *(1 Peter 2:21-22; Hebrews 4:15)* Jesus, our Master, denied Himself, and He taught His disciples (students) how to discipline (knowledge) themselves. In order to overcome corruption and to reconcile with God, disciples of Christ obey the Master's instructions. We deny the pleasures of the flesh, which separates us from the spirit. Although the lust within our blood yearns for the pleasures, we understand that the lust of the flesh is Satan's corruption. Since sin works death in us by that which is good, we crucify the flesh in order to obey God and do good works, which gives God the glory. *(Matthew 5:16)*

Through the knowledge of Jesus Christ, we learned that Satan rules the earth through witchcraft. The people, afraid of death, are desperate to survive. Betrayal, exploitation, and oppression have obliterated trust. Fear envelops the entire world. To reduce the anxieties of life, the devil offers the people pleasure of the flesh. Hence, the devil offers sinners the spiritual bricks they need to build his kingdom. Since slaves are powerless to escape, it makes sense to a spiritual slave when the false prophet teaches that he cannot be free from sin (perfect). Thus, slaves to sin cannot escape

Satan's power because the false prophets have taught them that they are unable to overcome the enemy. Further, in their ignorance, the people walk in darkness and are unaware of Satan's witchcraft that keeps them subject to his power. Emasculated of integrity and dignity, a sinner finds pleasure in committing fornication or adultery.

Children of Abraham have integrity and refuse to serve a false god. We know that Jesus is Lord. Accordingly, we are not afraid to exit out of the bondage of sin. We also understand that Satan uses the lust of the flesh and vanity to perpetuate our corruption and keep us separated from God. Through the knowledge of Jesus Christ, we know that it is our reasonable service to offer our bodies as a living sacrifice, holy and acceptable to God. Since all that is of the world is not of the Father, we know that we must overcome the things of the world to reconcile with the Father. We must overcome the lust of the flesh, the lust of the eyes, and the pride of life (what we inherited from Adam, our natural father) to inherit the Kingdom of God (what we will inherit from Jesus, our spiritual Father). *(1 John 2:15-16)* We must deny ourselves the ephemeral pleasure if we want be saved from the eternal torture.

The life of the flesh is in the blood. We have inherited corrupt blood from our corrupt forefathers. The corruption in our blood is the enemy of the spirit; thus, we must learn to love not our own lives. Not only must we understand that God does not love us unconditionally, which is why we cannot enter His kingdom unless we are born again, we must learn to hate our own life. *(Luke 14:26)* As corrupt souls, we are enemies of God. Those who want to inherit His kingdom must be willing, like the Master taught us, to take up our cross and shed our blood. *(Matthew 16:24)* If we want to be saved from destruction and inherit eternal life, we must overcome the blood (our natural life) and be redeemed from corruption (return to spirit).

Jesus promised that those who ate of His flesh and drank of His blood would have eternal life. *(John 6:54)* We would be reconciled with the spirit. To eat of Christ's flesh is to acquire the knowledge of Christ. He came to teach the people of His ways, so that we could walk in His path. He sent apostles throughout the world to teach His doctrine to all nations. Once the people know the truth (Jesus is Lord), they will come out of the bondage and be made free from sin.

It is not sufficient, though, for the people to eat of Christ's flesh and to acquire His knowledge. It is meaningless to profess Jesus as Lord, yet do not the things He commands. *(Luke 6:46)* Once we learn how the enemy corrupts us, we have to do the work necessary to overcome corruption. Just as the Master drank His blood out of the cup of sacrifice, we have to drink His blood out of the cup of sacrifice. *(Mark 14:23)*

The Cup of the Old Testament

The children of Israel had suffered for four hundred years in the bondage of Egypt. They cried unto the Lord for deliverance. God sent Moses to bring the people out of captivity. "And Moses took half of the blood, and put it in basons; and half of the blood he sprinkled on the altar. And he took the book of the covenant, and read in the audience of the people: and they said, All that the Lord hath said will we do, and be obedient. And Moses took the blood, and sprinkled it on the people, and said, Behold the blood of the covenant, which the Lord hath made with you concerning all these words." *(Exodus 24:8)*

God, through His servant, Moses, entered into a covenant with the children of Israel. Blood was sprinkled on the altar and on the people. The Lord wanted the people to witness for themselves whether they would obey or disobey His commandments. For example, many individuals say they love the Lord. They may not obey God, according to them, but their heart is right. "The heart is deceitful above all things, and desperately wicked: who can know it?" *(Jeremiah 17:9)* A man's heart is where his treasure is. *(Matthew 6:21; Luke 12:34)* Those who treasure the things of God will give up all that is of the world to worship God. *(Matthew 13:44)* Those who treasure the things of the world will reject the word of God and not seek to overcome the world. *(John 3:19-20)* The Lord put the people to the test to allow them to see if they loved Him. If they loved Him, they would keep His commandments. *(John 14:15)*

Moses told the people: "All the commandments which I command thee this day shall ye observe to do, that ye may live, and multiply, and go in and possess the land which the Lord sware unto your fathers. And thou shalt remember all the way which the Lord thy God led thee these forty years in the wilderness, to humble thee, and to prove thee, to know what was in thine heart, whether thou wouldest keep his commandments, or no." *(Deuteronomy 8:1-2)*

God and the children of Israel entered into a covenant. Moses sprinkled half of the blood on the altar and half of the blood on the people. According to the covenant, God would deliver the children of Israel out of Egypt and save them from their enemies. The people, having been saved from their enemies, would serve the Lord.

The Lord promised that He would deliver the people to a place that flowed with milk and honey, where He would put His laws in their hearts. They agreed that, having been delivered from the burden of slavery, they would obey His laws. However, the Lord was not going to reward the people with His blessings unless they were going to serve Him. Moses warned the people, "And it shall be, if thou do at all forget the Lord thy God, and walk after other gods, and serve them, and worship them, I testify against you this day that ye shall surely perish." *(Deuteronomy 8:19)*

After the death of Moses, Joshua warned the children of Israel of betrayal. "Ye cannot serve the Lord: for he is an holy God; he is a jealous God; he will not forgive your transgressions nor your sins. If ye forsake the Lord, and serve strange gods, then he will turn and do you hurt, and consume you, after that he hath done you good. And the people said unto Joshua, Nay; but we will serve the Lord. And Joshua said unto the people, Ye are witnesses against yourselves that ye have chosen you the Lord, to serve him. And they said, We are witnesses." *(Joshua 24:19-22)*

Unlike the lying false prophets who teach that God loves us unconditionally, Moses testified that there was a condition attached to God saving the people out of Egypt: they were to serve Him. If they served other gods, the Lord would destroy them. Unlike the lying false prophets who teach that once God has saved the people, the people will always be saved, Joshua explained that if the people forsook the Lord and served strange gods, the Lord would not forgive them of their sins and transgression. Further, although the Lord had saved the people from their enemies, if the people turned against Him, the Lord would destroy them.

The Lord does not tolerate lies and falsehoods, and will not give His glory to another. The people gave their word that they would serve Him. As the natural children of Abraham, the people agreed to walk upright before God as Abraham had walked and to reclaim the inheritance the Lord had granted to the seed of Abraham. According to His word, God defeated Pharaoh, brought them out of captivity, and defeated all the enemies they encountered on the way to the Promised Land.

Despite Moses' and Joshua's admonitions, the people failed to honor their covenant with God. The children of Israel lied to God. "Nevertheless they did flatter him with their mouth, and they lied unto him with their tongues." *(Psalms 78:36)* Each time the people encountered adversity, false teachers encouraged the people to rebel against God and return to Egypt. The children of Israel had cried out to the Lord for mercy from the bondage of Egypt. God heard their cry and saved them out of bondage. However, the people did not trust in the Lord and refused to serve Him. Although they pleaded with God for mercy and asked Him to deliver them out of Egypt, they chose to forsake the Lord and desired to return to Egypt. The Lord, after having saved the people, afterward destroyed practically all of them. *(Jude 1:5)*

It is reprehensible for people to verbally thank the Lord for saving them from their enemy, yet reject God's words of deliverance so they can remain in the bondage of sin and serve the enemy. The children of Israel declared that, if they had a choice between serving the Lord and serving Pharaoh, they would serve the Lord. After God delivered them out of Egypt and gave them a choice, they chose to serve Pharaoh. The Lord had demonstrated that Pharaoh was a fraud, yet the children of Israel were willing to renounce their own inheritance to work as slaves for Pharaoh. They esteemed a life of slavery above the promises of God.

The Cup of the New Testament

Adam rebelled against God. His unwillingness to separate from the woman indicated that he exalted the woman above God. As a result, God separated from Adam. Without the spirit, Adam died. Since Adam preferred the flesh over the spirit, he preferred that which would die over that which would live forever. He forsook his right to eternal life and the Kingdom of God. And, as the natural father and mother of all flesh, Adam's and Eve's lust of the flesh was passed down through the bloodline to all generations. All humans were conceived in sin; all flesh was created through the lust of the flesh; and all flesh is the enemy of the spirit.

Just as Moses delivered the people out of the bondage of Egypt, Jesus came to deliver the people out of the bondage of sin. From the beginning of time, God had predestined that He would redeem mankind. To the natural mind, God had placed mankind in a losing position. There could be no remission of sin without the shedding of blood. Further, if a sacrifice could be found, it had to be the perfect sacrifice. After all, the soul that sinned had to die. A sinner could not sacrifice his life to save another sinner. The human family appeared to be in a deleterious position. Everyone in Heaven was spirit and had no blood to sacrifice. Everyone on earth was flesh and had sinned. God looked around the altar and could not find anyone who could redeem the people.

It was not a problem at all. Before He created man, God had a purpose. He would allow all humans to die. He would redeem those who had integrity, those who were willing to bear witness to the truth. However, since the soul that sinned had to die, a perfect sacrifice had to be offered for the remission of sin. God counseled with His own will. *(Ephesians 1:11)* He would create mankind. He would allow mankind to witness its ignorance and weakness. He would allow mankind to witness His knowledge and power. He would allow mankind to witness the foolishness of those who rebelled against Him. He would redeem those who were wise enough to admit that He was Lord and obey His commandments. The Lord formed man from the womb, and the Lord redeemed man from the grave. *(Isaiah 44:24)* Jesus was both Lord (Almighty God) and Christ (sacrificial lamb). *(Acts 2:36)*

Accordingly, Jesus and His saints made a covenant by sacrifice. *(Psalm 50:5)* Although a spirit, Jesus took on flesh-and-blood and gave His natural life to redeem His people from spiritual death. *(Hebrews 2:14)* In exchange, His people give their natural lives (corruption) to reclaim their spiritual lives (incorruption). Redeemed from corruption, His people are able to serve Him in the spirit. Hence, Jesus reconciled the world to Himself. "And that he died for all, that they which live should not henceforth live unto themselves, but unto him which died for them, and rose again." *(2 Corinthians 5:15)* Jesus drank out of the cup of sacrifice. When Peter tried to save Christ from death, Jesus told him to put up his sword; Jesus had to drink His cup of sacrifice. *(John 18:11)* Although Jesus later agonized and prayed that His cup would pass, He inevitably acquiesced, "Nevertheless not as I will, but as thou wilt." *(Matthew 26:39)* Jesus was obedient to the cross, even unto death. *(Phillippians 2:8)*

God made a covenant to deliver the people out of the bondage of sin. "And as they did eat, Jesus took bread, and blessed, and brake it, and gave to them, and said, Take, eat: this is my body. And he took the cup, and when he had given thanks, he gave it to them: and they all drank of it. And he said unto them, This is my blood of the new testament, which is shed for many." *(Mark 14:22-24)* Jesus had to drink His cup of blood; He had to sacrifice the life of the flesh. And the covenant of the New Testament requires those who serve the Lord also to drink out of the cup of sacrifice; drink all of the blood of Jesus. *(Matthew 26:27-28)* The blood of Jesus is drink to those who thirst for righteousness.

Form Follows Function

We cannot serve two masters. We must either be obedient to the Father like Jesus or rebel against the Father like Satan. The form we take as individuals follows the function we want to perform. Those whose function is to serve the Lord will take on the form of a servant like Christ and exalt the spirit above the flesh. Since all flesh is corrupt, those who want to exalt the spirit above the flesh must overcome the things of the world and be redeemed from corruption. We must renew the way we think in order to transform the way we live. We want the type of mind that Christ had: we shed our blood and renounce the life of the flesh to walk in the Spirit of God.

Those whose function is to exalt flesh above spirit will simply conform to this world. Satan is the god of this world, and all that is of the world—the lust of the flesh, the lust of the eyes, and the pride of life—is not of the Father. Thus, to serve Satan requires us to exalt the desires of our flesh and the vanity we derive from promoting the flesh above the Spirit of God. Sinners reject the knowledge of Jesus Christ, because they love the world. They are glad to partner with Satan and deny that Jesus is their Lord.

Life and Death

Jesus came to integrate us with God. Satan wants to keep us separated from God. Jesus wants us to exalt the spirit. Satan wants us to exalt the flesh. Jesus wants us to have power. Satan wants us to remain weak. Jesus wants us to have life. Satan wants us to remain dead. The life of the flesh is in the blood, which we inherited from rebellious Adam and Eve. God made Adam and Eve both human and divine. Since they exalted flesh above spirit, they were separated from the spirit. If we do not want to be separated from the spirit, we have to shed our blood. Jesus Christ was conceived of the spirit and of the flesh. He was both human and divine. Since He exalted the spirit above the flesh, He gave up the life of the flesh. He sacrificed His flesh to remain spirit. We reveal our God and demonstrate what we treasure by who we choose to obey: Do we exalt Jesus as Lord and obey His commandments? Or do we exalt ourselves and reject Jesus as God?

Those who want to overcome Satan's corruption will drink out of Jesus' cup and place our corrupt lives on the altar of sacrifice. Just as Jesus shed His blood to demonstrate that He exalted the Spirit of God above His natural life, we take up our cross and follow Christ. We jettison the things of the world and renounce Satan's kingdom. To overcome sin, we love not our own lives, even unto death. We deny our flesh and die out to the things of the world.

Remember: Master means teacher. Disciples are students. Knowledge means discipline. The knowledge of Jesus Christ is to discipline ourselves. We must commit ourselves to a course of conduct to achieve our desired goals. We must deny ourselves. "Then said Jesus unto his disciples, If any man will come after me, let him deny himself, and take up his cross, and follow me." *(Matthew 16:24)* When we discipline ourselves, we demonstrate that we treasure the Spirit of God above the lust of the flesh; accordingly, we will not entertain Satan's witchcraft or indulge the lust within our flesh. We will renew our minds and bring our bodies under subjection. "He openeth also their ear to discipline, and commandeth that they return from iniquity. If they obey and serve him, they shall spend their days in prosperity, and their years in pleasures. But if they obey not, they shall perish by the sword, and they shall die without knowledge." *(Job 36:10-12)* Servants of Jesus Christ obey their Master—He has the knowledge of eternal life. *(Colossian 3:22-24)*

Covenant

A covenant is built upon trust. The only way a king can empower his subjects is if the subjects submit to his authority. The only way subjects will submit to the king is if they trust the king. God has all power. If we show that we are faithful and exalt the Lord above ourselves, the Lord will increase our power. God needs servants who know how frail they are and not get lifted up with pride when they enter into His glorious kingdom.

Consider: God gives His people knowledge and power (Holy Ghost). Satan manipulates his people and bewitches them to lust after weakness. God is going to destroy Satan. Further, the Lord is going to destroy all who rejected Him and served Satan. Despite all the demonic madness and corruption in the earth, the people exalt Satan. They reject God's knowledge and choose to be ignorant. They reject God's power and desire to be weak. They permit Satan to rule over them. God is not mocked. He is not about to let weak and ignorant people into His kingdom. His kingdom is a reflection of His power and glory. Those who enter the Kingdom of God will be like Christ—they will exhibit integrity in the earth and bear witness to the truth: Jesus is king. They will bow before God and renounce Satan's witchcraft.

The Lord Wants to Prove Us

The Lord did not take the Hebrews through the wilderness to destroy them. If God did not want the people to inherit the Promised Land, He would not have sent Moses to deliver them. He would have allowed their enemies to continue to oppress them. He took them through the wilderness to see if the people would serve Him. Consider: the Egyptians abused the Hebrews for 400 years. In contrast, God defeated the Egyptians within a matter of weeks and demonstrated that He was Lord. Although God defeated the Egyptians, provided the Hebrews with everything they needed, and followed them to ensure their safety, the children of Israel nonetheless preferred to go back to Egypt. In Egypt, they could reject God's knowledge and rely upon their own survival skills. They would not have to trust in the Lord. How presumptuous could they be? After 400 years of miserable slavery, they were too arrogant to trust the One who had delivered them from their enemies and blessed them with their inheritance.

Similarly, if God wanted the human family to perish, Christ would not have come into the earth to save the people from their sin. God could have allowed Satan to maintain power over the people and kept them corrupted. When He came to destroy Satan's kingdom, He could have destroyed Satan and all the people. Instead, God so loved the world until He himself likewise took on a body of flesh and blood, taught the people how to overcome, suffered sorrow and grief, and endured the cross. All He asks the human family is to acknowledge the truth: We live in sin, which is an unspoken way of admitting that we do not walk in integrity. We have all lied; we have all capitulated to corruption, which means that all of us know that we do not have all power. God does. Why are we willing to live as slaves to ignorance and weakness than to obey the holy commandments of God and live in peace? Why are we unwilling to keep our integrity and bear witness to the truth?

The Lord cast Satan and the rest of the sinners out of Heaven. A God who is holy in all His ways and with wisdom beyond measure, the Lord cannot stand those who are foolish. *(Psalm 5:5)* He allowed men and women to be taken into captivity and made to suffer. He wanted the people to see that only the weak engages in corruption. Oppression is nothing more than the weak cloaking their fear in the guise of power. Vanity is nothing more than the insecure exhibiting themselves to make people take notice of them. The Lord not only cast Satan out of Heaven but defeated Satan in the earth. He wanted the people to understand that He had superior knowledge and power. Those who live in His kingdom must submit to Him and obey His commandments. God cannot use those who choose to substitute their judgment above His. He is perfect and demands His servants to execute His will exactly as commanded.

The Lord came into the earth and suffered along with the people. He simply wants the people to show that they are aware of their frailties, recognize He is Lord, and obey His commandments. He wants the people to drink out of the cup of sacrifice that He drank and to be baptized with the same baptism as He was baptized. *(Mark 10:38-39)* The spirit and the flesh are enemies. There is the Creator, and there is the creation. Most of creation rejected the Creator. *(Psalm 115:16; 1 John 2:16)* Those who confess Jesus as Lord and exalt Him in the earth will inherit the Kingdom of God. Those who reject the Lord as God and exalt themselves will be destroyed.

────────── **Sin, that it Might Appear to be Sin** ──────────

The life of the flesh is corrupt. Men and women are weak and engage in all manner of evil to preserve their lives. They are so corrupt, until it literally kills them to do good. "Sin, that it might appear to be sin, by working death in us by that which is good." *(Romans 7:13)* We live in a world where people become furious when they are encouraged to serve the Lord. And what does God require? He commands the people to tell the truth, to love one another, and to do unto others as they would have others do unto them. He commands the people to have self-respect, and to treat others with comparable respect. In a few words, God tells the people that they should exalt integrity and promote trust. *(Micah 6:8)*

What is Satan's response? Satan tells the people to live and let live. No one should have morals or values. People should do whatever they want. Men can seduce their neighbors' wives and daughters. People can lie, steal, cheat, defraud, and do whatever that float their boat. People should disregard how their evil hurts others; they need to look out for themselves and the ones they love. Satan encourages men and women to attract attention to their flesh: show cleavage and muscles; promote seduction and lust. Satan knows, "For the flesh lusteth against the Spirit, and the Spirit against the flesh: and these are contrary the one to the other."

(Galatians 5:17) Hence, Satan has bewitched the people to join him in the fight against God.

It is a sad but damning indictment of the human family: the world is filled with violence and oppression. The world worships decaying flesh. Everyone knows that the Almighty commands the people to exhibit dignity and integrity towards others. Everyone knows that Satan entices the people to engage in evil. Yet the people reject the teachings of Jesus Christ and follow the example of Satan.

CHAPTER TEN
DELIVERANCE

The false prophets suborned perjury and persuaded the people to reject Christ. The Romans beat Him, humiliated Him, and hung Him from a tree. As Jesus hung there—His body lacerated by the whip, head pricked by a crown of thorns, and feet punctured by iron spikes—two thieves who had also been crucified with Him began to criticize and attack Him. *(Matthew 27:44)* They repeated the mocking accusations of the false prophets. If Jesus was indeed the Christ, He should show his power and save Himself. While He was at it, the thieves added, He should save them, too.

Surprisingly, after repeatedly criticizing Christ, one of the thieves displayed an honest heart and stopped complaining. "And one of the malefactors which were hanged railed on him, saying, If thou be the Christ, save thyself and us. But the other answering rebuked him, saying, Dost not thou fear God, seeing thou art in the same condemnation? And we indeed justly; for we receive the due reward of our deeds: but this man hath done nothing amiss." *(Luke 23:35-41)*

Both thieves had committed evil against innocent people, yet both complained that Jesus should save them from their sins. One of them was honest enough to admit the truth. Justice demanded that evil be destroyed. The humbled thief accepted responsibility for his corrupt actions and consented to death. He knew, however, that Jesus was an innocent man. "And he said unto Jesus, Lord, remember me when thou comest into thy kingdom. And Jesus said unto him, Verily I say unto thee, to day shalt thou be with me in paradise." *(Luke 23:42-43)* The remorseful thief had enough sense to realize that he should be worried about the life of his soul, not the life of his body.

Jesus was moved by the thief's decency. Jesus was not going to paradise that day; He was going to the grave. But, while He remained alive, He wanted the thief to know that he would be with Him in paradise. The thief was corrupt, but Jesus knew that He had sent famine into the land and allowed all humans to be corrupted. The thief's willingness to suffer death for his wickedness evidenced that, despite excruciating pain, he had no right to ask Jesus to save his natural life when Jesus had not chosen to save His own natural life. Jesus had compassion upon him and delivered his soul from eternal damnation.

The thieves epitomized the dishonesty of people. Both had hurt innocent people, but wanted God to save them from hurt. They reaped the pain for the pain they had sown, but criticized Jesus as if they were innocent men. Jesus, in contrast, was an innocent man. In His humiliation, His life was taken from Him, yet He opened not His mouth. Jesus accepted death without sin to ransom from the grave of sin those who repented of their sins. The humbled thief surrendered the death of his natural life and focused on saving his spiritual life.

Those who are honest know that the lust of the flesh requires us to disobey the spirit. If we have integrity, we will admit our corruption and ask God to teach us how to overcome. We walked in darkness, yet Jesus is the light. He knows how to overcome sin, and we entreat Him to teach us of His ways, so we can walk in His path. *(Isaiah 2:2-3)*

--------------------- **Die Out to the Flesh** ---------------------

It was not enough that Jesus gave His body as sacrifice; He was not living in sin. Jesus made a covenant with the people. He drank out of the cup of the New Testament, and His disciples are to likewise drink out of the cup of the New Testament. Drinking out of the cup of the New Testament confirms that the Master and His disciples agree that Jesus is Lord. The flesh is the enemy of the spirit, and the spirit is the enemy of the flesh. Jesus knew that He could defeat Satan and came into the earth to demonstrate He, despite walking in a flesh-and-blood body, had more power than Satan. He shed His blood and gave up His natural life to save the people from spiritual death. His disciples shed their blood to demonstrate that they renounce Satan's witchcraft and confess that Jesus is Lord. Since the body without the spirit is dead, and the life of the flesh is in the blood, disciples of Christ shed their blood—the life of sin—so that they can live in the Spirit of Jesus Christ. Jesus paid the ransom to redeem His servants from the grave of sin, and His servants come out of the grave of sin to restore their soul.

Body of Christ

Jesus went to Jerusalem and told some Jews, "Destroy this temple, and in three days I will raise it up." *(John 2:19)* The carnal-minded Jews retorted that it had taken forty-six years to build the temple. Jesus had spoken of the temple of His body. Most people who profess to be Christians have never been to church in their lives, which is why God will say to many, "I never knew you: depart from me, ye that work iniquity." *(Matthew 7:23)* They may have been clapping and singing, but they were not worshipping God. They may have been inside of a building, but they were not inside of the church. If they had been in the church, the Head of the body would have known them. However, they had never been in the body of Christ. They did not know the difference between a building and the Spirit of God. *(1 Corinthians Chapter 12)* The church, the body of Christ, is comprised of lively stones, individuals who have crucified the flesh, so that God can dwell within them. *(1 Peter 2:5; Psalm 23:3)* God is a spirit, and to be in the body of Christ is to dwell in the Spirit of Christ.

Keep in mind, the body without the spirit is dead. In Christ, all of us can be made alive. Hence, Christ will give us a new life. If we walk in the spirit, we will not fulfill the lust of the flesh. If we worship God, we will overcome the flesh and worship the Lord in the spirit. We cannot commit fornication and adultery (engage in uncleanness) and profess to be temples of God. If we love the world—the things of Satan—we are going to rebel against the spirit to please our flesh. Therefore, God is not mocked: if we walk after the flesh, which is the enemy of the spirit, we do not love God, which is why those who commit fornication and adultery cannot inherit the Kingdom of God—they are not heirs; they are not His children. *(1 Corinthians 6:9)* His Spirit does not dwell within them.

———————— Suffer with Me, Reign with Me ————————

Jesus made it clear that those who followed Him had to deny themselves, take up their cross, and follow Him. "If we suffer, we shall also reign with him: if we deny him, he also will deny us." *(2 Timothy 2:12)* Whoseover tried to save his life would lose it, but whosever chose to lose his life for Christ would save it. "What shall a man give in exchange for his soul?" *(Matthew 16:25-26; Mark 8:34-37)* We present our corrupt bodies as a living sacrifice and renounce idol worship. We do not exalt Satan—or ourselves—above the Lord. Those who exalt God over Satan—and themselves—will crucify that part of them that opposes God. Those who want to inherit the Kingdom of God will renounce their pagan worship.

We should not be surprised when wicked individuals are exalted. As the god of this world, Satan has the power to "bless" those who promote his kingdom. Ahab exalted the false prophets who supported his wickedness and incarcerated Macaiah who opposed his wickedness. Balak offered to promote Balaam to very great honor if Balaam would curse the children of Israel. *(Numbers 22:17)* In a corrupt world, those in power will typically be corrupt, and they will promote those who support their corruption.

The enemy is going to fight. Although no error was found

in Daniel, his enemies schemed to have him killed. Shadrach, Meshach, and Abednego were exceptional men, yet their enemies conspired to have them killed. Job was perfect. God had to warn Satan to spare Job's life. Jezebel sought to take Elijah's life. It is imperative that followers of Christ love not their own lives, even unto death. This is Satan's kingdom. He has the power of death and rules through fear of death. Christ's disciples must be prepared to pay the ultimate price.

Jesus was despised and rejected of men. The Master did not rob or hurt anyone, but lived a life of blessings and integrity. His enemies slandered His name and engendered hatred toward Him. Those who truly love the Lord will suffer libel and slander. "Woe unto you, when all men shall speak well of you! for so did their fathers to the false prophets." *(Luke 6:26)* The people of the world hate God, and those who love God. *(John 15:18)* Those who follow Christ are going to be hated and persecuted. *(Psalm 69:4; 2 Timothy 3:12)*

———————————— **Breaking Strongholds** ————————————

Jesus came into the earth to destroy the works of the devil. The people, through fear of death, allowed devils to control their lives. However, when the devils saw Jesus, they started shaking. *(James 2:19)* The devils knew that they were unable to defeat Jesus. Afterwards, Jesus gave power to His disciples and told them to go into various cities and heal the sick. Seventy of them returned with joy and told the Lord that, at the name of Jesus Christ, the devils were subject to them. *(Luke 10:17)* Jesus gave His disciples power over all the power of the enemy. *(Luke 10:19)* We have no need to fear Satan, despite his power of death. We have eternal life within us. Satan may kill our corrupt flesh, which is going to die anyway. The devil has no power over the Spirit of Jesus Christ, which lives within us. Satan does not intimidate us.

There were certain disciples who were unable to cast out a demon. They asked the Master why they did not possess the power to cast the demon out. Jesus answered that their unbelief had prevented them. If the disciples had more faith, they would have been successful. He added, "Howbeit this kind goeth not out but by prayer and fasting." *(Matthew 17:14-21)*

The entrenched demon had possessed a child from birth and caused the child to fall into fire, into water, and to engage in all manner of self-destructive behavior. The father of the child entreated Jesus to help him. Jesus said all things were possible if the father could believe. The father cried, "Lord, I believe; help thou mine unbelief." *(Mark 9:24)* The father, like many, had heard about God, but he did not know if God existed or was simply a myth created by man. He wanted his son to be healed, yet his faith was weak.

Those who come to God must first believe that He exists, and that He is a rewarder of them that seek Him. It is not necessary for the person to be initially strong in faith. God knows that He is a spirit, and He knows that mankind has been corrupted. Adam's sin separated the Creator from His creation. Further, the Lord knows that individuals who have known only bondage their entire lives are not going to have much faith. Many individuals, regardless of their positive mental attitude, will become disillusioned over time when they have not realized any material change in their circumstances. Faith is mockery to a slave.

The Lord knows that our enemies are too strong for us. He knows that fear of death prevents many from serving Him. There is no dispute that God's ways are the right ways. Many souls would love to always tell the truth, to walk upright before the Lord, to live a holy, sanctified life, and to walk in integrity. Few pay tithes and offerings to churches with the expectation that they will burn in hell. Many who go to houses of worship prefer to increase their faith and have a closer relationship with God. If they could increase their faith, they would improve their lives.

Satan has used witchcraft to induce us to lust after the flesh, which is the enemy of God. Additionally, we were conceived in sin. Satan bewitched Eve to consider the tree of the knowledge of good and evil. She saw lust of the flesh, lust of the eyes, and the pride of life—all of the evil things of the world—and rebelled against God. Adam's lust for Eve caused him to rebel against God. Since they are the mother and father of all the living, their corrupted blood has been passed down to all flesh. All of humanity was conceived in sin and shapened in iniquity. *(Psalm 51:5)* As always, the Master taught the people what to do to overcome: fast and pray.

Fasting

The spiritual transcends the natural. The true measure of a spiritual individual is whether he has control of his nature. "He that hath no rule over his own spirit is like a city that is broken down, and without walls." *(Proverbs 25:28)* Enemies can attack and overcome a defenseless man at any time. Jesus taught us how to defend ourselves against the enemies' attack: Drink of the cup of sacrifice and exercise self-control. *(John 18:10-11)* We can never go to Jesus and argue that he does not understand what it is to experience the temptations of the flesh. He was tempted but rejected the temptations. *(Hebrews 4:15)* Jesus taught the people to fast.

Fasting afflicts the body, requires the body to endure hardship, and brings the body under the control of the mind. When we fast, the body hungers and thirsts, which is what we seek after. The lust of the flesh is the enemy of the spirit. Our hunger and thirst for righteousness surpasses our hunger and thirst to please our corrupt flesh. We want to crucify the flesh and bring everything into captivity unto the obedience of the spirit. Moreover, Satan has bewitched mankind by seducing men and women to pursue the pleasures of the flesh. The lust of the flesh, however, keeps men and women separated from the spirit. Since the enemy is too strong for flesh-and-blood creatures, those who do not have the Spirit of God have no defense against Satan. Men and women are therefore unable to overcome the power of Satan because their lust of the flesh reinforces Satan's power over them.

Fasting allows us to overcome sin. In afflicting ourselves, we endure hardship, abstain from lust, and exercise self-control; we learn self-denial. Nothing has overtaken humans beside common things, and the Lord will not allow Satan to put anything upon us more than we can bear. Further, the Lord will make a way of escape from sin. Those who have disciplined themselves to deny the flesh will resist temptation and remain integrated with the spirit.

Fasting requires us to suffer, to exercise self-restraint. We know that lust resides within our bodies. When lust overtakes our rational thinking, we often engage in behavior that is self-destructive to ourselves and our families. As natural creatures, who adapted to our environment to survive, we adopted corrupt practices and behavior. It is difficult to renounce corrupt ways and relinquish corrupt behavior when such corruption provides pleasure to blunt the pain of life. Further, social pressure forces us to conform.

If we walk with God, our lives will be filled with comfort and blessing. We will have the security of knowing that God is real, and that He will reward us for serving Him. We must learn from those who were never slaves. Jesus and Moses were descendants of slaves, but they had never lived as slaves. Hence, they did not think like slaves. They refused to accept Satan's or Pharaoh's offer of physical pleasure in exchange for their integrity. Jesus and Moses fasted. They chose to afflict themselves in order to keep their bodies under subjection to the spirit.

Jesus knew that the body required food and drink to live. The Lord made the children of Israel to hunger. *(Deuteronomy 8:3)* He sent famine in the land—not for food or drink, but for His word. Without His word, the people were taken into captivity. *(Isaiah 5:13)* The people had natural food and drink to sustain natural life, but the absence of God's word led them into spiritual death. *(Matthew 4:4)* Unlike dumb beasts, children of God are not controlled by their genetic instincts. The corruption in our blood does not determine our conduct. The word of God instructs us how to overcome corruption and to defeat Satan. Therefore, we esteem the word of God above our necessary food. *(Job 23:12)* When we fast, we deliberately (knowingly) inflict pain upon ourselves to overcome our flesh's lust for pleasure. We invite suffering and hardship; we shun pleasure and comfort. We implement the knowledge of Jesus Christ and afflict our bodies to bring them under subjection. We exercise self-discipline and allow God to order our steps.

Fasting requires us to resist the desire and impulse to eat. When we fast, our mind exercises control over our decisions. Our mind determines when the body shall eat; the body does not control our behavior. When we treasure the things of the spirit, fasting conditions us to deny the temptations and impulses that our flesh craves. Fasting prepares our body to deny the desire, to resist the yearning, and to endure the hardship. Separation from God is death. Ergo, we fast and crucify the flesh, so the Spirit of God will live within us.

Daniel's Fast

Satan knows sinners can overcome sin through fasting and praying, so he sends false prophets to deceive the people. Many false prophets encourage their congregants to participate in a so-called "Daniel's fast." A "Daniel's Fast" may require church members to avoid eating certain foods for a limited period of time. For example, members may refrain from eating sweets, meats, or other food products. A "Daniel's Fast" is not a fast, has nothing to do with God, but is simply a trick of the devil.

First, Daniel did not fast. A fast, ordained by Jesus Christ, requires members to anoint their head and wash their face. *(Matthew 6:17)* Daniel did not anoint his head. *(Daniel 10:3)* Second, Jesus did not drink or eat anything during his fast. *(Luke 4:2)* Moses did not drink or eat anything during his fast. *(Exodus 34:28)* The men, women, children, and animals in Nineveh did not drink or eat anything during their fast. *(Jonah 3:7)* There is no indication that Daniel fasted; he simply altered his diet. Third, Jesus set the people free. Moses set the people free. Daniel remained in captivity. Deceived individuals participate in a "Daniel's fast"; disciples of Christ adhere to the teachings of Jesus Christ.

Satan knows that all "fasting" is not effective. "Wherefore have we fasted, say they, and thou seest not? wherefore have we afflicted our soul, and thou takest no knowledge? Behold, in the day of your fast ye find pleasure, and exact all your labours. Behold ye fast for strife and debate, and to smite with the fist of wickedness: ye shall not fast as ye do this day, to make your voice to be heard on high. Is it such a fast that I have chosen? a day for a man to afflict his soul? is it to bow down his head as a bulrush, and to spread sackcloth and ashes under him? wilt thou call this a fast, and an acceptable day to the Lord? Is not this the fast that I have chosen: to loose the bands of wickedness, to undo the heavy burdens, and to let the oppressed go free, and that ye break every yoke: Is it not to deal thy bread to the hungry, and that thou bring the poor that are cast out to thy house? when thou seest the naked, that thou cover him; and that thou hide not thyself from thine own flesh?" *(Isaiah 58:3-7)*

God does not take knowledge of a "Daniel's fast." He is not interested in your fasting to lose weight or to become physically healthier. He wants us to suffer—to afflict our bodies and endure pain. We fast to crucify the flesh, not to detoxify the body or to look more attractive. We fast to discipline ourselves and gain self-control. We fast to endure hardships so we can reject pleasure. With control of our emotions, we are able to reject the impulses and compulsions that drive us to give in to the lust of the flesh. Fasting helps to curb the impulse to please our flesh and keep our flesh subject to the will of God.

Praying

The scripture tells us that the conclusion of the whole matter is to fear God and keep His commandments. *(Ecclesiastes 12:13)* The world is not the Kingdom of God, and everyone should first seek the Kingdom of God and His righteousness. *(Matthew 6:33)*

Those who want to be saved from destruction need to overcome the world, which is filled with corruption. We have assimilated the ways of the world, and we need to be redeemed from witchcraft.

Ignorance may be preferable to a slave than knowledge; the less a slave understands about his ignominious life, the less pain and humiliation he may suffer. However, ignorance is not conducive to self-determination. Those who want to determine their own destiny must have sufficient knowledge to guide them in their chosen path. Those who want to be delivered from the slavery of sin must adopt a new way of thinking. We must let go of those things that comforted us in slavery, because a life of bondage does not comport with a life of freedom. Those who want to escape the bondage of sin must renounce Satan's witchcraft and false prophets' lying vanities—and elevate their minds above the things of the world.

All have sinned, and God does not hear sinners' prayers. *(Romans 3:23; John 9:31)* Yet, Jesus tells us that we should always pray. *(Luke 18:1)* Why should we always pray if God does not hear our prayer? We should always pray to do God's will. God has no interest in empowering and enriching us to rebel against Him. *(Ezra 9:6-14)* He knows what we need. Our prayer, therefore, should first be to do His will, and everything else will be added unto us.

God does not need us to pray. He already knows what we need and what we will petition. We need to pray. Prayer requires us to acknowledge that we need the Lord. Persistent prayer is transformative. Those who always pray will continuously seek to do the will of God. We cast down our own vain thoughts and imaginations and bring our minds into captivity unto the obedience of Christ. In our vanity, we pandered to the lust of the flesh and the vanity of self-promotion. Through the knowledge of Jesus Christ, we learned that Satan manipulated us to damn our own souls in exchange for the flattery of demon spirits. We want to come out of the bondage of sin and serve the Lord. *(Luke 1:17)* We have to pray because our enemies are too strong for us. We need the grace of God to overcome those who would force us to remain their slaves.

Once we have a mind to serve the Lord, the enemy is defeated. God has supreme power and promised to pour out His spirit upon us. If we cleanse ourselves from pollution through fasting and prepare our minds through praying, God will give us power over the enemy. The Spirit of God will dwell within us. An enlightened man cannot doubt the existence of God who dwells within him. A knowledgeable woman will not fear an enemy over whom she has power.

Victory through Christ

God, through Moses, went into Egypt and defeated Pharaoh in his own kingdom. God validated his power over Egypt. The Hebrews were free to leave captivity and to reclaim their inheritance. God, through Jesus Christ, defeated Satan in the devil's own kingdom. God validated His supremacy—He is the King of kings and Lord of lords. Children of God are free to leave the bondage of sin and to reclaim their birthright to inherit the Kingdom of God.

Jesus overcame sin and defeated death. The Master (teacher) taught His disciples (students) to discipline (knowledge) themselves. He taught us of His ways, so we could walk in His path. He ransomed us from the grave, so we could be reconciled with the Father. We emulate the ways of the Master: we fast and pray; we deny ourselves; we take up our cross and follow Him; we endure hardships; and we drink of His cup of sacrifice. Discipline (the knowledge of Jesus Christ) requires us to make a commitment to afflict ourselves to bring about the desired change in our lives. We subordinate our will to the will of God and bring everything into captivity unto the obedience of Christ. We walk free of sin.

Endure Hardness

Satan's power over us is in the weakness of our flesh. We lust after the flesh to derive some relief from the pain of life. Hence, the pleasure we derive from the flesh makes us unwilling to overcome the flesh. Yet, our unwillingness to overcome the flesh separates us from God and reinforces Satan's power. As a result of our ignorance, we remain separated from God, who wants to deliver us from Satan's heavy burdens that cause us so much unrest and pain. Thankfully, with the knowledge of Jesus Christ, we have been turned from darkness to light, from the power of Satan to the power of God. We understand that if we endure hardness like a good soldier, we can defeat the enemy. The enemy cannot make us self-destruct; he can only tempt us to self-destruct. Through the knowledge of Jesus Christ, we understand what the enemy is doing. Hence, we fast and pray to resist the temptation. The more we resist the temptation of the flesh, the more we grow in the spirit. When we overcome the witchcraft and walk in the Spirit of God, the lust of the flesh dissipates. We see how Satan manipulated us to give up the power and glory to become pathetic slaves.

Despise the Shame

In addition to overcoming witchcraft and crucifying the corruption within our blood, followers of Christ must be willing to subordinate their pride. Jesus was humiliated. Mary, an unmarried pregnant mother, was undoubtedly criticized. Hannah's adversary mocked her inability to have a child. *(1 Samuel 1:6)* Job observed, "But now they that are younger than I have me in derision, whose fathers I would have disdained to have set with the dogs of my flock." *(Job 30:1)* Humiliation is a part of salvation. When we exalt Christ in a self-absorbed and unbelieving world, we exhibit integrity. We demonstrate that we are not ashamed to admit that Jesus is Lord of our lives. Our dedication to the spirit in a natural world underscores our commitment to exalt God in the earth. Children of God will suffer scorn for Christ because they exalt the Lord over themselves. Let the deceived consider us fools – they will have eternity to reconsider.

———————————— **Living Sacrifice** ————————————

There is great peace to be found in sacrifice. Servants of God understand that "No weapon that is formed against thee shall prosper; and every tongue that shall rise against thee in judgment thou shalt condemn. This is the heritage of the servants of the Lord, and their righteousness is of me, saith the Lord." *(Isaiah 54:17)* Most individuals, like the impetuous prodigal son, want their inheritance now. They do not want to wait on God's blessings. Alas, the world is going to pass away. Those who walk after the things of this world will inherit nothing.

Those who trust in God's promises will esteem the word of God above their daily bread. They hunger and thirst for a kingdom wherein dwells righteousness, and renounce the lust of the flesh, the lust of the eyes, and the pride of life—all those vanities that bewitch men and women to rebel. Those who serve the Lord know that He will perform what He has promised. Therefore, believers are willing to wait upon the Lord, "Knowing that of the Lord ye shall receive the reward of the inheritance: for ye serve the Lord." *(Colossians 3:24)*

The only way we will deny ourselves, take up our cross, and follow Christ is to acknowledge that our sins have robbed us of our integrity. If we live in denial and cannot admit that sin is a manifestation of corruption, we will have little impetus to turn from sin. The thief cried out for deliverance, until he acknowledged that he deserved to die. His willingness to accept death underscored his integrity. Death delivered him from sin. His willingness to accept death earned him eternal life.

A person who wants to be forgiven of sin should rejoice when offered deliverance from sin. An individual who rejects God's knowledge, which would set him free from sin, does not want to be set free from sin. "And this is the condemnation, that light is come into the world, and men loved darkness rather than light, because their deeds were evil." *(John 3:19)* Sinners are deceived, but they are not crazy. They know that Jesus is despised and rejected in the earth, and they know that Jesus' knowledge is rejected because the people have no desire to overcome sin. Moreover, sinners know that Jesus did not die, so the people could remain in the bondage of sin and serve Satan. Jesus came that the people might have life, and the only life that will exist when the world ends will be spiritual. Those who chose to exalt Jesus will go into everlasting life in the Holy Ghost. *(Romans 14:17)* Those who chose to exalt Satan will go into everlasting damnation. *(2 Thessalonians 1:9)* God has challenged us to show that we exalt Him as king. We show our subserviency by repeatedly denying ourselves until we have completely surrendered.

The Lord has promised, "He that overcometh shall inherit all things; and I will be his God, and he shall be my son." *(Revelation 21:7)* It is the Lord's good pleasure to give us the kingdom, but He wants to ensure that we are going to be obedient to His word. Thus, those who want to serve the Lord will learn of His ways and overcome the power of Satan. They will take up their cross and follow Him. We fast because we want to keep all of God's commandments. We fast to bring our bodies under subjection, so that the power of Christ may rest upon us.

There will be those who will discourage us that we cannot overcome sin. Peter tried to discourage Jesus from dying. Jesus told Peter, "Get thee behind me, Satan." *(Matthew 16:23)* Jesus understood that Peter loved Him and meant well. However, Satan did not want Jesus to die. If Jesus did not shed His blood, there would have been no remission of sin. Further, Jesus would have allowed the desire of His flesh to override the will of the spirit. Similarly, if we do not shed our blood, we will continue to walk after the flesh. If we continue to sin, we cannot receive forgiveness of sin. *(Isaiah 55:7)* It is impractical to expect God to forgive us of sins, when we have deliberately chosen to join rebellious demons and fight against Him. God will not allow His enemies to inherit eternal life in His kingdom. Just as Jesus drank His cup, we must also drink our cup of sacrifice.

When we pursue the things of the spirit, we renounce the

things of the world. Satan's power over us is destroyed, because we have no interest in the things over which Satan has power. Our only interest is in pleasing the Lord. We are not afraid of Satan; Jesus has already promised to deliver us from the hands of our enemies. We do not need or want false prophets' lying vanities as a subterfuge to remain in the bondage of sin. We know the truth: Jesus is Lord. With His power, we are able to serve Him in holiness and righteousness all the days of our lives.

Through the knowledge of Jesus Christ, we are saved by grace, through faith, not by works. The enemy had us in the bondage of sin. Through fear of death, we served Satan. We committed adultery and fornication, lied, cheated, and engaged in all types of works of iniquity. While we yet rebelled against God, Christ died to deliver us from bondage. Now that we know the truth, we have no reason to rebel against God. Our God is the Almighty, and we should serve Him. We have no reason to serve Satan. Jesus is Lord, and He **must** deliver those who want to be delivered because we cannot serve Him if we are forced to serve another god. Since our enemy is stronger than us, the Lord has to fight our battle for us and defeat our enemy—and He is not only able to defeat our enemy, He already has. We are free to escape.

Recapitulate

Everyone is going to be judged according to the gospel of Jesus Christ. The apostle Paul observed, "But if our gospel be hid, it is hid to them that are lost: In whom the god of this world hath blinded the minds of them which believe not, lest the light of the glorious gospel of Christ, who is the image of God, should shine unto them." *(2 Corinthians 4:3-4)* Those who walk in the light as He is in the light will come out of darkness into the marvelous light, and will turn from the power of Satan unto God.

Since God does not want anyone to be destroyed, He does not want anyone deceived. Therefore, it is imperative that we acquire the knowledge of Jesus Christ and escape the pollution of this world. If we want to serve the Lord, God will resurrect us from the grave and save our soul from destruction. If we are determined to live the way we want and choose to reject the knowledge of Jesus Christ, we are going to be destroyed. In other words, those who are self-willed will destroy themselves.

Before we debunk the lying vanities of false prophets and other erroneous teachings, I will review what has been written in an attempt to make as plain as possible God's purpose for the human family.

Fear God and Keep His Commandments

The whole duty of man is to fear God and to keep His commandments. Jesus Christ is the King of kings and Lord of lords. He has superior knowledge and superior power. At His name, every knee must bow and every tongue must confess. He is the Supreme ruler. There are no legislators and judges to check His power. His subjects do not have the right to march and protest His decisions. He is the all-wise God. He allowed us to see for ourselves how weak and ignorant we are.

God created humans and allowed them to demonstrate whether they would follow the example of Christ and submit to the will of God or would follow the example of Satan and rebel. God deliberately allowed men and women to be taken into captivity and corrupted. We see how ignorant and frail we are. We see how humans, out of fear of death, oppress other humans. The Lord, therefore, has allowed us to witness how envy, strife, fear, and covetousness lead to corruption. Hence, we are witnesses to the madness in Satan's kingdom—and should readily understand why we should submit to God's supreme wisdom and power.

Individuals who acknowledge that Jesus Christ is Lord and turn from the wickedness in the earth will acquire His knowledge and power. They will denounce Satan's witchcraft and obey the commandments of God. Through the grace of God, obedient servants will overcome sin and demonstrate that they exalt the will of the Lord above their own will; they will give up their life of sin. They will be redeemed from corruption and prepared for the Master's use. Disobedient servants will refuse to acknowledge Jesus as Lord. They will continue to exalt their will above His and remain in the bondage of sin. Their stubborn refusal to obey the commandments of God indicates that they will not subject themselves to His commands. Such individuals have chosen Satan as their king and will remain in Satan's kingdom.

God entered into two covenants with His people: the natural children of Abraham and the spiritual children of Abraham. The natural children of Abraham were taken into the bondage of Egypt. The spiritual children of Abraham were taken into the bondage of sin. The Lord sent Moses to deliver the children of Israel out of bondage. Before the natural children of Abraham came out of the bondage of Egypt, the Lord commanded them to kill and eat an unblemished lamb. They were directed to put the lamb's blood around the door of the houses. The blood would signify to the death angel to pass over that house.

Before the spiritual children of Abraham came out of the bondage of sin, Jesus Christ (the Lamb of God) commanded them to eat of His unblemished flesh and to drink of His blood. The people did not put the blood around the door; Jesus was the door. (John 10:9) Those who drank His blood signified to the death angel to pass over them. They are a part of the body of Christ; they have the Spirit of Jesus Christ.

The Hebrews were taken into bondage after famine required them to leave their blessed land to go into Egypt, where there was food. They were stronger than the Egyptians, but they were too ignorant to know. The Egyptians, out of fear, enslaved the Hebrews and imposed harsh burdens upon the people. The Hebrews worked to build Pharaoh's treasure cities, which strengthened the power of Egypt over them. God saw the burdens the Egyptians imposed upon the Hebrews and had mercy upon them. Moses ultimately led the people out of Egypt. False prophets, to keep the children of Israel from having to confront their fear, lied to the people. The fearful people renounced their inheritance to serve the Egyptians. The children of Israel had cried out for mercy and asked the Lord to deliver them out of the bondage of Egypt. God had mercy and delivered them out of bondage. False prophets encouraged the people to forsake their own mercy and return to the bondage of Egypt. God destroyed nearly all of them.

The Lord sent famine into the earth—not for food or drink, but for the word of the Lord. The people, with the Spirit of God, were stronger than Satan. However, because of their ignorance, the people were separated from God. Sinners rejected the spirit of God, which would have given them power over their enemies; they lusted after the flesh, which gave their enemies power over them. Jesus saw the madness in the earth and had mercy upon the people. Jesus ultimately came and taught the people how Satan had bewitched them, so they could redeem themselves from corruption. Jesus died and paved the way for men and women to escape the bondage of sin. False prophets, however, lie to keep the people from having to confront their fear of death. *(Romans 7:13)* False prophets appeal to people's pride and vanity, which causes them to disobey God and remain in the bondage of sin. Although Jesus died so that sinners could receive remission of their sins and offered to ransom sinners from the grave of sin, those who have chosen to remain in the bondage of sin will be destroyed. They chose to forsake their own mercy.

Those who fear God do not want the false prophets' lying vanities. We want to be ready when the Lord comes and need the truth of God to set us free from sin. "Forasmuch then as Christ hath suffered for us in the flesh, arm yourselves likewise with the same mind: for he that hath suffered in the flesh hath ceased from sin; that he should no longer live the rest of his time in the flesh to the lusts of men, but to the will of God." *(1 Peter 4:1-2)* We will suffer in the flesh to cease from sin; we do not want to be separated from God.

Through the knowledge of Jesus Christ, disciples of Christ are able to come out of darkness and prepare ourselves to serve the

Lord. We need to purify ourselves to serve Him that is pure. *(1 John 3:1-3)* Since out of the Lord's mouth comes knowledge and understanding, we want messengers of God to teach us how to overcome sin and perfect ourselves. Messengers of God will turn us from the power of Satan to the power of Christ.

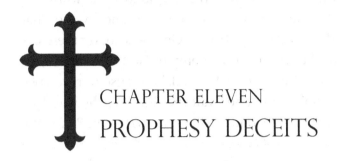

CHAPTER ELEVEN
PROPHESY DECEITS

Rebellious individuals reject the knowledge of Jesus Christ. "For that they hated knowledge, and did not choose the fear of the Lord." *(Proverbs 1:29)* Although ignorance led them into the bondage of sin, fools despise wisdom and instructions. *(Proverbs 1:7)* They despise and reject Jesus. *(Isaiah 53:3)* They despise and reject His knowledge. *(Hosea 4:6)* Most sinners want to remain in sin, and they do not want to hear anything that will trouble them to turn from their wickedness. Since they do not want their lives to comport with the word of God, they want preachers who will change the word of God to comport with their lives. Hence, they have refused to turn from evil and taken refuge in lies. *(Isaiah 28:15)*

Narrow is the gate that leads to eternal life. Most people are going to be destroyed because, since they do not believe the word of God, Satan has blinded their minds and persuaded them to believe adulterated versions of the gospel. *(2 Corinthians 4:3-4)* Those who ignore the testimony of Jesus Christ will remain ignorant; those who remain ignorant will remain in the bondage of sin; and those who remain in the bondage of sin will receive the wages of sin: death. Nearly the entire world has chosen to observe false prophets' lying vanities and to forsake their own mercy, which is why only a few will enter the gate that leads to eternal life.

God tells His people, "Love not the world, neither the things that are in the world. If any man love the world, the love of the Father is not in him." *(1 John 2:15)* Those who love the world are enemies of God. "Ye adulterers and adulteresses, know ye not that the friendship of the world is enmity with God? whosoever therefore will be a friend of the world is the enemy of God." *(James 4:4)* In Satan's kingdom, despite many individuals' pretense of reverence for Christ, most despise Him and exalt the things of the world.

Men and women were wonderfully made. *(Psalm 139:14)* We were created for the glory of God. *(Isaiah 43:7)* When sinners turn from their evil way and do good works, we give God the glory. *(Matthew 5:16; 1 Peter 2:12)* When we turn from wickedness and obey God, we demonstrate that we trust God with our very lives. However, the people of the world, like their god, refuse to glorify the Almighty. Men display their wealth, which many have obtained through corruption, and appear as successful. Women exhibit their flesh and captivate the lust of men. Women's partial nudity, tattoos, makeup, and lipstick—all of the things of the world—attest to their desire to attract attention to themselves and to promote their vainglory. "The shew of their countenance doth witness against them; and they declare their sin as Sodom, they hide it not. Woe unto their soul! for they have rewarded evil unto themselves." *(Isaiah 3:9)* Like the children of Israel, almost everyone rejects the Spirit of God to remain in sin. Keep in mind, they are not in the bondage of sin. They are not slaves to sin. Jesus paid the ransom to set them free and offered them the truth to make them free; they have rejected the truth to continue to sin against God. They volitionally serve Satan.

Consider: All that is of the world—the lust of the flesh, the lust of the eyes, and the pride of life—is not of the Creator. The things of the world are examples of Satan's witchcraft—vainglory. Those who love the world and are friends of the world are enemies of God. *(James 4:4)* Adulterers, for example, are enemies of God. The word of God denotes that fornicators and adulterers cannot enter the Kingdom of God. *(1 Corinthians 6:9; Galatians 5:16-21)* Jesus observed that if a man looked on a woman to lust after her, the man had committed adultery in his heart. *(Matthew 5:28)* Hence, Satan has so bewitched men and women to look sexy and promote lust, until such deceived individuals delight in helping Satan to condemn men and women's souls to hell. Lotharios and vixens, who would demand a divorce if they discovered their spouses had cheated on them, rejoice in their hearts when they see others ogling and lusting after their flesh. They take pleasure in destroying the souls of the weak, just as Satan is doing to them.

Jesus Christ requires servants who will humble themselves and acquiesce to His wisdom and power. As a result of famine for the Word of God, the people went into captivity. In due time, Jesus came to set them free from captivity. Before He ascended upon high, Jesus commanded His disciples to go and teach all nations, "Teaching them to observe all things whatsoever I have commanded you." *(Matthew 28:20)* The apostles were commanded to teach the people how to perform all the commandments of God.

Satan also sent pastors to feed the sheep. False prophets taught the same vomit that had caused the people to go into captivity. They taught the people that they could not live holy, although Jesus came to deliver the people out of the hands of their enemies, so the people could serve God, without fear, in holiness and righteousness. *(Luke 1:74-75)* They taught the people that God loved them unconditionally, although God hates sinners. *(Psalm 5:5)* They taught the people that they could not work and earn their salvation, although people are going to be judged according to their works. *(Revelation 20:12-13)* They taught the people that Jesus was their personal savior, although the people have never seen Jesus or heard His voice. *(John 5:37)* They taught the people that once they were saved, they were always saved, yet God saved the children of Israel out of Egypt and afterwards destroyed them. *(Jude 1:5)*

False prophets would not exist if sinners wanted to know the truth. False prophets and those that rebel against God have a mutual relationship: the false prophets lie to sinners, and sinners encourage false prophets to lie. "That this is a rebellious people, lying children, children that will not hear the law of the Lord: Which say to the seers, See not; and to the prophets, Prophesy not unto us right things, speak unto us smooth things, prophesy deceits." *(Isaiah 30:9-10)* Sinners love false prophets. They encourage false prophets to distort the word of God and to misrepresent Jesus' teachings. They have no desire to serve God; they want to be perverted. *(Isaiah 30:11-12)*

The children of Israel assured Moses that they wanted to be delivered from bondage and would obey God's commandments. God put them to the test. After He demonstrated His miraculous power of deliverance, He humbled them to see what was in their hearts. Would they exalt Him as their God and trust in His salvation? Would they reject Him and rely upon their own frailty? When they had to give up the only life they had ever known—the life of slavery—and trust in the Lord, they preferred to return to slavery. "Nevertheless they did flatter with their mouth, and they lied unto him with their tongues. For their heart was not right with him, neither were they stedfast in his covenant." *(Psalm 78:36)* The people declared they would serve the Lord if He delivered them out of the bondage of Egypt. When they perceived that freedom from bondage required them to place their lives in God's hand, they retracted. They preferred to serve Pharaoh and survive as slaves than to trust in God and reclaim their inheritance.

Jesus came to set those in the bondage of sin free. The Master taught his disciples, if they want to overcome sin, to deny themselves. Sinners reject such knowledge. They refuse to give up their lust of the flesh, lust of the eyes, and pride of life. They refuse to overcome sin. When the Lord commands the people to renounce the corruption that allows Satan to rule over them, the people reject God. They honor Jesus with their lips but Satan with their lives. They love pleasure more than they love God; thus, they choose to walk after the flesh. They reject Jesus' knowledge and choose not to walk like the Master walked.

Hypocrites do not taste the Lord and see that He is good. *(Psalm 34:8)* They do not eat of His flesh or drink of His blood; they eat from the table that is filled with vomit. They do not serve the Lord in holiness and righteousness; they want to remain polluted. They encourage false prophets to twist the scriptures and distort what it means to be saved by grace, not by works. If sinners are not saved by works, they feel safe when they disobey God and indulge the works of the flesh. They want the false prophets to tell them that once they are saved, they are always saved. If sinners do not have to obey the Lord to enter His kingdom, they can obey and disobey God according to their whim. They want false prophets to tell them that God hates the sin but loves the sinner. If such foolishness were true, sinners, like their father, the devil, could fight against God, yet God would continue to love them.

Satan Cannot Save Himself

Just as the Hebrews chose to serve Pharaoh, whom the Lord defeated, the people today want to serve Satan, whom the Lord defeated. "Wherefore the anger of the Lord was kindled against Amaziah, and he sent unto him a prophet, which said unto him, Why hast thou sought after the gods of the people, which could not deliver their own people out of thine hand?" *(2 Chronicles 25:15)* Satan is unable to deliver himself from the wrath of God to come. Nonetheless, the false prophets have persuaded the people that they can emulate Satan, rebel against God, and yet be delivered from the wrath of God.

It takes faith in God to reject the corruption of the world. We were born in sin, which is the only life we have ever known, and change requires exercising the courage to face unknown dangers. People want to feel safe. Those who do not have faith in God will conform to the world. Although they know they are wrong, they are willing to do whatever they believe necessary to survive. If that means they must engage in corruption, they will engage in corruption. Of course, they do not want to suffer punishment for their corruption, so they gravitate toward the lies of the false prophets, who are happy to accommodate.

When people want to sin, they know how to manipulate their

minds. Satan told Eve that she would not die if she ate from the tree. *(Genesis 3:4)* Satan's message appealed to her vanity. Eve did not ask God any questions or rebuke the devil. She began to imagine the possibilities of what Satan had told her and allowed her imaginations to overtake her. When the Hebrews wanted to rebel against God, they did not discuss how the Lord had brought them out of the bondage of Egypt. They began to rhapsodize about the cucumbers and melons they had eaten in Egypt. *(Numbers 11:5)* Unrepentant sinners distort their own perception; they love to have a kaleidoscope of lies to select from. When they disobey the word of God, they take comfort in the lying vanities that shade the truth and distort their rebellion.

Further, those who do not want to confront their fears do not want to hear about their cowardice. They do not want Joshua and Caleb to encourage their faith in the Lord; they want false prophets to use subterfuge to justify their lack of courage. Those who want to commit adultery and fornication do not want to hear about how they exalt flesh above spirit. They want to hear that they are only human and are going to sin. False prophets' lying vanities allow the wicked to feel justified when they rebel against the Lord.

Utter Error against the Lord

Many souls hunger and thirst for righteousness. False prophets tell the people that they cannot live holy. "For the vile person will speak villany, and his heart will work iniquity, to practise hypocrisy, and to utter error against the Lord, to make empty the soul of the hungry, and he will cause the drink of the thirsty to fail." *(Isaiah 32:6)* Thus, many who seek the Lord are worse off after listening to the false prophets than they were before. Remember: Jesus told the scribes and Pharisees that they traveled across sea and land to convert people to God. After they had converted the people, the proselytes were twice the children of Satan than the false teachers. *(Matthew 23:15)* Rather than teach the people how to overcome sin, the false prophets tell the people that they must remain in sin—nobody is perfect.

The implication is that Satan, who has the people in bondage, is more powerful than Jesus, who came to set the people free from bondage. If Jesus could not deliver the people out of the hands of Satan, that would make Satan the Almighty God. Of course, Jesus came to bear witness to the truth: He is Lord. And Jesus, manifested in a flesh-and-blood body, defeated Satan in Satan's kingdom to demonstrate that He is Lord. Alas, the people do not challenge the false prophets' error against the Lord. The lie is obvious, but lies are what the people want to hear.

——————————— **There is No Soundness** ———————————

The Lord looked at the mentally ill people and lamented. "Why should ye be stricken any more? ye will revolt more and more: the whole head is sick, and the whole heart faint. From the sole of the foot even unto the head there is no soundness in it; but wounds, and bruises, and putrifying sores: they have not been closed, neither bound up, neither mollified with ointment." *(Isaiah 1:5-6)* We are transmitting diseases, reveling in deviancy, and engaged in all manner of wickedness and corruption. Despite our public pretense of enjoyment, we are abusing drugs and alcohol, taking pills, and doing everything we can to avoid the demons that trouble us. The Lord has bestowed mercy upon the people and sent messengers to teach them how to overcome Satan's witchcraft. Sinners reject the message; they do not want to overcome.

——————————— **Spiritual Wickedness** ———————————

The fight against spiritual wickedness will not take place with clanging swords and charging chariots. The fight takes place in the heart. Men and women will devote their time and effort in pursuit of those things they treasure. If they treasure the Lord, they are going to seek out the knowledge of Christ. If they treasure themselves, they are going to seek out corruption. Ergo, a man who desires to serve the Lord will read the Holy Bible, bring his body under subjection through fasting and praying, and do those things that will elevate his mind above the flesh.

A sinner who wants to please himself does not want to overcome the lust of the flesh. His objective is to preserve and pleasure his natural life. For example, those that lust after the flesh may look at pornography. They know that porn is nothing but fiction, in which actors and actresses deliberately engage in histrionics that completely distorts reality. Their hazardous performances appeal to the sickness of men and women, yet people crave such sickness. Since it is in the hearts of the people to maximize the pleasure of the flesh, they volitionally give their minds over to Satan to manipulate their lust.

Many people, however, are not so inane to deny God completely. They go to church, clap, sing, and appear to worship God. They expect the preacher to talk about pleasant things and have no interest in hearing about their disobedience. "Also, thou son of man, the children of thy people still are talking against thee by the walls and in the doors of the houses, and speak one to another, every one to his brother, saying, Come, I pray you, and hear what is the word that cometh forth from the Lord. And they come unto thee as the people cometh, and they sit before thee as my people, and they hear thy words, but they will not do them: for with their mouth they shew much love, but their heart goeth after their own covetousness. And, lo, thou art unto them as a very lovely song of one that hath a pleasant voice, and can play well on an instrument: for they hear thy words, but they do them not." *(Ezekiel 33:30-32)*

Worship in Vain

Jesus knew that people were not sincere. They may have fooled themselves, but they did not fool God. "This people draweth nigh unto me with their mouth, and honoureth me with their lips; but their heart is far from me. But in vain they do worship me, teaching for doctrines the commandments of men." *(Matthew 15:8-9)*

People sit in buildings with false prophets and profess to worship God. The Lord looks upon the people and can hardly wait to destroy them. In fact, He is so angry until He will help them to believe their own lies. "He that killeth an ox is as if he slew a man; he that sacrificeth a lamb, as if he cut off a dog's neck; he that offereth an oblation, as if he offered swine's blood; he that burneth incense, as if he blessed an idol. Yea, they have chosen their own ways, and their soul delighteth in their abominations. I also will choose their delusions, and will bring their fears upon them; because when I called, none did answer; when I spake, they did not hear: but they did evil before mine eyes, and chose that in which I delighted not." *(Isaiah 66:3-4)* Just as God was not pleased with Saul's decision to save the best of the sheep and oxen, He is not pleased with pagan sacrifices. Rebellion is as the sin of witchcraft. Those who reject God's commandments and counter with their own version of worship are wasting their time. Satan has made fools of them.

Sinners engage in wickedness and listen to the false prophets who tell them what they want to hear. The people lie, steal, cheat, fornicate, commit adultery, and do anything they want in violation of God's commandments, yet many false prophets never discuss the wages of sin. There are preachers who hardly utter the words "sin," "commandments," or "repent."

Like those who rose up against Moses, many false teachers have gained immense fame and prominence among the people. They do not know how to deliver the people out of bondage, but they know how to motivate and inspire the people. The people are still Satan's slaves—captured, corrupted, and incapable of inheriting the Kingdom of God—but the false prophets pander to the vanity of the people. Jesus told His disciples that they had to hate mother, father, even themselves. *(Luke 14:26)* The false prophets tell the people that God loves them unconditionally. Jesus told His disciples that if they suffered with Him, they would reign with him. *(2 Timothy*

2:12) False prophets tell their disciples there is nothing they can do to earn salvation—Jesus paid it all.

───────────── **Will Not Acquit the Wicked** ─────────────

The Lord does not want anyone to perish. He is ready to forgive and mighty to save. He simply wants men and women to be honest. If we admit our wrong and turn from evil, God will deliver us. We must realize, however, that God is not mocked. He knows sincere individuals will seek knowledge to overcome sin. "The Lord is slow to anger, and great in power, and will not at all acquit the wicked." *(Nahum 1:3)* The Lord cannot lie: those who reject His knowledge are going to be destroyed. He will not acquit the wicked.

Despite their spiritual pretensions, sinners love false prophets. The false prophets prophesy lies, and the people love them for it. *(Jeremiah 5:31)* The people do not want to know the truth. If they knew the truth, the truth would make them free from sin. They would not commit adultery and fornication. They would not promote their own vanity and attract attention to the flesh. "To whom shall I speak, and give warning that they may hear? Behold, their ear is uncircumcised, and they cannot hearken: behold, the word of the Lord is unto them a reproach; they have no delight in it." *(Jeremiah 6:10)* The people know they are corrupt; they know the Lord has the knowledge and power to deliver them; yet the people reject the knowledge because they want to remain corrupt. The people love the flesh. They know it is of Satan, but they love the pleasures of the flesh more than they love God. *(2 Timothy 3:4)*

As sinners, we have done much evil and hurt many people. In our ignorance, we have contributed to the madness in the world. God is willing to forgive our sins, if we demonstrate that, after having been given an opportunity to overcome ignorance, we repented of our wickedness. Most will not. "Thus saith the Lord, Stand ye in the ways, and see, and ask for the old paths, where is the good way, and walk therein, and ye shall find rest for your souls. But they said, We will not walk therein. Also I set watchmen over you, saying, Hearken to the sound of the trumpet. But they said, We will not hearken." *(Jeremiah 6:16-17)* The Lord told the people to turn from their wickedness. The people rejected the word of the Lord. Although our sins hurt others and contribute to the madness in the earth, most people reject God and follow Satan.

────────────── **Naked and Unashamed** ──────────────

There are false prophets who lie and tell the people that God wants them to have a great sex life. In support of such blasphemy, the false prophets say that Adam and Eve were naked and unashamed. "Every day they wrest my words; all their thoughts are against me for evil." *(Psalm 56:5)* Adam and Eve were created by the spirit. They were spiritual beings and knew only good. They were unaware of their flesh and did not know they were naked. Once Satan deceived them, the spirit departed from them. After the spirit departed, they knew both good and evil. They realized they were naked. Their nakedness indicated they had fallen for Satan's witchcraft and lost their souls—they had committed evil.

Nakedness is shame. *(Isaiah 47:3; Revelation 16:15; Exodus 32:25)* Individuals are deceived who exhibit their nakedness and are unashamed. Such individuals are so caught up in pride and vanity—attracting attention—until they do not realize that they are displaying their own ignorance. Satan manipulated Adam and Eve to rebel against God and to lose their soul. Those who promote the weakness of the flesh (lust) to capture attention (vanity) cause their own destruction (enemy of God). They signal that they exalt Satan over God; they exalt witchcraft above truth and are not ashamed of their display.

God created spiritual beings. "That born of the spirit is spirit." *(John 3:6)* Satan deceived Eve, who was flesh of Adam's flesh. *(Genesis 2:23)* Thus, Adam disobeyed the Spirit to walk after the lust of his own flesh. Those who love the truth will renounce Satan's witchcraft, forsake their wicked ways, and return unto the Lord. Those who refuse to exalt Jesus as Lord have chosen to renounce their right of redemption, remain in corruption, and forsake their own mercy.

The flesh is the enemy of the spirit. All that is of the world—the lust of the flesh, the lust of the eyes, and the pride of life—is of the devil. Jesus came into the earth to save the people from their sins—the works of the flesh. Jesus came to destroy the works of the devil, which is why we have to be born again of the spirit to enter the Kingdom of God. The Spirit of God will give us power and victory over Satan's witchcraft. Just as the children of Israel chose to remain in the bondage of Egypt and were destroyed without mercy, those who remain in the bondage of sin are going to be destroyed without mercy. There will be no need for God to have mercy upon those who chose to reject His mercy. To be naked and unashamed is to accept separation from God. It is to accept the death and destruction of your depraved soul.

The apostle Paul, filled with the Spirit of God, exhorted saints that, if possible, he would encourage them to remain single and give their lives completely to God. False prophets observed that Paul must have had problems with women. Not only was Paul's comment directed to men and women, the flesh is weak. If individuals have overcome Satan's witchcraft, why should they seek to be entangled again with lust? Why risk losing their souls? Why should an individual who walks in the Spirit of God lust after the weakness of the flesh? Jesus gave believers power over the flesh. Paul simply encouraged those who had the Spirit of God to walk after the things of God.

Men of God try to reason with the people. "And Moses sent to call Dathan and Abiram, the sons of Eliab: which said, We will not come up: Is it a small thing that thou hast brought us up out of a land that floweth with milk and honey, to kill us in the wilderness, except thou make thyself altogether a prince over us? Moreover thou hast not brought us into a land that floweth with milk and honey, or given us inheritance of fields and vineyards: wilt thou put out the eyes of these men? we will not come up." *(Numbers 16:12-14)*

Sinners delude themselves. Moses delivered the Hebrews out of bondage, yet the former slaves perverted their own minds and pretended they had enjoyed the wealth of Egypt. Rather than trust in the Lord, they yearned to return to slavey. Similarly, despite the madness in Satan's kingdom, the people are unwilling to separate themselves from the world. They will attend religious services, clap their hands, and praise the Lord in songs. But they will not obey God's commandments. They seek preachers who will tell them that they will nonetheless inherit the Kingdom of God. They deceive themselves.

──────────── **Additional Edifying Scriptures** ────────────

"This people draweth nigh unto me with their mouth, and honoureth me with their lips; but their heart is far from me. But in vain they do worship me, teaching for doctrines the commandments of men." (Matthew 15:8-9)

"For my people is foolish, they have not known me; they are sottish children, and they have none understanding: they are wise to do evil, but to do good they have no knowledge." (Jeremiah 4:22)

"To whom shall I speak, and give warning that they may hear? behold, their ear is uncircumcised, and they cannot hearken: behold, the word of the Lord is unto them a reproach; they have no delight in it." (Jeremiah 6:10)

"Pride goeth before destruction, and an haughty spirit before a fall." (Proverbs 16:18)

CHAPTER TWELVE

SAVED BY GRACE

A servant does the work of his lord. The Lord works in His servants both the will and the do of His own good pleasure. *(Philippians 2:12)* Those who are disobedient do not the work of the Lord. They seek their own pleasure. Hence, they take comfort when the false prophets teach that we are saved by grace, through faith, and not by works. Since the phrase is likely the biggest misrepresentation of the entire Bible, I will address this lying vanity first and show how false prophets have twisted the scriptures and deceived the people.

Please remember that God did not want anyone to perish. Jesus spoke in parables, because He did not want His people deceived. False prophets would see but not perceive; they would read the scriptures but not comprehend. As a result of their ignorance, false prophets would teach heresies—and the Spirit of truth would expose the false teachers as liars. *(Revelation 2:2)*

I will preface my exposition by reminding the reader why sinners live in sin: The people, through fear of death, live all their lifetime in the bondage of sin. *(Hebrews 2:15)* The devil knows that, "skin for skin," people are not going to give up their life. *(Job 2:4)* In other words, people want to survive, and, as demonstrated by the children of Israel who preferred to return to the bondage of Egypt rather than confront the giants in Canaan, most individuals do not trust God to save them. *(Psalm 78:22)* Yet, God mandates that we exalt Him in the earth. *(Psalm 46:10)* God requires that we do His will in the earth, as it is in Heaven. *(Matthew 6:10)* Jesus' kingdom, however, is not of this world. *(John 18:36)* This is Satan's kingdom. *(Luke 4:6)* Those who exalt the Lord in the earth must denounce Satan, a demonic king, who possesses the power of death. *(Hebrew 2:14)*

As a result of Adam's disobedience, all died. God separated from Adam and Eve. Sin, separation from God, is death, and we were all conceived in sin. We were all dead in sin. The prophecy went out that God would come and ransom His people from the power of the grave of sin. Jesus Christ would come and destroy the grave. "I will ransom them from the power of the grave; I will redeem them from death: O death, I will be thy plagues; O grave, I will be thy destruction: repentance shall be hid from mine eyes." *(Hosea 13:14)* Jesus Christ came to destroy him that had the power of death, that is, the devil, and to deliver them, who through fear of death, were all their lifetime in the bondage of sin. *(Hebrew 2:14-15)* Hence, Jesus came to break the power of Satan over our lives and to liberate us from the bondage of sin. Once the power of the enemy was broken, we were free to leave; we were no longer forced to work for Satan. Those who wanted to serve the Lord could serve Him, without fear, in holiness and righteousness all the days of our lives. *(Luke 1:71-75)*

God sent famine into the earth—not a famine for food or water, but for the word of the Lord. *(Amos 8:11)* As a result, the people had gone into captivity because of the lack of knowledge. *(Isaiah 5:13)* We were forced to eat the vomit of ignorance, which polluted us with pagan beliefs. *(Isaiah 28:8)* Jesus promised that those who hungered and thirsted for righteousness would be filled. *(Matthew 5:6)* The Master told us, if we wanted to live forever, to eat of His flesh and drink of His blood. *(John 6:47-54)* His flesh was meat indeed. *(John 6:55)* Jesus taught us knowledge, which allowed us to escape the pollution of this world. *(2 Peter 2:20)* Although we were polluted in our own blood, He sent His word and healed us. *(Ezekiel 16:6; Psalm 107:20)* Through the word of His grace, God built us up and sanctifed us through the truth. *(Acts 20:32; John 17:17)* The truth made us free from sin. *(John 8:32)* Jesus saved us from our sins. *(Matthew 1:21)* We were saved by grace, through faith, not by works.

Saved by grace, through faith, not by works: the children of Israel worked to build Pharaoh's treasure cities. Despite all of their work, they could not deliver themselves out of the bondage of Egypt. The children of Israel could not boast about their labor, because their labor enriched their enemies and strengthed the power of Egypt over them. The children of Israel were slaves. Powerless. No integrity. No dignity. However, the Almighty, by grace, defeated Egypt and delivered them out of the bondage of Egypt. Those who trusted in Him, by faith, entered the Promised Land and were saved from their enemies. Israel had served a false god, Pharaoh, and engaged in evil works that destroyed themselves, but their deliverance from Egypt allowed them to serve the Lord and do good works, which gave the Almighty the glory. *(Matthew 5:16)*

Terminology

It will be helpful, as we go forward, if readers understand the definition of certain words and phrases that will be discussed. Mercy implies that someone had the right to impose harsher punishment upon an individual, but chose to extend leniency usually because there were mitigating circumstances. Grace implies that someone has offered help and/or support. Work implies that a person has engaged in a particular course of action. A worker of righteousness is a person who does the will of God. A worker of iniquity is someone who rebels against God.

Scriptures

In his epistle to the church at Ephesus, the apostle Paul wrote, "But God, who is rich in mercy, for his great love wherewith he loved us, Even when we were dead in sins, hath quickened us together with Christ, (by grace ye are saved;)" *(Ephesians 2:4-5)* In an epistle to Timothy, Paul added, God "who hath saved us, and called us with an holy calling, not according to our works, but according to his own purpose and grace, which was given us in Christ Jesus before the world began." *(2 Timothy 1:9)* Moreover, Paul wrote to the Romans: "And if by grace, then is it no more of works: otherwise grace is no more grace. But if it be of works, then is it no more grace: otherwise work is no more work." *(Romans 11:6)*

Abraham

In an epistle, Paul observed, "For if Abraham were justified by works, he hath whereof to glory; but not before God. For what saith the scripture? Abraham believed God, and it was counted unto him for righteousness. Now to him that worketh is the **reward** not reckoned of grace, but of debt. But to him that worketh not, but believeth on him that justifieth the ungodly, his faith is counted for his righteousness. Even as David also describeth the blessedness of the man, unto whom God imputeth righteousness without works." *(Romans 4:2-6)* As a result of the foregoing scriptures, the false prophets have taught the people that their works will not save them. *(Ephesians 2:4-5; Romans 4:2-6; 2 Timothy 1:9; Romans 11:6)*

The apostle James asked, "Was not Abraham our father justified by works, when he had offered Isaac his son upon the altar? Seest thou how faith wrought with his works, and works was made perfect? *(James 2:21)*

James and Paul were apostles of Jesus Christ. According to Paul's letter to the Romans, Abraham was not justified by works. **"For if Abraham were justified by works, he hath whereof to glory; but not before God."** According to James's letter, Abraham was justified by works. **"Was not Abraham our father justified by works, when he had offered Isaac his son upon the altar?"** To the carnal minded, there appears to be a contradiction. Paul implied Abraham was not justified by works, yet James implied that Abraham was justified by works. The paradox is simple to understand.

The whole duty of man is to fear God and to keep His commandments. A faithful servant is obedient. A rebellious servant is disobedient. Abraham was created to serve the Lord. As a child, Abraham served pagan gods. "And Joshua said unto all the people, Thus saith the Lord God of Israel, Your fathers dwelt on the other side of the flood in old time, even Terah, the father of Abraham, and the father of Nachor: and they served other gods." *(Joshua 24:2)* Since Abraham served pagan gods, the works he had performed was not for the glory of the Lord, but for the pagan gods of his father.

Abraham wanted to serve the true God. The Lord perceived that Abraham wanted to walk in integrity and told Abraham to come out from among his family. Abraham obeyed. *(Genesis 12:1-4)* The patriarch trusted God and was willing to leave the safety and security of his pagan family to serve the Lord. As Terah's eldest son, Abraham was entitled to inherit his father's property. The Lord promised Abraham if he left his father's house and stopped worshipping false gods, He would bless him. Abraham knew what he would inherit from his father. He did not know what God would give him. Regardless, he believed God and trusted in His word. He renounced his father's inheritance and separated from his natural family. Abraham wanted to walk in integrity, which mandated that he had to separate from pagan worshippers to walk with God. *(Genesis 12:1-5)* He wanted a righteous inheritance and trusted in the Lord to provide it. "By faith Abraham, when he was called to go out into a place which he should after receive for an inheritance, obeyed; and he went out, not knowing whither he went." *(Hebrews 11:8)*

Abraham walked by faith. He was willing to renounce a known inheritance from his father for an unknown inheritance from God. He believed in the word of God so much, until he was willing to accept God's promise over his father's guarantee. Abraham was willing to risk his life to serve the true God. The Lord told Abraham, "I am thy shield, and thy exceeding great **reward**." *(Genesis 15:1)* Abraham trusted in the Lord, and the Lord rewarded him. God created Abraham. He did not owe Abraham; He was not in debt to Abraham. Yet, the Lord rewarded Abraham. A reward is something an individual receives for having done the right thing.

Abraham had undoubtedly been raised and nurtured by his mother and father. He had bonded with his family and kinsmen. In addition to the strong emotional ties, his family offered financial and physical protection. Most people would not have left their native land and their families to walk with the Lord in an unknown territory, but Abraham did not allow fear to cause him to reject God. By faith, he departed from his people and their pagan worship. Moreover, when God later commanded him to offer up Isaac, his only son, Abraham obeyed.

Despite their apparent contradictions, the apostle Paul and apostle James were both correct. We are justified by our works, and we are condemned by our works, which is why God will **reward** all people according to their works. *(Revelation 20:12-13)* Abraham was not justified by works when God told him to come out from among his family. He, along with the rest of the unlearned, engaged in pagan worship. If he had not come out, he would have been on the other side of the flood like his father; he would have been destroyed with the rest of the heathens who served pagan gods. However, Abraham was justified by faith. Abraham had not served the Lord, but obeyed God and came out from pagan worship. He understood that the Lord was God and exalted Him above himself, his son, his erstwhile family, and his people. Hence, God was indeed supreme in his life.

Abraham's works demonstrated his faith in and submission to the Almighty. As a result of his works, God became his exceeding great reward. When the kings attacked Abraham's family, Abraham slaughtered them. God saved him from his enemies. "Ye see then how that by works a man is justified, not by faith only." *(James 2:24)* Faith without works is dead. *(James 2:26)*

In contrast, the Hebrews cried unto the Lord for deliverance from Egypt. After the Lord delivered them, they did not trust in the Lord for their safety and survival. Instead, they rebelled against God and yearned to return to Egypt. Through fear of death, they were willing to spend all their lifetime in bondage. By their words, they were condemned; they had lied unto the Lord and said they would serve him. When they came up against the giants in Canaan, they did not believe they could overcome the giants. They refused to trust the Lord and wanted to return to Egypt. "Because they believed not in God, and trusted not in his salvation." *(Psalm 78:22)* The Hebrews did not trust in the Lord because they did not believe in Him. Without faith, they chose to return to bondage; God destroyed them.

Works of Abraham

Abraham was the father of many nations. "He staggered not at the promise of God through unbelief; but was strong in faith, giving glory to God; and being fully persuaded that, what he had promised, he was also able to perform." *(Romans 4:20-21)* When believers have faith in God and obey God's commandments, they become workers of righteousness—children of Abraham. They do the works of Abraham. *(John 8:39)* Abraham did not say that he trusted God but continued to serve pagan gods. He separated from the pagan worshippers and trusted in the Lord for his safety. God told him what to do, and he did what the Lord told him. *(Genesis 17:1)* "Seest thou hath faith wrought with his works, and by works was faith made perfect?" *(James 2:22)*

Abraham was saved by grace, through faith, not by works. Abraham worshipped pagan gods. The Lord would not have saved him from his enemies had he remained among his family and worshipped pagan gods. He would have died on the other side of the flood, like his father, Terah, who refused to serve the Lord but worshipped pagan gods. *(Joshua 24:2)* Despite his pagan worship, the pagan gods could not save Terah. Abraham's pagan works would not have saved him, either. Abraham believed God and came out from paganism. He was justified in asking God to save him from his enemies. By faith, he trusted in the Lord and did the works of the Lord (obeyed God's commandments). God saved Him and gave him victory over his enemies.

Ruth

During a famine in Bethlehem, a certain man took his wife, Naomi, their two sons, and went to live in the country of Moab. In the course of time, the man died. His two sons married two women of Moab: Ruth and Orpah. Approximately ten years later, the two sons died. Naomi learned that the famine had ended in her homeland and decided to return to the land of Judah. She encouraged her daughters-in-law to return to their mothers' houses, and prayed that the Lord would bless them with husbands.

Both daughters expressed disagreement with Naomi's decision to leave Moab and return back to her people. They observed, "Surely we will return with thee unto thy people." *(Ruth 1:10)* Naomi explained that she did not have any more sons who could provide for them. In fact, if Naomi had any more boys, the two daughters-in-law would have to wait many years before the boys could become old enough to provide for the women. Orpah cried loudly. She loved her mother-in-law and did not want to be separated from her. Yet, without any visible means of survival, she chose to separate from her mother-in-law and remain among the pagans. Fear of death caused Orpah to remain among the heathens and serve false gods.

Ruth also cried with a loud voice. She undoubtedly loved her mother and experienced separation anxiety in leaving the land of her birth. Nonetheless, she refused to exalt anyone or anything above the truth. She was determined to worship the Almighty. "And Ruth said, Intreat me not to leave thee, or to return from following after thee: for whiter thou goest, I will go; and where thou lodgest, I will lodge: thy people shall be my people, and thy God my God." *(Ruth 1:16)* Ruth left her people and place of birth to serve the true God.

With no husband to provide for her and no assurance that Naomi would have more boys, Orpah did not know how she would survive. She chose to exalt her natural life above her spiritual life; she remained among the pagans. Ruth, in contrast, esteemed her spiritual life above her natural life. She chose to return with Naomi to Judah and be among the chosen people of God. She did not know how she would survive. She knew the Lord was God, and to worship Him required her to give up her pagan life.

Ruth did not have a husband, but her faith was not in a man. She requested and received permission from Naomi to work in the field. "And Ruth the Moabitess said unto Naomi, Let me now go to the field, and glean ears of corn **after him in whose sight I shall find grace.** And she said unto her, Go, my daughter." *(Ruth 2:2)* Without a husband to provide for her, Ruth was nonetheless willing to work for herself—as long as she could serve the Lord and keep her integrity.

Boaz, a distant relative and wealthy landowner, permitted Ruth to work in his field. She asked him, **"Why have I found grace in thine eyes,** that thou shouldest take knowledge of me, seeing I am a stranger? And Boaz answered and said unto her, It hath fully been shewed me, all that thou hast done unto thy mother in law since the death of thine husband: and how thou hast left thy father and thy mother, and the land of thy nativity, and art come unto a people which thou knewest not heretofore. **The Lord recompense thy work, and a full reward be given thee of the Lord God of Israel, under whose wings thou art come to trust.**" *(Ruth 2:10-12)*

To paraphrase, Ruth asked Boaz, "Why have you helped me? You don't know me." Boaz replied, "God saw that you were willing to forsake your mother, father, and home to serve Him. He rewarded you for trusting in Him." Ruth was saved by grace, through faith, not by works. In her pagan land, she served pagan gods; therefore, she did not serve the Lord. Her works did not save her; she was headed to destruction. Although Naomi had no boys for her to marry, Ruth put her trust in the Lord God of Israel. Through her faith, the Lord **rewarded** her works. *(Revelation 22:12)* He saved her from natural death (she worked for Boaz) and spiritual death (she served the Lord).

Ruth and Orpah had been blessed to marry children of the living God. After the death of their husbands, they were widowed. When Naomi decided to return to her homeland, both daughters said they would return with their mother-in-law. When the time came to see who would keep their word, the fear of death caused Orpah to reject the true God to remain among the pagans. Ruth had faith. She renounced her kinsmen, homeland, and pagan gods—the only life she had ever known—to serve the Lord. God saw her commitment and dedication to serve Him, and showed her grace. He blessed Boaz to be in a position to help Ruth, because she trusted in Him.

Like Abraham, Ruth was willing to leave her mother and father, her people, and the land of her birth. She certainly experienced emotional and familial resistance in departing from the people who had loved and nurtured her. Irrespective, she overcame the resistance to walk in integrity. Like Abraham, she had worshipped pagan gods. When she demonstrated that she was willing to serve the Lord and placed her life into His hands, the Lord provided the help she needed to live. She was saved by grace, through faith, not by works. She had previously served pagan gods and was not justified in the sight of God. If she had stayed in Moab, she would have been destroyed like Orpah. After Ruth learned the truth, she trusted in the Lord and renounced paganism. God did not owe Ruth anything; she was supposed to exalt the Lord above the heathens. God nonetheless rewarded her as recognition of her trust in Him.

Under the law, to ensure that widows would not be destitute or abandoned, God required relatives of widows' husbands to raise up seed unto them to preserve the family name in the earth. Naomi had land that she wanted to sell. By right, Naomi's sons had a right to inherit the property. Since the sons were dead, whoever purchased the property also was required to buy the rights to the deceased sons' widows, to raise up the name of the dead upon their inheritance. Hence, the kinsman who bought the land would also have to give Ruth a child in order to preserve her deceased husband's inheritance—his right of redemption.

As a kinsman, Boaz exercised his right to purchase the land and Ruth. In purchasing the land, Boaz redeemed Ruth's deceased husband's inheritance. In marrying Ruth, he ensured her natural survival. Boaz and Ruth bore a son, Obed, who was the grandfather of King David. *(Ruth 4:22)* The Messiah, Jesus Christ, came from the house of David. Jesus was a Jew; His lineage can be traced through the tribe of Judah. Although salvation is of the Jews, the blood of Ruth, a Gentile, was in the blood of Jesus Christ. *(Matthew 1:5-6)* Jesus was a kinsman of both Jews and Gentiles. Accordingly, in shedding His blood, Jesus paid the price for the wages of sin and redeemed all humans' right to be delivered from death—to be ransomed from the grave of sin. Jesus redeemed all humans' right to reclaim their birthright to inherit the Kingdom of God. *(Matthew 22:9)*

God promised to redeem the people. Abraham, a Jew, by faith, trusted God, and came out from among the pagans. God saved him. Ruth, a Gentile, by faith, trusted God and came out from among the pagans. God saved her. They were not justified when they served pagan gods; they had no reason to boast about their ignorance; but they were justified when they learned the truth and came out of paganism. They did not allow fear of death to make them remain among the heathens. Their obedience to the Lord demonstrated that they believed He was the Almighty. Since they had integrity, they trusted in the Lord, and He saved them.

Jonah

The word of the Lord came unto Jonah and commanded him to go to Nineveh and cry out against the wickedness of the people.

Jonah refused to obey the commandment of the Lord. Instead he took a ship and fled from the presence of the Lord. While Jonah was in the ship, the Lord sent a great wind into the sea, which endangered the lives of all that were on the ship. After an inquiry, the men learned that Jonah's rebellion had brought about the tempest in their lives. They reluctantly threw Jonah into the sea.

A great fish swallowed Jonah. For three days and three nights, Jonah was inside the belly of the fish, deep into the midst of the sea. Weeds wrapped around his head. There was no way Jonah could escape. He was powerless. He was captured. In great distress, with death closing upon him, he remembered the Lord. *(Jonah 2:7)* He prayed and beseeched the Lord to save him. Although he had been disobedient, he vowed that if the Lord saved him from death, he would do what God had commanded, and he would do it with thanksgiving.

The Lord heard Jonah's cry. Although Jonah had not obeyed His commandment, the Lord had mercy upon Jonah and spoke to the fish, which vomited Jonah upon dry land. Jonah was saved by grace (God made the fish vomit him up), through faith (he believed God had the power to redeem him), and not by works (he was unable to deliver himself). God delivered Jonah out of the fish, despite his disobedience. When the word of the Lord came unto him the second time, Jonah did not hesitate to pay his vows. "So Jonah arose, and went unto Nineveh, according to the word of the Lord." *(Jonah 3:3)* The prophet cried out and warned the people that they had forty days before Nineveh would be destroyed.

"So the people of Nineveh believed God." *(Jonah 3:5)* The people did not waste time debating with unbelievers. They proclaimed a fast. All the men, women, children, and animals went without food and drink. Everyone was ordered to turn "from his evil way." *(Jonah 3:8)* "Who can tell if God will turn and repent, and turn away from his fierce anger, that we perish not?" *(Jonah 3:9)* The people were wise. God is merciful and slow to anger, but will not acquit the wicked. The entire city of Nineveh humbled itself before the Lord. "And God saw their **works**, that **they turned from their evil way;**

and God repented of the evil, that he had said that he would do unto them; and he did it not." *(Jonah 3:10)*

God gave the people a grace period—forty days—before He destroyed them. While God withheld His wrath, the people humbled themselves, turned from their wickedness, and obeyed the commandments of God. When the Lord saw their works, that they turned from their evil ways, He did not destroy the people. The Lord warned the people (grace), which gave them a chance to save themselves from destruction.

Jonah had disobeyed and was headed for destruction. His works, his disobedience, should have resulted in death. Through the grace of God, Jonah was delivered out of the belly of the fish. His works did not save him out of the belly of the fish; he was powerless. He was saved by the power of God; saved by grace. As Jonah was facing death, his soul fainting within, he remembered the Lord's loving-kindness and tender mercies. His prayer indicated that he had faith that God could save him. After the Lord delivered (saved) him, he kept the commandment of God. If he had not obeyed, the Lord would have destroyed him.

In Nineveh, the people had disobeyed the Lord. They were not saved by their works; their wicked works were the reason God purposed to destroy them. God sent Jonah to warn them. (Grace) Because the people feared God (faith in His word), they turned from their wickedness. If they had not turned from their wickedness, they would have been destroyed. When the Lord saw their works—they turned from their evil—He did not destroy them. Their obedience to the work of the Lord saved them from destruction.

Cornelius

"For the promise, that he should be the heir of the world, was not to Abraham, or to his seed, through the law, but through the righteousness of faith. For if they which are of the law be heirs, faith is made void, and the promise made of none effect: because the law worketh wrath: for where no law is, there is no transgression. Therefore, it is of faith, that it might be by grace; to the end the promise might be sure to all the seed; not to that only which is of the law, but to that also which is of the faith of Abraham; who is the father of us all." *(Romans 4:13-16)*

As a child who descended from Jews and Gentiles, Jesus had the blood of all humanity. Accordingly, He had right to redeem the inheritance of all of mankind. The first man, Adam, had caused all to die. The second man Adam, Jesus Christ, had given all a chance to be born again of the spirit. *(1 Corinthians 15:22)* Anyone who wanted to worship the true God had a right to be redeemed from corruption. Just as the Lord showed grace to Ruth and blessed her for leaving her pagan home and trusting in Him, salvation has been offered to all those who are willing to come out of darkness and walk in the light of Christ.

In Caesarea lived an officer in the Roman army whose name was Cornelius, a devout man who feared God. He continuously prayed to God and sacrificed to help others. Despite his sincere spiritual devotion, he had been deceived. Further, he was not of the natural seed of Abraham, the chosen people of God. *(Acts 10:1-2)*

The Lord perceived Cornelius' honesty and sent an angel to the Gentile. When the angel appeared, Cornelius asked him, "What is it, Lord?" Cornelius was deceived, but he knew that the Lord was God. The angel told Cornelius that the Lord recognized his prayers and generous spirit. In other words, God saw that the sinner wanted to live holy. He instructed Cornelius to send men to Joppa and ask for Simon Peter, "he shall tell thee what thou oughtest to do?" *(Acts 10:6)* Although God recognized his spiritual devotion, Cornelius was still a barbarian. It was not enough that Cornelius did good works. He was not walking in the truth, which meant that he was not a servant of God.

Jesus had ascended into Heaven and delegated teaching duties to the apostles. He ordered Cornelius to send for Simon Peter. The apostles were responsible for telling the people what they had to do to inherit eternal life. Those who wanted to overcome needed to hear the apostles' testimonies. *(Revelation 12:11)* Those who wanted to be obedient to God had to follow the apostles' doctrines. *(Acts 2:42)* Any individual could have told Cornelius to live holy and obey God. Cornelius could not live holy and obey God unless he knew the truth. God had opened the apostles' understanding and commanded them to teach the people how to be saved. *(Luke 24:45; Matthew 28:19)*

Peter went to Caesarea and preached the gospel to Cornelius and his household. "While Peter yet spake these words, the Holy Ghost fell on all them which heard the word. And they of the circumcision which believed were astonished, as many as came with Peter, because that on the Gentile also was poured out the gift of the Holy Ghost." *(Acts 10:44-45)* The Gentiles received the Spirit of God, and Peter commanded them to be baptized. *(Acts 10:48)* Jesus said no one could enter the Kingdom of God unless he had been born again of the water and spirit. *(John 3:5)*

As a deceived man, Cornelius had not served the Lord; he was a pagan. He was not saved by his works. Yet, because of Cornelius' sincerity, God offered grace to Cornelius. God told Cornelius whom to send for, and where to find him. Peter told Cornelius what he had to do to be saved. After the Gentiles had been born again of the water of the spirit, "Then Peter opened his mouth, and said, Of a truth, I perceive that God is no respecter of persons: but in every nation he that feareth him, and **worketh righteousness** is accepted with him." *(Acts 10:34-35)* God promised Abraham that He would justify the heathens through faith. *(Galatians 3:8)* The Lord was willing to save all from sin (workers of iniquity) that turned from their wickedness and trusted in Him. In other words, since famine had covered the entire earth, all had sinned. Those who turned from their wicked ways and obeyed demonstrated that they acknowledged Jesus as Lord.

Cornelius was saved by grace (God told him to send for Peter) through faith (he trusted the angel, obeyed his word, and sent for Peter), and not by his works (he was a barbarian and participated in pagan worship). Once Cornelius learned the truth, he received the Holy Ghost and was baptized. If he continued in the apostles' doctrine, he was saved from his sins and positioned to inherit eternal life.

──────────── **Saul of Tarsus** ────────────

There was a man who truly wanted to give his life to God; his name was Saul. He had studied the Law of Moses under the tutelage of an eminent scholar, Gamaliel. *(Acts 5:34)* He was very dedicated to his faith and zealous in its defense. *(Acts 22:3)* As a result of his dedication and conviction, he persecuted Jesus Christ.

He was on his way to Damascus to destroy more saints when Jesus spoke to him from Heaven: "Saul, Saul, why persecutest thou me?" *(Acts 9:4)* Despite his sincere desire to serve God, Saul had been deceived and fought against God. He had attended theology school and been taught by a renowned scholar, but his teacher had not been sent by God. As a result, Saul had been taught wrong. In his zeal to defend his beliefs, he fought against the truth. *(Galatians 1:13-14; Acts 22:3-4)* Thus, Saul had been doing Satan's work while under the illusion that he was doing the work of the Lord.

Saul found grace in the sight of God and was given an opportunity to turn from his wickedness. "And he trembling and astonished said, Lord, what wilt thou have me to do? And the Lord said unto him, Arise, and go into the city, and it shall be told thee what thou must do." *(Acts 9:6)* Despite his spiritual desire to worship God, Saul was an enemy of God. Thus, the Lord did not save him because of his works; Saul's work was evil. The Lord showed Saul grace; He brought it to Saul's attention that he was fighting against God. Once Saul knew the truth, he stopped doing the work of Satan. Although those who followed Christ suffered persecution, Saul followed Christ and trusted in Him to save him.

Saul was saved by grace (God showed him the error of his ways), through faith (he trusted in God's word), and not by works (before his conversion, he persecuted the church). If Saul did the work God required of him, he would be saved from destruction. If Saul failed to do the work, he would be destroyed. "For thou I preach the gospel, I have nothing to glory of: for necessity is laid upon me; yea, woe is unto me, if I preach not the gospel!" *(1 Corinthians 9:16)*

Ezekiel

The word of the Lord came unto Ezekiel the priest: Go to the children of Israel, "to a rebellious nation that hath rebelled against me: they and their fathers have transgressed against me . . . for they are impudent children and stiffhearted. I do send thee unto them; and thou shalt say unto them, Thus saith the Lord God." *(Ezekiel 2:3-4)* The Lord warned the prophet, "But thou, son of man, hear what I say unto thee; Be not thou rebellious like that rebellious house." *(Ezekiel 2:8)* God had delivered the children of Israel out of bondage and saved them from their enemies. Nonetheless, they would not serve the Lord.

The Lord continued: "So thou, O son of man, I have set thee a watchman unto the house of Israel; therefore thou shalt hear the word at my mouth, and warn them from me. When I say unto the wicked, O wicked man, thou shalt surely die; if thou dost not speak to warn the wicked from his way, that wicked man shall die in his iniquity; but his blood will I require at thine hand." *(Ezekiel 33:7-8)* The Lord gave Ezekiel a commandment: The prophet was ordered to warn the people to turn from their wickedness and obey the commandments of God.

Each individual has a duty to fear God and to keep His commandments. The Lord did not want to destroy the children of Israel. However, He is a just God. He metes out reward and punishment according to what is right. Since all must reap what they sow, the Lord exercises patience and warns the people to turn from their wickedness. "Say unto them, As I live, saith the Lord God, I have no pleasure in the death of the wicked; but that the wicked turn from his way and live: turn ye, turn ye from your evil ways; for why will ye die, O house of Israel?" *(Ezekiel 33:11)* The Lord showed grace to the people. Although they deserved to be destroyed, the Lord did not want to destroy them. If the people feared God and turned from their wickedness, He would save them; yet, if the people refused to obey His commandments, He would be forced to destroy them. He is holy in all His works.

Ultimately, God does not decide who will be saved or lost; each individual does. God destroys the power of the enemy over us and allows each of us to choose life or death. Are we going to obey or disobey His commandments? As Abraham denoted, "That be far from {God} to do after this manner, to slay the righteous with the wicked: and that the righteous should be as the wicked, that be far from thee: Shall not the Judge of all the earth do right?" *(Genesis 18:25)* God will always do what is right. He will reward every man according to his works. *(Revelation 22:12; Romans 2:6; Matthew 16:27)* Workers of righteousness (those who obey the commandments of God) will be saved from destruction; workers of iniquity (those who disobey the commandments of God) will be destroyed.

"Nevertheless, if thou warn the wicked of his way to turn from it; if he do not turn from his way, he shall die in his iniquity; but thou hast delivered thy soul." *(Ezekiel 33:9)* The Lord did not take pleasure in the destruction of the wicked. He warned (grace) them. If the people stopped being stubborn and obeyed the Lord, He would not have destroyed them. They would not have been saved because of their works; they had been disobedient. They would have been saved by grace (God warned them), through faith (they believed God's word), and not by works (they had been rebellious). They would have been foolish to boast about their wicked works.

Nehemiah

Nehemiah asked certain men of Judah how things went in Jerusalem. They answered that the people were in great distress. The walls had been broken down, and the gates burned with fire. Nehemiah sat down and cried; the people of God, with no protection from their enemies, were destroyed. Although the children of Israel had rebelled against God, Nehemiah remembered God's tender mercies. He fasted and prayed. Nehemiah asked the Lord to move on the king to show him mercy. *(Nehemiah 1:1-11)*

The king granted Nehemiah's request to return to Jerusalem. Nehemiah and the men who went with him wanted to rebuild the wall. Critics called them feeble and laughed at them. Some said the wall would be so weak, until a fox could knock it down. From all indications, the city was ruined. Rubble and decay were everywhere. Nonetheless, the children of Israel who wanted to be saved from their enemies, "strengthened their hands for this good work." *(Nehemiah 2:18)* Although their enemies discouraged them, "So built we the wall; and all the wall was joined together unto the half thereof: for **the people had a mind to work.**" *(Nehemiah 4:6)*

——— Save Ourselves from This Untoward Generation ———

The people of God must rebuild the walls in their lives. Satan has sent messengers to tell them that they cannot overcome sin; they cannot live holy; and other heresies. However, those who have a mind to work can rebuild the walls in their lives. Jesus sent apostles to testify how we can overcome. *(Revelation 12:11)* Through fasting and praying, we can restore our integrity. "But, ye, beloved, building up yourselves on your most holy faith, praying in the Holy Ghost." *(Jude 1:20)* We cannot be only hearers of the word; we must be doers. If we believe in the Lord Jesus Christ, we will take His knowledge and discipline ourselves. We will exercise self-control and not acquiesce to Satan's witchcraft.

Through the knowledge of Jesus Christ, we can stop building Pharaoh's treasure cities. We can stop strengthening Satan's power over our lives. We can cleanse ourselves from the pollution of this world. We must build ourselves up on our most holy faith. But, please understand: holiness is not a faith. Holiness is a way of living. Faith is what you believe. You can believe in living holy and yet live in sin. You can believe you are right and yet be wrong. That is what is meant by being deceived. Therefore, it is necessary to understand that when we build ourselves up our most holy faith, we build ourselves up on the teachings of the apostles. *(Jude 1:20)* They were the men whom Jesus commanded to go and teach all nations. *(Matthew 28:19)* God put the apostles first in the church, because they are His messengers. *(1 Corinthians 12:28)*

God's name is holy, but holy is not His name. "For he that is mighty hath done to me great things; and holy is his name." *(Luke 1:49)* Holy is His name connotes that His name is sacred. "Hallowed be thy name." *(Matthew 6:9)* God's promise is holy, which implies that God word is sacred; He cannot lie. *(Psalm 105:42)* Jesus commanded His apostles to go and teach all nations. It is through the apostles' testimonies that we are able to overcome. *(Revelation 1:1-2; Revelation12:11)* The apostles' doctrine—the one faith taught by the apostles—is the faith that was delivered unto the saints. *(Jude 1:3)* When we build ourselves up on our most holy faith, we remain steadfast in the apostles' doctrine, lest we also be led away with the error of the wicked and fall from our own stedfastness. *(2 Peter 3:17)*

The apostles opened our ears to discipline (knowledge). "He openeth also their ear to discipline, and commandeth that they return from iniquity." *(Job 36:10)* They fed us the word of God and taught us how Satan had bewitched us. They exhorted us to reconcile with God. Like Nehemiah and his supporters, although we are corrupt, we appreciate God's grace. The Lord has given us space to rebuild the wall in our lives.

The enemy bewitched us to lust after our own destruction. "He that hath no rule over his own spirit is like a city that is broken down, and without walls." *(Proverbs 25:28)* Our walls were broken down. However, the King granted those who had a mind to work the space to rebuild the walls in our lives. We learned to exercise self-discipline and to deny ourselves. Through the grace of God, we have learned how the enemy captured us and what we can do to escape. If we obey His commandments, He will save us out of the hands of our enemies.

Empowering the Enemy

When the scripture denotes that we are saved by grace not by works, it means that, as sinners, we served Satan, a false god, who had deceived us. He had the power of death, and, through our fear of death, we did the works of Satan and disobeyed the works of God. The irony was, in our fear of Satan and desire to save our natural lives, we disobeyed God and were positioned to lose our spiritual lives. We had nothing to boast about. We were ignorant. We were weak. Our enemy, smarter and stronger than we, made us work to destroy our own soul. Further, we taught our children how to destroy their souls.

In His mercy, Jesus Christ came to save us from our sins and to deliver us from our enemies. He taught us of His ways, so we could walk in His path. He gave us a gift—the Holy Ghost. Since we had taken steps to obey Him, God gave us His power to help us. He knew that if we walked in the spirit, we would not fulfill the lust of the flesh. He knew that the spirit would comfort us when the inevitable fiery trials attempted to overtake us. Through God's knowledge and power—His grace—we were saved from the enemy. We turned from the power of Satan to the power of God. We refused to worship a false god, trusted in the Lord to deliver us, overcame the witchcraft, and walked in integrity. We were saved by grace, through faith, not by the wicked works we had ignorantly performed. Once He delivered us, we performed the work He commanded; He saw our good works and forgave our sins.

Thy Rod and Staff

The psalmist observed that, although he walked through the valley of the shadow of death, he did not fear any evil. His shepherd's rod and staff comforted him. *(Psalm 23:4)* The staff was a heavy wooden stick with a crook at the end. When sheep tried to go astray from the flock, the shepherd would place the rod of instruction around the sheep's neck and bring it back into the right path. When a wolf tried to attack the sheep, the shepherd used the powerful staff to beat away the beast and save the life of the sheep.

Through the grace of God—His knowledge and power—we are saved from the enemy. Though we live in Satan's kingdom and walk through the valley of death, we are not afraid. Jesus guides us in the path of righteousness. When false prophets attempt to lure us away from the truth, the Holy Ghost reminds us to remain stedfast in God's word. When our enemies attempt to overtake us, our faith in God's word empowers us to remain strong in the Lord and in the power of His might.

———————— Faith without Works is Dead ————————

"What doth it profit, my brethren, though a man say he hath faith, and have not works? Can faith save him? If a brother or sister be naked, and destitute of daily food, and one of you say unto them, Depart in peace, be ye warmed and filled; notwithstanding ye give them not those things which are needful to the body; what doth it profit? Even so, faith, if it hath not works, is dead, being alone." *(James 2:14-17)* It is not enough to speak faith. We show faith by trusting in the Lord. If we confess that Jesus is Lord, then we trust in Him to save us from the enemy. We cannot profess to believe that God is the Almighty, yet allow fear of the enemy to make us disobey the Almighty. We demonstrate our faith in the selection of the god we serve. "And Elijah came unto all the people, and said, How long halt ye between two opinions? if the Lord be God, follow him: but if Baal, then follow him. And the people answered him not a word." *(1 Kings 18:21)*

———————— Justify the Heathen through Faith ————————

Abraham, Ruth, and Cornelius worshipped pagan gods. Saul of Tarsus believed in the God of Abraham, but persecuted the God of Abraham. Jonah disobeyed the Lord. All of them turned from their wicked works to obey God's commandments. When the Lord observed their works, He saved each of them from death. He blessed Abraham to slaughter the kings; He helped Ruth find grace in the sight of Boaz; He guided Cornelius to Peter. "And the scripture, foreseeing that God would justify the heathen through faith, preached before the gospel unto Abraham, saying, in thee shall all nations be blessed." *(Galatians 3:8)* No one will enter the Kingdom of God by virtue of their birth (by operation of law). Our natural inheritance will be destroyed. Everyone who inherits the Kingdom of God will be justified by the spirit—through the grace of God, we overcame corruption. They did not allow the fear of death to make them remain in the bondage of sin. We renounced Satan's witchcraft and sacrificed the life of the flesh. We put our faith in God's promises of a better kingdom, and He saved us by grace.

Work Out Your Salvation

Satan has sent false prophets to tell the people that there is nothing they can do to be saved. According to the false teachers, people cannot work to earn their salvation. The apostle Paul exhorted the saints to work out their salvation with fear and trembling. *(Philippians 2:12)* The only way the people can be saved from destruction is to obey God's commandments. "Let us hear the conclusion of the whole matter: Fear God, and keep his commandments: for this is the whole duty of man. For God shall bring every work into judgment, with every secret thing, whether it be good, or whether it be evil." *(Ecclesiastes 12:13-14)* Obedience to God is good works; disobedience is evil works. Workers of righteousness obey God. Workers of iniquity disobey God. God will reward all according to their works. *(Revelation 22:12)* Remember: God created us for His glory; therefore, He does not owe us anything. Yet, He rewards the obedient and punishes the disobedient.

------------------ **Of Your Father the Devil** ------------------

Jesus told some Jews that they would know the truth, and the truth would make them free. *(John 8:32)* They responded that they were children of Abraham and had never been in bondage. Of course, Jesus, speaking in parable, was implying that the truth would deliver them from the bondage of sin. The people were thinking from a natural perspective: they had never been in natural bondage. In their minds, they did not need to be made free; they were already free.

Jesus explained that whoever committed sin was the servant of sin. *(John 8:34)* Satan is the god of sin, and those who commit sin do the works of Satan. The Jews thought, because they were descendants of Abraham, they were children of God. Jesus wanted them to understand that a new covenant had been established. The Messiah had come to redeem the people. The old covenant was coming to an end; a new covenant was being established.

The Master acknowledged that the Jews were the seed of Abraham. The people were Abraham's seed but they were not Abraham's children. God's covenant with Abraham was not based upon the natural; it was based upon the spiritual. Those who followed Abraham's example of faith in God, who put their trust in His word, would receive the promise of the Father. Ishmael, the son of Hagar, was Abraham's seed, but he was not Abraham's child. Ishmael was born under normal conditions. The promise to Abraham was based upon faith. *(Romans 4:13-16)* Accordingly, Ishamel did not have a right to inherit from Abraham. Isaac was Abraham's only son, because Isaac was conceived by faith. The blessings of God flow not through natural blood, but through faith in His word.

The men, not understanding the words of Jesus, became angry and told Jesus that they were not born of fornication. They only had one father, even God. Jesus told them that if God were their father, they would believe Him. Instead he told them, "Ye are of your father the devil, and the lusts of your father ye will do. He was a murderer from the beginning, and abode not in the truth, because there is no truth in him. When he speaketh a lie, he speaketh of his own: for he is a liar, and the father of it." *(John 8:44)*

A father is the source from which a child comes. According to the natural life, the gender of the child is determined by the father's chromosome. According to the spiritual life, the character of the individual is determined by his father's spirit. We do the deeds of our father. *(John 8:41)* Since Satan corrupted man, we were all born in sin. Satan, the father of sin, is the father of sinners. He is the father of those who walk in corruption.

The Jews were of the seed of Abraham but were not children of Abraham. In the flesh, they were Abraham's seed, because they were natural; however, just as Abraham had been captured and corrupted by Satan, so had his seed. Abraham was natural, but Abraham did not walk after the natural. Abraham refused to serve his father's pagan gods. He had integrity and exalted the Lord above his people. The natural children of Abraham, through fear of death, walked after their natural lives and renounced their spiritual inheritance. Like the patriarch, the spiritual children of Abraham refuse to serve pagan gods or exalt the life of the flesh above their soul. They do not serve Satan, Pharaoh, or themselves. They do the deeds of their father Abraham and exalt the Lord God.

Jesus told the Jews that they were of their father, the devil, because they walked after the flesh. Remember, Adam and Eve did not know they were flesh until they had been corrupted. Those who walk after the flesh walk after corruption. Unlike Adam and Eve, who did not know any better, those who walk after the flesh have volunteered to indulge Satan's witchcraft. Hence, they have chosen to destroy themselves. The works of the flesh is death. *(Galatians 5:19-21)*

Children of Satan walk after the things of this world. Like the prodigal son, they want their inheritance now and are willing to corrupt themselves in its pursuit. Abraham walked after the spirit. They that are after the spirit are concerned about the things of the spirit. Children of God renounce the the life of the flesh to redeem their soul from death. We refuse to conform to the corruption of this world, but trust in God's promise that He will give us a better life in His kingdom. Therefore, we subordinate ourselves to the Lord and do His will on earth as it is done in Heaven.

Abraham did not conform to the pagan ways of his people. He came out from among the corruption of his father to walk in the truth, and the spiritual descendants of Abraham—whether Jew or Gentile—will do the same. The natural descendants of Abraham are Abraham's seed, but—like Ishmael—their natural lives do not entitle them to inherit the spiritual blessings of God. The promise was not to Abraham or to his seed based upon the natural; it was based upon the spiritual. They had faith in God and kept His commandments.

Shall We Continue in Sin?

Paul acknowledged that man had received an abundance of grace. He asked, "What shall we say then? Shall we continue in sin, that grace may abound? God forbid. How shall we, that are dead to sin, live any longer therein? Know ye not, that so many of us as were baptized into Jesus Christ were baptized into his death? Therefore we are buried with him by baptism into death: that like as Christ was raised up from the dead by the glory of the Father, even so we also should walk in newness of life." *(Romans 6:1-4)* We cannot be saved by grace and remain in bondage. To be saved by grace means that, through the power and knowledge (grace) of God, we have been saved from the enemy. God has delivered us from sin.

To be saved does not mean that we are going to Heaven. God saved the people out of Egypt but most of them did not make it into the Promised Land. God saved the people meant that God delivered the people from the hands of their enemies. The Egyptians oppressed the Hebrews, and the children of Israel cried unto the Lord by reason of their bondage. The Lord heard the cry of the people and had mercy upon them. He broke the power of

Egypt over His people and set them free. However, the people did not trust in the Lord and did not want to confront the giants in Canaan. If they had trusted in the Lord, they would have inherited the Promised Land. Because they did not trust in the Lord but feared the giants would destroy them, they preferred to return to Egypt, where they knew how to survive. They chose to forsake God's mercy and were destroyed.

Jesus came to save us from our sins. Remember: the word sin is short for the phrase "sin of witchcraft." *(1 Samuel 15:23)* Satan is crafty; he simply makes up lying vanities to appeal to our emotions. Jesus Christ is the King of kings. Just as Moses was learned in all the ways of the Egyptians and knew how to escape from Egypt, Jesus, the all-wise God, knows all of Satan's tricks and knows how to escape from the pollution of this world. Hence, since Satan creates lies out of thin air to deceive the people, Jesus spoke in parables and performed in mysterious ways to save His people. Jesus is not the author of confusion, but He knows how to use Satan's confusion to help His people. Those who have the Spirit of Jesus Christ will see through Satan's witchcraft and not be deceived by false prophets.

False prophets have deceived the people and persuaded them to believe that Jesus died for our sins means that Jesus has already paid for our sins. Jesus died to ransom us from the grave of sin; Jesus died to deliver us from the power of death. Since He allowed us to go into captivity, He died to redeem us from captivity. The covenant was reciprocal. He died for the sins that we had committed. Now that we know that Jesus is Lord, we must bury the old man in the water of baptism and rise up in the newness of life. Hence, we crucify the flesh (life of corruption) and become born again of the spirit (redeem our soul from the grave). Having been resurrected from the grave and delivered out of the hands of our enemies, we are commanded to serve Him in holiness and righteousness all the days of our lives. *(Luke 1:67-75)*

To be saved means that Jesus has taught us how to overcome sin and given us power over the enemy. Now that our eyes have been opened, those who want to come out of the bondage of sin are free to serve Him. However, if we continue to disobey His commandments, God will destroy us just as He destroyed the children of Israel. "Know ye not, that to whom ye yield yourselves servants to obey, his servants ye are to whom ye obey; whether of sin unto death, or of obedience unto righteousness? *(Romans 6:16)*

Servants of God are in Satan's kingdom but are not subject to Satan. Accordingly, we do not perform the works of Satan. We exalt God in the earth and do His will on earth as it is done in Heaven. If we must suffer for the truth, we will suffer. We know that our God will save us from the enemy and do not fear Satan. "If it be so, our God whom we serve is able to deliver us from the burning fiery furnace, and he will deliver us out of thine hand, O king. But if not, be it known unto thee, O king, that we will not serve thy gods, nor worship the golden image which thou hast set up." *(Daniel 3:17-18)* We fear the Almighty God, He who can destroy the body and cast our soul into eternal fire—not the god of this world who can only destroy the flesh.

Garden of Eden

The Garden of Eden served as a microcosm of the Kingdom of God. It should be understood as an example of Heaven on earth. God walked with Adam and Eve in the spirit. Holiness and peace prevailed. The tree of life, eternal life, was there. Alas, Satan was there. The devil beguiled Eve and led her to believe that she could disobey God and not die. After listening to the devil, the woman looked at the tree of the knowledge of good and evil. She lusted after the flesh; she lusted with her eyes; and pride rose within her. She chose to rebel against God to promote her own glory. Adam chose to disobey the spirit and side with his helpmate. Adam and Eve destroyed their own souls. God drove them out of the garden; out of His kingdom.

Similarly, Satan has perverted and caused us to lust after our own destruction. Like Legion, who repeatedly engaged in self-mutilation, the people are driven by their own corruption to destroy themselves. Their fear of the Lord mollified by the lies of the false prophets, the people fail to consider that Adam and Eve died because they rebelled against the spirit. When we indulge the lust of the flesh, we destroy our own souls. "Now the works of the flesh are manifest, which are these; adultery, fornication, uncleanness, lasciviousness, . . . as I have also told you in time past, that they which do such things shall not inherit the kingdom of God." *(Galatians 5:19-21)*

Do not allow false prophets to lead you to believe that you can disobey God and enter His kingdom. "Let no man deceive you with vain words: for because of these things cometh the wrath of God upon the children of disobedience. Be not ye partakers with them. For ye were sometimes darkness, but now are ye light in the Lord: walk as children of light:" *(Ephesians 5:6-8)*

―――――――――――――― **Recapitulate** ――――――――――――――

Saved by grace, through faith, and not by works simply means that God allowed men and women to be overtaken by the enemy. Their enemy was too strong for them. In due time, God saved the people out of the enemy's hand. The Lord allowed the people to see that they could not deliver themselves; the people were weaker than their enemy. Yet the Lord was able to defeat all of their adversaries that came up against them. Hence, the Lord demonstrated that He was the Almighty. The Lord wanted to see what was in the people's hearts. Would they humble themselves and trust in Him? Or would they rebel against Him and make their own decisions? In other words, do the people have faith in God to obey His instructions?

The whole purpose of man is to fear God and to keep His commandments. We are to exalt the Lord and to do His will in the earth as it is done in Heaven. Yet, this is Satan's kingdom, and he is stronger than us. He has the power of death, and most individuals, skin for skin, are not going to give up their lives to serve the Lord. They rather remain in bondage before they give up their natural lives. Those who trust in the Lord will not serve Satan. Through faith, they are willing to confront the giants in Canaan; they are willing to go into the lion's den; they are willing to enter the fiery furnace. They exalt their spiritual life above their natural life. They have faith in God and will not submit to pagan worship. Such individuals are saved by grace, through faith, not by works. They could not save themselves from the enemy, but they trusted in the Lord to save them. Further, they knew the Lord was God and was not going to sacrifice their integrity. They were willing to lose their lives to serve the Lord, because they knew that the Lord would redeem them from death. As a result of their obedience, the Lord saved them and delivered them out of the bondage of sin.

Satan has sent false prophets to tell the people that saved by grace, through faith, and not by works implies that there is nothing the people can do to save themselves; it is God's unmerited favor. The devil knows that if the people do not work, they will not work out their salvation. *(Philippians 2:12)* They will continue to indulge in the works of the flesh and remain corrupt. Their unredeemed souls will be destroyed. *(Galatians 5:19-21; Romans 6:23)*

The Lord has commanded the people to come boldy before the throne of grace and get the help they need to overcome. Remember: In Adam all died. In Christ all shall be made alive. The entire human family lost its soul because of Adam's disobedience; we were conceived in sin. The nature of the flesh is sin. Christ came to set the people free from sin. Through the grace (knowledge and power) of God, we are redeemed from corruption (delivered from the enemy), sanctified through the truth (cleansed from pollution), and prepared for the Master's use (holy and obedient). Jesus ransomed us from the grave and destroyed the power of the enemy over our lives. We no longer, through fear of death, work for Satan. We have been set free to serve the Lord. Jesus died on the cross that we might receive the forgiveness of sin, and we take up our cross and follow Him to demonstrate that our forgiveness of sin was justified. When delivered from the enemy, we were obedient unto God and refused to sin against Him.

——————— Additional Edifying Scriptures: ———————

"And the sea gave up the dead which were in it; and death and hell delivered up the dead which were in them: and they were judged every man according to their works." (Revelations 20:13)

"And I saw the dead, small and great, stand before God; and the books were opened: and another book was opened, which is the book of life: and the dead were judged out of those things which were written in the books, according to their works." (Revelation 20:12)

"And, behold, I come quickly, and my reward is with me, to give every man according as his work shall be." (Revelation 22:12)

"And I heard a voice from heaven saying unto me, write, blessed are the dead which die in the Lord from henceforth: yea, saith the spirit, that they may rest from their labours; and their works do follow them." (Revelation 14:13)

"And if ye call on the Father, who without respect of persons judgeth according to every man's work, pass the time of your sojourning here in fear: forasmuch as ye know that ye were not redeemed with corruptible things, as silver and gold, from your vain conversation received by tradition from your fathers; but with the precious blood of Christ, as of a lamb without blemish and spot: who verily was foreordained before the foundation of the world, but was manifest in these last times for you." (1 Peter 1:17-19)

"Therefore, my beloved brethren, be ye stedfast, unmoveable, always abounding in the work of the Lord, forasmuch as ye know that your labour is not in vain in the Lord." (1 Corinthians 15:58)

"Wherefore lay apart all filthiness and superfluity of naughtiness, and receive with meekness the engrafted word, which is able to save your souls. But be ye doers of the word, and not hearers only, deceiving your own selves. For if any be a hearer of the word, and not a doer, he is like unto a man beholding his natural face in a glass: for he beholdeth himself, and goeth his way, and straightway forgetteth what manner of man he was. But whose looketh into the perfect law of liberty, and continueth therein, he being not a forgetful hearer, but a doer of the work, this man shall be blessed in his deed." (James 1:21-25)

"Let your light so shine before men, that they may see your good works, and glorify your father which is in heaven." (Matthew 5:16)

"But which of you, having a servant plowing or feeding cattle, will say unto him by and by, when he is come from the field, go and sit down to meat? And will not rather say unto him, make ready wherewith I may sup, and gird thyself, and serve me, till I have eaten and drunken; and afterward thou shalt eat and drink? Doth he thank that servant because he did the things that were commanded of him? I trow not. So likewise ye, when ye shall have done all those things which are commanded of you, say, We are unprofitable servants: we have done that which was our duty to do." (Luke 17:7-10)

"He taught me also, and said unto me, Let thine heart retain my words: keep my commandments, and live." (Proverbs 4:4)

"For there are many unruly and vain talkers and deceivers, specially they of the circumcision: whose mouths must be stopped, who subvert whole houses, teaching things which they ought not, for filthy lucre's sake. . . . Unto the pure all things are pure: but unto them that are defiled and unbelieving is nothing pure; but even their mind and conscience is defiled. They profess that they know God; but in works they deny him, being abominable, and disobedient, and unto every good work reprobate." (Titus 1:10-16)

"Ye see then how that by works a man is justified, and not by faith only. Likewise also was not Rahab the harlot justified by works, when she had received the messengers, and had sent them out another way? For as the body without the spirit is dead, so faith without works is dead also." (James 2:24-26)

"Not every one that saith unto me, Lord, Lord, shall enter into the kingdom of heaven; but he that doeth the will of my Father which is in heaven. Many will say to me in that day, Lord, Lord, have we not prophesied in thy name? and in thy name have cast out devils? And in thy name done many wonderful works? And then will I profess unto them, I never knew you: depart from me, ye that work iniquity." (Matthew 7:21-23)

"But we had the sentence of death in ourselves, that we should not trust in ourselves, but in God which raiseth the dead: Who deliver us from so great a death, and doth deliver: in whom we trust that he will yet deliver us." (2 Corinthians 1:9-10)

"And it shall be said in that day, Lo, this is our God; we have waited for him, and he will save us: this is the Lord; we have waited for him, we will be glad and rejoice in his salvation." (Isaiah 25:9)

"Fear thou not; for I am with thee: be not dismayed; for I am thy God: I will strengthen thee; yea, I will help thee; yea, I will uphold thee with the right hand of my righteousness." (Isaiah 41:10)

"The Lord is my light and my salvation; whom shall I fear? The Lord is the strength of my life; of whom shall I be afraid?" (Psalm 27:1)

"Many are the afflictions of the righteous: but the Lord delivereth him out of them all." (Psalm 34:19)

"The Lord is my strength and song, and is become my salvation." (Psalm 118:14)

"And Jethro said, Blessed be the Lord, who hath delivered you out of the hand of the Egyptians, and out of the hand of Pharaoh, who hath delivered the people from under the hand of the Egyptians. Now I know that the Lord is greater than all gods: for in the things wherein they dealt proudly he was above them." (Exodus 18:10-11)

"The Lord is their strength, and he is the saving strength of his anointed. Save thy people, and bless thine inheritance: feed them also, and lift them up for ever." (Psalm 28:8-9)

"Shew thy marvelous loving-kindness, O thou that savest by thy right hand them which put their trust in thee from those that rise up against them." (Psalm 17:7)

"Though I walk in the midst of trouble, thou will revive me: thou shalt stretch forth thine hand against the wrath of mine enemies, and thy right hand shall save me." (Psalm 138:7)

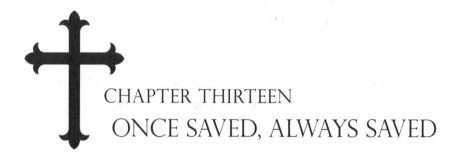

CHAPTER THIRTEEN
ONCE SAVED, ALWAYS SAVED

The devil, through the false prophets, has so blinded the people, until they believe that saved means they are going to Heaven. In biblical parlance, saved does not connote that anyone is going to Heaven; saved implies that God has delivered His people out of the hands of their enemies. They were too strong for us and forced us to serve them. Through the grace of God, we were delivered (saved) from death (sin). Jesus set us free, which allowed each of us to decide who we wanted to serve. Those with integrity acknowledged the supremacy of God and served the Lord. Those who lacked integrity rejected the truth, capitulated to the fear of death, and served a false god.

Those who obeyed God's commandments are going to inherit eternal life. "Then shall the King say unto them on his right hand, Come, ye blessed of my Father, inherit the kingdom prepared for you from the foundation of the world:" *(Matthew 25:34)* Those who failed to serve the Lord shall burn in eternal damnation. "Then shall he say also unto them on the left hand, Depart from me, ye cursed, into everlasting fire, prepared for the devil and his angels:" *(Matthew 25:41)*

Even more ridiculous, false prophets have taught the people that once they are saved, they are always saved. Satan dwelled in the Kingdom of God. He disobeyed the commandment of God and was cast out of the kingdom. Adam and Eve were living souls.

They disobeyed the commandment of God and were damned. God cast them out of the garden. There is not one scripture in the Holy Bible that supports the concept that once we are saved, we are always saved. In fact, the Holy Bible teaches just the opposite. Jesus came into the earth to bear witness to the truth: We are to serve only God. If we serve another god, we are going to be destroyed. Jesus warned the people to beware of wolves in sheep's clothing. The sheep were safe as long as they remained with the shepherd. If the wolves disguised themselves and succeeded in luring the sheep away from their savior, the wolf would destroy them. Satan's objective is to destroy you. In this chapter, we will debunk the lying vanity of once saved, always saved.

Children of Israel

The children of Israel had the right to inherit the land that God had promised their father, Abraham. However, the Lord wanted to see if the people would obey His commandments or not. He sent a famine into Canaan and forced the people to go into Egypt, whereupon they were subsequently enslaved and corrupted. In time, God heard the Hebrews' cry for mercy by reason of their bondage in Egypt and sent Moses to bring the people out of captivity. The Egyptians tried to overtake the Hebrews and return them into bondage. The Lord opened the sea and allowed the children of Israel to escape. After the children of Israel crossed the sea on dry land, the Lord drowned the Egyptians. "Thus the Lord **saved** Israel that day out of the hand of the Egyptians; and Israel saw the Egyptians dead upon the sea shore." *(Exodus 14:30)*

Moses told the people that God wanted them to prove that they would obey Him and keep His commandments. *(Exodus 20:20)* Moses wrote all the words of the Lord and His judgments. "And he took the book of the covenant, and read it in the audience of the people; and they said, All that the Lord hath said will we do, and be obedient." *(Exodus 24:7)* The Lord gave Moses laws and commandments, which Moses used to teach the people. *(Exodus 24:12)*

The Hebrews said that if they had the option between serving the Egyptians and serving the Lord, they would serve the Lord. Nonetheless, the Lord took them through the wilderness to see if the people would honor their word. He perceived that the people had lied to him. Each time the people encountered adversity, they began to murmur and complain. They did not trust in the Lord and wanted to go back to Egypt and serve the Egyptians. He destroyed nearly all of them. "For he said, Surely they are my people, children that will not lie: so **he was their Saviour**. In all their affliction he was afflicted, and **the angel of his presence saved them**: in his love and in his pity he redeemed them; and he bare them, and carried them all the days of old. But they rebelled, and vexed his holy Spirit: therefore **he was turned to be their enemy**, and **he fought against them**." *(Isaiah 63:8-10)*

God delivered the children of Israel out of the land of Egypt. Yet, the people rebelled against Him and yearned to return to Egypt. Thus, the people trusted the Egyptians with their lives more than they trusted God. "I will therefore put you in remembrance, though ye once knew this, how the Lord, having **saved** the people out of the land of Egypt, afterward **destroyed** them that believed not." *(Jude 1:5)* Since the children of Israel told Moses and Joshua that, despite the Egyptians' oppression, they preferred to serve the Egyptians rather than the Lord, there was no need for the Lord to have any more mercy upon them. God destroyed them without mercy. *(Hebrews 10:28)*

"Because ye have turned away from the Lord, therefore the Lord will not be with you." (Numbers 14:43)

The Dog Went Back to Its Vomit

Under the Old Testament, God sent famine into the land. He caused Joseph to be taken into Egypt and positioned him to interpret the Pharaoh's dream. God used Joseph to warn the king that famine was going to take place, and advised Egypt to store up food to wait out the famine. Although Joseph was a Hebrew, the Lord did not allow anyone to warn the Hebrews. Hence, the Lord created the conditions for His people to go into Egypt, where they were predestined to be taken into bondage.

In time, Moses delivered the children of Israel out of bondage. The Egyptians had corrupted the Hebrews and taught them paganism. Despite being delivered out of Egypt, the Hebrews did not trust God. They chose to serve as slaves to the Egyptians before they chose to serve God. Ergo, the Hebrews trusted corrupted Egyptians with their lives more than the Holy One of Israel. The Lord destroyed nearly all of them. He could not use corrupt servants.

Under the New Testament, God sent famine into the land—not for food or drink, but for the word of the Lord. During the famine, all tables were filled with vomit. *(Isaiah 28:8)* The only spiritual food the people had to eat was the pollution of the false prophets. "They are all gone aside, they are altogether become filthy: there is none that doeth good, no, not one." *(Psalm 53:3)* In their ignorance, the people were taken into the captivy of sin. *(Psalm 53:2-4)* None of the people understood. They were all dumb dogs. Their preachers were blind and ignorant. *(Isaiah 56:10)* Satan had deceived the entire world. *(Revelation 12:9)*

In due time, the prophecy went out: "Whom shall he teach knowledge? and whom shall he make to understand doctrine? them that are weaned from the milk, and drawn from the breasts." *(Isaiah 28:9)* The famine ended. Jesus Christ came to feed the people with knowledge. Those who hungred and thirsted for righteousness were going to be filled. *(Matthew 5:6)* His flesh was meat indeed. *(John 6:55)* Jesus was the word of God made flesh. *(John 1:1; John 1: 14)* The people had gone into captivity (darkness; ignorance) because of famine. Jesus came and ended the famine. He came to feed those who hungered and thirsted for righteousness. *(John 6:31-35)* Those who sat in darkness saw a great light. His words were a lamp unto our feet, and a light unto our pathway. We ate the flesh of Jesus Christ and learned of Him. Through His knowledge, Jesus led us out of the captivity of sin.

Those who ate of His flesh and drank of His blood would be sanctified by the truth. *(John 17:17)* We would be washed in the blood of the lamb. There would be no more hunger for righteousness. *(Revelaton 7: 14-17)* We would dwell in Christ, and Christ would dwell in us. *(John 6:56)*

Jesus Christ came and taught us of His ways, so that we could walk in His path. *(Isaiah 2:2-3)* He ransomed us from the grave of sin. Those who took heed to the word of God cleansed themselves from the pollution of this world. *(Psalm 119:9)* The people were able to escape the pollution of this world through the knowledge of Jesus Christ. *(2 Peter 2:20)*

However, there were those who turned and went back into sin. God had saved them from the enemy and allowed them to escape from captivity. The people had been set free from sin, but turned from the holy commandments. The dog went back to its vomit. *(2 Peter 2:22)* The word of God tells us plainly, "For it had been better for them not to have known the way of righteousness, than, after they have known it, to turn from the holy commandments delivered unto them." *(2 Peter 2:21)* The false prophets have deceived the people. Once you are saved from sin, you are not always saved from sin. Those who escaped from the pollution of this world, yet chose to backslide into sin, are going to be tormented more than those who never knew the way of righteousness. *(Luke 12:47-48)* They rejected the knowledge of Jesus Christ and are going to be destroyed. *(Hosea 4:6)*

Many people "thank the Lord for saving them." Yet, most of them remain in the bondage of sin. Jesus paid the ransom for us to come out of the grave of sin. We were required, quid pro quo, to come out of the grave of sin once the ransom was paid. There was no need to pay the ransom, if the captives remained in the grave. We cannot be "saved" from death and remain in the grave of sin. The living should never be found among the dead. Christ died to redeem our soul, i.e., to restore our spiritual life. Jesus set us free from sin and indeed "saved" us from our enemy. Satan, through fear of death, had kept us in the bondage of sin. We were dead, separated from God. Jesus came to reconcile us back to God. He died and broke the power over our lives. Now that we are free, we have no need to fear Satan or serve false gods. We are to serve the Lord in holiness and righteousness.

─────── **If My People Turn From Their Wicked Ways** ───────

Adam and Eve walked with God. Satan bewitched them and caused them to separate from God. They went from eternal life to instant death because of Satan's ability to persuade them to exalt themselves above God. Satan, a spirit, is not subject to the laws of nature. As long as humans exalt the flesh (weakness) and reject God (power), Satan will have power over them. The Lord entreats His people to turn from their wicked ways, so He can heal them. "If my people, which are called by my name, shall humble themselves, and pray, and seek my face, and turn from their wicked ways; then will I hear from heaven, and will forgive their sin, and will heal their land." *(2 Chronicles 7:14)*

Our God is mighty to save; but, He will save us only if we serve Him. If we turn against Him, He will turn against us. "And he went out to meet Asa, and said unto him, Hear ye me, Asa, and all Judah and Benjamin; **the Lord is with you, while ye be with him**; and if ye seek him, he will be found of you; but **if ye forsake him, he will forsake you.**" *(2 Chronicles 15:2)* The Lord could not forsake the people unless He had been with the people. He had saved them from their enemies, but warned the people to obey His commandments. If they forsook Him, He would forsake them. In other words, God had saved the people—and would continue to save the people while they were with Him. However, if the people rebelled against Him, He would allow their enemies to destroy them.

The false prophets have deceived the people and persuaded them that God will forgive them; all the people have to do is say they are sorry and ask for forgiveness. Satan's messengers do not tell the people that repent does not mean uttering a few words of sorrow. Repent means to turn from evil and keep God's commandments. Forgiveness comes after sinners have turned from wickedness and obeyed. "Let the wicked forsake his way, and the unrighteous man his thoughts: and let him return unto the Lord, and he will have mercy upon him; and to our God, for he will abundantly pardon." *(Isaiah 55:7)* There is no forgiveness or mercy without redemption. "Except a man be born of water, and of the Spirit, he cannot enter into the kingdom of God." *(John 3:5)*

————————— **The Lord Is Our Shepherd** —————————

The Lord is our shepherd. Jesus came to save the lost sheep. He will save us if we remain among the flock (remain with Him). Nonetheless, he has warned us to beware of wolves in sheep's clothing. If we allow wolves to deceive and lure us away from the shepherd, we will be destroyed. If we forsake the Lord and depart from the flock, the Lord will forsake us. Our enemy is too strong for us. We must remain with the shepherd and not allow the wolves to bewitch us to depart from the truth.

The prodigal son was saved (alive) while he remained in his father's house. When he departed from his father, he fell under the witchcraft of riotous living (death). "For this my son was dead, and is alive again; he was lost, and is found." *(Luke 11:24)* "Alive again" implies that the son was previously saved when he lived with his father. When he departed and lived in the bondage of sin, he was dead. "He was lost" connotes that the child had been deceived and lost his soul, but "is found" implies that his father has redeemed him back to life. His willingness to turn from his wickedness and return home gave the father an opportunity to restore the son's life. Here is another way of understanding the prodigal son: God (Father) created Adam (Son). The Lord breathed into Adam and made him a living soul. Adam separated from God and died. "He was lost; he lost his soul." In Adam, all died. All of us were separated from the Father. All of us lost our soul. The entire human family went into the pollution of this world (the bondage of sin) and engaged in riotous living. Those who are humble enough to return to God will be redeemed from corruption. Christ will give a new life, "alive again," to those who were once dead (lost) but returned home and reconciled (is found) with the Father.

Jesus observed, "For whosoever will save his life shall lose it: and whosoever will lose his life for my sake shall find it." (Matthew 16:25) The prodigal son is emblematic of those who want to enjoy themselves in Satan's kingdom and refuse to return to God. They do not want to sacrifice the life of the flesh but prefer to remain separated from God to live in sin. Such rebellious children will lose their soul. Those who are humble enough to repudiate the pollution of this world and return to God will restore their soul—and inherit eternal life.

Satan has sent false prophets into the world to tell the people who have departed from God that, although their sins have separated them from the Father, they are still saved. The devil knows that the wages of sin is death. He knows that if the wicked refuses to forsake his ways and the unrighteous man his thoughts and return unto the Lord, their soul will be lost forever.

Eli Falls Over Backward

Eli the priest oversaw the house of the Lord in Shiloh. The Lord had planned to bless Eli's house forever. Sadly, the priest had two disobedient sons, and the Lord could not tolerate disobedient servants. The Lord sent a man of God to tell Eli that God was going to destroy his house. *(1 Samuel 2:27-30)*

The Lord had saved the children of Israel out of Egypt. He had saved them during the Battle of Jericho. *(Joshua chapters 5 and 6)* The Lord had repeatedly saved the children of Israel from their enemies. At the time of Eli, Israel was at war with the Philistines, and the heathens were defeating the people of God. Israel needed the help of the Lord to defeat its enemies and sent for the Ark of the Covenant. The ark represented the agreement God had established with the children of Israel: If the people served the Lord, the Lord would defeat their enemies. When the ark came among the people, they expected God to "**save** us out of the hand of our enemies." *(1 Samuel 4:3)*

The ark was brought into the camp, and Israel shouted with a great noise. When the Philistines learned that the Ark of the Covenant had been brought into Israel's camp, they became afraid; they knew that the God of Israel, the Almighty God, had defeated the powerful Egyptians. The Philistines, expecting defeat, chose to fight like men rather than surrender. However, the children of Israel had disobeyed the Lord and violated the covenant. Since the people had forsaken the Lord, the Lord had forsaken them. He did not save them from their enemies. The Lord allowed the Philistines to destroy 30,000 of His people. Further, the Philistines took possession of the Ark of the Covenant and killed the two sons of Eli. *(1 Samuel 4:10-11)*

An Israelite ran from the battle and went back to Shiloh. When Eli the priest asked how the battle was going, the response was that the Philistines were defeating Israel. Additionally, Eli's two sons had been killed. Of course, Eli was troubled by such news. When the Israelite added that the Ark of the Covenant had been taken, the priest could not take anymore. Eli fell off his seat and broke his neck. *(1 Samuel 4:18)* The loss of the Ark of the Covenant signaled that, although God had saved them previously, as a result of their continuous rebellion, God had forsaken His people and given them over into the hands of their enemies. God is with us while we are with Him. If we forsake God, God will forsake us.

——— **Gave Them into the Hands of Their Enemies** ———

The Lord pleaded with the children of Israel to stop rebelling against Him. The people refused to obey. God gave them over to their enemies. "And the heathen shall know that the house of Israel went into captivity for their iniquity: because they trespassed against me, therefore hid I my face from them, and gave them into the hand of their enemies: so fell they all by the sword." *(Ezekiel 39:23)* The Lord had saved them before. When the people continued to rebel, the Lord turned His back and allowed their enemies to destroy them.

──────────────── **King Solomon** ────────────────

It had been in King David's heart to build a house for the Lord. The Lord was pleased with David's devotion; nonetheless, the Lord told the king that He would allow his son, Solomon, to build the house. King Solomon subsequently built and dedicated the house to the Lord.

During his dedication, Solomon asked the Lord: **if** the people sinned, and the heaven shut up and did not give rain because of the sins of the people, "yet **if** they pray toward this place, and confess thy name, and turn from their sin," to forgive the sins of the people and send rain upon the land. The king continued: **if** the people went out to war against their enemies, and they sinned against the Lord, whereby the Lord gave them over to their enemies, "**If** they return to thee with all their heart and with all their soul in the land of their captivity," to hear from Heaven and forgive the people. Time and again the king implored God to forgive the people and bless the children of Israel, **if** they turned from their wickedness. After Solomon finished praying, fire came down from heaven and consumed the prepared sacrifices. *(2 Chronicles 6:1-42)*

The Lord answered Solomon that He had heard his prayers and his supplications, and that He would keep the covenant He had made with David. "**If** my people, which are called by my name, shall humble themselves, and pray, and seek my face, and turn from their wicked ways; then will I hear from heaven, and will forgive their sin, and will heal their land." *(2 Chronicles 7:14)* The Lord made it clear that the covenant was a reciprocal agreement. He would save them from destruction in exchange for their service to Him. "**But if ye turn away, and forsake my statutes and my commandments,** which I have set before you, and shall go and serve other gods, and worship them: then will I pluck them up by the roots out of my land which I have given them; and this house, which I have sanctified for my name, **will I cast out of my sight**, and will make it to be a proverb and a byword among all nations." *(2 Chronicles 7:21)*

The Lord had saved the children of Israel from the Amalekites at Ziklag. *(1 Samuel 30:23)* The Lord had saved Israel from the Philistines. *(1 Samuel 17:47)* The Lord would be with His people as long as they obeyed Him. The Lord told Solomon that if he walked upright before Him as David walked, He would establish his kingdom forever. If Solomon rebelled against Him, the Lord would turn against the king. *(1 Kings 9:1-9)* Further, if the people sinned against God and refused to turn from their wickedness, God would turn against them, too.

Solomon had excellent understanding and made contingency plans. He knew Israel would sin, and He knew the Lord would forsake them: the king entreated the Lord to forgive the people **if** they turned from their wickedness and returned to Him. The Lord made it clear that He would preserve Solomon's kingdom and forgive the people if they turned from their wickedness and obeyed: "Then will I hear from Heaven." If they did not obey, they would be destroyed: "I will cast you out of my sight." Not only did Solomon lose his kingdom, God gave the children of Israel into the hands of their enemies. *(1 Kings 11:1-11)* He had saved them before; He destroyed them afterwards.

"Only fear the Lord, and serve him in truth with all your heart: for consider how great things he hath done for you. But if ye shall still do wickedly, ye shall be consumed, both ye and your king." (1 Samuel 12:24-25)

─────────── **Stand in the Gate of the Lord's House** ───────────

The children of Israel had again been disobedient. The Lord had saved them out of the hands of their enemies time and again. Yet, despite His mercy, the people refused to obey. The Lord commanded the prophet Jeremiah to go and stand in the gates of the Lord's house and warn the people who came to worship that they had better change their ways. The Lord asked the people if they thought they were going to steal, murder, commit adultery, engage in other forms of wickedness, "And come and stand before me in this house, which is called by my name, and say, We are delivered to do all these abominations?" *(Jeremiah 7:10)* The Lord had delivered (saved) the people out of the hands of their enemies. He had not delivered (saved) the people, so the people would rebel against Him.

The Lord told the people not to trust in lying word, "saying, The temple of the Lord, The temple of the Lord, The temple of the Lord." *(Jeremiah 7:4)* Yes, it was the Lord's house, but the building would not save them. God was willing to destroy the building and the people, too.

He told Jeremiah to tell the people, "But go ye now unto my place which was in Shiloh, where I set my name at the first, and see what I did to it for the wickedness of my people Israel." *(Jeremiah 7:12)* The Lord had established Eli the prophet and others in Shiloh. When the people refused to obey, he allowed the Philistines to destroy them. The Lord told Jeremiah to let the people know, "Therefore will I do unto this house, which is called by my name, wherein ye trust, and unto the place which I gave to you and to your fathers, as I have done to Shiloh. And I will cast you out of my sight." *(Jeremiah 7:14-15)* The chosen people of the Lord worshipped in the house of the Lord. The Lord had repeatedly saved them from their enemies, and had given them and their fathers the house to worship in. Yet if the people refused to obey, the Lord would do to them just like he had done to the rebellious in Shiloh: He would hide His face and allow their enemies to destroy them.

They Went Backward and Not Forward

God established a covenant with the people. "But this thing commanded I them, saying, Obey my voice, and I will be your

God, and ye shall be my people: and walk ye in all the ways that I have commanded you, that it may be well unto you. But they hearkened not, nor inclined their ear, but walked in the counsels and in the imagination of their evil heart, and went backward, and not forward." *(Jeremiah 7:23-24)* The Lord, through Moses and Joshua, told the people that He, pursuant to the covenant, would save them from their enemies **if** they obeyed Him. He told the people, through Jeremiah, that if they obeyed His voice, He would be their God, and they would be His people. If the people wanted things to be well with them, they had to walk in the way He had commanded. If the people rebelled against Him, He would turn and fight against them.

"For the children of Judah have done evil in my sight, saith the Lord: they have set their abominations in the house which is called by my name, to pollute it." *(Jeremiah 7:30)* The children of Israel were not interested in being redeemed from the pollution and corruption of the enemies, whereby they would be ready to serve the Lord. The self-willed rebels were committed to engaging in the pagan practices they had learned from the heathens. The Lord made it clear that if they continued to disobey, "Then **will I cause to cease** from the cities of Judah, and from the streets of Jerusalem, the voice of mirth, and the voice of gladness, the voice of the bridegroom, and the voice of the bride: **for the land shall be desolate**." *(Jeremiah 7:34)* The children of Israel were the people of God; however, the Lord is holy in all his ways. If the children of Israel chose not to serve Him, the Lord would do to them just as He had done to their enemies: destroy all of them—the land would be desolate.

Continue in the Doctrine

The apostle Paul exhorted Timothy to "Take heed unto thyself, and unto the doctrine; **continue** in them: for in doing this thou shalt both save thyself, and them that hear thee." *(1 Timothy 4:16)* The apostle understood that being saved did not mean that a person was going to Heaven. It simply meant that those who obeyed the apostles' doctrine would not go into sin. They would be saved from sin, because the apostles' doctrine was the knowledge of Jesus Christ, who came to teach us of His ways, so that we could walk in His path. *(Isaiah 2:2-3)* Disciples of Christ walked the way the Master walked.

Saints who had wisdom and judgment "**continued** steadfastly in the apostles' doctrine." *(Acts 2:42)* Unlike the foolish Galatians, who had allowed ignorant false prophets to deceive them and turn them away from the truth, wise men and women knew, "For if after they have escaped the pollutions of the world through the knowledge of the Lord and Saviour Jesus Christ, they are again entangled therein, and overcome, the latter end is worse with them than the beginning. For it had been better for them not to have known the way of righteousness, than, after they have known it, to turn from the holy commandment delivered unto them." *(2 Peter 2:20, 21)* The people could not turn from the holy commandment, unless they had walked in the holy commandments. The people could not have escaped the pollution of the world, unless God had saved them from the pollution. We have to continue in God's word until the end.

———————————— **Abide in Me** ————————————

Jesus told the people: "I am the true vine, and my Father is the husbandman. . . Abide in me, and I in you. As the branch cannot bear fruit of itself, except it abide in the vine; no more can ye, **except ye abide in me.** . . . **If a man abide not in me**, he is cast forth as a branch, and is withered; and men gather them, and **cast them into the fire**, and they are burned." *(John 15:1-6)* Jesus made it clear that a man should abide in him, yet can become withered if he did not remain. A man has to first be a part of something to abide in it. If a man walked with God, he was saved. If he did not remain with God, he was destroyed. Jesus exhorted the people to abide in Him. If they did not remain with Him, they would be cast into the fire and burned.

God breathed into Adam, and man became a living soul. As long as Adam ate from the tree of life, he lived. When he rebelled against God and ate from the tree of the knowledge of good and evil, he died. Adam had life, but chose to bring death upon himself. Jesus died, but rose from the grave. The spirit restored His soul. Those who obey God will inherit eternal life; those who disobey God will inherit eternal damnation.

If Ye Rebel Against the Lord

Samuel told the chosen people of God: "**If** ye will fear the Lord, and serve Him, and obey His voice, and not rebel against the commandment of the Lord then shall both ye and also the king that reigneth over you **continue** following the Lord your God: But **if** ye will not obey the voice of the Lord, but rebel against the commandment of the Lord, then shall the hand of the Lord be against you, as it was against your fathers." *(1 Samuel 12:14-15)* The only way the people could have continued following the Lord is if He had saved them. If the people turned against the Lord, the Lord would turn against them.

The Lord Is Not Among You

God saved the children of Israel out of Egypt, but the people continued to rebel. Moses told the people: "Go not up, for the Lord is not among you; that ye be not smitten before your enemies. For the Amalekites and the Canaanites are there before you, and ye shall fall by the sword: **because ye are turned away from the Lord, therefore the Lord will not be with you.**" *(Numbers 14:42-43)* The people disregarded Moses' warning and went up the hill. "Then the Amalekites came down, and the Canaanites which dwelt in that hill, and smote them, and discomfited them, even unto Hormah." *(Numbers 14:45)*

Who Gave Jacob for a Spoil?

The prophet Isaiah asked, "Who gave Jacob for a spoil, and Israel to the robbers? did not the Lord, he against whom we have sinned? for they would not walk in his ways, neither were they obedient unto his law." *(Isaiah 42:24)* God saved the children of Israel. They refused to obey. He gave them over into the hands of their enemies.

Being Led Away with the Error of the Wicked

Paul told the church at Corinth: "Moreover, brethren, I declare unto you the gospel which I preached unto you, which also ye have received, and wherein ye stand; By which also **ye are saved, if** ye keep in memory what I preached unto you, unless ye have believed in vain." *(1 Corinthians 15:1-2)* Paul wanted the people to know that if they did not remain steadfast in the apostles' doctrine, the people would be led away from the truth. Without truth, like the foolish Galatians, they would disobey God's commandments and be destroyed. Peter reaffirmed Paul's admonition when he added: "Ye therefore, beloved, seeing ye know these things before, beware lest ye also, being led away with the error of the wicked, **fall from your own stedfastness.**" *(2 Peter 3:17)* The people were saved when they walked in the truth. If they turned from the truth, they would be destroyed with the rest of the deceived.

He Gave His People Over to the Sword

The psalmist observed that God established a testimony in Jacob and appointed a law in Israel. God told the people to keep His commandments and to teach their children. *(Psalm 78:5)* "Nevertheless they did flatter him with their mouth, and they lied unto him with their tongues. For their heart was not right with him, neither were they stedfast in his covenant. But he, being full of compassion, forgave their iniquity, and destroyed them not." *(Psalm*

78:36-38) The Lord exhibited great patience with the children of Israel. He had saved them from their enemies. However, after they continued to rebel, "He gave his people over also unto the sword, and was wroth with his inheritance." *(Psalm 78:62)*

―――――――――― **Saved by Hope** ――――――――――

The apostle Paul explained to the church at Rome: "And not only they, but ourselves also, which have the firstfruits of the Spirit, even we ourselves groan within ourselves, waiting for the adoption, to wit, the redemption of our body. For we are saved by hope: but hope that is seen is not hope: for what a man seeth, why doth he yet hope for? But if we hope for that we see not, then do we with patience wait for it." *(Romans 8:23-25)*

Saved individuals do not have a guarantee of eternal life. We are saved by grace, through faith. We patiently endure hardness as good soldiers and obey the commandments of God. We remain steadfast in the apostles' doctrine and look forward to the day of redemption when God will save us from the wrath to come upon the earth. "And you, that were sometime alienated and enemies in your mind by wicked works, yet now hath he reconciled in the body of his flesh through death, to present you holy and unblameable and unreproveable in his sight: **if ye continue in the faith** grounded and settled, and **be not moved away** from the hope of the gospel." *(Colossians 1:21-23)*

――――――― **We Are Not of Them Who Draw Back** ―――――――

Similarly, the Hebrews were exhorted to continue to obey the Lord. They were not going to receive an instant reward for serving the Lord. Those who serve the Lord must endure until the end, which is why Jesus told the disciples if we continue in his word, we are his disciples indeed. *(John 8:31)* "But we are not of them who draw back unto perdition; but of them that believe to the saving of the soul." *(Hebrews 10:39)* Many individuals went to church and professed to have given their lives to the Lord. When tribulations came, the people rejected God and went back to their corrupt ways. Those who want to save their soul from death will not return to their former life of sin but will continue to obey God's commandments.

The Lord has made it plain: spiritual children of Abraham must obey the Lord if they want to inherit the spiritual Promised Land. If they, like the natural children of Abraham turn from the Lord, He will destroy them just as He destroyed the natural children of Abraham. "Now the just shall live by faith: But **if** any man draw back, my soul shall have no pleasure in him." *(Hebrews 10:38)* The people had to obey God's commandments until the end. If anyone turned back, God would not be pleased. Those who had put their hands to the plow and turned back were not worthy to be with the Lord. *(Luke 9:62)*

Paul told the Romans how the Lord had not spared the disobedient Hebrews. Hence, he entreated the Romans to "Behold therefore the goodness and severity of God: on them which fell, severity; but toward thee, goodness, **if thou continue** in his goodness. **Otherwise, thou also shalt be cut off.**" *(Romans 11:22)* The Lord had destroyed the Hebrews who had rebelled. If the Romans continued to obey the Lord, God would bless them. If the Romans rebelled, God would also destroy them as He destroyed the backsliding Hebrews.

Ezra

The children of Israel rebelled against the Lord, and the Lord allowed them to be taken into captivity. The king allowed some of the Jews to leave Babylon and return to Jerusalem.

Ezra the priest "had prepared his heart to seek the law of the Lord, and to do it, and to teach in Israel statutes and judgments." *(Ezra 7:10)*

The children of Israel suffered great persecution while in captivity, but the Lord saved some from destruction. *(Ezra 9:7-9)*

When Ezra learned that some of the children of Israel and priests had not separated themselves from the heathens, but continued to rebel against God, he shaved his head and sat astonished. He knew that the Lord had punished the children of Israel for their disobedience, but the Lord would have been within His rights to have destroyed all of them—the people had forsaken the covenant. In His mercy, the Lord delivered some of the people out of captivity. Ezra asked: "Should we again break thy commandments, and join in affinity with the people of these abominations? wouldest not thou be angry with us till thou hadst consumed us, so that there should be no remnant nor escaping?" *(Ezra 9:14)*

Ezra knew that, just as God had saved the Hebrews out of Egypt and destroyed them in the wilderness, the Lord, having saved many of the children of Israel in Babylon, would destroy them if they continued to disobey. The people were terrified and cried; they trembled at the thought of breaking the commandment of God. *(Ezra 9:4)* They knew God had allowed their enemies to carry away the others who had been disobedient. If the people continued to rebel against God, the Lord would also cast them out of His sight. *(Ezra 9:15)*

"But he knoweth the way that I take: when he hath tried me, I shall come forth as gold. My foot hath held his steps, his ways have I kept, and not declined. Neither have I gone back from the commandments of his lips: I have esteemed the words of his mouth more than my necessary food." (Job 23:10-12)

Be Thou Faithful unto Death

God is merciful. He delivered Abraham, Ruth, and Cornelius out of ignorance. He will deliver anyone who wants to serve Him out of the hands of the enemy. "If that nation, against whom I have pronounced, turn from their evil, I will repent of the evil that I thought to do unto them" *(Jeremiah 18:8)* The Lord is slow to anger and great in power, but He will not allow the wicked to live.

(Nahum 1:3) God requires individuals to remain faithful, even unto death. "Fear none of those things which thou shalt suffer: behold, the devil shall cast some of you into prison, that ye might be tried; and ye shall have tribulation ten days: be thou **faithful unto death**, and I will give thee a crown of life." *(Revelation 2:10)* If the people do not remain faithful unto death, God will destroy them.

Sealed Unto the Day of Redemption

The false prophets have taught the people that their salvation is sealed unto the day of redemption: "And grieve not the holy Spirit of God, whereby ye are sealed unto the day of redemption." *(Ephesians 4:30)* The apostle Paul wanted the people of God to know that God would save us until the end if we did not grieve His Holy Spirit. How do we grieve His Holy Spirit? What happened to those who grieved God's Holy Spirit? "But **they rebelled**, and vexed his holy Spirit: therefore **he was turned** to be their enemy, and he fought against them." *(Isaiah 63:10)* We are sealed unto the day of redemption if we continue steadfastly in the apostles' doctrine and do not rebel against the Lord. If we rebel against Him, He will turn against us.

Those who have received God's testimony have set to their seal that God is true. *(John 3:33)* Therefore, those who believe God will obey His commandments and remain steadfast in the apostles' doctrine—and the Lord will save them from their enemies. "Let the redeemed of the Lord say so, whom he hath redeemed from the hand of the enemy." *(Psalm 107:2)* God redeemed those who humbled themselves and obeyed His commandments, and turned to be the enemy of those who rebelled against Him. "And the anger of the Lord was hot against Israel, and he delivered them into the hands of spoilers that spoiled them, and he sold them into the hands of their enemies round about, so that they could not any longer stand before their enemies." *(Judges 2:14)*

──────── **Don't Turn Aside From the Lord** ────────

Do not allow false prophets to deceive you. God made a covenant with His people that He would save us from our enemies if we served Him. If we forsake Him, He will also forsake us. "As a dog returneth to his vomit, so a fool returneth to his folly." *(Proverbs 26:11)* Do not be a fool and believe that you can reject the salvation of Jesus Christ and be saved from destruction. Jesus Christ destroyed the power of death and paved the way for everyone to be saved from their sins. Christ came to set us free. If we have been saved from sin, we need to "Stand fast therefore in the liberty wherewith Christ hath made us free, and be not entangled again with the yoke of bondage." *(Galatians 5:1)*

The apostle Paul called the Galatians foolish and asked, who hath bewitched them to depart from the truth? *(Galatians 3:1)* "Ye did run well; who did hinder you that ye should not obey the truth? This persuasion cometh not of him that calleth you." *(Galatians 5:7-8)* Only fools will fall for Satan's witchcraft and believe that once they are saved they are always saved. God will not deliver us out of bondage, have us to reject Him to return to the bondage of sin, yet allow us to enter into His holy kingdom. Just as He destroyed the children of Israel who preferred to serve in the bondage of Egypt, He will destroy those who prefer to serve in the bondage of sin.

──────── **Additional Edifying Scriptures** ────────

"If my people, which are called by my name, shall humble themselves, and pray, and seek my face, and turn from their wicked ways; then will I hear from heaven, and will forgive their sin, and will heal their land." *(2 Chronicles 7:14)*

"And he went out to meet Asa, and said unto him, Hear ye me, Asa, and all Judah and Benjamin; The Lord is with you, while ye be with him; and if ye seek him, he will be found of you; but if ye forsake him, he will forsake you." *(2 Chronicles 15:2)*

"Her adversaries are the chief, her enemies prosper; for the Lord hath afflicted her for the multitude of her transgressions: her children are gone into captivity before the enemy." (Lamentations 1:5)

"The yoke of my transgressions is bound by his hand: they are wreathed, and come up upon my neck: he hath made my strength to fall, the Lord hath delivered me into their hands, from whom I am not able to rise up." (Lamentations 1:14)

"Take heed unto thyself, and unto the doctrine; continue in them: for in doing this thou shalt both save thyself, and them that hear thee." (I Timothy 4:16)

"The wicked have laid a snare for me: yet I erred not from thy precepts . . . I have inclined my heart to perform thy statutes alway, even unto the end." (Psalm 119:110,112)

"But Christ as a son over his own house: whose house are we, if we hold fast the confidence and the rejoicing of the hope firm unto the end." (Hebrews 3:6)

"But now, after that ye have known God, or rather are known of God, how turn ye again to the weak and beggarly elements? Whereunto ye desire again to be in bondage?" (Galatians 4:9)

"For we are made partakers of Christ, if we hold the beginning of our confidence stedfast unto the end." (Hebrews 3:14)

"If ye continue in the faith grounded and settled, and be not moved away from the hope of the gospel." (Colossians 1:23)

"Seek ye the Lord while he may be found, call ye upon him while he is near: Let the wicked forsake his way, and the unrighteous man his thoughts: and let him return unto the Lord, and he will have mercy upon him; and to our God, for he will abundantly pardon." (Isaiah 55:6-7)

"And the Lord commanded us to do all these statutes, to fear the Lord our God, for our good always, that he might preserve us alive, as it is at this day." (Deuteronomy 6:24)

"The highway of the upright is to depart from evil: he that keepeth his way preserveth his soul." (Proverbs 16:17)

"For if after they have escaped the pollutions of the world through the knowledge of the Lord and Saviour Jesus Christ, they are again entangled therein, and overcome, the latter end is worse with them than the beginning." (2 Peter 2:20)

"They on the rock are they, which, when they hear, receive the word with joy; and these have no root, which for a while believe, and in time of temptation fall away. And that which fell among the thorns are they, which, when they have heard, go forth, and are choked with cares and riches and pleasures of this life, and bring no fruit to perfection." (Luke 8:13-14)

"Brethren, if any of you do err from the truth, and one convert him; Let him know, that he which converth the sinner from the error of his way shall save a soul from death, and shall hide a multitude of sins." (James 5:19-20)

"Only fear the Lord, and serve him in truth with all your heart: for consider how great things he hath done for you. But if ye shall still do wickedly, ye shall be consumed, both ye and your king." (1 Samuel 12:24-25)

"The Lord is with you, while ye be with him; and if ye seek him, he will be found of you; but if ye forsake him, he will forsake you." (2 Chronicles 15:2)

"But the mercy of the Lord is from everlasting to everlasting upon them that fear him, and his righteousness unto children's children; to such as keep his covenant, and to those that remember his commandments to do them." (Psalm 103:17-18)

"Then said Jesus to those Jews which believed on him, If ye continue in my word, then are ye my disciples indeed." (John 8:31)

"Behold therefore the goodness and severity of God: on them which fell, severity; but toward thee, goodness, if thou continue in his goodness: otherwise thou also shalt be cut off." (Romans 11:22)

"As also in all his epistles, speaking in them of these things; in which are some things hard to be understood, which they that are unlearned and unstable wrest, as they do also the other scriptures, unto their own destruction. Ye therefore, beloved, seeing ye know these things before, beware lest ye also, being led away with the error of the wicked, fall from your own steadfastness." (2 Peter 3:16-17)

"Because with lies ye have made the heart of the righteous sad, whom I have not made sad; and strengthened the hands of the wicked, that he should not return from his wicked way, by promising him life." (Ezekiel 13:22)

"And he said, What have I sinned, that thou wouldest deliver thy servant into the hand of Ahab, to slay me?" (1 Kings 18:9)

"For now we live, if ye stand fast in the Lord." (1 Thessalonian 3:8)

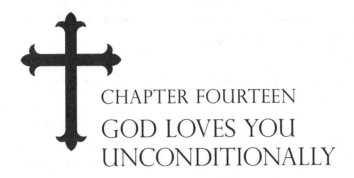

CHAPTER FOURTEEN

GOD LOVES YOU UNCONDITIONALLY

The idea that God loves you unconditionally is one of the most foolish statements ever expressed. Satan wants to destroy us. He knows that the fear of the Lord is the beginning of knowledge. *(Proverbs 1:7)* He knows that the conclusion of the whole matter is to fear God and keep His commandments. *(Ecclesiastes 12:13-14)* As a result, the devil does not want us to fear God. He wants us to believe that nothing will happen to us if we rebel against the Almighty. Those who walk after the flesh will rebel against the spirit and lose their soul.

God commanded us, before the foundation of the world, to live holy. *(Ephesians 1:4)* The people went into captivity because of the lack of knowledge; during the famine, all they had to eat was the false prophets' vomit, which kept them in pollution. Jesus came to set the captives free and to fill those who hungered and thirsted for righteousness. However, most people, through fear of death, will not serve the Lord. Those who do not fear God will not keep His commandments. Hence, the false prophets' job is to persuade the people that they do not have to live holy. God will love them, regardless of whether they obey or disobey His commandments. "For the vile person will speak villany, and his heart will work iniquity, to practise hypocrisy, and to utter error against the Lord, to make empty the soul of the hungry, and he will cause the drink of the thirsty to fail." *(Isaiah 32:6)* The deceived will reject God's knowledge and remain in the bondage of sin. Unredeemed, they will forsake God's mercy and be destroyed.

Unconditional

Webster's dictionary defines "unconditional" as "not limited by condition" and "absolute." The definition simply means that, regardless of the circumstance, everything will remain the same. In this context, "God loves you unconditionally" implies that God will always love you, regardless of whether you obey or disobey His commandments.

Commandment

According to Webster's dictionary, a "commandment" is "an order or mandate." A command is "to have or exercise authority or control over; be master of; have at one's bidding or disposal." A person who issues commands has power and authority over his subjects. Hence, a commandment is not a suggestion or recommendation. A commandment is an order that must be followed.

Jesus Christ is the King of kings and Lord of lords. He sent famine into the earth and allowed men and women to bear witness to their own ignorance and frailty. In defeating our enemies, Jesus demonstrated that He has all power and authority in Heaven and on earth. *(Matthew 28:18)* He will not countenance rebellion. His commandments must be obeyed. Those who disobey His commandments and challenge His kingship will be destroyed.

The Lord tells His people: "Keep my commandments, and live; and my law as the apple of thine eye." *(Proverbs 7:2)* In contrast, the Lord has a word for those who disobey His commandments. "But he that sinneth against me wrongeth his own soul: all they that hate me love death." *(Proverbs 8:36)* Those who believe that

God loves them unconditionally have been deceived. A condition of God allowing you to live is to keep His commandments. If you sin against Him, you will die. *(Ezekiel 18:20)* Since He is superior to you, your rebellion indicates that you hate Him. As His enemy, you will be destroyed. God's love or hate for you—your salvation or damnation—depends upon whether you obey or disobey His commandments.

Covenant

God and the human family entered into a covenant. A covenant is an agreement: the agreement is conditioned on the basis that both parties will honor their word. If you serve me, saith the Lord, I will save you. If you forsake me, I will forsake you. *(2 Chronicles 15:2)* If you deliver me out of the hands of my enemy, saith the people, we will serve you in holiness and righteousness all the days of our lives. (Luke 1:67-75)

Satan has sent false prophets to tell the people that God will love them regardless of whether they serve Him or serve Satan. "Thus saith the Lord of hosts, Hearken not unto the words of the prophets that prophesy unto you: they make you vain: they speak a vision of their own heart, and not out of the mouth of the Lord. They say still unto them that despise me, The Lord hath said, Ye shall have peace; and they say unto every one that walketh after the imagination of his own heart, No evil shall come upon you." *(Jeremiah 23:16-17)* The false prophets tell the people, "No evil shall come upon you." Satan told Eve, "Ye shall not surely die." *(Genesis 3:4)*

God Hates the Sin but Loves the Sinner

False prophets lie to the people and say, "God hates the sin but loves the sinner." It is foolish to hate the act and not hate the person who committed the act. Without the sinner, there would be no sin. According to the word of God, God hates sinners: "The foolish shall not stand in thy sight: **thou hatest** all workers of iniquity." *(Psalm 5:5)* Jesus Christ is the King of kings, the supreme ruler. All of His ways are holy. Those who rebel against Him are evil and must be destroyed. Accordingly, He hates all sinners. He will cast them out of His sight. *(Matthew 7:23; Luke 13:27)*

----------------------------- **God Loves Everybody** -----------------------------

Satanic messengers tell the people that God loves everybody. "Was not Esau Jacob's brother? saith the Lord: yet I loved Jacob, and **I hated Esau**." *(Malachi 1:2-3)* The Lord blessed Jacob and destroyed Esau. Esau said he would build; the Lord said He would tear it down. *(Malachi 1:4)*

Esau and Jacob were both sons of Isaac, and grandsons of Abraham. They were among the chosen people of God, yet God loved Jacob and hated Esau. The Lord is no respecter of person. *(Acts 10:34)* Why did He love Jacob and hate Esau? Why did the children of Israel (Jacob's descendants) have a right to inherit the Promised Land, whereas the children of Esau were destroyed? *(Obadiah 1:18)*

----------------------------- **Children of Israel** -----------------------------

Moses led the children of Israel out of the bondage of Egypt. The people had not made it across the sea before they began to rebel. When the Egyptians came after them, they complained to Moses that they would have preferred to serve the Egyptians than to die in the wilderness. *(Exodus 14:12)* Despite their lack of faith, the Lord, in accordance with the covenant, delivered the people and destroyed their enemies. The Lord told the people, "**If** ye walk in my statutes, and keep my commandments, and do them; . . . I will walk among you, and will be your God, and ye shall be my people . . . And **if** ye will not for all this hearken unto me, but walk contrary unto me; Then I will walk contrary unto you also in fury; . . . and my soul shall *abhor* (hate) you." *(Leviticus 26:3, 12, 27, 28, 30)* "If" means "on the condition."

The Lord, through Moses, spoke in plain language to the people: If the people walked upright before Him and kept His commandments, He would defeat their enemies. He would be their God, and they would be His people. *(Exodus 23:22; Jeremiah 32:38)* However, if the people turned against Him, He would turn against them. As we know, the children of Israel refused to obey, and the Lord abhorred (hated) them. "Therefore was the wrath of the Lord kindled against his people, insomuch that he **abhorred** (hated) his own inheritance." *(Psalm 106:40)*

God told the children of Israel, as they exited out of Egypt, that they were going to pass through lands that were inhabited by other people. He told His people to learn not the ways of the heathens. But His people "were mingled among the heathen, and learned their works." *(Psalm 106:35)* He hated His own people, "And he gave them into the hand of the heathen; and they that hated them ruled over them." *(Psalm 106:40-43)*

It has been previously observed that the Lord, after having saved the children of Israel out of Egypt, afterwards destroyed them that did not believe. Out of 600,000 men and an unknown number of boys, only two males who left Egypt made it into the Promised Land. *(Numbers 14:1-10; Numbers 26:64-65; Numbers 32:11-12)* The covenant made with the children of Israel was based upon certain conditions: He would be their God and deliver them from their enemies *if* (on the condition) they would keep His commandments and serve Him. Since they refused to serve Him, He hated (abhorred) them and gave them over to their enemies.

God Hates All Murderers

The Lord has made it clear that all liars and murderers shall have their part in the lake that burneth with fire and brimstone. *(Revelation 21:8)* "Thou shalt destroy them that speak leasing

(lies): the Lord will **abhor** (hate) the bloody and deceitful man."
(Psalm 5:6)

───────── **Jacob Have I Loved; Esau Have I Hated** ─────────

Abraham, as the first born of his father, Terah, had the right
to inherit his father's property. Abraham could live comfortably
among his family, people, and culture. However, his family
and people served pagan gods. God made Abraham a promise:
If Abraham came out from among his family and served Him,
God would bless him. A man of integrity, Abraham trusted God
and renounced his father, mother, family, land of his birth, and
inheritance to serve the Lord. Abraham esteemed the spiritual
blessings of God above the natural blessings of his father, his love
for his people, and the safety of his home. *(Genesis 12:1-4)*

Abraham was 100 years old when his only son, Isaac, was
born. His wife, Sarah, was 90 years old, well past her child-bearing
years. Further, she had been barren from the womb. *(Genesis 22:2)*
Although Abraham had another child, Ishmael, the child's mother,
Hagai, was in normal conditions and had conceived under natural
circumstances. As far as God was concerned, Ishmael was not
Abraham's son. God is a spirit. His children are those who are
conceived by faith. *(Galatians 3:7)* The covenant with Abraham
and his seed was based upon those who trusted in the Lord. Isaac
was a child of promise *(Galatians 4:28)*; Abraham's seed was going
to inherit the Promised Land *(Acts 7:5)*; people of God walk by faith
in God's promises. *(2 Peter 1:4)* Our faith in Him is according to
His word. *(Luke 1:38; Psalm 119:9; Genesis 6:22)*

God told Abraham that in him and his seed, all the nations of the
earth were going to be blessed. Jesus Christ, the Messiah, was going
to come through the seed of Abraham. Thus, it was necessary for
God to have faithful servants, like Abraham, who exalted spiritual
blessings above natural blessings—individuals who exalted the
things of God above the things of the flesh. Further, since Jesus
had to come through the seed of Abraham, God had to preserve

the Jewish people. Whoever inherited Abraham's blessings was guaranteed God's protection. Abraham's blessing was passed on to his son, Isaac, the child of promise.

It is important to note that Ishmael was Abraham's seed, but he was not Abraham's child. Accordingly, he did not have a right of inheritance. Isaac, conceived by faith, was considered as Abraham's only child. Sarah, Abraham's wife, told her lord to put the bond woman, Hagai, and her son, Ishmael, out of the house. Ishmael had been conceived under normal conditions. Sarah did not want Ishmael to inherit along with her son—and God told Abraham to obey his wife. The promise to Abraham was based upon faith—those who trusted in the Lord.

If Ishmael had been entitled to inherit the promises of God because he was a natural child of Abraham, all of the seed of Abraham could inherit the Promised Land, regardless of whether they trusted in the Lord or obeyed His commandments. God will not allow those who are in the bondage of sin to inherit along with those who have been conceived by faith (born again of the spirit). God's promises are for those who believe in them.

Before he died, Abraham expressed concern about Isaac's prospective wife. He made the eldest servant of his house swear that he would not allow Isaac to marry an unwise woman. Abraham told his servant to secure Isaac a wife from among his natural people. As always, the Lord blessed Abraham. *(Genesis 24:1)* The servant went to Mesopotamia, unto the city of Nahor, and prayed to God that the Lord would show kindness to Abraham. He asked the Lord to show him the wife to give Isaac out of respect for Abraham. *(Genesis 24:14)* The Lord led the servant to the right spot for the blessing. The Lord had the perfect wife waiting: Rebekah.

Rebekah had a similar mindset as Abraham. She was willing to leave paganism to serve the true God. Just as Abraham left his family by faith and moved away, Rebekah left her family by faith to marry Isaac. She did not know Abraham or Isaac, but she trusted in the Lord. Just as Sarah, Isaac's mother, had been barren from the womb and required spiritual intervention to have a child, Rebekah was barren from the womb and required divine intervention to have children. *(Genesis 25:21)* God's blessings are activated by faith.

Rebekah, a virtuous woman, was critical to the birth of Jesus Christ and for the salvation of humanity. Although she was barren, her husband, Isaac, prayed, and, by faith, Rebekah conceived. The Lord blessed her with twins who wrestled inside her womb. When she inquired of the Lord, He told her that one of her sons would be stronger than the other, and the elder (Esau) would serve the younger (Jacob). *(Genesis 25:23)*

As Isaac's first born, Esau was positioned to inherit the birthright. God's promise to bless Abraham and his seed would have passed from Abraham to Isaac, and from Isaac to Esau. As heir to God's promise, Esau would have ensured that God protected and preserved him and his seed. The Lord had to bless Esau, because Jesus Christ, the Messiah, had to come through the seed of Abraham. *(Genesis 22:18; Matthew 1:1)*

Isaac loved his eldest son, Esau. Rebekah, however, loved Jacob. *(Genesis 25:28)* One day, Esau came home hungry. Jacob had cooked, and Esau asked Jacob for food. Jacob told Esau that he would give him food in exchange for his birthright. Esau scoffed at his birthright. In order to justify his renunciation of God's blessings, he exaggerated the situation and made it seem like he was about to starve to death. "And Esau said, Behold, I am at the point to die: and what profit shall this birthright do to me?" *(Genesis 25:32)* Accordingly, he sold his birthright to his brother for a morsel of meat.

Esau had the right to inherit the blessings of God, yet he had such little appreciation for God's promises, until he traded away thousands of years of spiritual blessings for one meal. The significant issue was not that Esau was hungry. If he had simply endured the light affliction of hunger for a little while, his mother would have fed him. His willingness to sell his birthright for a morsel of meat indicated that he exalted the comfort of his flesh over the blessings of God; he despised the fact that he had to suffer affliction to inherit God's blessings. *(Genesis 25:34)*

Jacob put on a hairy fur to pretend he was Esau, which caused Isaac, who could not see, to bestow the blessing upon Jacob. It is probable from Jacob's cooking and being at home that he was what many call a "mama's boy." The salient issue is that Jacob understood the importance of the birthright. When an opportunity presented itself to obtain the birthright, Jacob quickly seized upon it. Neither Rebekah nor Jacob defrauded Esau out of his birthright. Jacob made Esau an offer, and Esau accepted the offer. Jacob was the rightful heir to the birthright: Abraham's children are those who live by faith in God's promises. *(Galatians 3:7)* As a result, God's blessing passed down from Abraham to Isaac, and from Isaac to Jacob. The Lord subsequently changed Jacob's name to Israel, and only the children of Israel were able to inherit the Promised Land.

Ignorant false prophets have criticized Rebekah for her actions, yet God, in saving His people, predestined her to be Isaac's wife. Like her husband, Rebekah could have favored Esau, because he was most capable of providing food for the family. Rebekah knew, however, that the Lord had told her that the elder would serve the younger. Like Abraham, Rebekah esteemed her spiritual life above her natural life and left her pagan family to serve the Lord. Like Sarah, she knew that the blessings of God were contingent upon faith in God. She evidently prepared Jacob to secure the birthright, which would explain why Jacob quickly bartered food to Esau in exchange for the birthright.

While Esau was willing to renounce his birthright for a morsel of meat, Jacob would later wrestle with God all night. God whipped Jacob around so much while they wrestled, until the Lord threw Jacob's thigh out of joint. Nonetheless, Jacob would not turn God loose. *(Genesis 32:24-30)* Jacob is like those who, despite their natural afflictions, refuse to renounce God. The Lord wants servants who understand that He is our salvation. *(John 6:66-69)* We are not going back into Egypt; we are not going back into sin; but we cannot make this journey alone. We are going to wrestle with God until He blesses us.

Esau epitomizes those who, when they encounter affliction or temptation, are willing to renounce the things of God in deference to their natural desires. To survive or to derive pleasure, sinners will rebel against God. They will engage in behavior that indicates they value the flesh above the spirit. They exalt their will above God's will. Esau repeatedly exercised poor judgment. He took wives from the daughters of Canaan, which grieved his mother and father. *(Genesis 36:2; Genesis 26:34-35)* As we know from Solomon and Samson, those who exalt lust over spirit will ultimately lose everything. "For he that soweth to his flesh shall of the flesh reap corruption; but he that soweth to the Spirit shall of the Spirit reap life everlasting." *(Galatians 6:8)*

Consider: Sarah made Abraham put Hagai and Ishmael out of the house to ensure that Isaac, conceived by faith, would inherit God's blessing. Abraham wanted to ensure that Isaac married a God-fearing woman. The Lord blessed Isaac with Rebekah, who ensured that the blessings of God would remain within her family. Isaac, because of Rebekah, charged Jacob not to marry heathen women. *(Genesis 28:1)* Isaac would ultimately bless Jacob with the inheritance. *(Genesis 28:4)* Wise women build their houses, but fools tear it down with their own hands. *(Proverbs 14:1)* Sarah and Rebekah exhibited great understanding: They knew God was supreme and exalted their spiritual lives above their natural lives, which ensured that their families would walk with the Lord. Unlike foolish women, who promote the lust of the flesh and empower Satan to overtake their families, Sarah and Rebekah exalted the spirit and saved their families from death.

Esau despised his birthright--a veritable denunciation of the blessings of God. God hated Esau and destroyed him and his entire lineage. *(Obadiah 1:18)* Similarly, God hates all sinners. *(Psalm 5:5)* Workers of iniquity exalt their will—the will of the flesh—above the will of the spirit. Since stubbornness is as iniquity and idolatry, workers of iniquity refuse to forsake their evil ways; they exalt themselves above the Almighty. Like Satan, they refuse to accept Jesus as Lord. Although the Lord died to redeem their right to inherit His kingdom, workers of inqiuity reject the inheritance of

God to exalt their natural lives. God hated the rebellious children of Israel, who renounced their inheritance and desired to return to Egypt to save their natural lives. God hated Esau, who renounced his birthright to please his flesh. Just as God destroyed the children of Israel and Esau, God hates those who renounce His deliverance to serve as Satan's slaves. He will destroy them, too.

God Greatly Abhorred Israel

God rained manna down from heaven and fed the children of Israel angels' food, but they refused to keep His covenant. They did not trust Him to save them from their enemies. The Hebrews had gone into Egypt to buy corn and had been taken into captivity. God led them out of captivity and gave them corn from heaven. *(Psalm 78:24)* Yet the people placed more trust in the Egyptians than their Savior. "When God heard this, he was wroth, and greatly **abhorred** (hateth) Israel." *(Psalm 78:59)* The children of Israel did not exalt the Lord like Abraham, Isaac, and Jacob. They exalted the natural above the spiritual; they exalted weakness over power; they exalted temporal over eternal. They had no integrity and did not deserve their inheritance. God destroyed them.

"I have hated the congregation of evildoers; and will not sit with the wicked." (Psalm 26:5)

God Hates the Covetous

Greed is rampant in the earth. Those in power exploit the powerless and rejoice in their abuse of power. Those not in power abuse others to increase their power. Proud men and women refuse to humble themselves before God. In fact, their minds are so corrupt, until they either do not believe in God or have no fear of God. The weak look upon those in power and admire their corruption. They desire such power. "For the wicked boasteth of his heart's desire, and blesseth the covetous, whom the Lord **abhorreth** (hates)." *(Psalm 10:3)* God hates the wicked and covetous.

———— God Hates Those Who Rebel Against Him ————

The children of God were losing a battle to the Philistines. They sent for the Ark of the Covenant and shouted with joy when the ark was brought into the camp. The Lord, however, did not protect His people but allowed their enemies to destroy them. "I have forsaken mine house, I have left mine inheritance; I have given the beloved of my soul into the hand of her enemies. Mine heritage is unto me as a lion in the forest; it crieth out against me: therefore have I **hated** it." *(Jeremiah 12:7-8)*

The Lord loved the children of Israel, who were like lions in the forest; they were where they did not belong. The Lord suffered enough of their rebellion and allowed their enemies to destroy them. There are people who profess to love the Lord. They patronize strip clubs, frequent whore houses, and support places that promote Satan's kingdom. They rejoice in Satan's witchcraft and have become enemies of God. The Lord hates them and has given them over to a reprobate mind. *(Romans 1:28)*

———— If You Forsake the Lord, He Will Forsake You ————

Those who forsake the ways of the Lord will be forsaken by the Lord. "The Lord is with you, while ye be with him; and **if** ye seek him, he will be found of you; but **if** ye forsake him, he will forsake you." *(2 Chronicles 15:2)* The Lord hates those who are lifted up with pride. All flesh is weak; all the glory belongs to God. The Lord hates liars. God hates those who breed distrust. God hates those who take innocent lives. God hates those who are constantly imagining ways to hurt other people. God hates those who create conflict among others. "These six things doth **the Lord hate**; yea, seven are an **abomination** (hatred) unto him: A proud look, a lying tongue, and hands that shed innocent blood, an heart that deviseth wicked imaginations, feet that be swift in running to mischief, a false witness that speaketh lies, and he that soweth discord among the brethren." *(Proverbs 6:16-19)*

—————————— **God Hates the Wicked** ——————————

The world is filled with wickedness. A common proverb in the earth is to trust no one. Nearly all agreements must be in writing. Individuals have to lock their vehicles and houses. Extortion and exploitation are common. Murder occurs throughout the day. The false prophets, rather than cry aloud and show the people their transgressions, tell the people that God loves them regardless of the people's rampant wickedness. God hates the wicked, yet the false prophets tell sinners that God loves them regardless of their evil. "The Lord trieth the righteous: but the wicked and him that loveth violence **his soul hateth.**" *(Psalm 11:5)*

—————————— **I Abhorred Them** ——————————

The children of Israel had been corrupted by the Egyptians. As corrupt souls, they could not serve the holy God. They had to be redeemed. Thus, the Lord told them that, as they passed through the land, they should not learn the ways of the barbarians. He hated those who served false gods, which was why He had separated the children of Israel from the other nations and given them their own territory. "Ye shall therefore keep all my statutes, and all my judgments, and do them: that the land, whither I bring you to dwell therein, spue you not out. And ye shall not walk in the manners of the nation, which I cast out before you: for they committed all these things, and therefore **I abhorred** (hated) **them.**" *(Leviticus 20:22-23)*

We are pilgrims and strangers in the earth. If we adopt the ways of the wicked, God will turn and fight against us. He will unleash His plagues also upon us. "God judgeth the righteous, and God is angry with the wicked every day. If he turn not, he will whet his sword; he hath bent his bow, and made it ready. He hath also prepared for him the instruments of death." *(Psalm 7:11-13)* Those who love the world do not love God. *(1 John 2:15-16)* Those who love God must overcome the world to inherit the Kingdom of God. *(Revelation 12:11; Revelation 21:7)* If we seek to save our life of corruption, we will lose our soul.

My Soul Lothed Them

The Lord spoke through the prophet Zechariah and observed that He would have no more pity upon the people of the land. He would not save them from their enemies, but would allow their enemies to destroy them. He would let them die. He hated the people, and they hated Him. "Three shepherds also I cut off in one month; and my soul **lothed** (hated) them, and their soul also **abhorred** (hated) me." *(Zechariah 11:8)*

Those that God Hates Will Fall in the Bottomless Pit

We live in a world filled with lust of the flesh, lust of the eyes, and the pride of life. Satan uses deceived women to promote his kingdom. Such women display their cleavage, wear tight-fitting outfits, paint their nails, color their hair, put on lipstick, and wear makeup to attract attention to their flesh. Satan knows that the lust of the flesh is the enemy of God. *(Romans 8:5-8)* Hence, men who lust after the flesh are enemies of God, and women who pander to men's lust are enemies of God. *(1 John 2:16-17)* In hell, they will lift up their eyes and realized that they chose to make a Faustian bargain with Satan. God hated them. "The mouth of strange women is a deep pit: he that is **abhorred** (hated) **of the Lord** shall fall therein." *(Proverbs 22:14)*

Men and women of the world have an internecine relationship: all that is of the world—the lust of the flesh, the lust of the eyes, and the pride of life—are not of the Father. *(1 John 2:16)* Thus, Satan has most of his female servants exhibiting their flesh to appeal to the lust of men. In return, the men ogle the women and compliment them on their sex appeal, which panders to the women's pride and vanity. Their collusion conceals the fact that they are helping to damn each other's soul. *(Galatians 6:7-8)*

—————————— **We Have Sinned Against Thee** ——————————

The people had been wicked and sinned against God. The cry went out: "Hast thou utterly rejected Judah? hath thy soul **lothed** Zion? . . . Do not **abhor** us . . . break not thy covenant with us." *(Jeremiah 14: 19-21)* When we violate the covenant of God, God will reject us; God will loath (hate) us; God will abhor (hate) us. A covenant is an agreement. God is a jealous God; He will not give His glory to another. When we lie and say that we are His servants, yet serve other gods, we mock Him. The Lord hates deceitful people and will destroy liars. "Thou shalt destroy them that speak leasing: the Lord will **abhor** (hate) the bloody and deceitful man." *(Psalm 5:6)*

—————————— **I Will Love Them No More** ——————————

God's people revolted against Him. The Lord spoke through the prophet Hosea and told the people that He would drive them from His house. The Lord did not love them anymore. He hated the children of Israel. "All their wickedness is in Gilgal: for there **I hated them**: for the wickedness of their doings I will drive them out of mine house, **I will love them no more**: all their princes are revolters." *(Hosea 9:15)* God loved the people, but they revolted against Him. His love turned to hatred. Those who love the world are enemies of God. *(1 John 2:15-16)*

—————————— **Destruction for Those Who Turn Back** ——————————

The apostle Paul made it clear that God did not spare the children of Israel. He saved them out of Egypt. He saved them out of the hands of the Amalekites and their other enemies. However, the people repeatedly provoked the Lord to anger, and the Lord gave them over to their enemies. The Lord turned against those whom He once loved and hated them. God will also turn against us and destroy us if we rebel against Him. "Behold therefore the goodness and severity of God: on them which fell, severity; but toward thee, goodness, **if thou continue** in his goodness: **otherwise thou also shalt be cut off.**" *(Romans 11:22)* Paul made it clear that God's goodness toward the people was conditioned upon whether the people continued to do good. If the people did not continue in God's goodness, they would also be destroyed.

———— There Was No Remedy for God's Wrath ————

From the beginning of time, the Lord has pleaded with the human family. "Hate the evil, and love the good, and establish judgment in the gate: it may be that the Lord God of hosts will be gracious unto the remnant of Joseph." *(Amos 5:15)* He has shown wicked men and women the error of their ways. The people reject the word of the Lord. They rejoice in their wickedness and revel in their sin. They display their nakedness and take pride in their corruption. "The shew of their countenance doth witness against them; and they declare their sin as Sodom, they hide it not. Woe unto their soul! for they have rewarded evil unto themselves." *(Isaiah 3:9)* Licentious individuals flaunt their six-pack abdomens and cleavages as a testimony that they promote the lust of the flesh. They exalt Satan's witchcraft over the Spirit of God. When the messengers of God show them their transgressions, they stone, kill, and/or imprison the prophets of the Lord. They despise God's word. There shall come a day when God will reward them for exalting themselves above Him. "And the Lord God of their fathers sent to them by his messengers, rising up betimes, and sending; because he had compassion on his people, and on his dwelling place. But they mocked the messengers of God, and despised his words, and misused his prophets, until the wrath of the Lord arose against his people, till there was no remedy." *(2 Chronicles 36:15-16)*

----------------------- **Continue in My Love** -----------------------

Jesus told his disciples, "As the father hath loved me, so have I loved you: **continue** ye in my love. **If** ye keep my commandments, ye shall abide in my love; even as I have kept my father's commandments, and abide in his love." *(John 15:9-10)* The Master made it clear that his love was conditional—"If ye keep my commandments, ye shall abide in my love." If we love the Lord, we will keep His commandments and abide in His love. *(John 14:15)* When we disobey God's commandments, we have violated the New Testament and have turned against God. The Lord loves those who obey him—"I love them that love me." *(Proverbs 8:17)* He hates and will destroy those who disobey him—"But he that sinneth against me wrongeth his own soul: all they that hate me love death." *(Proverbs 8:36)* If we do not keep God's commandments, we hate God, and God hates us. *(Psalm 5:5)*

The prophet Malachi warned the people not to allow Satan's messengers to deceive them with such foolishness as "God loves you unconditionally." He told the people, "Ye have wearied the Lord with your words. Yet ye say, Wherein have we wearied him? When ye say, Every one that doeth evil is good in the sight of the Lord, and he delighteth in them; or Where is the God of judgment." *(Malachi 2:17)* The Lord is tired of the lies of the false prophets. The Lord does not love sinners, and He does not delight in their evil. Without sinners, there would be no sin.

----------------------- **We Must Hate Our Own Life** -----------------------

Jesus told Nicodemus that, **except** a man was born again of water and spirit, he could not enter the Kingdom of God. *(John 3:5)* Adam and Eve allowed Satan to bewitch and separate them from the spirit. As natural beings, separated from the spirit, we have been corrupted. God does not love us as natural beings, which is why Adam died. God does not love corruption. The Lord hates every false way. *(Psalm 119:104; Psalm 119:128)* The Lord hates workers of iniquity. *(Psalm 5:5)* God made it clear: we cannot enter His kingdom **except** we are born again. A condition of entering into the Kingdom of God is that we must be born again. We must be redeemed. In other words, God does not love us regardless of our condition. In fact, we cannot love ourselves unconditionally. **"If any man** come to me, and **hate not** his father, and mother, and wife, and children, and brethren, and sisters, yea, and **his own life** also, **he cannot be my disciple.** And whosoever doth not bear his cross, and come after me, cannot be my disciple." *(Luke 14:26-27)* Remember: we have to keep His commandments to abide in His love. *(John 8:31; John 15:10)* God is holy in all His ways. We have to crucify the corruption of our flesh to abide in His love. We have to continue in His word to demonstrate that we are His disciples indeed.

The scripture plainly tells the people that those who engage in the works of the flesh—fornication, adultery, and such things— cannot inherit the Kingdom of God. *(Galatians 5:19-21)* Satan corrupted Adam, and separated him from the Spirit of God. The entire human family died. Satan wants you to believe that God loves you unconditionally, because he knows that corruption cannot inherit incorruption; as sinners, we cannot enter into God's kingdom. "So then they that are in the flesh cannot please God." *(Romans 8:8)* Jesus made it clear that we have to hate our own life and be born again of the spirit. We have to be reconciled with the spirit. We have to obey God's commandments. As children of Satan, separated from the spirit, we are workers of iniquity. *(John 8:34-44)* Just as Adam died because of the wages of sin, we are dead because of the wages of sin. Except we are born again of the spirit, we will not be redeemed from the first death but will be cast into an everlasting lake of fire. *(Revelation 20:14)*

——— **If You Do Wickedly, You Shall Be Destroyed** ———

The prophet Samuel knew that God did not love people unconditionally. He admonished the children of Israel to walk upright before the Lord and to obey his commandments. "**If** ye will fear the Lord, and serve him, and obey his voice, and not rebel against the commandments of the Lord then shall both ye and also the king that reigneth over you continue following the Lord: **But if** ye will not obey the voice of the Lord, but rebel against the commandment of the Lord, then shall the hand of the Lord be against you, as it was against your fathers." *(1 Samuel 12:14-15)* "If ye will fear the Lord, and serve him, and obey his voice" were conditions the people had to satisfy to please God. If the people refused to obey those conditions, God would destroy them, as He did their fathers.

Samuel warned the people, "For the Lord will not forsake his people for his great name's sake: because it hath pleased the Lord to make you his people. Moreover, as for me, God forbid that I should sin against the Lord in ceasing to pray for you: but I will teach you the good and the right way: Only fear the Lord, and serve him in truth with all your heart: for consider how great things he hath done for you. **But if** ye shall still do wickedly, ye shall be consumed, both ye and your king." *(1 Samuel 12:22-25)* The prophet taught the people the good and right way. He wanted the people to fear God and obey Him. God had done great things for them. If they feared the Lord and obeyed Him, God would continue to do great things for them. If the people continued to do wickedly, God would destroy them.

——————— **Ye Are My Friends, If** ———————

Jesus told some Jews that if they continued in His word, they would be made free. They responded that they had never been in bondage. How would Jesus' words make them free? Jesus added that whosoever committed sin was the servant of sin. The

Jews responded that Abraham was their father. Jesus corrected them: if Abraham were their father, they would do the works of Abraham. *(John 8:39)* The people were indeed natural descendants of Abraham; however, their sinful works were the works of Satan. Therefore, since they did not obey the word of God, they were the children of the devil. *(John 8:44)* They were enemies of God. Those who are friends of God obey His commandments. "Ye are my friends, **if** ye do whatsoever I command you." *(John 15:14)* Abraham was a friend of God; he was obedient to God's word. *(James 2:21-24)*

The Lord loved the children of Israel, the descendants of Abraham, Isaac, and Jacob. However, when Ehud died, the people rebelled. Did God love the people unconditionally? The Lord rejected them and sold them into the hand of their enemies. "And the children of Israel again did evil in the sight of the Lord, when Ehud was dead. And the Lord sold them into the hand of Jabin king of Canaan." *(Judges 4:1-2)*

God is slow to anger, but He will not acquit the wicked. "But the mercy of the Lord is from everlasting to everlasting upon them that fear him, and his righteousness unto children's children; To such as keep his covenant, and to those that remember his commandments to do them." *(Psalm 103:17-18)* The Lord did not create us, so that we could rebel against Him; He could have kept Satan in Heaven if He wanted rebellious servants. The Lord did not die for us, so we could serve false gods; He could have allowed us to remain in the bondage of sin. The Lord created and redeemed us to serve Him, and we show our love for Him by keeping His commandments. His mercy and righteousness are for those who keep His commandments.

The prophet Jeremiah observed, "I have seen also in the prophets of Jerusalem an horrible thing: they commit adultery, and walk in lies: they strengthen also the hands of evildoers, that none doth return from his wickedness: they are all of them unto me as Sodom, and the inhabitants thereof as Gomorrah." *(Jeremiah 23:14)* The false prophets pacify sinners by pretending that God loves them unconditionally. This is not the fear of the Lord as written in the scriptures. This is Satan's witchcraft as taught by blind false prophets. Instead of warning the people to turn from their wickedness, Satan's messengers tell people that no evil is going to come upon them—God loves them unconditionally. Satan knows that if the people believe that God loves them unconditionally, then the people will not fear the Lord. Hence, there will be practically no impetus for the people to overcome sin.

Hell

Many false prophets teach their congregants that there will be no hellfire. According to Satan's messengers, God would not put His own children in hell. That is true. God loves His children. *(Malachi 3:17)* God, however, hates Satan's children. *(Psalm 5:5)* Sinners are not children of God; they are children of Satan. *(John 8:44)* Satan and his children are going to burn in fire that shall never be quenched. *(Revelation 20:10; Mark 9:43-44)* Jesus warned the people to beware of false prophets, who would deceive many. Unfortunately, like Eve, such individuals have chosen to believe Satan's lying vanities and distrust Jesus Christ.

"And the woman said unto the serpent, We may eat of the fruit of the trees of the garden: But of the fruit of the tree which is in the midst of the garden, God hath said, Ye shall not eat of it, neither shall ye touch it, lest ye die. And the serpent said unto the woman, Ye shall not surely die." *(Genesis 3:2-3)* Satan told Eve that if she disobeyed, she would not die. In other words, Satan told her to believe him and not God. Satan, through false prophets, has persuaded the people to believe him and not God. God said He hated workers of inquity; false prophets tell the people that God loves them unconditionally. The people believe the false prophets. Jesus has warned sinners that they will be cast into an eternal lake of fire. *(Mark 9:45; Matthew 13:41-50)* Yet, sinners believe the false prophets who tell them that God will not put them in such a fire.

"Ye that love the Lord, hate evil: he preserveth the souls of his saints; he delivereth them out of the hand of the wicked." (Psalm 97:10)

God is Love

God is love. "He that loveth not knoweth not God; for God is love." *(1 John 4:8)* The Lord is indeed merciful, compassionate, kind, and loving. "The Lord trieth the righteous: but the wicked and him that loveth violence **his soul hateth.**" *(Psalm 11:5)* God loved the children of Israel. When they refused to obey Him, He hated them. What did God do after He hated them? He destroyed them. God loved Esau. When Esau despised his birthright, God hated him. What did God do after He hated Esau? He destroyed him. What will happen to the lying false prophets? They shall have their part in the lake that burneth with fire and brimstone. *(Revelation 19:20)* The Lord hates the wicked. *(Psalm 11:5)* What shall happen to the wicked? "Upon the wicked he shall rain snares, fire and brimstone, and an horrible tempest: this shall be the portion of their cup." *(Psalm 11:6)*

God has a spirit of love. God also has an evil spirit. *(1 Samuel 16:14)* God has seven spirits. *(Revelation 4:5)* God is complete. He has whatever spirit is needed to execute righteous judgment. He loves those who obey and hates those who disobey. He will save those who obey and destroy those who disobey. He is a just God and will reward every man according to his works.

Evil is Good

A false prophet told his massive congregation that 99.9% of the people in the world are good people. When the false prophet told such an obvious lie, the audience should have been horrified. The world is filled with wicked people, which is why Jesus stated that only a few would enter the narrow gate that leads to eternal life. According to the false prophet, only a relative few are wicked.

It was clear that the preacher contradicted the words of Jesus, yet the congregation gave him a thunderous ovation. They believed the false prophet more than they believed Jesus Christ.

The Lord was displeased with the people in Sodom and Gomorrah and purposed to destroy them, "because their sin is very grievous." *(Genesis 18:20)* Abraham questioned whether God would destroy everyone in the city: "That be far from thee to do after this manner, to slay the righteous with the wicked: and that the righteous should be as the wicked, that be far from thee: Shall not the Judge of all the earth do right." *(Genesis 18:25)* Abraham knew that God would not destroy innocent people. "But the men of Sodom were wicked and sinners before the Lord exceedingly." *(Genesis 13:13)* The Lord is a just God; He destroyed the cities of Sodom and Gomorrah. Yet He saved the few souls who obeyed his command to separate themselves. If 99.9% of the people were good, the gate that leads to eternal life would not be narrow.

The same false prophet told his congregation that God loves Muslims just as much as He loves Christians, and He loves atheists just as much as He loves believers. "The eyes of the Lord are upon the righteous, and his ears are open unto their cry. The face of the Lord is against them that do evil, to cut off the remembrance of them from the earth." *(Psalm 34:15-16)* The Lord does not love sinners, unbelievers, or those who worship false gods; sinners, unbelievers, and pagan worshippers are going to burn in an everlasting lake of fire. *(Revelation 21:8)* God loves the way of righteousness, and He hates every false way. *(Proverbs 12:28; Psalm 119:128)* Those who sin against God love death; they destroy their own soul. *(Proverbs 8:36)*

The scripture is replete with example after example where God saved those who served him and destroyed those who rebelled. Nonetheless, despite the false prophets' reprehensible lie, the audience gave him another thunderous ovation. The Lord is not a respecter of persons. He will save the Jew or the Gentile; He will save all who obey His commandments. He will destroy all who do not. *(Acts 10:34-35)*

Will Not Give His Glory to Another

Just as God loved Jacob and hated Esau, God loves those who exalt Him above themselves and hates those who exalt themselves above Him. When we exalt our frail, weak, dying bodies above His everlasting power and spirit, we have chosen to worship false gods. It is complete idiocy for weak humans to exalt Satan and themselves above the Almighty God, and expect God to love them. God, holy in all His ways, hates every false way. The Lord hated Satan, which is why He cast Satan out of His kingdom and will destroy him. The Lord hated Esau, who exalted a little hunger over God's blessings. The Lord hates all workers of iniquity, those who exalt themselves above Him and rebel against His commandments.

Keep His Word

God loves us when we love Him. "Jesus answered and said unto him, if a man love me, he will keep my words: and my Father will love him, and we will come unto him, and make our abode with him." *(John 14:23)* If we want God to love us, we have to obey His word and keep His word. If we refuse to obey His commandments, it is because we have the same disobedient spirit as Satan and refuse to exalt the Lord above ourselves.

Those who refuse to serve the Lord are like Esau, who renounced his spiritual birthright to please his flesh. God hated Esau. The Lord observed that Esau could build, but He was going to tear it down. *(Malachi 1:3-4)* God destroyed Esau. *(Obadiah 1:18)* We can be like Esau and despise our birthright. We can reject the word of God and remain in the bondage of sin. God will destroy us, too. *(Hosea 4:6)*

Holy in All His Ways

Let me be clear for those who pretend that God is all love and goodness. The Lord told Saul to kill all the Amalekites: men, women, children, babies, and animals. The Lord commanded the slaughter of newborn babies and dumb animals. *(1 Samuel 15:3)* What evil had they done? The people of Nineveh had wisdom. When Jonah told them to turn from their wickedness, men, women, children, babies, and animals refrained from water and food. The people knew that God was going to destroy everything associated with wickedness. "The face of the Lord is against them that do evil, to cut off the remembrance of them from the earth." *(Psalm 34: 16)*

God made sure that those who had the right to inherit the natural Promised Land—His chosen people—spend 400 years in slavery. Keep in mind, the children of Esau were not entitled to inherit the Promised Land—all of them had already been destroyed. *(Obadiah 1:18)* The Lord put a lying spirit in the mouth of Ahab's prophets to induce the king to get killed. *(1 Kings 22:22; 2 Chronicles 18:21)* The Lord sends strong delusions to those who are determined to believe a lie. *(2 Thessalonians 2:11)* The Lord allows men and women to be raped, beaten, and killed every second of the day. The Lord is love, but He also has an evil spirit. *(1 Samuel 18:10)* He is a complete God and is able to faithfully execute judgment upon those whom He loves and hates. Vengeance is mine, saith the Lord, I will repay. *(Romans 12:19)*

God is not some namby-pamby fictitious Santa Claus who has nothing but joy and love for everyone. He is not some God that comports with humans' idea of how a God should conduct himself. Abraham slaughtered some kings. How did God feel about Abraham killing those men? He brought forth bread and wine, and He and Abraham celebrated. *(Genesis 14:18)* Melchizedek was God. *(Hebrews 7:1)* God's blessing passed down from Abraham, Isaac, and Jacob to Judah. How did God describe Judah's blessing? He rejoiced—Judah's hands were going to be in the neck of his enemies; his eyes would be red with wine; his teeth would be white with milk. *(Genesis 49:8-12)* David was a man after God's own heart. How did God bless David? "Thou hast given me the necks of mine enemies; that I might destroy them that hate me. They cried, but there was none to save them: even unto the Lord, but he answered them not. Then did I beat them small as the dust before the wind: I did cast them out as the dirt in the street." *(Psalm 18:40-42)* Jesus went to Jerusalem to celebrate the Passover. How did He celebrate? He allowed the Romans to hammer iron spikes into His hand and feet. How did God feel about the Romans' abuse of Jesus? It pleased the Lord to make Jesus suffer. *(Isaiah 53:10)*

God, the defender of integrity, is the King of righteousness. He is holy in all His works. *(Psalm 145:17)* Satan is an evil spirit, who was willing to rise up against holiness and righteousness. If Satan had prevailed, as he has in the earth, he would have tormented God throughout eternity. God is going to torment Satan (and his followers) throughout eternity. Sinners are those who engage in wickedness when the truth will not allow them to have their way. As humans, we have to admit that Satan, our slavemaster, has corrupted us and perverted our thinking. We exploit others to promote ourselves. We must become like the contrite thief on the cross and consent to the death of sin in our lives. We cannot expect the defender of integrity to save our evil souls from death. We must take up our cross and crucify the wickedness within us and be thankful that Jesus is Lord and not Satan.

The devil knows the wrath of God to come. If people knew the wrath of God to come, they would turn from their wickedness and obey all of God's commandments. *(Luke 16:19-31)* The people are so vain, however, until some actually believe such nonsense as God loves them unconditionally. People who have fallen for Satan's witchcraft and believe God loves them unconditionally are like the apocryphal rooster who thought the sun came up to hear him crow. They are deluded. He is the Almighty! God does not exalt anyone above Himself. He did not create us, so He could serve us; He created us, so we could serve Him. *(Isaiah 43:7; Romans 1:25)*

Satan, through the false prophets, has caricatured God. The Holy One of Israel has been transmogrified from the defender of holiness to the preserver of wickedness. Yet, God hates every false way. *(Psalm 119:104; Psalm 119:128)* He cast Satan out of Heaven because Satan refused to obey. God cast Adam and Eve out of the garden because they refused to obey. God dethroned Saul because the king failed to obey. "For thou art not a God that hath pleasure in wickedness: neither shall evil dwell with thee." *(Psalm 5:4)* False prophets have deceived you: God does not love you unconditionally. God will tell sinners to depart from Him and cast them into an eternal lake of fire. *(Luke 13:27-28)* If you want God to love you, keep His commandments. *(1 John 5:3)*

——————— Additional Edifying Scriptures ———————

"Thus saith the Lord of hosts, the God of Israel; behold I will bring upon this city and upon all her towns all the evil that I have pronounced against it, because they have hardened their necks, that they might not hear my words." (Jeremiah 19:15)

"The way of the wicked is an abomination to the Lord: but he loveth him that followeth after righteousness." (Proverbs 15:9)

"But thou hast utterly rejected us; thou art very wroth against us." (Lamentations 5:)

"My flesh trembleth for fear of thee; and I am afraid of thy judgments." (Psalm 119:120)

"And I prayed unto the Lord my God, and made my confession, and said, O Lord, the great and dreadful God, keeping the covenant and mercy to them that love him, and to them that keep his commandments;" (Daniel 9:4)

"Therefore hath the Lord watched upon the evil, and brought it upon us: for the Lord our God is righteous in all his works which he doeth: for we obeyed not his voice." (Daniel 9:14)

"Go, enquire of the Lord for me, and for them that are left in Israel and in Judah, concerning the words of the book that is found: for great is the wrath of the Lord that is poured out upon us, because our fathers have not kept the word of the Lord, to do all that is written in this book." (2 Chronicles 34:21)

"But ye, beloved, building up yourselves on your most holy faith, praying in the Holy Ghost, keep yourselves in the love of God, looking for the mercy of our Lord Jesus Christ unto eternal life." (Jude 1:20-21)

"For thus saith the Lord God; behold, I will deliver thee into the hand of them whom thou hatest, into the hand of them from whom thy mind is alienated. And they shall deal with thee hatefully, and shall take away all thy labour, and shall leave thee naked and bare: and the nakedness of thy whoredoms shall be discovered, both thy lewdness and thy whoredoms. I will do these things unto thee, because thou hast gone a whoring after the heathen, and because thou art polluted with their idols." (Ezekiel 23:28-30)

"Surely thou wilt slay the wicked, O God: depart from me therefore, ye bloody men. For they speak against thee wickedly, and thine enemies take thy name in vain. Do not I hate them, O Lord, that hate thee? and am I not grieved with those that rise up against thee? I hate them with perfect hatred: I count them mine enemies." (Psalm 139:19-22)

"I hate and abhor lying: but thy law do I love." (Psalm 119:163)

"Thou lovest righteousness, and hatest wickedness: therefore God, thy God, hath anointed thee with the oil of gladness above thy fellows." (Psalm 45:7)

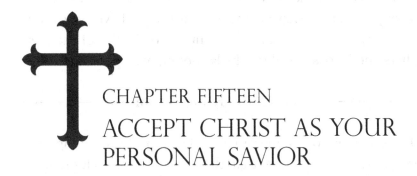

CHAPTER FIFTEEN

ACCEPT CHRIST AS YOUR PERSONAL SAVIOR

False prophets have taught the people to accept Jesus Christ as their personal savior. It sounds humbling when a man says that he accepts Christ as his personal savior. The implication is that the sinner has disobeyed God and acknowledges that he needs forgiveness. If Jesus had not died for his sins, the contrite soul implies, he would be lost. That is true. However, if the speaker walked in the light as Christ is in the light, he would know that Christ cannot be anyone's personal savior. This lying vanity is another trick of the devil.

Satan, the most subtle beast of the field, is highly intelligent. When God sent famine into the land for truth, everyone was taken into captivity. Without the knowledge of Jesus Christ, everyone would remain corrupt and be destroyed. Thank the Lord we are able to catch the devil in his craftiness. *(Ephesians 4:14)*

It will be easy to understand why Satan wants you to believe this lying vanity if you keep these words in remembrance: (1) the people were taken into captivity and corrupted by the lack of knowledge *(Isaiah 5:13)*; (2) the people can escape the pollution of this world through the knowledge of Jesus Christ *(2 Peter 2:20)*; and (3) the people are going to be destroyed by the lack of knowledge. *(Hosea 4:6)* Satan, to succeed in damning our souls, must divert our attention from false prophets and cause us to reject the knowledge of Jesus Christ. Satan knows that Jesus has returned to Heaven and does not personally teach anyone. Hence, if we believe Jesus is our personal savior, we will not pay attention to the lies of the false prophets and be destroyed for the lack of knowledge.

Jesus Is Our Lord and Savior

There is none other name under Heaven given among men where we can be saved, other than the name of the Lord Jesus. *(Acts 4:12)* Jesus, our redeemer, died for the sins of the people. *(John 1:29)* The prophet Isaiah wrote, "I, even I, am the Lord; and beside me there is no saviour." *(Isaiah 43:11)* Jesus is Lord. *(Acts 9:5)* Jesus is indeed the King of kings and the Lord of lords. As a result of Jesus' death on the cross, all humans have the right to be resurrected from the grave of sin. *(1 Corinthians 15:22; Job 33:27-28)*

Personal

According to Webster's dictionary, "personal" means "done in person without the intervention of another" or "carried on between individuals directly." Jesus is a spirit. In Adam all died. Hence, we are humans. The people have never seen Jesus or heard His voice. *(John 5:37)* The people are destroyed by the lack of knowledge, and Jesus is not in the earth in a physical body to personally teach the people.

The Master (Teacher) opened His disciples' (students') understanding and told them to go and teach all nations. *(Luke 24:45; Matthew 28:19)* The Master told Peter to feed His lamb, to feed His sheep. *(John 21:15-17)* Jesus delegated the teaching of the gospel to His disciples. The Master would later send Paul as His ambassador to the Gentiles. *(2 Corinthians 5:20)* Paul had the duty to turn the people from darkness to light. *(Acts 26:18)* Paul, instead of Christ, taught us how to overcome Satan's witchcraft.

Corruption cannot inherit incorruption—and we were conceived in corruption. *(1 Corinthians 15:50; Psalm 51:5)* In order to be saved from the wrath of God and to inherit eternal life, we have to be redeemed from corruption. How did the people become corrupt? Our enemies overtook us. Ignorant priests taught us their vomit and filthiness. *(Isaiah 28:7-8)* We went into the captivity of sin because of the lack of knowledge. *(Isaiah 5:13)* Why was there a lack of knowledge? God sent famine of His word into the land. *(Amos 8:11)* The people could not learn the word of God; they had to eat the vomit of the heathens. Jesus died for the sins of the people, because He caused the people to go into the captivity of sin. He allowed the heathens to overtake and corrupt us. During the time of our ignorance, Jesus winked. *(Acts 17:30)* He subsequently came into the earth and taught the people how to overcome. Now that Jesus has come and taught us, we have no excuse to remain polluted. *(John 15:22; 2 Peter 2:20)*

God winked at our ignorance but now commands us to obey. We cannot obey the commandments of God and serve Him, if we remain corrupt. Remember: God was in Christ reconciling the world unto Himself. All of His ways are holy, and we have learned the ways of the heathens. In order to serve the Lord, we must be delivered out of the hands of our enemies and redeemed from corruption. Jesus came to set us free from the sin of witchcraft (spiritual lies) and to reconcile us with the Father. Jesus came to redeem us, to sanctify us through the truth. Jesus came to turn everyone—like Abraham, Ruth, Cornelius, and others who had been deceived—from darkness to light, from the power of Satan to God. Since He died and went back to spirit, who will teach us of His ways, so we can overcome corruption? His apostles will teach us of His ways. *(Matthew 28:19)* They will feed us. *(John 21:17)* We can overcome corruption "by the word of {the apostles'} testimony." *(Revelation 12:11)*

What Shall We Do?

On the day of Pentecost, after the disciples in the upper room were filled with the Holy Ghost, there were individuals who thought the disciples were drunk. Peter explained that they were not drunk but had been filled with the Holy Ghost. He explained that the unbelievers had wrongfully crucified Jesus but God had made that same Jesus both Lord and Christ. "Now when they heard this, they were pricked in their heart, and said unto Peter and to the rest of the apostles, Men and brethren, what shall we do? Then Peter said unto them, Repent, and be baptized every one of you in the name of Jesus Christ for the remission of sins, and ye shall receive the gift of the Holy Ghost." *(Acts 2:37-38)* The apostle Peter, having been personally taught by the Master, told the people what they needed to do to be saved. Peter did not tell the people to bow their head and accept Christ as their personal savior. The apostle knew, "Except a man be born of water and of the Spirit, he cannot enter into the kingdom of God." *(John 3:5)* Peter had understanding and taught the people in accordance with Jesus' instructions.

Moreover, the people were not saved because they had been baptized in water or because they had received the Holy Ghost. The new birth was just the beginning. They had to change their entire nature and move on to perfection. *(Hebrews 6:1)* They had to be redeemed from corruption. How would the people escape the pollution of this world if the Master was not around to teach them? The apostles testified to the Master's teachings. *(Revelation 12:11)* Jesus had opened the understanding of His apostles and commanded them to teach all nations. *(Matthew 28:19)* Those who wanted to save themselves from sin and escape the pollution of this world needed the knowledge of Jesus Christ—and Jesus sent apostles to teach all nations. Those who believed "continued stedfastly in the apostles' doctrine." *(Acts 2:42)*

No human today has been personally taught by Jesus Christ. The Master shed His natural life circa 2,000 years ago and went back to spirit. However, Jesus personally taught Peter; Jesus personally gave Peter the keys to the kingdom; and Jesus personally washed Peter's feet. Yet, Jesus did not personally save Peter. When Jesus left the earth and ascended on high, neither Peter nor Mary, the mother of Jesus, could inherit the Kingdom of God. They did not receive the Holy Ghost, one of the requirements to enter the Kingdom of God, until the day of Pentecost. *(Acts 1:13-14; Acts 2:4)* The Holy Ghost could not come until Jesus left. *(John 16:7)* If they had not subsequently received the Holy Ghost, they could not enter the Kingdom of God. *(John 3:5)*

Remember: God entered into a New Testament with the human family. *(Luke 22:20)* Jesus came and ransomed the people from the grave of sin. *(Hosea 13:14; Hebrews 2:14-15)* He drank out of the cup of sacrifice, and He commanded us to drink out of the cup of sacrifice. *(John 18:11; Matthew 26:27-28)* He shed His blood, and He commanded us to take up our cross and shed our blood. *(Matthew 16:21-25)* He was obedient unto death, even the death of the cross; and we love not our lives even unto death. *(Philippians 2:8; Revelation 12:11; 1 Corinthians 10:21)* We had gone into captivity because of the lack of knowledge, and, without the lack of knowledge, we would be destroyed. *(Isaiah 5:13; Hosea 4:6)* God did not want anyone destroyed. *(John 3:16)* Thus, Jesus came to teach us of His ways, so that we could come out of captivity and walk in His path. *(Isaiah 2:2-3)* We can overcome ignorance today and be saved from sin through the apostles' testimony. *(Revelation 12:11)*

Cornelius

There was a devout man in Caesarea named Cornelius, who made great sacrifices and entreated God to help him. As a Roman officer, Cornelius had been taught pagan worship and, despite his noble deeds, was lost and on his way to destruction. God perceived Cornelius' sincere desire to live right and had mercy upon him. God, through an angel, told Cornelius to send to Joppa, for Simon Peter, "He shall tell thee what thou oughtest to do." *(Acts 10:6)*

Jesus did not personally save Cornelius, nor did the angel personally save Cornelius; Jesus sent the angel to tell Cornelius to send for Peter, who personally told Cornelius how to be saved. Jesus delegated responsibility to Peter to teach Cornelius how to be saved. "And he shewed us how he had seen an angel in his house, which stood and said unto him, Send men to Joppa, and call for Simon, whose surname is Peter; Who shall tell thee words, whereby thou and all thy house shall be saved." *(Acts 11:14)* Although Peter personally told Cornelius how to be saved, Peter could not personally save him. He taught Cornelius "words, whereby thou and all thy house shall be saved." Cornelius was a pious man but not a holy man. He was a barbarian. If he wanted to be saved from destruction, he needed to know the truth. Peter taught Cornelius and his house how to be saved; it was up to them whether they obeyed the instructions. They had to save themselves. *(Acts 2:40)*

Peter knew that "saved" meant "delivered." To be saved means that God has delivered an individual out of the hands of the enemy. "And the Lord shall help them, and deliver them: he shall deliver them from the wicked, and save them, because they trust in him." *(Psalm 37:40)* "And it shall come to pass, that whosoever shall call on the name of the Lord shall be delivered." *(Joel 2:32)* "For whosoever shall upon the name of the Lord shall be saved." *(Romans 10:13)* Those who have the Spirit of Jesus Christ understand prophecy. To be saved means to be delivered out of the hands of your enemy. In the days of Moses, to be saved meant that God had delivered the people out of the bondage of Egypt. *(Exodus 14:30)* In contemporary terms, to be saved means that God has delivered the people out of the bondage of sin. *(Matthew 1:21)* We are saved from sin when disciples (students) acquire the discipline (knowledge) of the Master (teacher) and follow His example (take up our cross and follow Christ).

For example, God set the children of Israel free from the bondage of Egypt. He allowed the people to choose for themselves life and death. *(Deuteronomy 30:15-16)* God destroyed those who wanted to return to death in Egypt; and He saved those who wanted a new life in the Promised Land. Similarly, Jesus has set us free from the power of Satan and allowed each of us to choose whether we want to serve the Lord or Satan. Those who choose to remain in the bondage of sin will be destroyed. Those who want to serve the Lord will be redeemed from the grave and given a new life. *(Joel 2:27-28)*

Jesus taught Peter; hence, Peter had the knowledge of Jesus Christ, which is why the angel told Cornelius to send for Peter. It was Peter's responsibility to feed the lamb, to feed the sheep; it was Peter's duty to teach the people and impart the knowledge of salvation. *(John 21:17)* Peter taught Cornelius what he "oughtest to do" to save himself. *(Acts 10:6)* Jesus was not going to personally save Cornelius. Jesus told Cornelius whom to send for (Simon Peter), and Peter told Cornelius what he needed to do to save himself. Cornelius had the choice whether to save or destroy himself.

Turn from Darkness to Light

Saul of Tarsus fought against the church. Jesus called Saul and told him to stop persecuting His people. After Saul humbled himself, the Lord told Saul (Apostle Paul) that He was going to send him to the Gentiles: "To open their eyes, and to turn them from darkness to light, and from the power of Satan unto God, that they may receive forgiveness of sins, and inheritance among them which are sanctified by faith that is in me." *(Acts 26:18)*

It was Paul's duty to turn the people from darkness to light, from Satan's witchcraft to God's deliverance, that the people "may receive forgiveness of sin, and inheritance among them which are sanctified." Jesus did not turn the people from Satan; He delegated the responsibility to Paul to teach the people and set them free from sin. Although Jesus had shed His blood, the people were still in darkness and subordinated to the power of Satan. They could not inherit eternal life because they remained corrupt. Only the truth could set the people free—and Jesus sent Paul to open the eyes of the Gentiles and lead them out of ignorance and captivity.

If the people wanted to receive forgiveness of sins and inherit the Kingdom of God, they had to open their eyes and turn from darkness to light. Forgiveness comes after we have forsaken our wickedness and returned unto the Lord. *(Isaiah 55:7)* We must turn

304 | ELVIS CARDELL BANKS

from Satan to God. We cannot choose Satan as our god and expect the Almighty to forgive us for exalting a false god above Him, and exalting witchcraft above truth.

Save Yourself

If the Good Shepherd were our personal savior, there would have been no need for Him to warn us to beware of wolves in sheep's clothings; He would personally save us from them. If the Good Shepherd were our personal savior, He would not have commanded the apostles to feed His sheep and to teach all nations. He would personally teach us. If Satan can persuade someone that Christ is his personal savior, the deceived will fail to take heed to the lies of the false prophets and be destroyed. We save ourselves by obeying the apostles' doctrine. *(Acts 2:40-42)*

Covenant by Sacrifice

There is a major difference between Jesus as our savior and Jesus as our personal savior. God has entered into a covenant with mankind. He has done His part; now we must do ours. We must save ourselves. *(Acts 2:40)* He shed His blood, so that we might receive the remission of sin. *(Hebrews 9:22)* We must turn from our wickedness and obey His commandments. In other words, Jesus went into the grave to ransom us from the grave. He sacrificed His natural life to redeem our right to a spiritual life (He offered us forgiveness of sin), and we sacrifice our natural life (we turn from wickedness to righteousness) to redeem our spiritual inheritance.

As we learned from Saul of Tarsus, it is not enough to want to worship the Lord. There are many spiritual-minded people who are fighting against God. *(John 16:2; Acts 9:5; 1 Timothy 1:13)* We must worship the Lord in spirit and in truth. Satan, the most subtle beast of the field, is an old serpent. *(Genesis 3:1)* He has been deceiving people for thousands of years. *(Revelation 12:9)* In order to overcome that deceiver, we must be as wise as serpents. *(Matthew 10:16)* Jesus, the all-wise God, will teach us how to overcome. He has the knowledge that will help us see through Satan's witchcraft. Yet, Jesus is not in the earth to teach us. His life was taken from the earth, and He had to return to where He came from. *(Acts 8:33)* Who will teach the people? Jesus opened the apostles' understanding and commanded them to teach the people. *(Luke 24:45; Matthew 28:19)* We overcome Satan through the words of the apostles' testimonies. *(Revelation 12:11)*

———————— **Destroyed by the Lack of Knowledge** ————————

God tells us plainly that the people are destroyed by the lack of knowledge. *(Hosea 4:6)* Unless we have the knowledge of Jesus Christ, all of us will be destroyed. Who has the knowledge of Jesus Christ? "And I will give you pastors according to mine heart, which shall feed you with knowledge and understanding." *(Jeremiah 3:15)* "For the priest's lips should keep knowledge, and they should seek the law at his mouth: for he is the messenger of the Lord of hosts." *(Malachi 2:7)* If the pastors and priests do not have the correct knowledge, we are going to be destroyed for the lack of knowledge. Hence, Satan wants you to believe that Jesus is your personal savior, so his false teachers can keep you separated from the way of truth.

———————— **Satan Deceived the Whole World** ————————

The people can only call upon the Lord, if they believe in the Lord. The people cannot believe in the Lord, unless they hear from the Lord. The people can only hear from the Lord through his preacher. *(Romans 10:14)* The apostles were required to preach the word of faith. *(Romans 10:8)* In teaching sinners that Christ is their personal savior, Satan knows that fewer people will question false teaching or turn from wickedness. "And the great dragon was cast out, that old serpent, called the Devil, and Satan, which deceiveth the whole world; he was cast out into the earth, and his angels were cast out with him." *(Revelation 12:9)* The people will confess that Jesus is Lord and believe in their hearts that He died for their sins. As a result of the false prophets' lies, they will say they are saved by the grace of God, and not by works; therefore, they will continue to engage in the works of the flesh. *(Galatians 5:19:21)* Since the wages of sin is death, workers of iniquity will be destroyed. *(Romans 6:23; Matthew 7:23; Luke 13:27; Psalm 5:5)*

Keys to the Kingdom

Jesus told His disciples that it was needful that He went away. If He did not leave, the Holy Ghost could not come. *(John 16:7)* Jesus did not stay in the earth to personally save anyone. "In his humiliation his judgment was taken away: and who shall declare his generation? for his life is taken from the earth." *(Acts 8:33)* Jesus' natural life was taken away. He went back to spirit. The Lord gave Peter the keys to the Kingdom of God and observed that whosoever Peter loosed on earth would be loosed in Heaven, and whosoever Peter bound on earth would be bound in Heaven. *(Matthew 16:19)* Jesus needed earthen vessels to teach the people on the earth. *(2 Corinthians 4:5-7)* Jesus needed natural messengers to communicate His message to natural people.

How Can They Hear Without a Preacher?

Life is filled with danger, and people are in bondage because of fear of death. In writing to the Romans, the apostle Paul made it clear that whosoever that called upon the name of the Lord would be saved. *(Romans 10:13)* Paul added that the people would not call on the Lord, unless they believed He would deliver them. The apostle asked, "How shall they believe in him of whom they have not heard?" *(Romans 10:14)* The people had never heard God. How could they trust God to save them, if they did not know whether God was able to save them? God sends preachers to teach the people. "So then faith cometh by hearing, and hearing by the word of God." *(Romans 10:17)* How do we hear the word of God, so we can have faith? "The word of faith, which we preach." *(Romans 10:8)* Our faith in God is based upon the apostles' teachings.

Paul made it clear that the people had not heard the voice of God, which is exactly what Jesus told the people. We have never seen God's shape or heard His voice. *(John 5:37)* We need the truth to overcome corruption. We need the knowledge to escape the pollution of this world. Without the knowledge of Jesus Christ, we are going to be destroyed. Yet Jesus is not going to personally teach us. He sends preachers to teach the people. *(Romans 10:14)* We hear from God through preachers, which is why Jesus warned the people to beware of false prophets. He is not going to personally save us. He has sent His word. We must pay earnest heed to what preachers are teaching. If we disregard what the preachers are telling us, we will allow them to deceive us—and, of course, most people will be deceived. *(Matthew 24:11; Matthew 7:13)*

"Men and brethren, children of the stock of Abraham, and whosoever among you feareth God, to you is the word of this salvation sent." (Acts 13:26)

My Sheep Hear My Voice

Jesus observed, "My sheep hear my voice, and I know them, and they follow me." *(John 10:27)* Jesus told His disciples, "He that heareth you heareth me." *(Luke 10:16)* Jesus is a spirit and does not preach to the people. God sent an angel, who told Cornelius to send for Peter, who had previously assured Jesus that he would feed His sheep and feed His lamb. *(John 21:15-17)* Honest souls who want to know the truth of God will seek the priest. "For the priest's lips should keep knowledge, and they should seek the law at his mouth: for he is the messenger of the Lord of host." *(Malachi 2:7)* God sends priests to deliver His message of salvation.

—————————— **Neither Pray I for These Alone** ——————————

Everything we have read or heard about God and Jesus Christ is hearsay—information that has been taught based upon what someone else spoke or wrote. If the messenger is a liar, we cannot trust the message. We need the truth to be delivered from sin, which is why Jesus prayed, "Neither pray I for these alone, but for them also which shall believe on me through their word." *(John 17:20)* Matthew, Mark, Luke, and John wrote the gospel of Jesus Christ. Paul wrote much of the New Testament. When we understand that Jesus is not here to personally teach us, we will take earnest heed to the things we have heard, lest at any time we should let them slip. *(Hebrews 2:1)* If we pay close attention to the preachers' words, we will soon discover that most of them are found to be liars— remember, narrow is the gate and straight is the way that leads to eternal life, and only a few will find it. *(Matthew 7:14)*

—————————— **Ambassadors for Christ** ——————————

The apostle Paul wrote to the church in Corinth. "Now then we are ambassadors for Christ, as though God did beseech you by us: we pray you in Christ's stead, be ye reconciled to God." *(2 Corinthians 5:20)* He told them that he was an ambassador for Christ. An ambassador is an individual who has been authorized to speak on behalf of another; he is a messenger or envoy. The apostle added that he was in Christ's stead, which simply connotes that Christ had sent him to teach the people on His behalf—"unto whom now I send thee." *(Acts 26:17)* God commanded His apostles to teach the people, and we are going to be judged by the teachings of the apostles. *(Galatians 1:8)*

—————————— **Joseph Saved the Hebrews from Starvation** ——————————

Joseph's brothers envied him and sold him into bondage. Joseph was taken into Egypt and imprisoned. He ultimately reconciled with and forgave his brothers. He explained: "But as for you, ye thought evil against me; but God meant it unto good, to bring to pass, as it is this day, to save much people alive." *(Genesis 50:20)* When famine covered Egypt and Canaan, God had positioned Joseph to interpret the king's dream. Joseph's interpretations allowed the king to store food "to save much people alive." God used Joseph to ensure that the people had food during the natural famine; God uses servants to ensure that the people have food during spiritual famine.

Receive Him Not Into Your House

The disciples who followed Peter and the other apostles continued steadfastly in the apostles' doctrine. *(Acts 2:42)* Unlike the foolish Galatians, they did not allow false prophets to manipulate them to depart from the word of God. "Whosoever transgresseth, and abideth not in the doctrine of Christ, hath not God. He that abideth in the doctrine of Christ, he hath both the Father and the Son. If there come any unto you, and bring not this doctrine, receive him not into your house, neither bid him God speed: For he that biddeth him God speed is partaker of his evil deeds." *(2 John 1: 9-11)* John made it clear to the people that God would only be with those who abided in the doctrine of Christ. Jesus opened the apostles' understanding, and the apostles taught the doctrine of Christ. Those who take heed and continue in the apostles' doctrine "shalt both save thyself, and them that hear thee." *(1 Timothy 4:16)* Jesus did not personally save them. He sent the apostles to teach us His knowledge of salvation—"Teaching them to observe all things whatsoever I have commanded you." *(Matthew 28:20)*

Jesus instructed His apostles how to overcome Satan's witchcraft, and the apostles communicated the gospel unto us. Those who want to be delivered from sin must observe all that Jesus has commanded. Obedience to the doctrine of Christ (apostles' doctrine) determines whether we are holy or unholy. Cornelius was a pious man but corrupt; Mohandas Gandhi was a pious man but corrupt; Socrates was a pious man but corrupt. They were men of faith, but they were not holy men. They may have had faith in their false gods and believed in living holy, but they could not live holy without the holy word of God. There is only one faith: the apostles' doctrine. *(Ephesians 4:5; Galatians 1:8)* We must believe upon Christ according to what is written in the scriptures. *(John 7:38)*

— I Have Sent Mine Angels . . . To Testify In the Churches —

Jesus sent His angels in the churches to testify: "Blessed are they that do his commandments, that they may have right to the tree of life, and may enter in through the gates into the city. For without are dogs, and sorcerers, and whoremongers, and murderers, and idolaters, and whosoever loveth and maketh a lie. I Jesus have sent mine angel to testify unto you these things in the churches. I am the root and the offspring of David, and the bright and morning star." *(Revelation 22:14-16)* His angels are the apostles, prophets, teachers, and others. Jesus did not come to personally tell us what His commandments were. He sent others to testify of His words, which is why we are able to overcome "through the words of their testimony." *(Revelation 12:11)*

—————— Confirmeth Words of His Servants ——————

The prophecy in the old time came not by the will of men, but holy men of God spake as they were moved by the Holy Ghost. *(2 Peter 1:21)* God speaks to His messengers and send them to the people. The Lord "confirmeth the word of his servant, and performeth the counsel of his messengers; that saith to Jerusalem, Thou shall be inhabited; and to the cities of Judah, Ye shall be built, and I will raise up the decayed places thereof." *(Isaiah 44:26)* The Lord does not want His people to perish and admonishes them to observe whether the words of the preachers are true. If the prophet prophecy something, and it does not come to pass, God has not spoken by that prophet. *(Deuteronomy 18:22)* If the preachers utter lies against the Lord and walk in darkness, they have not been sent by God. *(Proverbs 14:5)*

Most people, like the Galatians, have been taught foolishness. The deceived false prophets have perverted the scriptures. The people, however, do not know that the preachers are deceived; hence, the blind follows the blind. Peter warned the people not to allow deceived false teachers to lead them to destruction. The apostle Peter reaffirmed the teachings of Paul. "As also {Paul} in all his epistles, speaking in them of these things; in which are some things are hard to be understood, which they that are unlearned and unstable wrest, as they do also the other scriptures, unto their own destruction. Ye therefore, beloved, seeing ye know these things before, beware lest ye also, being led away with the error of the wicked, fall from your own stedfastness." *(2 Peter 3:16-17)* God has given many commandments. Those who follow false prophets will disobey God's commandments and be destroyed.

Lord, Let it Alone

Many times, prophets, such as Moses, had to calm God down. The Lord would become so enraged, until He was ready to destroy the people. *(Psalm 106:23)* The prophet would have to ask the Lord to destroy him if He was going to destroy the people. *(Exodus 32:32)* "And I sought for a man among them, that should make up the hedge, and stand in the gap before me for the land, that I should not destroy it: but I found none. Therefore have I poured out mine indignation upon them; I have consumed them with the fire of my wrath: their own way have I recompensed upon their heads, saith the Lord." *(Ezekiel 22:30-31)* The prophets often saved the people from God's wrath.

"He spake also this parable; A certain man had a fig tree planted in his vineyard; and he came and sought fruit thereon, and found none. Then said he unto the dresser of his vineyard, Behold, these three years I come seeking fruit on this fig tree, and find none: cut it down; why cumbereth it the ground? And he answering said unto him, Lord, let it alone this year also, till I shall dig about it, and dung it: And if it bear fruit, well: and if not, then after that thou shalt cut it down." *(Luke 13:6-9)* The prophet asked the Lord to give him more time to work with the people. The preacher was responsible for feeding the sheep and teaching the people. If the people continued to disobey, the prophet would step back and allow God to execute His wrath.

Before I Formed Thee, I Knew Thee

The prophet Jeremiah denoted that God had chosen him before he was born. Why did the Lord ordain him a prophet? The Lord wanted him to show the people their transgression, encourage the people to serve the Lord, and build the people up. "Before I formed thee in the belly I knew thee; and before thou camest forth out of the womb I sanctified thee, and I ordained thee a prophet unto the nations . . . for thou shalt go to all that I shall send thee, and whatsoever I command thee thou shalt speak." *(Jeremiah 1:5-7)* "Then the Lord put forth his hand, and touched my mouth. And the Lord said unto me, Behold, I have put my words in thy mouth. See, I have this day set thee over the nations and over the kingdoms, to root out, and to pull down, and to destroy, and to throw down, to build, and to plant." *(Jeremiah 1:9-10)*

The Lord put His words in Jeremiah's mouth and set the prophet over the nations and over the kingdoms to build and destroy. It is the messengers' job to do the Lord's work in the earth. God sends them to tell the people: "Thus saith the Lord . . ."

The Word of the Lord is With Him

When people are in trouble and need help from the Lord, they communicate with the man of God. The man of God communicates with God. Jehoshaphat and two other kings were on their way to fight the king of Moab. As they traveled, they had no water for the people or for the cattle to drink. "And the king of Israel said, Alas!

that the Lord hath called these three kings together to deliver them into the hand of Moab!" *(2 Kings 3:10)* Without water, the people and their animals would be weak and easy victims for the Moabites. "But Jehoshaphat said, Is there not here a prophet of the Lord, that we may enquire of the Lord by him? And one of the kings of Israel's servants answered and said, Here is Elisha the son of Shaphat, which poured water on the hands of Elijah. And Jehoshaphat said, The word of the Lord is with him." *(2 Kings 3:11-12)* Jehoshaphat, a God-fearing man, knew they were in trouble and needed God's help. He did not pray to God. He asked if there was a prophet of the Lord near; he needed to hear from God. And God, through the prophet, told the three kings what to do. The people obeyed God, and God gave them victory over the Moabites. *(2 Kings 3:8-27)*

I Make Them to Know

There are those who believe they can read the scripture and divine the word of God for themselves. We are exhorted to search the scripture but we cannot completely understand the scripture on our own. *(John 5:39; Acts 8:27-35)* God sends messengers to teach the people. "And Moses said unto his father in law, Because the people come unto me to enquire of God: When they have a matter, they come unto me; and I judge between one and another, and I do make them know the statutes of God, and his laws." *(Exodus 18:15-16)*

They Caused Them to Understand

Messengers of God teach the people and give them understanding. "And Ezra blessed the Lord, the great God. And all the people answered, Amen, Amen, with lifting up their hands: and they bowed their heads, and worshipped the Lord with their faces to the ground. . . and the Levites, caused the people to understand the law: and the people stood in their place. So they read in the book in the law of God distinctly, and gave the sense, and caused them to understand the reading." *(Nehemiah 8:6-8)*

Except Some Man Guide Me

An Ethiopian eunuch was sitting in his chariot and reading the book of Isaiah the prophet. The Spirit of the Lord moved on the apostle Philip and told him to go and meet with the eunuch. Philip asked the eunuch if he understood what he was reading. "And he said, How can I, except some man should guide me?" *(Acts 8:31)* Jesus did not go and sit with the eunuch. He sent the apostle. Jesus is a spirit. The eunuch needed a man to guide him.

Apostles' Doctrine

Jesus told the people to destroy the temple, and He would raise it up in three days. Jesus died and rose again. His death and resurrection gave men and women the right to redeem themselves from corruption. In order for Christ to build His church, He had to teach the people of His ways, so that we could walk in His path. *(Isaiah 2:2-3)* However, the Master had to return to spirit. *(John 16:7)* Thus, He delegated responsibility to the apostles to teach the people. *(Matthew 28:19)* The apostles' doctrine—the apostles' teaching—is the gospel of Jesus Christ. We overcome through the words of the apostles' testimonies. *(Revelation 12:11)*

The human family's only hope of salvation is through the knowledge of Jesus Christ. Satan can only deceive the people if they reject the knowledge of Jesus Christ. Thus, the knowledge of Jesus Christ will determine whether the people are saved or destroyed. If Satan bewitches the people to believe that Jesus is their personal savior, the people will be deceived. God's commandments and instructions are communicated by His preachers. If the people are following messengers of Satan, they are not receiving the instructions or commandments of God. When the Lord comes and find them in sin, the people will be destroyed.

There are preachers who profess to be apostles but have been found to be liars. *(Revelation 2:2)* Some churches have preachers under contract, which, of course, is contrary to the word of God. A preacher cannot oversee the house of God if others have the authority to influence his control. "The heads thereof judge for reward, and the priests thereof teach for hire, and the prophets thereof divine for money: yet will they lean upon the Lord, and say, is not the Lord among us? None evil can come upon us." *(Micah 3:11)* Many preachers are hired based upon their style of preaching, and people are gullible enough to think that God is with them just because they are in a building called church. The people pay the preacher to tell them what they want to hear; the preacher tells them what they want to hear; and all of them are deceived and headed to destruction.

Paul thanked the Lord for the Thessalonians who believed the truth—what he taught them. The truth sanctified the people. *(John 17:17)* "But we are bound to give thanks always to God for you, brethren beloved of the Lord, because God hath from the beginning chosen you to salvation through sanctification of the Spirit and belief of the truth." *(2 Thessalonians 2:13)* The Lord knew that the truth would cleanse the people and renew within them a right spirit. Paul was a truthful witness of Christ; those who obey his word will be saved. "A true witness delivereth souls: but a deceitful witness speaketh lies." *(Proverbs 14:25)*

———————— **Knowledge in Earthen Vessels** ————————

Jesus preached in parables deliberately to confuse the people. *(Matthew 13:13)* The knowledge of salvation through Jesus Christ was given to earthen vessels—men—who would preach the word to all creatures. "For God, who commanded the light to shine out of darkness to shine in our hearts, to give the light of the knowledge of the glory of God in the face of Jesus Christ. But we have this treasure in earthen vessels, that the excellency of the power may be of God, and not of us." *(2 Corinthians 4:6-7)* God sends messengers to teach the people how to be saved. *(Acts 11:14; Malachi 2:7)* Jesus departed from the earth and went back to spirit. He delegated teaching duties to His apostles.

They Have Moses and the Prophets

There was a certain rich man who died and went to hell. The tormented soul pleaded with the Lord for mercy. The Lord explained to the man that there is a great gulf between Heaven and Hell. After a person enters, he cannot exit. Once the damned soul recognized that he could not escape the torment of hell, he realized that his wicked relatives had no idea how much suffering awaited them. He asked the Lord to allow him to go and warn them to turn from their wickedness, lest they came into the place of indescribable torment. In writing about hell, Isaiah observed that those in hell were so miserable, until it was vexation just to understand the report. *(Isaiah 28:19)* Governor Felix trembled when Paul explained to him about the wrath of God to come. *(Acts 24:25)* The former rich man—burning in hell—wanted to impress upon those who still had a chance to obey God and avoid His wrath. The Lord answered that the people had Moses and the prophets; they were God's messengers. If the people did not believe God's messengers, they would not believe one that returned from the dead. *(Luke 16:19-31)*

Jesus is not going to personally save anyone. If the people want to be saved, they must follow the apostles' doctrine. God sends preachers to save them that believe. *(1 Corinthians 1:21)* Preachers are God's messengers, which is why Jesus admonished us to beware of false prophets. Satan wants us to believe Jesus is our personal savior. If the people believe Christ has personally saved them, they will not take heed to the lies of the false prophets and be deceived.

Additional Edifying Scriptures

"And thou, child, shalt be called the prophet of the Highest: for thou shalt go before the face of the Lord to prepare his ways; to give knowledge of salvation unto his people by the remission of their sins." (Luke 1:76-77)

"To open their eyes, and to turn them from darkness to light, and from the power of Satan unto God, that they may receive forgiveness of sins, and inheritance among them which are sanctified by faith that is in me." (Acts 26:18)

"Forbidding us to speak to the Gentiles that they might be saved, to fill up their sins always: for the wrath is come upon them to the uttermost." (1 Thessalonians 2:16)

"And when the children of Israel cried unto the Lord, the Lord raised up a deliverer to the children of Israel, who delivered them, even Othniel the son of Kenaz, Caleb's younger brother." (Judges 3:9) See also Judges 3:15; Judges 3:31; Judges 6:14; Judges 6:36; and Judges 7:7.

"And he gave some, apostles; and some, prophets; and some, evangelists; and some, pastors and teachers; For the perfecting of the saints, for the work of the ministry, for the edifying of the body of Christ:" (Ephesians 4:11)

"For he whom God hath sent speaketh the words of God: for God giveth not the Spirit by measure unto him." (John 3:34)

"And many people shall go and say, Come ye, and let us go up to the mountain of the Lord, to the house of the God of Jacob; and he will teach us of his ways, and we will walk in his paths." (Isaiah 2:3)

"He that heareth you heareth me; and he that despiseth you despiseth me; and he that despiseth me despiseth him that sent me." (Luke 10:16)

"Ye have neither heard his voice at any time, nor seen his shape. And ye have not his word abiding in you: for whom he hath sent, him ye believe not." (John 5:37-38)

"And Moses said unto his father in law, Because the people come unto me to enquire of God." (Exodus 18:15)

"Now then do it: for the Lord hath spoken of David, saying, By the hand of my servant David I will save my people Israel out of the hand of the Phillistines, and out of the hand of all their enemies." (2 Samuel 3:18)

"Nevertheless, they were disobedient, and rebelled against thee, and cast thy law behind their backs, and slew thy prophets which testified against them to turn them to thee, and they wrought great provocations. Therefore thou deliveredst them into the hand of their enemies, who vexed them: and in the time of their trouble, when they cried unto thee, thou heardest them from heaven; and according to thy manifold mercies thou gavest them saviours, who saved them out of the hand of their enemies." (Nehemiah 9:26-28)

"And he said unto me, Son of man, go, get thee unto the house of Israel, and speak with my words unto them. For thou art not sent to a people of a strange speech and of an hard language, but to the house of Israel. . . Son of man, I have made thee a watchman unto the house of Israel: therefore hear the word at my mouth, and give warning from me." (Ezekiel 3:4, 5, 17)

"And moreover, because the preacher was wise, he still taught the people knowledge; yea, he gave good heed and sought out, and set in order many proverbs. The preacher sought to find out acceptable words; and that which was written was upright, even words of truth." (Ecclesiastes 12:9-10)

"Then Manoah intreated the Lord, and said, O my Lord, let the man of God which thou didst send come again unto us, and teach us what we shall do unto the child that shall be born." (Judges 13:8)

"Then answered Amos, and said to Amaziah, I was no prophet, neither was I a prophet's son; but I was an herdman, and a gatherer of sycomore fruit. And the Lord took me as I followed the flock, and the Lord said unto me, Go, prophesy unto my people Israel." (Amos 7:14-15)

"And it shall come to pass, that every soul, which will not hear that prophet, shall be destroyed from among the people." (Acts 3:23)

"And other sheep I have, which are not of this fold: them also I must bring, and they shall hear my voice; and there shall be one fold, and one shepherd." (John 10:16)

"In his humiliation his judgment was taken away: and who shall declare his generation? For his life is taken from the earth." (Acts 8:33)

"In the day when God shall judge the secrets of men by Jesus Christ according to my gospel." (Romans 2:16)

"They forgat God their savior, which had done great things in Egypt; wondrous works in the land of Ham, and terrible things by the Red sea. Therefore he said that he would destroy them, had not Moses his chosen stood before him in the breach, to turn away his wrath, lest he should destroy them." (Psalm 106:21-23)

"And by a prophet the Lord brought Israel out of Egypt, and by a prophet was he preserved." (Hosea 12:13)

"And God sent me before you to preserve you a posterity in the earth, and to save your lives by a great deliverance. (Genesis 45:7)

"Thou leddest thy people like a flock by the hand of Moses and Aaron." (Psalm 77:20)

"Yet he sent prophets to them, to bring them again unto the Lord; and they testified against them: but they would not give ear." (2 Chronicles 24:19)

"Fools because of their transgression, and because of their iniquities, are afflicted. Their soul abhorreth all manner of meat; and they draw near unto the gates of death. Then they cry unto the Lord in their trouble, and he saveth them out of their distresses. He sent his word, and healed them, and delivered them from their destructions." (Psalm 107:17-20)

"And my temptation which was in my flesh ye despised not, nor rejected; but received me as an angel of God, even as Christ Jesus." (Galatians 4:14)

"Son of man, I have made thee a watchman unto the house of Israel: therefore hear the word at my mouth, and give them warning from me. When I say unto the wicked, Thou shalt surely die; and thou givest him not warning, nor speakest to warn the wicked from his wicked way, to save his life; the same wicked man shall die in his iniquity; but his blood will I require at thine hand." (Ezekiel 3:17-18)

"Behold, I send an Angel before thee, to keep thee in the way, and to bring thee into the place which I have prepared.

Beware of him, and obey his voice, provoke him not; for he will not pardon your transgressions: for my name is in him. But if thou shalt indeed obey his voice, and do all that I speak: then I will be an enemy unto thine enemies, and an adversary unto thine adversaries. . . Thou shalt not bow down to their gods, nor serve them, nor do after their works: but thou shalt utterly overthrow them, and quite break down their images." (Exodus 23:20-22, 24; Joshua 5:13-14)

"For {Moses} supposed his brethren would have understood how that God by his hand would deliver them: but they understood not." (Acts 7:25)

"And it shall come to pass, that every soul, which will not hear that prophet, shall be destroyed from among the people." (Acts 3:23)

"And by a prophet the Lord brought Israel out of Egypt, and by a prophet was he preserved." (Hosea 12:13)

"This Moses whom they refused, saying, who made thee a ruler and a judge? the same did God send to be a ruler and a deliverer by the hand of the angel which appeared to him in the bush." (Acts 7:35)

"Now then do it: for the Lord hath spoken of David, saying, By the hand of my servant David I will save my people Israel out of the hand of the Philistines, and out of the hand of all their enemies." (2 Samuel 3:18)

CHAPTER SIXTEEN

NOBODY IS PERFECT

G od is perfect. *(Matthew 5:48)* God was in Christ reconciling the world unto Himself. *(2 Corinthians 5:19)* God is a spirit, and He wanted us to be integrated with Him. *(John 4:24)* He wanted to walk in us, and He wanted us to walk in Him. *(Galatians 5:16)* Yet many who profess to believe in Him do not believe they can be redeemed from the natural back to the spiritual; they do not believe that God can deliver them out of the grave of sin. False teachers, as they did the children of Israel, have persuaded the people that they cannot overcome the enemy. As a result of their unbelief in the power of God, many have concluded that they cannot walk perfect before God and keep all of His commandments

Neither Jesus nor any of His messengers ever taught the people that they were expected to disobey God. If we disobey one commandment of God, we demonstrate that there is one thing we exalt above God. Thus, God is not our God, because He is not supreme in our lives. For example, Adam disobeyed God one time and was cast out of the garden. Saul disobeyed God one time and was removed as king. Judas betrayed Christ one time and was destroyed. If we offend in one point, we are guilty of everything. *(James 2:10)* God commands His people to be perfect. *(Matthew 5:48)* Since the wages of sin is death, the Savior would not have given us a command that we could not perform. *(Romans 6:23)*

———————————— **Mark the Perfect Man** ————————————

The scripture tells us plainly to mark the perfect man and behold the upright for the end of that man is peace. *(Psalm 37:37)* Job was a perfect man. *(Job 1:1)* Noah was a perfect man. *(Genesis 6:9)* Daniel was a perfect man. *(Daniel 6:4)* "And when Abram was ninety years old and nine, the Lord appeared to Abram and said unto him, I am the Almighty God; walk before me, and be thou perfect. And I will make my covenant between me and thee, and will multiply thee exceedingly." *(Genesis 17:1-2)* God told Abraham that if he walked perfect before Him, He would make a covenant with Abraham. Since God made a covenant with Abraham, we extrapolate from the scripture that Abraham was perfect.

The scripture further denotes that God put apostles and others in the church for the "perfecting" of the saints. *(Ephesians 4:12)* Those who have been born again must move on to perfection. *(Hebrews 6:1)* In fact, Jesus, the Lord of lord and King of kings, lived a perfect life in Satan's kingdom, and He taught us of His ways, so that we could walk in His path. *(Isaiah 2:2-3)* He was our example. There is not one scripture in the Bible that implies that people cannot live without sin. However, Satan, through the teachings of the false prophets, has persuaded the people that no one can live a perfect life. And most of the people have chosen to believe Satan.

———————————— **Perfect** ————————————

According to Webster's dictionary, the word perfect means "without fault," "error free," and "complete." Jude observed that Jesus Christ was able to keep us from falling and to present us faultless (without fault) before the presence of His glory with exceeding joy. *(Jude 1:24)* Daniel was without fault or error. "Then the presidents and princes sought to find occasion against Daniel concerning the kingdom; but they could find none occasion nor fault; forasmuch as he was faithful, neither was there any error or fault found in him." *(Daniel 6:4)* Jesus asked the man at the well if he wanted to be made whole. Jesus came to redeem us back to the way humans were created. Remember: Adam was spirit and flesh. God had breathed into him and made him a living soul. Jesus came to reconcile us with the spirit. Jesus came to resurrect us from the grave of sin, to restore our lost soul, so we could inherit eternal life. *(1 Corinthians 15:22)* We must be integrated with God to enter His kingdom. We must be perfect.

God created Adam and Eve. God was perfect; His creation was perfect. Adam and Eve committed one sin each and were corrupted; they were separated from God. Those who have learned the truth and walk in the light know that where there is Christ, there is liberty. *(2 Corinthians 3:17)* Children of God overcome sin and keep His commandments.

—————— Who Hath Believed Our Report ——————

The prophet Isaiah asked, Who hath believed our report? He wanted to know to whom the arm of the Lord had been revealed. The arm of the Lord is not shortened that it cannot save. Jesus Christ has the power to resurrect the dead from the grave of sin—but the people do not believe. Unlike those who are still wallowing in corruption, the redeemed know that the world was not fortuitously created by a big bang. Humans did not walk up out of a sea. Theories are for those who are ignorant of the facts. The Spirit of God confirms God's existence; the knowledge of God delivers us out of darkness; and the grace of God saves us from the power of the enemy. When we exalt the Lord in spirit and in truth, we are made free. Followers of Christ do not walk in darkness, subject to the power of Satan. Through the knowledge of Jesus Christ, we have been redeemed from corruption.

Satan enticed the human family to promote its own vanity, which gave him power over our lives. The Lord allowed men and women to witness their own weakness. If they were too ignorant to escape Satan's witchcraft, what made them presumptuous enough to believe they were smarter than God? If the people did not have the strength to overcome Satan, how were they going to withstand God? *(Jeremiah 12:5)* Jesus Christ demonstrated He is Lord and commanded the people to obey His commandments. Those who exalt Jesus as Lord recognize they cannot defeat Him; therefore, they obey Him. Those who refuse to exalt Jesus as Lord and continue to rebel will be destroyed.

──────────── **Whosoever the Son Has Set Free** ────────────

God sent famine into Canaan and forced the children of Israel into Egypt. He turned the hearts of the Egyptians against the Hebrews and caused the Egyptians to enslave His own people. He predestined for them to be taken into captivity. *(Psalm 105:16-25)* Jesus ultimately followed the children of Israel out of bondage; God had caused the people to go into bondage. *(1 Corinthians 10:4)* Similarly, God sent famine into the world and forced men and women into the bondage of sin. *(Isaiah 5:13)* Jesus came to set the people free from sin. *(John 8:32-36)*

Further, just as God sent Moses to deliver the people out of the bondage of Egypt to reclaim their natural inheritance, God sent Jesus to deliver the people out of the bondage of sin to reclaim their spiritual inheritance. Just as Abraham renounced his pagan inheritance from his father, Terah, to bear witness to the truth, the spiritual children of Abraham renounce their pagan inheritance from our father, the devil, to bear witness to the truth. We do not walk after corruption and do the deeds of our father. We demonstrate to God that we are not servants of Satan. We would not have fought against God in Heaven, and we renounce disobedient to God in the earth. We exalt the Lord and separate ourselves from the wicked. We want to be redeemed; we want to be made whole; we want to reclaim our birthright—we want to walk in the Spirit of God and, as heirs by adoption, inherit His kingdom.

Why are we heirs by adoption? God did not create us. We were born in sin, through the lust of the flesh. We were spiritually dead. Jesus came and offered us a new life. We renounced the life of sin and came out of the grave. We were born again of the spirit. God adopted us as His children.

The purpose of the gospel of Jesus Christ is to open the eyes of the blind, to turn the people from darkness to light, from the power of Satan to God. *(Acts 26:18)* Those who do not believe they can live perfect do not believe the truth, because the truth makes the people free from sin. Whosoever the Son has set free is free indeed. *(John 8:36)* And those who do not believe they can be perfect cannot be integrated with God because He is perfect. "This I say then, walk in the Spirit, and ye shall not fulfil the lust of the flesh." *(Galatians 5:16)* Those who walk after the flesh are subject to Satan. *(Hebrews 2:14-15)* Those who walk in the Spirit of God have Satan subject to them. *(Luke 10:17-18)* It is Satan's objective to persuade the people that they cannot live a perfect life; to not be perfect is to be separated from God, and to be separated from God means death.

Ransomed From the Grave

God prophesied that He would ransom the people from the power of the grave; He would redeem the people from death. *(Hosea 13:14)* The sting of death is sin. *(1 Corinthians 15:56)* Jesus came and destroyed him that had the power of death, that is, the devil, and delivered those, who through fear of death, were all their lifetime subject to the bondage of sin. *(Hebrews 2:14-15)* Jesus destroyed the power of the grave and redeemed the people from death. *(Isaiah 25:8-9)* Jesus set us free and saved us from our sins. *(Matthew 1:21)* Further, He asked the man at the well if he wanted to be made whole, which is the same as complete. He wanted to know if the man wanted his natural body to be made whole. The man was sick; he wanted to be healed, but he needed help to get into the pool. *(John 5:7)* The spiritual equivalent under the new covenant "to be made whole" was to heal the man's soul. We were powerless to sin; our enemy was too strong for us, and he had the power of death. *(Hebrews 2:14)* We were dying in our own blood.

We needed someone to save us from our sins, save us from death. Jesus came and saved us from sin and death. "He sent his word, and healed them, and delivered them from their destructions." *(Psalm 107:20)*

———————————— **Be Ye Holy** ————————————

God, before the foundation of the world, commanded men and women to live holy. *(Ephesians 1:4)* Adam and Eve were perfect creatures, who walked in the Spirit of God. They became imperfect when Satan corrupted them and caused them to exalt their will over God's will. Without the Spirit of God, Adam and Eve were weak human beings. Satan, a spirit, possessed the power of death and became god of this world. It was his kingdom, and he had the ability to elevate whomever he chose to elevate; and he invariably elevated those who promoted his evil intentions. In the course of time, fear of death—masked by envy, pride, and lust—caused men and women to strive against each other. Corrupt individuals who wanted to promote their vanity and preserve their lives persecuted others. Those who wanted to survive persecution had to acquiesce to the corruption of those in power. Self-preservation prevailed. Men and women rejected integrity. Skin for skin, they did whatever they had to do to survive.

And God often sat back and watched. He withheld His knowledge and power, and allowed men and women to witness their own wickedness. Without God, men and women bartered their soul to the devil. Many worshipped the sun and moon, and they passed such pagan worship down through the generation. Those who worshipped the sun started the pagan festival that subsequently became known as Christmas. Those who worshipped the moon started the pagan festival that subsequently became known as Easter. Although Easter was named after Eastra, the goddess of spring, the false prophets persuaded the people that the celebration honored Jesus Christ.

The people were so corrupted and deceived by false prophets, until they turned the truth of God into fables—Peter Cottontail, Santa Claus, Rudolph the Red-Nose Reindeer, Frosty the Snowman, et al. *(2 Timothy 4:3-4)* Satan, through the teachings of the false prophets, deceived those who professed to walk in the light to perpetuate the ignorance of those who walked in darkness. God told the people to not learn the ways of the heathens; the people not only learned the ways of the heathens, they attached the name of Christ to the paganism. *(Jeremiah 10:1-4)* Christ never had any fellowship with pagan gods, yet the false prophets persuaded the people that pagan worship honored the birth and resurrection of Jesus Christ. *(2 Corinthians 6:14-15)* Few ever stopped to question why the date of Easter changed every year.

Although God told His people to learn not the ways of the heathens, the Lord sent famine into the world—not for food or for drink, but for the word of God. Hence, despite the Lord's admonition to learn not the ways of the heathens, the people went into captivity because God did not have a prophet in the land to teach the people the truth. All of the priests and prophets were ignorant. In due season, just as Moses came to deliver the children of Israel out of the bondage of Egypt, Jesus Christ came to deliver the people out of the bondage of sin. The Master did not want anyone to perish and came to teach the people the truth.

───────── **He Sent His Word and Healed Them** ─────────

"In the beginning, God created the heaven and the earth." *(Genesis 1:1)* Darkness covered the earth. "And God said, Let there be light: and there was light." *(Genesis 1:3)* God created and breathed into Adam and Eve, and they became living souls. The breath of God—the Spirit of God—is our soul. Satan deceived Adam and Eve. As a result of their disobedience, man and woman lost their souls; they were separated from the spirit. Their children—conceived through lust of the flesh—were born in sin.

Jesus Christ came into the earth to teach us of His ways, so that we could walk in His path. The darkness had passed; the light had come into the world. The Lord knew how to overcome Satan's corruption, and the people could escape the pollution of this world through His knowledge. Jesus taught His disciples, and sent them to teach all nations how to overcome. The apostles bore witness that light had come into the earth, and those who received the apostles' testimonies no longer walked in darkness.

Just as God did not create Adam and Eve until after He created light, which allowed them to see, God did not create new creatures, until after Jesus Christ came and gave us the light of the gospel, which allowed us to see Satan's witchcraft. *(2 Corinthians 4:1-6)* We do not grope in darkness and ignorance, blinded by Satan. Those who walk in darkness are subject to the power of Satan. Those who walk in the light as He is in the light have overcome Satan's witchcraft; they have been set free from sin. *(Acts 26:18)*

Through the knowledge of Jesus Christ, we learned that humans are an heritage of God. *(Psalm 127:3)* We are His offsprings. Jesus ransomed us from the grave and redeeded our right to inherit eternal life. All we have to do is to renounce Satan and bear witness to the truth: Jesus is Lord. Those who make a covenant with Christ by sacrifice shall redeem themselves from the grave of sin and become joint-heirs with Christ. *(Romans 8:14-17)* Moreover, we learned that Satan kept the people in bondage through fear of death. *(Hebrews 2:14-15)* As a result of the fear of death, people lusted after the flesh to find some pleasure and comfort from the burdens of sin. Ergo, Satan had us lusting after weak, dying human tissue (flesh), which required us to rebel against the Almighty God. In our ignorance, Satan corrupted our minds and made us despise our own birthright. We renounced our own salvation to lust after Satan's witchcraft and chose to destroy our own soul.

We Can Overcome the Enemy

The scripture is divided between the Old Testament and the New Testament. Each testament represents a covenant God made with the human family. Under the first covenant, God agreed to deliver the natural descendants of Abraham out of the bondage of Egypt. In exchange, the people agreed to serve the Lord and inherit the Promised Land. "And Caleb stilled the people before Moses, and said, Let us go up at once, and possess it; for we are well able to overcome it." *(Numbers 13:30)* Caleb believed God and inherited the Promised Land.

Unfortunately, false prophets persuaded nearly all of the people that they could not overcome the giants in the land. "But the men that went up with him said, We be not able to go up against the people; for they are stronger than we." *(Numbers 13:31)* As a result, the people rebelled against God and purposed to return to the bondage of Egypt. Although God had defeated Pharaoh in Pharaoh's kingdom, the people lacked faith in the Almighty. They chose to serve a false god (Pharaoh) who they believed would save their lives more than they trusted their Saviour. God destroyed His own inheritance. *(Jeremiah 12:7-8)*

Similarly, under the second covenant, Jesus Christ came into the earth and overcame sin. *(John 6:33)* Jesus was in all points tempted like we, yet without sin. *(Hebrews 4:15)* He knew the wages of sin was death and did not capitulate to Satan's witchcraft. As a flesh-and-blood being, Jesus was subordinated to the spirit. Jesus could only remain integrated with God if He walked in integrity. In walking in obedience (Remember: all God's ways are holy), Jesus walked in perfect holiness and remained integrated with the Spirit of God.

Jesus did not live a perfect life because His name was Jesus. He fasted and prayed to keep His body under subjection. He understood that He could not put hot coal in His bosom and not be burned. *(Proverbs 6:27)* He prayed that He would not be led into temptation. In praying to keep His minds on the things of the spirit, not allowing His mind to entertain wickedness, and offering His body as a living sacrifice, He committed Himself to obedience to the spirit. He knew that the flesh was the enemy of the spirit and fasted to bring His body under subjection. He was tempted like other men, yet He denied Himself the pleasure of the flesh. Jesus refused to corrupt Himself; He refused to walk after the lust in His blood.

The spirit is not subject to the laws of nature. Jesus, conceived of the spirit, was a spirit. Jesus, conceived of the flesh, was flesh. *(John 3:6)* As a man of integrity and with the knowledge that the Spirit of God was the Almighty, Jesus did not indulge Satan's witchcraft. He had the power to refrain from sin because greater was the Spirit within Him than the spirits in the world. *(Luke 10:17-20)* Additionally, since Jesus did not want to sin (which is why He prayed not to be tempted) and had the power to abstain from sin (Holy Ghost), Jesus walked perfect before God. "This I say then, walk in the spirit, and ye shall not fulfil the lust of the flesh." *(Galatians 5:16)*

Although Satan's kingdom offered pleasure of the flesh for those who rebelled against God and pain for those who rebelled against Satan, Jesus chose to suffer the pain and bruises. He chose to deny Himself. The Master knew that the life of the flesh was in the blood; therefore, Satan, in bewitching the people to lust after the flesh, had the people lusting after the corruption they inherited within their blood. Ergo, the people were dying in their own blood. *(Ezekiel 16:6)* Deceived individuals—walking after the lust of the flesh, lust of the eyes, and the pride of life—chose to remain under the power of Satan and to damn their own souls to hell.

For example, many individuals, during times of financial hardships, have been tempted to commit crimes to alleviate their monetary troubles. Most do not commit crimes because they fear the loss of their freedom if captured. Jesus knew that if He committed sin, He would be separated from the Spirit of God and captured by Satan. He resisted the temptation. Those who fear God and know that the wages of sin is death will repudiate Satan's witchcraft and pride, and humble themselves. They will disregard their vanity and submit themselves to the will of God. *(2 Corinthians 10:5)*

Crucify the Flesh

God loved His creation and did not want any to perish. Jesus came and set an example for us to follow. In crucifying the flesh, the

Master overcame death. Jesus knew that the flesh was the enemy of the spirit. If we walk after the flesh, we cannot walk in the spirit. If we do not have the spirit, we do not have eternal life. God gave us a choice: choose life (spirit; incorruption) or death (flesh; corruption). Adam, exalting flesh, chose death. Jesus, exalting spirit, chose life. Jesus knew that the spirit could never die, whereas the flesh was going to pass away. Since the life of the flesh is in the blood, Jesus shed His blood to demonstrate that He rejected the life of the flesh. He exalted the Spirit of God and trusted in God's promises. He refused to sacrifice eternal life for ephemeral pleasures. He obeyed the commandments of God and renounced the things of the world.

Before He ascended upon high, the Master (Teacher) commanded His disciples (students) to feed His sheep, to teach (discipline) them how to take up their cross and follow Him. For example, Peter, who had betrayed Christ three times on the same night that Judas betrayed Christ once, never betrayed Christ again. Once Peter saw that Jesus rose from the grave, he did not fear death anymore. He knew that Christ had the power to also raise him from the dead. Those who believe Jesus is Lord have no need to fear death. Skin for skin, we renounce the life of the flesh and its inherent corruption, because we have faith in the promises of God. We crucify the flesh (stop indulging the lust within our blood) and overcome Satan's witchcraft. We come out of the grave of sin to walk in the newness of a spiritual life. As His disciples, we followed Jesus, who led us out of the bondage of sin and taught us to walk as He walked.

Through the words of the apostles' testimonies, we ate of Christ's flesh and drank of His blood. We learned of Jesus' ways and walked in His path. With the knowledge of Jesus Christ, we reconciled with the spirit. "The disciple is not above his master: but every one that is perfect shall be as his master." *(Luke 6:40)* Christ was our example. *(1 Peter 2:21-22)* Jesus Christ, through His apostles, taught the people to walk as He walked. In crucifying the flesh and overcoming sin, we submitted to the will of the spirit. Our steps are ordered by the Lord. *(Psalm 37:23)* Since He is perfect, when we obey all of His commandments, we are perfect. *(Psalm 145:17; Matthew 28:20; Luke 1:74-75; Matthew 5:48)*

──────── **Those Who Call Upon the Name of the Lord** ────────

Those who call upon the name of the Lord shall be saved from their sins. *(Romans 10:13)* The people only have the incentive to call upon the Lord if they want to be saved. God sends preachers to communicate words of faith to the people—"We are well able to overcome the enemies." Just as the spies told the Hebrews that they could not overcome the giants in Canaan, false prophets have persuaded people that they cannot overcome sin. If the people cannot overcome sin, Jesus cannot be God.

God means supreme. If Jesus does not have the power to deliver His people out of bondage and save them from the enemy, He does not have all power. If Satan has the people in the bondage of sin and Jesus cannot deliver the people out of bondage, Satan is God. A preacher who teaches that Satan is Lord is a liar who has been sent to keep the people subject to the power of Satan. Yet, a preacher who teaches that we cannot be perfect—free from sin—is conveying the same message. If we cannot be perfect, then Jesus has commanded us to do something that we cannot do—and He does not have the power to deliver us from the enemy, so that we are able to perform His commandment.

Those who walk in the light are able to catch Satan in his craftiness. "Rebellion is as the sin of witchcraft." Only the ignorant and deceived do not believe they can live a perfect life. Individuals whose God is the Lord know that they can overcome the enemy. The apostle John said that he was in the spirit and God revealed to him that the people were able to overcome. *(Revelation 12:11)* The apostles testified to the teachings of Jesus Christ, who came to teach us of His ways, so that we could walk in His path. *(Isaiah 2:2-3)* Those who follow after Christ should walk as He walked. "He that saith he abideth in him ought himself also so to walk, even as he walked." *(1 John 2:6)* The scripture admonished the people to move on to perfection. *(Hebrew 6:1)* Anyone who teaches any doctrine other than what the apostles taught, angel or anyone else, has been sent from Satan and will be condemned. *(Galatians 1:8)* Jesus taught us to observe all that He had commanded us, and He commanded us to be perfect. *(Matthew 5:48)*

──────────── **Go in Peace and Sin No More** ────────────

Some men found a woman in the act of adultery and wanted to stone her. They brought the woman to Jesus. Since Jesus knew that those who sinned had to die, He permitted the men to stone the woman. He told the one without sin to cast the first stone. The Master, of course, knew that all had sinned. When all the men left, Jesus asked the woman where were her accusers. She answered, they had all left. The Master, since He had not committed sin, was the only one who had the right to stone her. However, He told the woman that He would not *condemn* her either. Jesus saved the woman from her sin. Nonetheless, He cautioned her to go in peace and sin no more. She might be destroyed the next time. *(John 8:1-11)*

Jesus came to save all of us from our sins. Satan wants God to destroy us. He accuses us before the Lord day and night. *(Revelation 12:10)* As of now, Jesus has saved us from our accuser and has not condemned us. However, we are to go in peace and sin no more. The next time we might be destroyed. Remember, Zacharias observed that God would save us from our enemies and all those that hated us. Jesus came into the earth not to condemn but to save. *(John 3:17)* Jesus taught us how to overcome the enemy and to escape from captivity. Now that we have the ability to overcome the power of the enemy, we have no cloak for our sins. *(John 15:22)* We are to go in peace and sin no more. If we reject the knowledge of Jesus Christ and continue in sin, we are going to be destroyed. *(2 Peter 2:20; Hosea 4:6; Matthew 7:21-27)*

Jesus forgave the woman, and He offers us the remisson of sin. The first covenant had fault—men and women, without the power of God, were weaker than Satan. Men and women, without the knowledge of God, were less intelligent than Satan. *(Hebrews 8:7)* Those who walk in the light as He is in the light should have turned from the power of Satan unto God. Our enemies have been made subject to us; we should have overcome them. We should be sanctified through the truth. *(Acts 26:18)*

Confess Your Fault

The Lord tells the human family to stop living in denial. We are not God; we are weak creatures. Despite all our pretensions, we are highly insecure and live in fear. The Lord wants humans to admit Satan has them in the bondage of sin, confess their faults, humble themselves, and ask God to deliver us from slavery. "If we say we have no sin, we deceive ourselves, and the truth is not in us. If we confess our sins, he is faithful and just to forgive us our sins, and to cleanse us from all unrighteousness." *(1 John 1:8-9)* If we stop living in denial and admit the truth (we are corrupt), God will forgive us of our sins and save us from our enemies. We need to emulate the prodigal son: admit our fault, humble ourselves, and return to the Father.

The salient issues come down to integrity and faith. If we are honest with ourselves, we will humble ourselves and acknowledge that we are nothing but weak flesh. We are afraid of death and engage in all manner of corrupt behaviors in order to survive. The devil offers us pleasure to give us temporary relief from the pain; ironically, it is the pleasure that causes our pain. In kowtowing to our weakness, we empower our enemy and allow him to manipulate us to self-destruct. In other words, Satan corrupted Adam and Eve through the lust of the flesh. Without the spirit, they only had natural lives. The life of the flesh is in the blood; hence, Adam and Eve transmitted corruption through their blood. When we indulge the lust within our blood, we perpetuate our own corruption and reinforce Satan's power over our lives. When we commit to a life of sin, we commit to a life of rebelliousness—a life of wickedness and evil.

With the knowledge of Jesus Christ, we learn to take up our cross and crucify the flesh. Since the natural life is a corrupt life, we crucify the flesh and overcome nature. Unlike unbelievers, believers are not going to forsake our own mercy to save our natural life. Jesus taught us the truth: the Spirit of God is supreme. Ergo, we exalt the Spirit of God (our soul) over our flesh-and-blood life (flesh). We are willing to overcome Satan's corruption in order to reconcile with the spirit. Not only do we not fear death, we consent to death and die out to sin. We know that Jesus came out of the grave. When He came out of the grave, He defeated death and raised up His temple out of the grave of sin. Those of us who are a part of the body of Christ—spiritual beings, lively stones, new creatures, children of God—have chosen to be buried with Christ, so that the power of God might dwell within us. We have made a covenant of sacrifice: We die with Him, so that we can live with Him. *(2 Timothy 2:11)* Ergo, we bury our life of sin in the grave, so that we can rise up in the newness of life with Christ.

Of course, since Satan has the power of death, we must believe that God has the power to save us from death. If we believe that God raised Jesus from the grave, we believe that God has the power to raise us from the grave. If we believe that Jesus is not a God of the dead but a God of the living—and raised Lazarus from his sleep—we believe that God "even now" can resurrect us from sin—sleep—our first death. Jesus, the all-wise God, lived a perfect life. He knew how the people could overcome corruption. Those who have learned of His ways and walked in His path should walk as the Master walked—free of sin.

If the people believe the messengers of Satan, they will remain mired in the sin of witchcraft. They will continue to engage in works of iniquity and remain separated from God. When the Lord comes, just as He destroyed the children of Israel who chose to serve as slaves in the bondage of Egypt, He will destroy those who serve as Satan's slaves in the bondage of sin. "They believed not in God, and trusted not in His salvation." *(Psalm 78:22)*

Know Ye That the Lord is God

It is important to remember that to serve the Lord is to exalt the spirit above the flesh. Honest individuals recognize that the Lord is God; it is He that has made us, not we ourselves. We are the sheep of His pasture. *(Psalm 100:3)* Therefore, to become integrated with God, we subordinate our will to His will. We magnify the Lord when we walk after the things of the spirit. Satan became god of this world through deception. He rules the world through deception. Those who walk after the flesh refuse to submit to Jesus Christ. They refuse to confess Jesus as Lord and reject His commandments. Satan knows that the wages of sin is death, but he does not want the people to know. Accordingly, he has sent false prophets to teach the people that they are human; they are going to sin. If the people are human, they are not children of God. *(Romans 8:9)* That which is born of the spirit is spirit. *(John 3:6)* Children of God have crucified the flesh and have been raised up in the newness of life—they are spiritual beings. Jesus came to ransom humans (those who are dead) from the grave of sin and reconcile them with the spirit. If humans do not come out of the grave of sin, they will suffer the second death. *(Revelation 20:6; 20:14)*

Nothing Will Happen to You

False prophets are never going to explicitly tell their followers to disobey God. Remember, Satan is the most subtle beast of the field. He did not tell Eve explicitly to disobey God. He simply told Eve that nothing would happen to her if she disobeyed. Thus, by reducing Eve's fear of the Lord, Satan acquired greater ability to stimulate Eve's vanity and pride. The woman ultimately fell for Satan's witchcraft and lost her soul. Similarly, when the false prophets tell the people that no one is perfect, they are not explicitly telling the people to sin. They are in a subtle way telling the people that they cannot refrain from sin, which is an unspoken way of telling the people that they are not expected to do all that Jesus has commanded.

To mitigate sinners' fear of the Lord, false prophets tell them that they are saved by grace, not by works of righeousness. Of course, the people were not saved by works of righteousness; they were workers of iniquity. Hence, false prophets twist the scriptures to deceive the people. The people believe that since they are saved by grace, they will not be lost if they disobey God. They do not understand that saved by grace implies that we were saved by God's knowledge and power. The Master taught us how to overcome Satan's witchcraft; His word cleansed us from the pollution of this world; the truth He spoke sanctified us. *(Revelation 12:11; 2 Peter 2:20; John 17:17)* His word healed us from our sickness and infirmities—and saved us from destruction. *(Psalm 107:20)* We are saved by grace: Jesus' word is grace. *(Acts 20:32)*

Those who are not deceived know that we have to obey all that God has commanded. *(Matthew 28:20)* We have to work out our salvation with fear and trembling, because if we offend in one point, we are guilty of it all. *(Philippians 2:12; James 2:10)*

────── **Saved by Grace, Not by Works--Revisited** ──────

Satan's objective is to damn your soul. In order to deceive the people, Satan must persuade the people that they can disobey God and still inherit eternal life. False prophets must persuade the people that no one is perfect in order for the people to believe that their sins will not lead to destruction. Satan will remind the people, if a person says he has no sin, we deceive ourselves. *(1 John 1:8)* The devil knows that, without holiness, no one can see God. *(Hebrews 12:14)* Just as Eve's disobedience caused her death, our disobedience likewise will cause our death. We must walk in integrity to remain integrated with God. If we overcome sin—and we are well able to overcome the enemy through the power of Jesus Christ—God will forgive our sins.

We do not want God to drive us away from the tree of life, as He did Adam and Eve. *(Genesis 3:24)* We do not eat from the tree of evil. We eat only from the tree of life, so we can enter through the gates into the city. "Blessed are they that do his commandments, that they may have right to the tree of life, and may enter in through the gates into the city." *(Revelation 22:14)* We acquire the knowledge of Jesus Christ and overcome sin. "But now being made free from sin, and become servants to God, ye have your fruit holiness, and the end everlasting life." *(Romans 6:22)* Sinners, like Adam and Eve, know they are evil and disobedient, yet they refuse to repent and stop eating from the corrupt tree.

To be saved by grace, not by works, simply means that our enemies were too strong for us. We have nothing to boast about. Just as the children of Israel built Pharaoh's treasure cities and worked to empower their enemies, those who walk after the flesh work to empower Satan. The Lord had mercy upon us because He knew we were ignorant: "but I obtained mercy, because I did it ignorantly in unbelief." *(1 Timothy 1:13)* The people had gone into captivity because of ignorance (lack of knowledge). The Lord was willing to forgive the people for the lack of knowledge, because He had sent famine into the land—not for food or for drink, but for His word. The people were ignorant because God refused to teach them.

Jesus ended the famine and came to feed the people. He gave us His word (His grace) and delivered us from destruction. He raised us out of the grave of sin and renewed within us a new life. *(1 Peter 2:24)* "So he fed them according to the integrity of his heart; and guided them by the skillfulness of his hands." *(Psalm 78:72)* Jesus taught us the truth. Further, He gave His life, so we could receive the forgiveness of sin. Since He hid His word, He bore the stripes of those who had sinned, and sent His word and healed those who were sick. Our ransom for sin has been paid. We are commanded

to come up out of the grave of sin and walk in the newness of life—
new creatures in Christ Jesus.

No Cloak for Their Sins

Please do not allow false prophets to bewitch you: there is no
cloak for sin. Those who reject the knowledge of salvation and
remain corrupt will be destroyed. *(Hosea 4:6)* "Unto you first God,
having raised up his Son Jesus, sent him to bless you, in turning
away every one of you from his iniquities." *(Acts 3:26)*

Remember: Stubbornness is as iniquity and idolatry. *(1 Samuel
15:23)* Those who rebel against God exalt themselves above Him;
they worship themselves. They know they are sinners, weak and
frail creatures, yet they refuse to change. They have chosen to
preserve their corruption than to redeem their integrity. Ergo,
they prefer to save their corrupt flesh-and-blood life than to be
reintegrated with the Spirit of God. They rather live as slaves to sin
than to confess Jesus is Lord. "Fools because of their transgression,
and because of their iniquities are afflicted. Their soul abhorreth
all manner of meat; and they draw near unto the gates of death."
(Psalm 107:17-18) Unlike the prodigal son, who recognized that a
life of sin is death, most sinners despise wisdom and instructions.
They rather sacrifice their integrity and destroy their own souls.

Works of Abraham

Abraham, the prototype of the faithful servant, was a perfect
man. There are many who note that Abraham lied. *(Genesis 20:2)*
When afraid of death, Abraham denied that Sarah was his wife;
he said she was his sister. Similarly, Isaac said Rebekkah was not
his wife. *(Genesis 26:7)* Jacob said he was Esau. *(Genesis 27:19)*
Rebekkah helped Jacob to secure Esau's blessings. *(Genesis 27:6-17)*
Their deceitfulness seems to contradict the belief that Abraham,
Isaac, Jacob, and Rebekkah were faithful to God.

Abraham, Isaac, Jacob, and Rebekkah lived before the Ten

Commandments were given. There was no commandment against lying. Since there was no law, there was no transgression. *(Romans 4:15; Romans 5:13)* Each of them obeyed the commandments of God. "For in many things we offend all. If any man offend not in word, the same is a perfect man, and able also to bridle the whole body." *(James 3:2)* If God did not issue a command, they did not disobey His command. As long as they obeyed God's commandments, they were perfect.

Make Ready a People

Many readers will not readily understand how people can live free from sin. God is very much aware that most people have been deceived. The Master knows that slaves who have never known anything besides slavery will have great trust issues. They will also have great difficulty believing they can be free. Further, no slavemaster wants his slaves to know the truth; slaves will never volitionally serve another master if they believe they are stronger than the master.

Satan is a liar. He sends false prophets to deceive the people because he knows that the people, with the Spirit of God, are stronger than he. Thus, his power is in the slaves' weakness; he is god only to those who are ignorant. He has sent false prophets to teach lies; in teaching that nobody is perfect, the false prophets tacitly tell the people that they are expected to sin, which separates them from God. Those who are foolish enough to sin against God and separate from the spirit unsuspectingly give the devil power over them. If the people knew the truth, they would know that they have a right to walk with God, who would give them power over Satan.

God never owned slaves. He always set the people free from bondage and allowed all individuals the right to choose whom they wanted to serve. The Lord allowed Satan, Pharaoh, drugs, alcohol, and other gods to overpower the people. He wanted the people to recognize their own frailty. Those who succumbed to Satan's and the world's witchcraft were overcome and taken into captivity. They were dying in their own blood; the corruption within them was leading them to self-destruct. The Lord told the people to come to Him; He would deliver them out of bondage and give them rest for their soul. Those who were humble enough to exalt Jesus as Lord learned from Him and were delivered. Those who exalted the life of sin above integrity, who refused to admit the truth (they need Jesus), and exalted corrupt flesh above the power of God chose to destroy themselves. Hence, God allowed everyone to bear witness to the truth and gave everyone the right to choose life or death.

The purpose of this chapter is simply to get people to recognize that God came to save us from our sins, because the wages of sin is death. He entered into a covenant with His creation and promised to deliver us out of captivity. God has superior knowledge. Those who want to serve Him must trust in His word. When we are integrated with Him, He will guide us in the way of holiness. Since all of His ways are holy, when we obey all of His commandments, we are holy. Perfection requires us to be complete. When we walk in the Spirit of God through obedience, we walk in the spirit and in the flesh. We have both the Father and the Son. God was in Christ reconciling us to Himself. The redeemed have been made whole. Perfect. The way the Lord made them.

————— **Observe All that I Have Commanded Them** —————

Adam and Eve disobeyed God only one time; they lost their soul. Saul disobeyed God one time; he lost his kingship. Judas betrayed Christ one time; he was damned forever. The people of God, those who have been delivered from sin, walk steadfastly in the apostles' doctrine and work out their salvation with fear and trembling. The Lord is indeed slow to anger and willing to forgive, but He will not acquit the wicked.

————————— **Spirit of God is Perfect** —————————

Adam and Eve were flesh-and-blood, yet they were perfect. God created them. He breathed into them, and they became living souls. They were integrated with God. As long as they obeyed God, they walked in the Spirit of God, who led them in the path of righteousness. Their separation from God came when Satan persuaded Eve to lust after the tree that contained evil, which led to their corruption. Hence, Adam's and Eve's imperfection did not come about because they were flesh; their imperfection came about because of the sin of witchcraft. Eve allowed Satan to beguile her to rebel against God, and Adam chose to walk after his flesh (Eve was flesh of his flesh) rather than to deny himself and obey God. Neither the man nor the woman had known evil before they ate from the tree. Flesh is the manifestation of evil. Those who have chosen to walk after flesh have chosen to exalt Satan's witchcraft and live a life of corruption. They have chosen to reject the word of God to walk after evil and to destroy their own soul. Those who have chosen to crucify the flesh admit that Jesus is Lord and exalt the Spirit of God above the lust within our flesh. We have chosen to bury the life of sin, and to rise up in the newness of life.

Our objective as believers is to be redeemed from corruption. We cannot be a follower of Christ and walk in sin. Christ is holy, and He leads His people in the way of holiness. *(1 Peter 1:16; Leviticus 11:44)* It is impossible to walk in the Spirit of God and not live a perfect life. The Almighty God is perfect. All of His ways are perfect. Children of God are perfect. *(Matthew 5:48; Genesis 17:1; Job 1:1)* Only those who are disobedient and unfaithful are not perfect.

Servants of God have been freed from sin and have obtained mercy. *(Romans 6:22)* We sinned against the Lord out of ignorance. Jesus offered us grace—knowledge and power—and delivered us out of the hands of our enemies. We believed in the Lord and trusted in His salvation. We learned of Satan's witchcraft, denied ourselves the pleasing corruption of the flesh, and came out of the grave of sin. We serve the Lord in holiness and righteousness. We obey all that He has commanded us and walk perfect before God.

———————— Additional Edifying Scriptures ————————

"Now the God of peace, that brought again from the dead our Lord Jesus, that great shepherd of the sheep, through the blood of the everlasting covenant, make you perfect in every good work to do his will, working in you that which is wellpleasing in his sight through Jesus Christ; to whom be glory for ever and ever. Amen." (Hebrews 13:20-21)

"Again, the kingdom of heaven is like unto treasure hid in a field; the which when a man hath found, he hideth, and for joy thereof goeth and selleth all that he hath, and buyeth that field. Again, the kingdom of heaven is like unto a merchant man, seeking goodly pearls: Who, when he had found one pearl of great price, went and sold all that he had, and bought it." (Matthew 13: 44-46)

"Be watchful, and strengthen the things which remain, that are ready to die: for I have not found thy works perfect before God. Remember therefore how thou hast received and heard, and hold fast, and repent. If therefore thou shalt not watch, I will come on thee as a thief, and thou shalt not know what hour I will come upon thee." (Revelation 3:2-3)

"Depart from me, ye evildoers: for I will keep the commandments of my God." (Psalm 119:115)

"Blessed are they that keep his testimonies, and that seek him with the whole heart. They also do no iniquity: they walk in his ways. Thou hast commanded us to keep thy precepts diligently." (Psalm 119:2-4)

"The steps of a good man are ordered by the Lord: and he delighteth in his way." (Psalm 37:23)

"The Lord is righteous in all his ways, and holy in all his works."(Psalm 145:17)

"For wherein shall it be known here that I and thy people have found grace in thy sight? is it not in that thou goest with us? so shall we be separated, I and thy people, from all the people that are upon the face of the earth." (Exodus 33:16)

"For it became him, for whom are all things, and by whom are all things, in bringing many sons unto glory, to make the captain of their salvation perfect through sufferings. For both he that sanctifieth and they who are sanctified are all of one: for which cause he is not ashamed to call them brerthren," (Hebrews 2:10-11)

"My brethren, count it all joy when ye fall into divers temptations; Knowing this, that the trying of your faith worketh patience. But let patience have her perfect work, that ye may be perfect and entire, wanting nothing." (James 1:2-4)

"Though he were a Son, yet learned he obedience by the things which he suffered. And being made perfect, he became the author of eternal salvation unto all them that obey him." (Hebrews 5:8-9)

"I beseech you therefore, brethren, by the mercies of the God, that ye present your bodies a living sacrifice, holy, acceptable unto God, which is your reasonable service." (Romans 12:1)

"Forasmuch then as Christ hath suffered for us in the flesh, arm yourselves likewise with the same mind: for he that hath suffered in the flesh hath ceased from sin; That he no longer should live the rest of his time in the flesh to the lusts of men, but to the will of God." (1 Peter 4:1-2)

"And he gave some, apostles; and some, prophets; and some, evangelists; and some, pastors and teachers; For the perfecting of the saints, for the work of the ministry, for the edifying of the body of Christ." (Ephesians 4:11-12)

"Whosoever trangresseth, and abideth not in the doctrine of Christ, hath not God. He that abideth in the doctrine of Christ, he hath both the Father and the Son. If there come any unto you, and bring not this doctrine, receive him not into your house, neither bid him God speed: For he that biddeth him God speed is partaker of his evil deeds." (2 John 1:9-11)

"Sanctify them through thy truth: thy word is truth." (John 17:17)

"I press toward the mark for the prize of the high calling of God in Christ Jesus. Let us therefore, as many as be perfect, be thus minded: and if in any thing ye be otherwise minded, God shall reveal even this unto you." (Philippians 3:14-15)

"So he fed them according to the integrity of his heart; and guided them by the skillfulness of his hands." (Psalm 78:72)

"Behold, I have refined thee, but not with silver; I have chosen thee in the furnace of affliction." (Isaiah 48:10)

"Thus saith the Lord, thy Redeemer, the Holy One of Israel; I am the Lord thy God which teacheth thee to profit, which leadeth thee by the way that thou shouldest go." (Isaiah 48:17)

"Be ye therefore perfect, even as your Father which is in heaven is perfect." (Matthew 5:48)

"For as many as are led by the Spirit of God, they are the sons of God." (Romans 8:14)

"What fruit had ye then in those things whereof ye are now ashamed? for the end of those things is death." (Romans 6:21)

"For if ye live after the flesh, ye shall die: but if ye through the Spirit do mortify the deeds of the flesh, ye shall live." (Romans 8:13)

"But now being made free from sin, and become servants to God, ye have your fruit unto holiness, and the end everlasting life." (Romans 6:22)

"He that saith, I know him, and keepeth not his commandments, is a liar, and the truth is not in him. But whoso keepeth his word, in him verily is the love of God perfected: hereby we know that we are in him." (1 John 2:4-5)

"He that committeth sin is of the devil; for the devil sinneth from the beginning. For this purpose the Son of God was manifested, that he might destroy the works of the devil." (1 John 3:8)

"Because it is written, Be ye holy; for I am holy." (1 Peter 1:16)

"Seeing ye have purified your souls in obeying the truth through the Spirit unto unfeigned love of the brethren,

see that ye love one another with a pure heart fervently."
(1 Peter 1:22)

"Follow peace with all men, and holiness, without which no
man shall see the Lord." (Hebrews 12:14)

"that ye may stand perfect and complete in all the will of
God." (Colossians 4:12)

"For God hath not called us unto uncleanness, but unto
holiness." (1Thessalonians 4:7)

"And you, that were sometime alienated and enemies in
your mind by wicked works, yet now hath he reconciled in
the body of his flesh through death, to present you holy and
unblameable and unreproveable in his sight: if ye continue
in the faith grounded and settled, and be not moved away
from the hope of the gospel." (Colossians 1:21-23)

"For the upright shall dwell in the land, and the perfect shall
remain in it." (Proverbs 2:21)

"And his name through faith in his name hath made this
man strong, whom ye see and know: yea, the faith which
is by him hath given him this perfect soundness in the
presence of you all." (Acts 3:16)

"Mark the perfect man, and behold the upright: for the end
of that man is peace." (Psalm 37:37)

"And in every work that he began in the service of the house
of God, and in the law, and in the commandments, to seek
his God, he did it with all his heart, and prospered." (2
Chronicles 31:21)

"God is light, and in him is no darkness at all. If we say that we have fellowship with him, and walk in darkness, we lie and do not the truth: But if we walk in the light, as he is in the light, we have fellowship one with another, and the blood of Jesus Christ his Son cleanseth us from all sin. If we say that we have no sin, we deceive ourselves, and the truth is not in us. If we confess our sins, he is faithful and just to forgive us our sins, and to cleanse us from all unrighteousness." (1 John 1:5-9)

"The Lord will perfect that which concerneth me: thy mercy, O Lord, endureth for ever: forsake not the works of thine own hands." (Psalm 138:8)

"Blessed are they that keep his testimonies, and that seek him with the whole heart. They also do not iniquity: they walk in his ways . . . Wherewithal shall a young man cleanse his way? by taking heed thereto according to thy word. With my whole heart have I sought thee: O let me not wander from thy commandments. Thy word have I hid in mine heart, that I might not sin against thee." (Psalm 119:2,3,9,10,11)

"Let the redeemed of the Lord say so, whom he hath redeemed from the hand of the enemy;" (Psalm 107:2)

"As for God, his way is perfect: the word of the Lord is tried: he is a buckler to all those that trust in him. . . . It is God that girdeth me with strength, and maketh my way perfect." (Psalm 18:30,32)

"Nevertheless the foundation of God standeth sure, having this seal, The Lord knoweth them that are his. And, let every one that nameth the name of Christ depart from iniquity." (2 Timothy 2:19)

"And she shall bring forth a son and thou shalt call his name JESUS: for he shall save his people from their sins." (Matthew 1:21)

"Thou in they mercy hast led forth the people which thou hast redeemed: thou hast guided them in thy strength unto thy holy habitation." (Exodus 15:13)

"My foot hath held his steps, his ways have I kept, and not declined." (Job 23:11)

"There was a man in the land of Uz, whose name was Job; and that man was perfect and upright, and one that feared God, and eschewed evil." (Job 1:1)

"And now, brethren, I commend you to God, and to the word of his grace, which is able to build you up, and to give you an inheritance among all them which are sanctified." (Acts 20:32)

"Go ye therefore and teach all nations . . . teaching them to observe all things whatsoever I have commanded you." (Matthew 28:19)

"Teaching us that, denying ungodliness and worldly lusts, we should live soberly, righteously, and godly, in this present world; Looking for that blessed hope, and glorious appearing of the great God and our Saviour Jesus Christ: Who gave himself for us, that he might redeem us from all iniquity, and purify unto himself a peculiar people, zealous of good works." (Titus 2:12-14)

"There hath no temptation taken you but such as is common to man: but God is faithful, who will not suffer you to be tempted above that ye are able; but will with the temptation also make a way to escape, that ye may be able to bear it." (1 Corinthians 10:13)

"No weapon that is formed against thee shall prosper; and every tongue that shall rise against thee in judgment thou shalt condemn. This is the heritage of the servants of the Lord, and their righteousness is of me, saith the Lord." (Isaiah 54:17)

"Sanctify yourselves therefore, and be ye holy: for I am the Lord your God. And ye shall keep my statutes, and do them: I am the Lord which sanctify you." (Leviticus 20:7-8)

"Walk before me, and be thou perfect." (Genesis 17:1)

"Now unto him that is able to keep you from falling, and to present you faultless before the presence of his glory with exceeding joy." (Jude 1:24)

"Thou shalt be perfect with the Lord thy God." (Deuteronomy 18:13)

"For the upright shall dwell in the land, and the perfect shall remain in it." (Proverbs 2:21)

"Trust in the Lord with all thine heart; and lean not unto thine own understanding. In all thy ways acknowledge him, and he shall direct thy paths." (Proverbs 3:5-6)

"For the Lord hath redeemed Jacob, and ransomed him from the hand of him that was stronger than he." (Jeremiah 31:11)

"For they verily for a few days chastened us after their own pleasure; but he for our profit, that we might be partakers of his holiness. Now no chastening for the present seemeth to be joyous, but grievous; nevertheless, afterward it yieldeth the peaceable fruit of righteousness unto them which are exercised thereby." (Hebrews 12:10-11)

"Then spake Jesus again unto them, saying, I am the light of the world: he that followeth me shall not walk in darkness, but shall have the light of life." (John 8:12)

"Wherefore, beloved, seeing that ye look for such things, be diligent that ye may be found of him in peace, without spot, and blameless." (2 Peter 3:14)

"Thou wilt keep him in perfect peace, whose mind is stayed on thee: because he trusted in thee." (Isaiah 26:3)

"And be renewed in the spirit of your mind; and that ye put on the new man, which after God is created in righteousness and true holiness." (Ephesians 4:23-24)

CHAPTER SEVENTEEN

BORN AGAIN OF THE SPIRIT

As we near the conclusion of the book, it should be obvious—as Jesus prophesied—that false prophets have saturated the world with false teachings. It is impossible to address all of the lies false prophets teach. Nonetheless, many readers are honest enough to admit that they walk in sin and are separated from God, despite His commandment that we live holy. Since children of God must do the works of Abraham and walk perfect before the Lord, it is appropriate to discuss how individuals are able to live a perfect life. We will transition in the book from the lying vanities of the false prophets and directly address the transformative power of God.

God is not natural. He is neither a man nor woman. God is a spirit. *(John 4:24)* In Him, we live and move and have our being. *(Acts 17:28)* As the Almighty, God has all the power and deserves all the glory. Those who worship the Lord do not worship flesh; they worship spirit. Since the spirit transcends the flesh, we exalt the spirit above the flesh. We renounce Satan's witchcraft, false prophets' lying vanities, and our own corruption. We bring everything into captivity unto the obedience of Christ.

To the defiled, nothing is pure. *(Titus1:15)* The god of this world has blinded their minds to the truth: Jesus has the power to deliver the people out of the bondage of sin. Satan has corrupted the minds of spiritual Hebrew slaves and taught them through false prophets that they cannot overcome the enemies. Separated from God, the people do not have the power to defeat their enemies. Without any assurance that God exists, most do not have confidence in His word and lean to their own defiled survival skills. In order to save their corrupt flesh, they are willing to rebel against the commandments of God and destroy their own soul.

Anyone can profess to believe in God. There is a major difference, though, between theory and fact. It would be hypocritical for the people to confess Jesus as Lord, yet exalt Satan. It would be unjust for a holy God to command the people to confront the fear of death and entrust their lives to Him without giving the people any credible evidence to confirm His existence. People have children, parents, and others who depend upon them. Jesus knows that are our enemies are too strong for us. It would be suicide to confront our more powerful enemies – unless we have a God who is willing and able to save us from our enemies.

In the days of old, God performed visible miracles to demonstrate His existence. He dwells within His people today in the form of the Holy Ghost. Unbelievers may not be aware of His existence, but the Spirit of God is delivering His people out of the bondage of sin and redeeming us from corruption. We have been baptized in the name of Jesus Christ and received the gift of the Holy Ghost. We are journeying to perfection. *(Hebrews 6:1)*

———————— **Came That You Might Have Life** ————————

As corrupt souls, it is easy for many to fall for the witchcraft and believe that God does not exist. We were conceived through deception. We were born as slaves. Hence, our minds were distorted while we were yet in the womb. Further, Satan, the god of this world, has the power of death. *(Hebrews 2:14)* In fact, all that we have is within Satan's power. *(Job 1:12)* When our enemies are too strong for us and have power over our lives, we feel compelled to conform to their will. Since the life of the flesh is the only life the unredeemed have ever known, their survival requires them to depend upon their own knowledge and experience to survive. Since the life of the flesh is corrupt, the unredeemed only know the ways of corruption. Hence, those who lean to their own understanding to survive will remain corrupt. *(Proverbs 14:12)*

Jesus Christ came to save the people from their sins and to bear witness to the truth: He is the Almighty God. Satan, the god of this world, has the power of death; power over the natural. Jesus is Lord of Heaven and earth. He has power over the spiritual and the natural; Jesus has the power of life and death.

Our God, the God of the living (Jesus Christ) not the god of the dead (Satan), has the power to resurrect those who are dead. He promised to ransom sinners from the grave of sin and to restore their spiritual life. "I will ransom them from the power of the grave; I will redeem them from death." *(Hosea 13:14)* Remember: Satan corrupted Adam and Eve through witchcraft and made them die. We were all conceived through the lust of the flesh. Since the life of the flesh is in the blood, lust is our nature. We have to die out to the flesh to overcome the lust of the flesh within the blood. Yet, Satan, through the fear of death, has the people afraid to die. *(Hebrews 2:14-15)* As a result, the people cannot overcome the lust of the flesh, because the lust of the flesh is within their blood, which is the life of the flesh. We have to relinquish the only life we know—the life of the flesh—to overcome lust. Skin for skin, most people are not going to give up their natural life. They will embrace lust of the flesh and corruption before they accept death. The irony is, corruption is death.

Satan does not have power over those whose eyes are opened. *(Acts 26:18)* We know Jesus is Lord and do not fear death. We know that the life of the flesh is a life of corruption. The life of the flesh is death, and God is going to destroy death. Unlike the deceived, we know that Satan rules through the fear of death. Hence, those who walk after the flesh and remain in sin are going to be destroyed. Satan has positioned us to self-destruct, and he has sent false prophets to deceive us into believing that Jesus has already saved us. The deceived do not understand that Jesus did not die so we could serve Satan. *(Jeremiah 7:1-15; Ezra 9:10-15)* Jesus died so the honest in heart (those with integrity) would be free to serve God. Regardless of how much the people pretend that their heart is right, God knew how to find out who would serve Him or not: He placed everyone in captivity. He would deliver and redeem those who trusted in His word; and He would allow those who did not trust in Him to destroy themselves.

In other words, God offered everyone the right to come out of the grave of sin. Those who confessed that Jesus was Lord and came out of captivity were saved from their sins. They kept His commandments and inherited the right to enter in through the gates into the city. *(Revelation 22:14)* Those who confessed that Jesus was Lord but remained in the bondage of sin were condemned. They rejected His knowledge of salvation and chose to remain in the grave among the dead. *(Hebrews 2:2-3)* "For by thy words thou shalt be justified, and by thy words thou shalt be condemned." *(Matthew 12:37)* Those whose hearts were right obeyed His commandments; those whose hearts were not right disobeyed. "For their heart was not right with him, neither were they stedfast in his covenant." *(Psalm 78:37)*

Jesus died to redeem the people from the grave. He died to offer them remission of sins, so that they could return to God. Those who believe that Jesus is Lord and that God raised up Jesus out of the grave will trust in God to deliver them from the grave of sin. Those who walk in the light know that God commanded us to live holy, and we cannot live holy unless He delivers us out of the hands of our stronger enemy. Hence, we do not fear death because God has to save us. He is a God that cannot lie. *(Titus 1:2)* Not only has He given us His word, but we cannot serve Him unless He saves us from the enemy. He has promised to save us, so we can serve Him. *(Luke 1:67-75)*

Jesus Christ stumbled under the weight of the cross. He dreaded having iron spikes hammered through his hands and feet, yet He had supreme confidence that the spirit would raise Him from the dead. Followers of Christ dread suffering, but know that natural suffering reflects the death of sin in our life. Unlike unbelievers, who lust after pleasure and remain slaves to flesh, believers know that Satan rules through witchcraft. We reject the pleasure of the flesh and refuse to indulge the corruption within our blood. We refuse to allow the god of this doomed world to bewitch us to self-destruct along with him. We want to reconcile with God and reclaim our spiritual birthright to inherit eternal life.

When the Lord decided to deliver the children of Israel out of Egypt, Pharaoh did not have the power to stop Him. When the Lord decided to resurrect Lazarus from the grave, death could not stop Him. When God decided to raise Jesus from the grave, the body of Christ, despite the absence of blood, was restored to life. The flesh-and-blood body of Jesus Christ died, but the Spirit of Jesus Christ remained alive. Since Jesus coveted eternal life and the flesh was going to die anyway, Jesus made a wise choice. When we stop walking after the corruption within our blood and die out to sin, we resurrect our soul from the grave. Our flesh is going to die anyway; we want our soul to inherit eternal life. The Spirit of God raises us out of the grave of sin and gives us victory over our enemies. *(1 Corinthians 15:55-57)*

We derive our confidence in our ability to overcome sin from the knowledge that greater is He that is in us than he that is in the world. *(1 John 4:4)* Further, we trust our God, as He has promised, to save us from the enemy as we escape from sin. Thus, we admit that Jesus is Lord and refuse to allow fear of death or lust of the flesh to make us rebel against Him. We renounce the things of this world and embrace the things of God. We love not the world, nor the things that are in the world. We do not walk after the god of this world—or his embellishments. We walk after the Almighty. Just as Christ was resurrected from the grave and walked in the flesh despite the absence of blood, we walk in the flesh but do not walk after the corruption within our blood. The same spirit that resurrected Christ from among the dead resurrects us from among the dead. We have consented to sacrifice the life of the flesh to walk in the Spirit of God.

—————————— **Except A Man Is Born Again** ——————————

Except a man is born again of water and spirit, he cannot enter the Kingdom of God. *(John 3:5)* That which is born of flesh is flesh, and that which is born of spirit is spirit. Since we were conceived through the lust of the flesh, we were born separated from God. When we are born again of the spirit, we have been integrated with God. Just as a newborn baby will not experience puberty and wrestle with all of the weaknesses of the flesh at his birth, a spiritual newborn will not overcome all of the weaknesses of the flesh as soon as he is born again. Just as newborn babies will have to ultimately struggle with the lust of the flesh, spiritual newborns will have to ultimately overcome lust to remain reconciled with God.

God knows that individuals who have been born again must overcome lust of the flesh and move on to perfection. *(Hebrews 6:1)* Therefore, the Lord will do everything possible to help an individual to overcome. He tells the people to always pray. He tells the people to fast. He tells the people to come boldly before the throne of grace and get the help they need. *(Hebrews 4:16)* Our God, who is mighty to save, does not want any to perish, and will save those who call upon His name. In fact, our God is so committed to saving the people, until He gives us something that we do not deserve—the gift of the Holy Ghost. All of His ways are holy and perfect. Ergo, when we are led by His spirit, all of our ways are holy and perfect. We become children of God. "For as many as are led by the Spirit of God, they are the sons of God." *(Romans 8:14)* We crucify the flesh and allow the Spirit to guide us. He tells us what to do, and we obey His commandments. "I have chosen the way of truth: thy judgments have I laid before me. *(Psalm 119:30)*

Although we are polluted when we initially seek Him, the Lord bestows upon us His spirit. His presence empowers and comforts us. His spirit confirms His existence. Further, the spirit transcends the law of nature; therefore, the Holy Ghost gives us power over the flesh and this world. Thus, the Holy Ghost reassures us that there is a spiritual world, which corroborates that the life of the flesh is not the only life that exists; the Holy Ghost proves that God exists; and the Holy Ghost entreats us to walk in the power of the Almighty.

Consider: Peter was ready to fight when the Romans came to capture Jesus. Once Jesus was captured, Peter became afraid of death and betrayed Christ three times. However, after Peter received the Holy Ghost, he was ready to fight again. The Holy Ghost reinvigorated Peter's willingness to fight for Christ. He never betrayed the Master again. Likewise, the Holy Ghost gives us a new life. We do not have to betray Christ through the fear of death. If we obey God and crucify the flesh, we will overcome sin and live in the spirit with Christ throughout eternity.

––––––––– **Have Ye Received the Holy Ghost?** –––––––––

One of the very first things that preachers who have been sent by God want to know: "Have ye received the Holy Ghost since ye believed?" *(Acts 19:2)* God raised Lazarus from the dead, parted the Red Sea, delivered the children of Israel out of Egypt, opened the eyes of the blind, walked on water, made the wind to cease, and performed all manner of miracles. The Holy Ghost is the Spirit of God. With the Holy Ghost dwelling within us, we have transcendental power—power over all natural things, over all of the things of the world. The Holy Ghost confirms that our God is real, and we know from the scripture that He has all power. Therefore, with the power of the Almighty within us, we have power over all weaknesses, shortcomings, fears—all the power of the enemy. *(Luke 10:19)* We do not have to live in fear; we do not have to remain slaves to sin. Our God, who cannot lie, has assured us that He will save us during our escape.

––––––––––––– **Comforter** –––––––––––––

Receiving the gift of the Holy Ghost is without question the most important part of spiritual growth—we have returned home to the Father. The phrase "Holy Ghost" differentiates the Spirit of God from demonic spirits. If we are servants of God, we must serve Him in the spirit. Since all of His ways are holy, all of our ways must be holy. Through fasting, praying, and transforming our mind, we bring our natural desires under subjection. We offer our bodies as a living sacrifice, holy and acceptable unto God, which is our reasonable service. Just as God was in Christ, i.e, the spirit was inside the flesh-and-blood body, the Holy Ghost is God within us. Those who are obedient to His commandments—like Abraham, Job, Daniel, and Noah—are perfect; their steps are ordered by the Lord. *(Psalm 37:23)*

Just as Jesus, the Son, was God with us when He walked in the flesh, Jesus, the Holy Ghost, is God with us in the Spirit. *(Matthew 1:23; Philippians 1:19)* The Jesus Christ who followed the children of Israel as they journeyed from the bondage of Egypt to their natural Promised Land is the same Jesus Christ who walks with us as we journey from the bondage of sin to our spiritual Promised Land. *(1 Corinthians 10:4)* He promised, when He went away, that the Father would send the Comforter. The Holy Ghost, Jesus Christ, is our Comforter. He told us that He would be with us until the end. *(Matthew 28:20)*

The Holy Ghost spoke from Heaven and asked Saul why he persecuted Him. "And he said, who art thou, Lord? And the Lord said, I am Jesus whom thou persecutest: it is hard for thee to kick against the pricks." *(Acts 9:5)* Jesus came from spirit and went back to spirit. There is one Lord; Jesus is Lord; the Lord is God; and God is a spirit. *(Ephesians 4:5; Acts 9:5; Psalm 100:3; and John 4:24)*

The God that Answers by Fire

Ahab asked the prophet Elijah if he were the one who troubled Israel. Elijah answered that he had not troubled Israel. The people were troubled because they had forsaken the Lord and idolized pagan gods. Elijah, the only prophet of the Lord, told Ahab to send for his prophets. After the eight hundred and fifty false prophets appeared, Elijah told them to cut up two bullocks, which were subsequently laid on wood. "And call ye on the name of your gods, and I will call on the name of the Lord: and the God that answereth by fire, let him be God. And all the people answered and said, It is well spoken." *(1 Kings 18:24)* All the people agreed that if God existed and wanted the people to serve Him, the least He could do was to reveal who He was, so they would know whom to serve.

Elijah challenged the false prophets to call upon their god to see if he would answer. The false prophets called upon their god from morning until noon. After their god did not answer, they began to make blood sacrifices. Elijah mocked them and their god. The pagans called upon their god again to answer until the evening sacrifice. Their god did not answer. He could not answer: he did not exist.

Elijah told the people to come near him. He took twelve stones and built an altar. He built a trench around the altar. He told the people to pour water upon the bullocks and upon the wood. He told them to repeat the process a second and third time. The water drenched the bullocks and wood, and filled the trench. Elijah prayed and asked the Lord to demonstrate that He was the Lord God. "Then the fire of the Lord fell, and consumed the burnt sacrifice, and the wood, and the stones, and the dust, and licked up the water that was in the trench." *(1 Kings 18:38)* The God of Abraham, Isaac, and Jacob—the Lord Jesus Christ—is the only God who answers by fire. He is the only God who exists.

Pillar of Fire and Cloud

As the children of Israel exited the land of Egypt, the Lord went before them by day in a pillar of a cloud, to lead them the way; and by night in a pillar of fire, to give them light. *(Exodus 13:21)* Back in Egypt, Pharaoh could not rest. The slaves had worked and helped to build Egypt into the richest and most powerful nation on earth. Their exodus from bondage was a slap in the face to Egypt as a nation and to Pharaoh as a king. If Egypt was so powerful and Pharaoh a god, why were the slaves able to simply walk out of the land in peace? Pharaoh could not deny the preeminent power of

God. His wounded pride, however, made him rise up to fight again. He went after the children of Israel with the expectation to bring them back into captivity.

The children of Israel were encamped against the sea when they observed Pharaoh's chariots quickly approaching. Fear of death came upon the people, and they cried unto the Lord for deliverance. The angel of the Lord removed from the front to the back—between the children of Israel and the Egyptians. It was a cloud and darkness to Egypt, but it gave light by night to the Hebrews. *(Exodus 14:19-20)*

While the fire separated the two groups, God breathed upon the water and caused it to dry, and the Hebrews went through the sea on dry ground. *(Exodus 15:8)* In the morning, after the children of Israel had crossed the sea, the Egyptians pursued after the Hebrews into the water with the intention to overtake them. The Lord made the water return into the sea and drowned the Egyptians. Hence, while the people of God went through the water, the fire of the Lord protected and shielded them from their enemies. The children of Israel were baptized in the cloud and in the sea. *(1 Corinthians 10:1-2)* God destroyed the works of the Egyptians and delivered the children of Israel out of the bondage of Egypt. *(Exodus 14:30-31)* The people continued their journey toward the Promised Land to reclaim their inheritance.

Similarly, when we receive the Holy Ghost, we stop doing the works of the devil. Demons who once ruled over us have been made subject unto us. *(Luke 10:17)* Just as the Holy Ghost was a pillar of fire to protect the children of Israel from the Egyptians, the Holy Ghost is a cloven tongue like as of fire to protect the children of God from Satan. *(Acts 2:3)* Just as the children of Israel were baptized in the sea, the children of God are baptized in water. *(Acts 2:38)* God buried Israel's enemies in the sea, and we bury our sins in water baptism. *(Colossians 2:12)* God has given us a new life, which gives us the impetus to bury the life of corruption.

Those who do not have the Holy Ghost cannot see through spiritual darkness; they cannot see through Satan's witchcraft and false prophets' lies. "Judas saith unto him, not Iscariot, Lord, how is it that thou wilt manifest thyself unto us, and not unto the world." *(John 14:16-26)* Those who have the Holy Ghost are able to escape from the bondage of sin because the fire of the Holy Ghost is a light unto us, yet darkness to the world. "Even the Spirit of truth; whom the world cannot receive, because it seeth him not, neither knoweth him: but ye know him; for he dwelleth with you, and shall be in you. *(John 14:17)* Those who have the Holy Ghost understand prophecy, because holy men of old spake as they were moved by the Holy Ghost. *(2 Peter 1:21)* Hence, those who have the Spirit of God have the same spirit that moved on the prophets to write the scriptures, and they have the same spirit as those whom God sent to explain the scriptures. *(John 20:22)* We have all been baptized into the same spirit. *(1 Corinthians 12:13)*

While those who have the Holy Ghost are cleansing ourselves in the water of baptism and escaping the pollution of this world (redeemed), the fire of the Holy Ghost prevents our enemies from overtaking us (saved). The knowledge of Jesus Christ (light) illuminates our path through the darkness (ignorance) and helps us to escape from captivity (make us free from sin).

Remember: after God made Adam from the dust, He breathed into Adam, and Adam became a living soul. *(Genesis 2:7)* The breath of God is the Spirit of God. After God parted the sea, He breathed upon the water and dried up the sea, which allowed the people to pass over on dry land. "And with the blast of thy nostrils the waters were gathered together, the floods stood upright as an heap, and the depths were congealed in the heart of the sea." *(Exodus 15:8)* The breath of God that parted the waters was the Spirit of God, the Holy Ghost, that breathed life into Adam. Moreover, the breath of God that breathed life into Adam and parted the waters was the Holy Ghost that Jesus told His disciples to receive when He breathed upon them. "And when he had said this, he breathed on them, and saith unto them, Receive ye the Holy Ghost." *(John 20:22)* When we receive the Holy Ghost, we have received the breath of life; we have been born again of the spirit—the Spirit of God has come into our bodies. Our soul, which was lost in the Garden of Eden, has been restored.

Although the life of the flesh is in the blood, the Holy Ghost has given us a new life. Our life is no longer limited to flesh and blood; we have both the Father and the Son, the spirit and flesh. Like Adam (before he died) and Jesus, we are divine and human. Integrated with God. If we continue in the Spirit, we will be perfect, like Jesus; we will resurrect our soul from the grave of sin and inherit eternal life. Alas, if we sin against God, like Adam, we will die.

Since the Spirit of God has power over Satan, whereas Satan has power over the flesh, those who want to please the Father will follow the example of the Son. They will take up their cross and crucify the flesh. They will renounce the life of corruption within their blood and reclaim their right to inherit the Kingdom of God. Unlike the first man Adam, who sacrificed his spiritual life to exalt his natural life, those who follow the second man Adam, Jesus Christ, will sacrifice their natural life to retain their spiritual life. In crucifying the flesh and exalting the spirit, we demonstrate that we renounce corruption to save our soul. We exalt God (spirit) above ourselves (flesh).

The Holy Ghost, the Spirit of God, comforts us. We have God's knowledge, and we have His power within our bodies. *(John 14:26; John 3:8)* We are not afraid of death. His rod of instruction (knowledge) and staff (power) give us comfort. We overcome sin and love not our own lives, even unto death. *(Revelation 12:11)* We renounce the life of the flesh, which wars against our soul. *(1 Peter 2:11)* Accordingly, we walk in the spirit and deny the flesh. Those who have been born again of the Spirit and redeemed from corruption will inherit the Kingdom of God, where they, as holy spirits, will enjoy eternal life.

Endued With Power from On High

Jesus shed His blood on the cross. Since the life of the flesh is in the blood, Jesus did not have a natural life after He rose from the grave. He had flesh, but no blood. Once Jesus demonstrated that He was Lord, He had to leave. Having shed His blood, He was no longer in the form of a servant. He could not remain in the earth as a spirit. He was the Almighty, and His kingdom was not of this world. This was Satan's kingdom, and the Almighty could not be subordinated to a false god. Once He went back to Heaven as a spirit, He could return to the earth as a spirit. He had defeated the god of this world, and demonstrated that He was Lord of Heaven and earth. Therefore, Jesus had the authority to rule in the kingdom of men. *(Daniel 4:25)* Since He had paid the ransom, He had the right to deliver His servants out of captivity, and His servants acquired the right to leave captivity.

Jesus did not sacrifice His integrity, despite his life of flesh and blood. He rejected Satan's witchcraft and did not capitulate to the fear of death. With power over death, Jesus walked free of sin and defeated death. As a result, He did not have to die for His sin. His death paid for the sins of everyone else who had been conceived in sin. Jesus came to ensure that we would not have to die in sin. In other words, because of Adam's disobedience, the entire human family died. Jesus came to resurrect us from the dead, from the grave of sin, so we do not have to suffer the second death—eternal damnation. Jesus waited and allowed death to overtake Lazarus; Jesus allowed death—sin—to overtake all of us. However, just as He resurrected Lazarus from the grave, Jesus has the power to resurrect all of us from the grave of sin.

Sinners, who, through fear of death, were all their lifetime subject to bondage, do not have to fear death anymore. "O death, where is thy sting? O grave, where is thy victory? The sting of death is sin; and the strength of sin is the law." *(1 Corinthians 15:55-56)* Those who want to exit out of the bondage of sin are free to leave. All we need is the power that gave Jesus victory over Satan—the power of the Holy Ghost. The Holy Ghost—the Spirit of God—gives all believers power over death. Just as God breathed upon the waters and freed the children of Israel from the bondage of Egypt, God will breath upon us—the Holy Ghost—and free us from the bondage of sin. The power of the enemy has been broken over our lives. We are no longer forced to serve false gods. We can live with integrity and worship the Lord in spirit and in truth.

The prophets foretold that God was going to pour out His spirit upon the people and ransom them from the grave. *(Joel 2:28; Hosea 13:14)* Before Jesus ascended back to Heaven, He told His disciples to go to Jerusalem and wait there. "And, behold, I send the promise of my Father upon you: but tarry ye in the city of Jerusalem, until ye be endued with power from on high." *(Luke 24:49)* After His people received the Holy Ghost, they would be endued with the power of God—the same power that kept Jesus free from sin; the same power that destroyed the Egyptians and set the Hebrews free; and the same power that destroyed the works of the devil and set us free. *(Acts 1:8)* Now that we walk in the light, our eyes have been opened. We have turned from the power of Satan to God.

─────────────── **Rushing Mighty Wind** ───────────────

God breathed into Adam, and Adam became a living soul. *(Genesis 2:7)* God breathed upon the waters, in the form of the wind, and parted the sea. *(Exodus 14:21; Exodus 15:8)* God breathed upon His disciples and prepared them to receive the Holy Ghost. *(John 20:22)* On the day of Pentecost, God breathed upon His disciples, in the form of a rushing mighty wind, and they were all filled with the gift of the Holy Ghost. *(Acts 2:1-4)*

"And when the day of Pentecost was fully come, they were all with one accord in one place. And suddenly there came a sound from heaven as of a rushing mighty wind, and it filled all the house where they were sitting. And there appeared unto them cloven tongues like as of fire, and it sat upon each of them. And they were all filled with the Holy Ghost, and began to speak with other tongues, as the Spirit gave them utterance." *(Acts 2:1-4)*

In addition to hearing the wind, there appeared unto them cloven tongues like as of fire. Remember, the god that answers by fire is God. Elijah prayed and supplicated to the Lord to show the people that He was God; God answered by fire. *(1 Kings 18:38)* Solomon prayed and supplicated to the Lord; God answered by fire. *(1 Kings 9:3; 2 Chronicles 7:1)* On the day of Pentecost, the disciples continued in prayer and supplication; God answered by fire. *(Acts 1:14; Acts 2:3)* Just as the Lord appeared as a pillar of fire to light the way through the darkness for the children of Israel, the Lord appeared as cloven tongues, like as of fire, to those in the upper room. The Holy Ghost—the Spirit of God—guides the people through the darkness into the truth. *(John 16:13)* God's word, in the midst of the darkness, is a lamp unto our feet, and a light unto our pathway. *(Psalm 119:105)*

There were those in Jerusalem who heard the disciples speak in tongues and thought the disciples were drunk. Peter stood up and explained that those who spoke in tongues were not drunk. The noise that the people heard had been prophesied: "And it shall come to pass afterward, that I will pour out my spirit upon all flesh; and your sons and your daughters shall prophesy, your old men shall dream dreams, your young men shall see visions: and also upon the servants and upon the handmaids in those days will I pour out my spirit." *(Joel 2:28-29)*

Unlike what Nicodemus thought, men and women did not have to enter again into their mothers' wombs to be born again. The people had already been born of the flesh. God simply needed to pour His spirit upon the people. "That which is born of the flesh is flesh; and that which is born of the Spirit is spirit." *(John 3:6)* Those that received the Holy Ghost had been born again—not of the flesh—but of the spirit. God had filled them with His spirit. God had breathed into them and restored their souls. They had received a new life; they had become living souls.

Polluted In Our Own Blood

Many of us engage in deviant behavior. We are filled with self-loathing and hate how we live. We do things that we do not want to do and do not understand why we continue to do them. Our families and friends look upon us with disdain and wonder why we cannot seem to get our lives together, and we have no explanation. We do not understand that Adam and Eve lusted after the flesh and passed their corruption through the blood. We were conceived in sin and shapened in iniquity; we were born to self-destruct.

Not only was corruption within our blood, we were ignorant. Satan had bewitched us and enticed us to lust after the very corruption that caused us to self-destruct. We derived pleasure from the pain that killed us. Like Legion, we committed suicide on the installment plan—killing ourselves little by little. Yet, the Lord had mercy upon our soul. "And when I passed by thee, and saw thee polluted in thine own blood, I said unto thee, when thou wast in thy blood, Live, yea, I said unto thee when thou wast in thy blood, Live." *(Ezekiel 16:6)* If Jesus had not come and taught (discipline) us how to deny ourselves, we would have continued to indulge the very witchcraft that caused us to destroy ourselves.

The Spirit of the Lord took the prophet Ezekiel into a valley filled with very dry bones. Life had ceased long before. The Lord asked the prophet if the bones could live. Ezekiel told the Lord that He knew whether the bones could live. God told the prophet to prophesy to the bones. Ezekiel prophesied to the bones, and told them to hear the word of the Lord. The word of the Lord (grace) restores life to the dead. *(John 6:63)* The prophet prophesied to the wind; the wind was the breath of God. *(Ezekiel 37:5-6)* Skin returned upon the bones; breath went into them; life was resurrected. *(Ezekiel 37:14)*

The people had lost hope and thought they were forever dead. *(Ezekiel 37:11)* The Lord told the prophet to prophesy to the dead bones and tell the people that He would open up the graves and restore their life. "And ye shall know that I am the Lord, when I have opened your graves, O my people, and brought you up out of your graves. And shall put my spirit in you, and ye shall live, and I shall place you in your own land: then shall ye know that I the Lord have spoken it, and performed it, saith the Lord." *(Ezekiel 37:13-14)*

The word is God, and the Spirit of God is the breath of life! It does not matter how long we have been dead in sin. Satan bewitched us with the things of the world and kept us separated from God. The false prophets deceived us and led us to believe that we could not overcome the grave of sin. Thanks to the knowledge of Jesus Christ, we no longer walk in darkness. If we are willing to hear the word of the Lord, God will teach us how to overcome the enemy. He will breathe upon our dry bones and raise us from the dead. If we humble ourselves and return unto the Lord, though we were dead, we will come out of the grave of sin. God will put His spirit in us, and we will live.

Satan had bewitched us. Through the fear of death, we were buried in the grave of sin. We were afraid to relinquish the drugs, alcohol, and other palliatives that destroyed our lives, because they gave us temporary pleasure from our relentless pain. Yet, it was our indulgence in the works of the flesh—sin—that separated us from the Spirit, which allowed Satan to impose heavy burdens upon us. "But sin, that it might appear sin, working death in me by that which is good." *(Romans 7:13)* Satan had persuaded us that the things of the world would help us to enjoy life, yet the things of the world were of Satan. Hence, the devil bamboozled us and had us to believe that if we served God and gave up the things of the world, we would be miserable. He manipulated us to believe that we needed to try a different drug, engage in more debauchery, maybe immerse ourselves deeper into the things of the world, we would find nirvana. We became more and more sick—dying in our own blood. We were dead (slaves) in sin. Worse, when our Savior came to teach us how to escape, the enemy sent false prophets to tell us that we could not overcome the sin that killed us. They offered lying vanities to make us feel slightly better, but we remained in the grave of sin and suffered the sting of death. Thankfully, God sent His word and healed us. Jesus ransomed us from the grave of sin and taught us how to overcome the enemy; Christ awakened us out of sleep and caused us to arise from the dead. He taught us how to overcome, set us free from the bondage of sin, and gave us a new life in the Spirit of God. *(Ephesians 5:14)*

The Lord has taught the people how to overcome Satan. Remember: God so loved the world that He gave His only begotten son as sacrifice for the sins of the people; those who believed in Jesus would not die. *(John 3:16)* Jesus told Mary that if she believed, she would see the glory of God. Jesus resurrected Lazarus while He was yet buried and gave him a new life. "I am the resurrection, and the life: he that believeth in me, though he were dead, yet shall he live. And whosoever liveth and believeth in me shall never die." *(John 11:25-26)* Those who have the Spirit of God cannot die; they can only sleep. The spirit is eternal life.

Similarly, Jesus told Paul to open our eyes. Just as Jesus told Mary that if she believed, she would see the power of God, all believers will see the power of God and not be afraid of the power of Satan. The fear of death will no longer keep them in bondage; death would be swallowed up in victory. Christ overcame death; death was swallowed up in victory. Jesus came out of the grave, and, when He arose, He ransomed all believers out of the grave of sin. He went back to Heaven and poured out His spirit upon all believers. The power of the Holy Ghost—the power of God—makes all demons subject to us. We are not subject to any demons.

Our objective is to tell believers to ignore the lying vanities of false prophets. Satan wants to entice sinners to believe that it is expected for them to remain in the bondage of sin. The devil knows that the Lord will forgive us of our sins only if we come out of the grave. *(Colossians 2:13)* We cannot remain in the grave of sin and receive forgiveness; the grave is for those who have rejected God's words of eternal life. We are "warning every man, and teaching every man in all wisdom; that we may present every man perfect in Christ Jesus." *(Colossians 1:28)*

The Breath of Life

God breathed into the dust, and Adam became a living soul. *(Genesis 2:7)* God breathed upon the waters, and the children of Israel passed over on dry land and started a new life outside of

Egypt. *(Exodus 15:8)* God breathed upon the dry bones, and the dead regained life. *(Ezekiel 37:10)* God promised that He would ransom the people from the grave. "Therefore prophesy and say unto them, Thus saith the Lord God; Behold, O my people, I will open your graves, and bring you into the land of Israel. And ye shall know that I am the Lord, when I have opened your graves, O my people, and brought you up out of your graves, And shall put my spirit in you, and ye shall live." *(Ezekiel 37:12-14)*

Jesus did not come into the earth to leave our souls in hell. Although Satan had captured us with witchcraft and had us enslaved in the bondage (grave) of sin, Jesus came to destroy him. *(Hebrews 2:14-15)* He came to deliver us from the grave—the sting of death is sin. *(1 Corinthians 15:56)* After we have been delivered from Satan and the power of death, we are no longer forced to work as slaves anymore. We do not have to be afraid of death anymore; hence, we are free to serve the Lord without fear. We will remain stedfast in the apostles' doctrine and abound in the work of the Lord. *(1 Corinthians 15:58)*

——————————— **Recapitulate** ———————————

Of course, since no one can enter the Kingdom of God unless he has been born again, false prophets have deceived the people about how they have been born again. Accordingly, I will address how to know when an individual has been born again of the spirit.

First, I want to take a moment to help readers connect why Jesus observed that no one could enter the Kingdom of God unless he was born again of the water and of the spirit. Remember: before the children of Israel came out of Egypt, they sacrificed an unblemished lamb and placed the blood upon their door posts. They subsequently ate the lamb. Eating the lamb, of course, foreshadowed when we would eat of the flesh of Jesus Christ (the Lamb of God). Those of us who ate of His flesh (knowledge) and drank of His blood (sacrifice the life of the flesh; sin) cleansed ourselves from the pollution of this world. We washed ourselves in His blood. *(Psalm 119:9; Revelation 7:14)* We made a covenant by sacrifice.

Further, as the children of Israel exited out of bondage, Egypt attempted to overtake them. God breathed upon the water and allowed the children of Israel to escape. He destroyed the Egyptians. *(Exodus 14:30)* The people did not have to fear death anymore. When we bury our lust and corruption in water baptism, we are buried with Christ. We do not have to fear death anymore. God has ransomed us from the power of the grave (sin) and destroyed our enemies. *(Hebrews 2:14-15)* Ergo, when we are born again of water, we eat of His flesh and drink of His blood. We crucify the flesh. When we are born again of the spirit, we have a new life. God has breathed into us and made us into living souls. God gave everyone the option to choose life or death: Those who offered up their flesh as sacrifice to redeem their lost soul chose to inherit eternal life. Those who chose to save their natural life and its inherent corruption have renounced their spiritual life. They chose to inherit eternal damnation.

Caveat: In Adam all died; the sins of the father were visited upon the sons. In Christ, all have been made alive. The soul that sin, it shall die. We cannot blame anyone but ourselves.

———— These Signs Shall Follow Them That Believe ————

The scripture tells us, "And these signs shall follow them that believe; In my name, shall they shall cast out devils; they shall speak with new tongues; They shall take up serpents; and if they drink any deadly thing, it shall not hurt them; they shall lay hands on the sick, and they shall recover." *(Mark 16:17-18)* Those who believe will call upon the Lord, and our God will answer by fire. He will pour upon us His Spirit, which confirms His existence. Thus, we know that Jesus Christ is the true God, the living God.

For They Heard Them Speak With Tongues

Satan does not want us to be redeemed from corruption. Accordingly, the demon has sent blind false teachers to deceive the people about the meaning of born again. It is common for false prophets to exhort the people to pray and ask God to come into their lives; they receive Him as their Lord and Savior. If the people confess with their mouth and believe in their heart, according to the false prophets, the people have been born again. Satan is crafty but his deceitfulness will not prevail against the church—those who walk in the Spirit of Jesus Christ. *(Matthew 16:18)*

Peter said that Jesus was the Christ, the Son of the living God. *(Matthew 16:16)* When confronted with the fear of death, Peter betrayed Christ three times. To be born again is not to utter words; anyone can make gibberish sounds. To be born again is to be filled with the Holy Ghost. Those that walk after the flesh walk after the corruption within their blood. Those that walk after the spirit are guided by the Holy Spirit.

God breathed into Adam, and man became a living soul. God breathed upon the wind and divided the sea to restore life to the children of Israel. *(Exodus 15:8)* The prophet Ezekiel prophesied to the dead bones, and the breath of God restored life to the dead. *(Ezekiel 37:9-10)* Jesus breathed upon His disciples and told them to receive the Holy Ghost. *(John 20:22)* The Holy Ghost is the breath of God. It is critical that the people know when they have received the Holy Ghost, because no one can enter the Kingdom of God except he or she has been born again.

When the day of Pentecost was fully come, there came a sound from Heaven as of a mighty rushing wind. Peter and the other disciples received the Holy Ghost. "And they were all filled with the Holy Ghost, and began to speak with other tongues, as the Spirit gave them utterance." *(Acts 2:4)* The Spirit of God made them speak with other tongues. How do we know that speaking in other tongues indicated they had received the Holy Ghost? Peter verified that their speaking in tongues fulfilled the prophecy. "But this is

374 | ELVIS CARDELL BANKS

that which was spoken by the prophet Joel; And it shall come to pass in the last days, saith God, I will pour out of my Spirit upon all flesh." *(Acts 2:16-17)* God made the people speak in tongues as evidence that they had received new life; they had been born again of the spirit.

God also sent Peter to Cornelius and other Gentiles. While Peter was speaking to the Gentiles, the Holy Ghost fell upon them. The Jews were astonished when they saw that the Gentiles also received the Holy Ghost. How did the Jews know that the Gentiles had received the Holy Ghost? "For they heard them speak with tongues, and magnify God." *(Acts 10:46)*

Moreover, the apostle Paul met some of John's disciples at Ephesus. He asked them if they had received the Holy Ghost, since they believed. They responded that they did not know whether there was any Holy Ghost. Paul immediately knew something was wrong. He quickly identified the problem. "And when Paul had laid his hands upon them, the Holy Ghost came on them; and they spake with tongues, and prophesied." *(Acts 19:6)*

Paul warned the people that if they wanted to be ignorant, to be ignorant, but those who want the power of God are entreated to covet to prophesy and to forbid not to speak with tongues. *(1 Corinthians 14:38-39)* The Holy Ghost is the Spirit of God. "But as many as received him, to them gave he power to become the sons of God, even to them that believe on his name." *(John 1:12)* Jesus told His disciples to wait at Jerusalem until they were filled with power; believers received the power of the Holy Ghost. How do we know? They spoke in tongues. "And these signs shall follow them that believe: In my name shall they cast out devils; they shall speak with new tongues." *(Mark 16:17)*

——————— Like Fire Shut Up in My Bones ———————

The Holy Ghost is like fire shut up in our bones. *(Jeremiah 20:9)* The Holy Ghost is God. *(Romans 14:17)* When fear would have overtaken us, when we would have fainted in the time of trouble, the presence of God kept us strong. Our faith is bolstered by the presence of God and we remain upright in obedience. Jesus urged those who labored under the weight of bondage and were heavy laden with sin to come unto Him; He would give us rest for our souls. *(Matthew 11:28)* The Holy Ghost, the Comforter, gives us rest for our soul. Though fearful men and women engage in all manners of wickedness to survive, we fear no evil. Our God is with us. His knowledge (rod) and power (staff) comfort us. *(Psalm 23:4)*

─────────────── **He Became a Living Soul** ───────────────

God created man out of the dust. Adam's physical body was composed of the earth, which is going to pass away. Adam had no eternal life within him. The Lord breathed into Adam, and man became a living soul. With the Spirit of God, Adam had eternal life. Adam had two lives: a natural life that could live in a natural setting (earth), and a spiritual life, the Spirit of God, which allowed him to live in a spiritual setting (Garden of Eden). Adam was human and divine. Adam chose to follow after flesh. His decision to exalt the flesh above the Spirit separated him from God. The Spirit of God came out of Adam; Adam's eternal life ended the same day he sinned. Man was cast out of the garden.

Without the spirit, Adam's body was nothing more than natural compositions from the dust of the earth. Adam had a natural life but no spiritual life. He had unsuspectingly chosen to renounce life that was eternal for life that was ephemeral. Not only had he been reduced to decaying human tissue, but there were spirits in the earth: Satan and other fallen angels. Adam's disobedience to the Spirit of God to walk after the flesh gave Satan power over him. When the Spirit of God left him, Adam realized what a fool he had been. He was naked and ashamed.

The Lord cast Satan and his servants out of His kingdom. The Lord cast Adam and Eve out of the garden. The Lord always cast the evil and wicked out of His sight. *(Psalm 5:4-5)* Thankfully, Christ came to redeem man. To be redeemed means that God has restored human beings back to the original state when Adam and Eve were human and divine. Christ came to restore our soul. He came to redeem our right to inherit the Kingdom of God. However, we have to demonstrate that we will obey. The Lord requires those who enter His kingdom to acknowledge Him as king and obey His commands. He demands faithful servants who have the integrity to humble themselves and submit to His supreme wisdom and power.

──────── **Children of God Are Led By the Spirit** ────────

Jesus was the Son of God and the Son of Man. He was conceived of the spirit, and He was conceived of a flesh-and-blood woman. He was divine and human. Before Jesus' body on the cross could die, the spirit had to come out; the spirit cannot die. Before Jesus' body could enter into Heaven, the blood had to come out; flesh-and-blood (corruption) cannot inherit the Kingdom of God (incorruption). In order to save the people, Jesus must persuade the people to crucify the flesh and integrate with the spirit. In order to destroy the people, Satan must persuade the people to walk after the flesh and separate from the spirit. Hence, to damn our souls, Satan offers those things that are pleasing to the flesh. To save our soul, Jesus commands us to sacrifice the life of the flesh and be born again of the spirit.

Jesus' objective is to save the people from their sins and to give them an inheritance among them that are sanctified. When the Lord comes to destroy the earth, He cannot destroy those who have the Spirit of God; He cannot destroy Himself. "For as many as are led by the spirit of God, they are the sons of God." *(Romans 8:14)* He has to take those filled with His spirit—His children—to His kingdom. He will not leave His own soul in hell. *(John 1:12; Galatians 4:6-7; Romans 8:16-17)*

When we are born again of the spirit, we are spirit. *(John 3:6)* The Spirit of God has entered into our bodies and restored our soul. We become the sons of God. (God is a spirit. His children are those whom He created—spiritual beings. To the carnal mind, Father and Son describe male figures. In spiritual parlance, Father and Son describe Creator and created. A spirit is neither male nor female, which is why those who walk in the spirit are not flesh. *(Galatians 3:28; Romans 8:9)* When we have been born again of the Spirit, we have become new creatures. Not only does the power within us transcend the flesh, our spiritual minds are now on the things of the spirit. *(Romans 8:5)* Through the knowledge of Jesus Christ, we have been transformed through the renewing of our minds. We understand how Satan bewitches the people and make them lust after the flesh, which gives Satan power over them. When we walk in the spirit, we reject Satan's witchcraft and deny the flesh, so that we have power over Satan. We are no longer weak humans; we are filled with the power of God Almighty; we are more powerful than Satan. *(Luke 10:19)*

When we are born again of the spirit, we have a new Father (God); we are new creatures (spiritual beings); and we walk in the newness of life (redeemed from corruption). *(Romans 6:4)* We are children of God—children who do not lie—children whose Father cannot lie. We have integrity and are integrated with the Holy One. Whereas we once walked in the flesh and allowed Satan to have power over us, we now walk in the spirit and exercise power over Satan. Like Abraham, we renounced our pagan father (Satan) who deceived us and positioned us to be destroyed. We learned that Jesus is Lord, acknowledged the truth, and came out of paganism. We have been redeemed—we are spiritual and natural—complete— perfect—just the way God originally made Adam and Eve. We are now able to inherit the blessings of God. When we remain obedient, keep our integrity, do not fall for Satan's witchcraft, and exalt God above ourselves, we will remain perfect; we will remain integrated with God and run in the ways of His commandments— holy and sanctified. We have been transformed from flesh to spirit, from children of sin to children of obedience, from darkness to light, from the power of Satan to the power of God.

────────────── **Ye Are Not in the Flesh** ──────────────

Jesus did not have a natural life when He rose from the grave. The life of the flesh is in the blood, and Jesus had shed His blood. He had flesh but He was no longer human. "All flesh is not the same flesh: but there is one kind of flesh of men, another flesh of beasts, another of fishes, and another of birds. There are also celestial bodies, and bodies terrestrial: but the glory of the celestial is one, and the glory of the terrestrial is another." *(1 Corinthians 15:39-40)* Jesus had a body of flesh, but His life was spirit.

God gives us the Holy Ghost—His spirit—which means that we have a spiritual life. We walk in the flesh, but we are no longer flesh. Remember: Jesus said we had to be born again of the water and spirit. When we are born again of the water, we bury our life of the flesh and wash away our life of sin. When we are born again of the spirit, God gives us His power, so that we will have power over the enemy. Since we are no longer in bondage, we are able to overcome corruption. Through the renewing of our minds, we crucify the flesh and cultivate spiritual growth. Out of the ashes arise new creatures in Christ Jesus: redeemed, spiritual beings, who walk with God. We have become Christians—Christ-like. We are those in which God was in Christ reconciling unto Himself. We are the sons of God. Although we walk in the flesh, we do not walk after the flesh. Thus, we have overcome the life of the flesh. "But ye are not in the flesh, but in the Spirit, if so be that the Spirit of God dwell in you. Now if any man have not the Spirit of Christ, he is none of his. And if Christ be in you, the body is dead because of sin; but the Spirit is life because of righteousness." *(Romans 8:8-10)*

When we are born again of the spirit, we are spirits. We have a new life; we walk in holiness and righteousness. Ergo, when we walk in the spirit (walk in obedience to God's commandments), we will not fulfill the lust of the flesh. *(Galatians 5:16)* We take up our cross and crucify the flesh, because they that are in the flesh cannot please God. *(Romans 8:8)* When we walk in the spirit, we, like Jesus, will be flesh, yet we are celestrial beings—spirits in human form. Just as God was in Christ, the Holy Ghost is God in us.

The Lord and two angels appeared unto Abraham. They sat down and ate with him. After the meal, God told Abraham that his wife, Sarah, would have a child. *(Genesis 18:1-10)* God and the angels had flesh, but they did not have blood. Remember, God was Melchizedek, who drank wine and ate bread with Abraham. *(Genesis 14:18-20; Hebrew 7:3)* God wrestled with Jacob. *(Genesis 32:24-30)* When God pours out His Spirit—the Holy Ghost—upon us, although we walk in the flesh, we do not walk after the flesh. We do not walk after the blood. We do not walk after lust. We have set our affection on things above. *(Colossians 3:2)* When we deny the flesh (crucify the flesh) and overcome the lust of the flesh, our bodies become dead to sin. Death has no power over us. *(Romans 6:5; 1 Peter 2:24)*

None of His

False prophets have deceived the people and taught them to believe that their sins are covered by the blood of Jesus. If we want remission of sins, we must repent and be baptized into the death of Jesus Christ. *(Acts 2:38; Romans 6:3-4)* Christ did not walk after the flesh, and His disciples do not walk after the flesh. He took up His cross and shed the life of His flesh, and we take up our cross and shed the life of the flesh. Just as He shed His blood, we shed our blood. God and His children made a covenant by sacrifice. Jesus shed His blood for the remission of sins of those who turned from their wickedness to follow Him—those who crucified the flesh to walk in the spirit.

Jesus observed that many will say to Him upon His return that they had prophesied in His name, cast out devils, and done many wonderful works. He will answer them, depart from me, ye workers of iniquity; I never knew you. *(Matthew 7:22-23)* Why would Jesus, who knows all things, tell the people that He never knew them? The Shepherd knows His sheep. They follow Him. *(John 10:27)*

Adam and Eve rejected the word of God. After they sinned and perceived that Satan had bewitched them, they hid themselves from the presence of the Lord. "And the Lord God called unto Adam, and said unto him, Where art thou?" *(Genesis 3:9)* The Lord knew where Adam was, yet His question evidenced that, as a result of Adam's sin, man no longer walked with God. Without the Spirit of God, none of us are children of God. "Now if any man have not the Spirit of Christ, he is none of his." *(Romans 8:9)* Those who commit adultery and fornication cannot inherit the Kingdom of God, because they do not have the Spirit of Christ. *(1 Corinthians 6:9-10)* God cannot dwell in unclean temples. Therefore, polluted and defiled temples must be destroyed. *(1 Corinthians 3:16-17)*

Jesus told the people to destroy His temple, and in three days He would raise it up. It had taken forty six years to build the temple. The people questioned how He would rebuild the temple in three days. Jesus spoke in parables. He was not referring to the building; He was referring to the church. The Romans were going to crucify Him; they would destroy His flesh. After three days, however, the body of Christ would rise from the grave. Understand, the Jesus that died was not the Jesus that arose. The Jesus that died was flesh and blood. The Jesus that arose had no blood. Jesus' natural life had ended. Remember, Jesus told the people to destroy His temple, and in three days He would raise it up again. *(John 2:19)* The Spirit that came out of the body before it died was the Spirit that rose the body up out of the grave. *(Acts 2:24)* The body that arose was a spiritual body—the Lamb of God had shed His blood and sacrificed His natural life for the sins of the people. The Spirit is eternal life and could not remain in the grave.

The body that arose from the grave was the church; the temple. Jesus had defeated Satan and offered up sacrifice for the sins of the people. He had ransomed His people from the grave. Those who wanted to come out of the grave of sin had the right to receive the remission of their sins. They were set free from captivity and, once filled with the Holy Ghost, ready to serve the Lord. Members of the church were not temples made by hand. We were lively stones, filled with the Spirit of Jesus Christ. *(1 Peter 2:5)* Just as Christ was a spirit manifested in the flesh, we became spirits manifested in the flesh. We buried our natural bodies in water baptism and took on a new body—a spiritual body—and walked in the Holy Ghost. We had a new Father, the Holy Ghost, and we became the Sons of God. As spirits, we became a part of the body of the Christ, celestrial beings, the church. Those who possessed the Spirit of God could not remain in the grave of sin.

God did not know those who did not have His spirit; they were none of His. His body is spiritual, and sinners do not have His spirit. They have a natural body; Christ has a spiritual body. They have a terrestrial body; Christ has a celestial body. *(1 Corinthians 15:40)* Christ is a spirit, His children are those He created—spiritual creatures. They have a natural body, but live according to the spirit. Sinners are not children of God. Sinners are children of Satan, those who walk after the flesh and rebel against the spirit. *(John 8:34-44)* They have chosen, like Adam, to exalt flesh above spirit.

Since He died without sin, Jesus overcame the grave. Christ died for the sins of the people. The spirit resurrected Jesus' body from the grave. His servants—those who made a covenant with Him by sacrifice—were free to rise up out of the grave of sin and walk in the newness of life. "Now the Lord is that spirit: and where the spirit of the Lord is, there is liberty." *(2 Corinthians 3:17)* As new creatures, we walk in the power of Jesus Christ, who defeated Satan and set His people free. We are no longer in the bondage of sin. We have overcome the flesh, which gave Satan power over us, and walk in the Spirit of God, which gives us power over Satan. The Lord is perfect, and when we obey all that He has commanded us, we are perfect. *(Matthew 28:20; Luke 1:67-75)*

As lively stones—the church—we worship the Lord in spirit and in truth. Jesus destroyed the power of Satan over our lives. We crucified the life of sin (flesh) to walk in the Spirit of God (holiness). The Holy Ghost restored our soul. Just as Jesus resurrected Lazarus from the grave, He has resurrected us from the grave of sin—"even now"—in this sinful world.

———————— **Whosoever Will, Let Them Come** ————————

The Jews were astonished when the Gentiles received the Holy Ghost. *(Acts 10:45)* The Lord has called the whole earth to the bridal feast; whosoever that wants to come is welcome. *(Revelation 22:17)* It does not matter whether the person lives in India, Africa, Asia, or America. All those who walk in darkness have been called into His marvelous light. *(1 Peter 2:9)* The Lord has been found of them that did not seek Him; those who did not know have learned of Him. *(Isaiah 65:1; Romans 10:20)* Cornelius did not seek Christ. Cornelius sought to live right. The Lord revealed Himself to Cornelius. God will pour out His spirit upon all flesh – to as many who call upon His name. *(Joel 2:32; Acts 1:14)*

———————— **Servants of God Overcome Sin** ————————

Jesus did not die, so we could sin with impunity. Jesus died to offer us immunity. Jesus did not die, so we could continue in sin. *(Romans 6:1-2)* Jesus died to save us from our sins. *(Matthew 1:2)* Jesus came to destroy Satan and those who rebelled against Him. *(Hebrews 2:14-15)* He set the captives free. Those who separated from Satan and obeyed God would be spared destruction. *(1 Samuel 15:6)* Remember: God set the Hebrews free from bondage. Those who refused to serve the Lord but preferred to remain as slaves in Egypt were destroyed. God set all of the slaves free; He wanted to see who would or would not obey Him. Jesus invited everyone to the bridal feast. Everyone has a right to call upon His name. Although God does not want anyone to perish, He will destroy those who have accepted sin (slavery) as a way of life. Jesus came to ransom believers from the power of grave and to give them a new life in the Holy Ghost. Jesus came to transform our minds—to turn us away from the power of Satan to God. He did not set us free, so we could serve Satan and remain in the bondage of sin. He came to liberate us from sin and redeem us from corruption.

The reason many people do not believe in perfection is because they have never been born again of the Spirit. If the people had the Holy Ghost and walked in the Spirit of God, they would know that the Lord will guide them in the path of righteousness for His name's sake. At the appropriate time, the Holy Ghost will always bring the right thing to their remembrance. The Lord orders the steps of His servants and ensures that those who want to obey Him know His will. *(John 7:17)*

When we are born again, we do not return to our mother's womb. We do not want to be born again of the flesh. "That which is born of the flesh is flesh." Our natural father, Adam, was corrupt. He emulated Satan and sinned against God. To be born again of the flesh—conceived because of Satan's witchcraft—is to remain in the same state of sin—dead. Since the life of the flesh is in the blood, if we enter again into our mother's womb, we will again inherit the corruption passed down through the blood. Those who serve the Lord must overcome the flesh in order to serve the Lord in the spirit. The Holy Ghost assures us that God is real. Although God moves in mysterious ways, we trust in Him. We recognize that He has superior knowledge and power; therefore, we obey His commandments and allow His will to be done in our lives.

─────────── **There is One Lord** ───────────

There are false prophets who assert that "God is not a Christian." According to the false prophets, a person's religion is in large part dependent upon where the person was born. For example, a person born in Saudi Arabia will likely believe in Islam, a person born in India will likely believe in Hinduism, and a person born in America will likely believe in Christianity. Therefore, our religious beliefs are largely based upon what each culture promotes. Since all religions have certain common features, they argue, people should not be divided by arbitrary differences of theology and should worship God the best they can. And people actually believe such satanic philosophy.

Jesus said, "I am the way, the truth, and the life: no man cometh unto the Father, but by me." *(John 14:6)* Every human was conceived in sin. In order for us to be saved from the wrath of God to come, we have to be redeemed from the corruption within our blood. As a result of corruption, we sin against God. There is no other name under the heavens given among men whereby we must be saved from sin other than the name of the Lord Jesus. *(Acts 4:10-12)* Allah, Buddha, and other gods do not answer by fire; they do not answer when they are called because they do not exist. They cannot pour out their spirit and restore life to lost souls. They cannot teach corrupt souls how to overcome the enemy. Just as Abraham had to come out from his pagan family to worship God in truth, all who want to worship God in spirit and in truth must come out from corruption.

Remember: God will destroy unclean temples. *(1 Corinthians 3:17)* If the Spirit of God does not dwell within us, we cannot inherit the Kingdom of God. If the false prophets deceive us and persuade us to believe that we do not have to be perfect, we will be damned. We will commit adultery and fornication, for example, and think that we are saved by grace. If we had been taught the truth—those who commit fornication and adultery are going to be destroyed—we could have overcome and saved our souls. *(1 Corinthians 6:9)* We could have sanctified ourselves. *(John 17:17)* Instead, having been deceived, we damned our own soul.

Satan knows that those who have not been born again of the spirit cannot enter the Kingdom of God. He has sent blind false prophets to teach the people that they can live a good life according to their own preferred belief. Abraham, Ruth, Cornelius, and Saul of Tarsus had to renounce their pagan beliefs. In fact, since Satan has deceived the whole world, everyone has to renounce his or her pagan beliefs and come into the knowledge of the truth. All of us must be born again of the Holy Ghost and baptized into the One spirit, the Spirit of Jesus Christ.

——————————————— **Sabbath Day** ———————————————

There are false teachers who teach their congregants that they are to remember the Sabbath day and to keep it holy. Accordingly, the false teachers teach the people that God does not allow them to work on the Sabbath day; they are commanded to sit down and rest.

God told the children of Israel to remember the Sabbath day and to keep it holy. *(Exodus 20:8)* They were commanded to sit down and rest on the seventh day. *(Exodus 20:10)* Jesus, however, did not sit down and rest on the seventh day. The scribes and Pharisees believed Jesus was a demon, in part, because He worked on the Sabbath day, which was contrary to the Law of Moses. *(Luke 13:14)* Why did the scripture tell the people to sit down and rest on the seventh day, yet Jesus, who was God with us and holy in all His works, did not sit and rest? If Jesus was perfect and lived a life free of sin, how was He able to work on the Sabbath day and not disobey the commandment of God?

In the beginning, God created the Heaven and earth. He rested on the seventh day from all his work which He had made. *(Genesis 2:1-2)* He blessed and sanctified the seventh day as a day of rest. Remember: the Lord had not finished His work. He only rested from the work "which He had made." *(Genesis 2:2)* He did not create the earth in vain, but had a purpose in creating the earth. God cast Satan down into the earth. *(Revelation 12:9)* He created the earth to be inhabited by men and women. *(Isaiah 45:18)* The Lord rested from His labor and allowed His purpose to be fulfilled. Just as He allowed Satan to challenge Job to see whether Job would obey, the Lord allowed Satan to challenge all humans to see whether they would obey. Satan, day and night, reminds God of those who disobey His commandments and reject His salvation. *(Revelation 12:10)*

From the foundation of the earth, God commanded the people to live holy, but we could not live holy; our enemy was too strong and intelligent for us. *(Ephesians 1:4; Hebrews 2:14-15)* In carrying out His purpose, the Lord sent famine into the earth. The people lacked knowledge and went into the captivity of sin because of ignorance. *(Isaiah 5:13)* The Lord allowed us to see how ignorant and frail we were. Satan bewitched our minds and made us destroy ourselves. Satan, who had the power of death, corrupted the entire world. Through fear of death, we lied, stole, cheated, and/or engaged in other acts of wickedness. We sacrificed our integrity and did anything to survive. Satan had us so enslaved—and false prophets had us so deceived—until we accepted slavery as a way of life.

Since the Lord wanted us to live holy yet allowed us to be taken into the bondage of sin, He had the duty to deliver us from sin. We had the right to be redeemed. Unlike the ignorant false prophets who teach that grace is God's unmerited favor, those who walk in the light know that we have a right to be redeemed. We were conceived in sin. We cannot obey God's commandment to live holy, unless the Lord redeems us from corruption and gives us a new life—which is why the Lord commands His people to come boldly before the throne of grace. *(Hebrews 4:16)* We cannot obey His commandments unless He delivers us out of the hand of the enemy; our enemy is too strong for us. *(Psalm 18:17; 2 Samuel 22:18)* Further, God sent famine of His word into the land and made us walk in darkness. In our ignorance, we built our enemies' treasure cities. *(Exodus 1:11)* We built the kingdom for those who enslaved us. *(Luke 4:5-6)* In spiritual parlance, we were so bewitched until we rebelled against our Savior and served our destroyer. We were weak and ignorant. And God purposely created these conditions, which is why Jesus died for our sins. If we were compelled to obey His commandments—and we were—He had to break the power of the enemy over us and allow us the opportunity to redeem ourselves from corruption.

When the time came to redeem mankind, Jesus, as a spirit, did not have blood to redeem mankind. Yet, there could be no remission of sin or redemption without the shedding of blood. Therefore, Jesus manifested Himself in the flesh. *(1 Timothy 3:16; Matthew 1:23)* Once Jesus took on flesh and blood, He had the blood to offer up as sacrifice to redeem mankind. Jesus came in the flesh to finish the work that the Spirit had started in the beginning. *(John 17:4)* Remember: Jesus was in the beginning. *(Revelation 22:13)*

Jesus came into the earth and told the people, "Come unto me, all ye that labour and are heavy laden, and I will give you rest. Take my yoke upon you, and learn of me: for I am meek and lowly in heart: and ye shall find rest unto your souls." *(Matthew 11:28-29)* Men and women had rebelled against God. In seeking to save our natural lives, we lost our spiritual lives. In other words, in order to live, we engaged in all types of wickedness and evil. We worked ourselves to death. In our struggle to survive, we became more and more inured to corruption. Jesus exhorted the lost sheep to humble themselves and return to God. If they returned unto the Lord, He would feed them; He would restore their soul; and He would redeem them from corruption. Those who reconciled with the Father would not have to spend their entire life in the bondage of sin, but would find rest for their soul.

Jesus worked on the seventh day because He had already worked on the first six days in the beginning. When Jesus died on the cross, He completed the work necessary to fulfill His purpose. He observed, "It is finished." *(John 19:30)* Jesus' death destroyed the works of the devil and proved He was Lord. He had the authority to deliver His people out of the bondage of sin. As a spirit, He had created man and allowed him to be corrupted. As a spirit manifested in the flesh, He had died to redeemed man from corruption. Although Satan had imposed heavy burdens upon the people and caused them to submit to his will, there was no need for the people to sit down and rest to keep the Sabbath day holy. Jesus delivered the people out of bondage and offered us rest for our soul.

Jesus did not have to sit down and rest on the Sabbath, because He was Lord of the Sabbath. *(Matthew 12:8)* He had power over everything. Jesus lived holy all the days of the week. Children of God do not have to sit down and rest to keep the Sabbath holy. We have the Holy Ghost and are able to live holy every day.

We have been delivered from sin and taught to walk the way the Master walked. The people were commanded to obey **all** of God's commandments. *(Matthew 28:20)* The people, having been delivered out of the hands of their enemies, could serve the Lord in holiness and righteousness **all** the days. *(Luke 1:75)* Jesus' disciples do not have to sit down and rest anymore on the Sabbath day. He has given us rest for our souls. *(Matthew 11:29)*

The Lord knew that rebellious people would sin unless they sat down and did nothing. "And it came to pass, that there went out some of the people on the seventh day for to gather, and they found. And the Lord said unto Moses, How long refuse ye to keep my commandments and my laws? **See, for that the Lord hath given you the sabbath,** therefore he giveth you on the sixth day the bread of two days; abide ye every man in his place, let no man go out of his place on the seventh day. So the people rested on the seventh day." *(Exodus 16:27-30)* God commanded the people to save food on the sixth day, so they could rest on the Sabbath. Jesus knew if the people worked, they would sin, because they had been corrupted by the Egyptians. He knew that the people were weak and ignorant, which is why He commanded them to sit down and rest; Jesus wanted to keep one day as a holy day. **"Moreover also I gave them my Sabbaths, to be a sign between me and them, that they might know that I am the Lord that sanctify them."** *(Ezekiel 20:12)* The Sabbath day was a sign that God would deliver His people from corruption and sanctify them. Of course, Jesus came to take away the sin of the world and to sanctify His people through the truth. *(John 1:29; John 17:17)*

God rested on the seventh day. He gave us the Sabbath to let us know that He had not finished His work. Satan would corrupt us; but Jesus would come and finish the work the Father had started in the beginning. God wanted the people to know that He was the Lord that sanctified them. Remember: the people were in bondage because of the lack of knowledge. They had been in Egypt and corrupted by the Egyptians. The children of Israel had been taught paganism. Their enemies who worshipped false gods had deceived and corrupted them. Their enemies had forced them to sacrifice their integrity. The Sabbath day was a sign between God and His people that He was going to come and teach them the truth: He was Lord. He was the Almighty. With the truth, the people could come out of captivity and sanctify themselves. They could serve the God of their fathers and not serve strange gods anymore. In Jesus Christ, they could restore their integrity and find rest for their souls.

Jesus established a new covenant—New Testament—with the human family. We did not have to sit down and rest to keep the Sabbath day holy. He gave us His knowledge, which allowed us to escape the pollution of this world. *(2 Peter 2:20)* He gave us His power, which gave us power over all of the power of the enemy. *(Luke 10:19)* Just as God ransomed the children of Israel out of the bondage of Egypt, He ransomed His children out of the bondage of sin.

Jesus kept the Sabbath day: He lived holy. He did not have to sit down and rest, because He was Lord of the Sabbath. Satan had no power over Him. He worked on the seventh day (Sabbath) to finish the work started in the beginning. Once Jesus finished His work, no one had to sit down and rest on the Sabbath day. We were able to live holy every day. "Let no man therefore judge you in meat, or in drink, or in respect of an holyday, or of the new moon, or of the sabbath days." *(Colossians 2:16)* The people did not have to sit down and rest anymore to keep the Sabbath day holy; Jesus delivered us out of the bondage of sin and gave us the Holy Ghost, so we could remain free from sin. We are commanded to keep all of God's commandments, and to serve the Lord in holiness and righteousness **all the days** of our life. *(Matthew 28:20; Luke 1: 74-75)*

Immaculate Conception

According to some false teachers, God granted Mary, the mother of Jesus Christ, an exemption from sin. The concept is called Immaculate Conception. Although Mary was a virgin when Jesus was conceived, the false teachers theorize that she was born without sin. In Adam all died. The only way an individual could have been conceived without sin is that the person had been conceived by the Spirit of God. With the exception of Jesus Christ, all humans were conceived through the lust of the flesh between a man and a woman. There is no evidence in the scripture to support the concept that Mary was conceived by the spirit or born without sin.

Mary could not have been conceived without sin. The scripture tells us that Jesus was in all points tempted like the rest of the human family. *(Hebrews 4:15)* He could not have been tempted like the rest of the human family, unless He experienced the lust of the flesh, lust of the eyes, and the pride of life—the things of the world. *(1 John 2:16)* He had to experience all of the corrupting influences that bedeviled flesh-and-blood beings. After all, Jesus came here to demonstrate that humans, with the Spirit of God, can overcome Satan's witchcraft and walk free of sin in the flesh.

The Master knew that Satan's power over us was the fear of death. In our ignorance, we lusted after the very weakness that gave Satan power over us. Jesus knew He was Lord. Therefore, He did not fear Satan. He experienced the lust of the flesh and other temptations that had overtaken the human family. *(1 Corinthians 10:13)* Yet, He refused to please himself and allow Satan to have power over Him. *(Romans 15:3)* He knew everyone should obey the Spirit of God and not worship a pagan god who was determined to make his servants destroy themselves. With the Spirit of God, humans would have power over all demons and be resurrected from death (the grave of sin). We would rise up in the newness of life and walk as the Master walked—free from sin.

Jesus was the Son of God and the Son of Man. He was conceived of the Holy Ghost and conceived of a flesh-and-blood woman. *(Matthew 1:20; Isaiah 7:14)* That which is born of the spirit is spirit. That which is born of the flesh is flesh. *(John 3:6)* Since the spirit is the enemy of the flesh, and the flesh is the enemy of the spirit,

Christ walked in the spirit, so that He would not fulfil the lust of the flesh. *(Galatians 5:16)* Christ exalted His Father—the Holy Spirit. The only way Christ could have acquired lust was through His mother. The lust of the flesh is not of the Father. *(1 John 2:16)* Hence, Christ could not have acquired lust from His Father because His Father was Spirit and derived no pleasure from the flesh. "So then they that are in the flesh cannot please God." *(Romans 8:8)*

Remember: Adam and Eve had never known lust of the flesh until Satan beguiled Eve to separate from God. Jesus' mind was committed to do the will of the spirit and to deny the things of the flesh. *(Romans 8:5)* As a result, the will of His flesh and the will of His spirit were in conflict. *(Romans 8:7)* Jesus came to do the will of the Father. *(John 6:38-39)* He asked His mother, "Woman, what have I to do with thee?" *(John 2:4)* Jesus' devotion was not to His mother; He came to shed the blood that He had inherited from her. Jesus wanted to please His Father (Spirit) not His mother (flesh). *(Luke 22:42; Romans 15:3)* He exalted the spirit above the flesh. Jesus' devotion was to His Father, spirit. Therefore, Christ pleased not Himself. *(Romans 15:3)* His flesh wanted to live, but the spirit wanted Him to die. He surrendered to the will of His Father and shed His blood. *(Luke 22:42)* The cup of sacrifice required Jesus to die. He exalted the life of the spirit and consented to the death of the flesh. *(John 18:11)* He had taken on the flesh only because there could be no remission of sin without the shedding of blood. *(Hebrews 9:22)*

God could have created a body without a woman, just as He had created Adam. The sacrifice, though, had to be both holy yet have sinful blood within the body. The sacrifice had to have blood, because lust of the flesh was in the blood—the life of the flesh. Jesus had to demonstrate that humans, with the Spirit of God, had power over lust. Further, the sacrifice had to unblemished, because a sinner could not sacrifice his life for the sins of another; the soul that sinned had to die. *(Ezekiel 18:20)* Since no one in Heaven had blood and everyone on earth had been conceived in sin, Jesus, a spirit, manifested Himself in the flesh to shed His blood for the sins of the people. *(John 1:29; 1 Timothy 3:16)*

Adam and Eve walked in the spirit and were integrated with God. They discovered they were flesh and blood after they disobeyed. Since Satan had overtaken man through corruption, which caused man to separate from the spirit, Jesus came and demonstrated that flesh-and-blood humans, filled with the Spirit of God, could overcome the things of the world. *(John 16:33)* Jesus demonstrated that He was Lord; He had power over all of His enemies.

Jesus overcame sinful blood and proved His preeminence. "For what the law could not do, in that it was weak through the flesh, God sending his own Son in the likeness of sinful flesh, and for sin, condemned sin in the flesh." *(Romans 8:3)* Ergo, filled with the Spirit of God, Jesus' flesh-and-blood body had the power to overcome Satan's corruption. Jesus demonstrated that greater was the power in Him than the power in the world. Humans were not sinners because we were flesh-and-blood creatures; we were sinners because Satan had bewitched us to walk after the corruption within our blood. Those who walk after the flesh conform to the things of the world. Those who walk in the Spirit of God are able to overcome the things of the world, because Jesus has taught us how to discipline themselves and not give in to Satan's witchcraft.

Mary was a virtuous woman and highly favored. Nonetheless, she was not without sin. Jesus was in all points tempted like others in the world, and all that is of the world is not of the Father. *(Hebrews 4:15; 1 John 2:16)* The Father is spirit, and all that is of the world pertains to the flesh. Mary, His mother, was Jesus' only parent who had flesh-and-blood. Moreover, she was espoused to marry Joseph; hence, she had lust for a man. After the birth of Jesus, she married and had other children. *(Luke 8:20)* Joseph knew that Mary had lust for a man. When he found out that Mary was pregnant, he did not believe she had been faithful and prepared to terminate the relationship. An angel warned Joseph that he had to marry Mary; the angel confirmed that Mary's child was not by a man, but by God. *(Matthew 1:19-20)*

Mary, an extraordinary woman, was conceived in sin just like all other humans. She committed sin. Under the law, if a person had sinned, they had to offer a lamb as a sin offering. If they did not have a lamb, they had to offer two turtledoves or two young pigeons. *(Leviticus 2:19-24)* Mary and Joseph came to Jerusalem and offered up Jesus to the Lord. While there, they also offered up a pair of turtledoves or two young pigeons for their sins. *(Luke 2:24)* Of course, they also offered up the Lamb of God. Further, after Jesus' death, Mary could not enter the Kingdom of God. Jesus made it plain that no one could enter the Kingdom of God unless the person had been born again of water and spirit. Mary had been conceived like all other flesh-and-blood creatures and was not exempt from sin. (Immaculate Conception) Since the New Testament began after Jesus died, she had to be born again, too. Mary was in the upper room on the day of Pentecost and received the Holy Ghost. *(Acts 1:14; Acts 2:4)*

Additional Edifying Scriptures

"And, behold, I send the promise of my Father upon you: but tarry ye in the city of Jerusalem, until ye be endued with power from on high." (Luke 24:49)

"For with stammering lips and another tongue will he speak to this people. To whom he said, This is the rest wherewith ye may cause the weary to rest; and this is the refreshing: yet they would not hear." (Isaiah 28:11-12)

"And the seventy returned again with joy, saying, Lord, even the devils are subject unto us through thy name. And he said unto them, I beheld Satan as lightning fall from heaven. Behold, I give unto you power to tread on serpents and scorpions, and over all the power of the enemy: and nothing shall by any means hurt you." (Luke 10:17-19)

CHAPTER EIGHTEEN
BORN AGAIN OF THE WATER

Many people have believed the lying vanities of the false prophets and completely disregarded Jesus' admonition: Except a man is born again of water and spirit, he cannot enter the Kingdom of God. *(John 3:5)* We have addressed the need to be born again of the spirit. We will now address the need to be born again of the water. Since the Holy Ghost gives us a new life with God, we should renounce Satan and our old life of sin.

The Egyptians forced the children of Israel to serve them for more than 400 years. After Moses delivered the Hebrews out of Egypt, the people stopped and encamped against the sea. Suddenly, they realized that the Egyptians were approaching with the intention to take them back into captivity. The Lord told Moses to take the people into the sea. God parted the waters and allowed the people to escape over dry land. When the Egyptians pursued into the sea after the Hebrews, the Lord caused the waters to come together and drowned the Egyptians. The Hebrews were baptized in the cloud and in the sea; they escaped through the water but saw their enemies destroyed. *(1 Corinthians 10:2; Exodus 14:30)*

When we acquire the knowledge of Jesus Christ, we understand that Satan bewitched Adam and Eve through the lust of the flesh. Satan's power over us resides within the lust in our blood. When we lust after flesh, we lust after the very corruption that destroys our soul. Since sin works death in us by that which is good, we have to crucify the life of the flesh and its inherent sin to overcome death. *(Romans 7:13)* That is the knowledge the Master taught His disciples: discipline. The Master taught us to deny ourselves. Those who want to serve the Lord must discipline themselves and exercise self-control. We must understand that the corruption in our blood germinated from Satan's witchcraft and deny ourselves the illicit pleasures of the flesh. In other words, we need to fast and pray. We pray to condition our minds to obey the word of God and fast to exercise control over our behavior.

Everyone was born in the bondage of sin. The life of the flesh (life of sin) is the only life the unredeemed has ever known. We know Satan is corrupt; we know we are corrupt; yet do we want to serve the Lord? Are we willing to give up the life of the flesh and corruption to inherit the Kingdom of God? Are we willing to give up the bondage of sin to serve the Lord in holiness and righteousness? Children of Abraham do not serve false gods and have renounced their father's pagan worship. We separate from the things of the world and trust in the Lord to save us from those who would force us to conform to the world. We want a new life, a spiritual life, which will dwell in the Kingdom of God throughout eternity.

Jesus told Nicodemus that no one could enter the Kingdom of God who had not been born again of the water. Those who are baptized are baptized into the death of Jesus Christ. *(Romans 6:1-14)* Just as the children of Israel escaped through the water but saw their enemies destroyed, we go into the water to destroy the power of the enemy over us. We stop walking after the weakness in our blood and learn to deny ourselves. We have learned that the pleasure that we derive from indulging the flesh induces us to lust after the flesh, which entices us to commit adultery and fornication. We serve Satan and live in the bondage of sin in exchange for momentary pleasures. Ergo, we exchange damnation in an eternal lake of fire for short-lived enjoyment. Satan has bewitched us to destroy our own soul.

Through faith in Jesus Christ, we overcame the enemy and

discovered that there is indescribable joy in the Holy Ghost. We overcame Satan's witchcraft and realized that there is no comparison between those who are free and those who are enslaved—those who serve God Almighty, who empowers and those who serve the fraudulent Satan, who destroys. Accordingly, we deny our flesh and walk in the Holy Ghost, where we find rest for our soul. We have renounced slavery for freedom; temporary relief for eternal rest; damnation for salvation. We have been redeemed from corruption and prepared for the Master's use.

—————— Baptized in the Name of Jesus Christ ——————

The salient issue in this chapter is that we cannot enter the Kingdom of God unless we have been born again of the water (baptized), and many professed Christians have never been baptized. To be born again of water means that we have buried our enemies. Just as the Egyptians were buried in the sea, we have buried our enemy (life of the flesh) in the water of baptism. Hence, we have buried the life of the flesh and been baptized into the death of Jesus Christ, which is why we are baptized in the name of Jesus Christ.

False prophets have baptized the people in the "name of the Father, of the Son, and of the Holy Ghost," which they quote right but perform wrong. Remember, Jesus taught in parable because false prophets would not understand the scriptures. Since false teachers would not understand the Master, disciples of Christ would know that such blind teachers were not messengers of Christ.

Jesus commanded His disciples to "Go ye therefore, and teach all nations, baptizing them in the name of the Father, and of the Son, and of the Holy Ghost." *(Matthew 28:19)* Please remember that servants of God must do as Jesus commands. If Jesus tells us to build a window three cubit feet, we are to build the window three cubit feet. If the Lord tells us to go and wash in the Jordan River, it does not matter if we live adjacent to the Nile River. We are to go and wash in the Jordan River. The Lord is God. He has supreme wisdom and power.

Jesus told His disciples to baptize the people in the *name* of the Father, of the Son, and of the Holy Ghost. It was a simple commandment, and it is a mandatory requirement to inherit eternal life. Let me reiterate: Jesus told the disciples to baptize the people in the *name* of the Father, and of the Son, and of the Holy Ghost.

There is only one *name* under heaven given among men, whereby we can be saved, and that *name* is Jesus Christ. *(Acts 4:10-12)* At the name of Jesus, every knee is going to bow and every tongue is going to confess. *(Romans 14:11)* Jesus opened His apostles' understanding and commanded them to teach the people. On the Day of Pentecost, when the people cried out for salvation, they asked Peter what should they do. Peter told them to repent and be baptized in the **name** of Jesus Christ. *(Acts 2:38)*

Recall, this is the apostle Peter whom Jesus commanded to feed His sheep. *(John 21:15-17)* Jesus delegated responsibility to Peter to teach the people. This is Peter whom God told Cornelius to send to Joppa, for he "shall tell thee words, whereby thou and all thy house shall be saved." *(Acts 11:14)* Just as he commanded the Jews on the day of Pentecost to be baptized in the name of Jesus Christ, Peter also commanded Cornelius and the Gentiles to be baptized in the name of the Lord. *(Acts 10:48)* Of course, the name of the Lord is Jesus Christ. *(Acts 9:5)* Peter, an apostle of Jesus Christ, understood the scripture. Jesus gave him the keys to the Kingdom of God. *(Matthew 16:19)*

Similarly, God sent the apostle Paul to the Gentiles: "To open their eyes, and to turn them from darkness to light." *(Acts 26:14-19)* Paul met some of John's disciples at Ephesus and asked if they had received the Holy Ghost. The disciples answered that they did not know whether the Holy Ghost existed. Paul immediately perceived that the men could not have been properly taught if they did not know whether the Holy Ghost existed. Paul asked the disciples how they had been baptized. They responded that they had been baptized under John's baptism, which, of course, took place under the old covenant. The thief on the cross and others could be saved without baptism, because the old covenant did not require water baptism. The New Testament did not begin until the testator, Jesus Christ, died. *(Hebrews 9:16)* There was no need for the people to be baptized under the old covenant because, without the Holy Ghost, which God could not send until Jesus went away, the enemy was going to force them back into sin.

After Jesus' death, a new covenant was established with the human family. Disciples were required to turn from their wickedness and to become new creatures in Christ—bury the life of sin (flesh) and walk in the newness of life (spirit). We were to turn from the power of Satan to the power of God; to turn from (repent) disobedience to the wisdom of the just (obedience). *(Luke 1:17)* We were required to serve the Lord. Disciples came out of the bondage of sin and received the power of the Holy Ghost, which gave us power over all demon spirits. Paul told the disciples that John only prepared them for the coming Messiah; they were to believe on Christ Jesus. "When they heard this, they were baptized in the name of the Lord Jesus." *(Acts 19:5)* Paul turned John's disciples from darkness to light.

The apostles understood Jesus' instructions; their eyes were open. When they baptized in the name of the Father, and of the Son, and of the Holy Ghost, they baptized in the name of the Lord Jesus Christ. Those who want to obey the commandments of God will follow the apostles' example. The book of the Acts of the Apostles is included within the Holy Bible so that believers can compare the actions of the apostles with the actions of their preachers. If their preachers' teachings do not comport with the apostles' teachings, their blind preachers have been sent by Satan to damn their souls. *(Galatians 1:6-9)* Those who reject the apostles' teachings reject the teachings of Jesus Christ—and are going to be destroyed. *(Hosea 4:6; John 3:5; Luke 10:16)*

Those who want to inherit eternal life must submit to the word of God. "If any man think himself to be a prophet, or spiritual, let him acknowledge that the things that I write unto you are the commandments of the Lord." *(1 Corinthians 14:37)* No one can enter the Kingdom of God who has not been baptized in the name of the Lord Jesus Christ. If a person has been baptized in the name of the Father, and of the Son, and of the Holy Ghost—and not in the name of Jesus Christ—the person has not been baptized. No name was ever called. Repentance and forgiveness of sin must be preached in the name of Jesus Christ. *(Luke 24:47)* If the Lord commands us to be baptized in the **name**, we have to be baptized in His **name**—not in terms that describe Him.

Although it should suffice that the scripture explicitly observes that no one can enter the Kingdom of God except he is baptized, and that baptism must be in the name of Jesus Christ, my primary objective in writing this book was to expose some of the lies of the false prophets. Therefore, I will briefly discuss why false prophets are able to deceive the people and erroneously baptize them in the name of the Father, and of the Son, and of the Holy Ghost—and not in the *name* of Jesus Christ.

Most people are carnal minded and cannot understand the things of the spirit. Readers who do not believe the apostle Peter or the apostle Paul will not believe me if I wrote one thousand pages to explain the word of God. Therefore, I will not delve too deeply into the mystery of Christ. I will nonetheless provide sufficient information to help those who fear God and want to keep His commandments.

———————————— **To The Unknown God** ————————————

Paul's spirit was stirred in him when he visited Athens and observed that the entire city had been given to idolatry—worship of false gods. *(Acts 17:16)* The Athenians, highly intelligent people, had literally built an altar to the unknown God. *(Acts 17:23)* It was common for spiritually ignorant people to worship many gods. For example, when the people needed rain, they prayed to the rain god. When they needed help on the battlefield, they prayed to the war god. When they needed sunshine, they prayed to the sun god. When they needed moonlight, they prayed to the moon god. They had a god for whatever they needed; however, just in case they had unsuspectingly omittted a god, the Athenians built a monument to the unknown god to demonstrate that they did not intend any disrespect.

Paul condemned the Athenians' pagan beliefs and observed, "Whom therefore ye ignorantly worship, *him* declare I unto you." *(Acts 17:23)* The apostle wanted the people to understand that God was not comprised of idols, figurines, and ornaments. There was only one God. Paul declared "Him"—ONE—to the Athenians. Paul knew that there was one Lord; the Lord was God; and Jesus Christ was Lord and God. *(Ephesians 4:5; Psalm 100:3; Acts 9:5; John 20:28)*

Peter and Paul baptized in the name of Jesus Christ, because they understood that the **name** of the Father, and of the Son, and of the Holy Ghost was Jesus Christ. However, despite their examples, which are recorded in the scriptures, false prophets read Jesus' statement to baptize in the **name** of the Father, and of the Son, and of the Holy Ghost and refuse to baptize in the **name** of Jesus Christ. The ignorant false prophets know that Jesus was the name of the Son, but evidently fear that, if they baptize in the name of Jesus Christ, they will omit the names of the Father and Holy Ghost. Thus, they repeat Jesus' command but disobey His commandment. Their followers, therefore, cannot enter the Kingdom of God. They have not been born again of the water; they have not been baptized in the name of Jesus Christ. *(John 3:5; Acts 2:38)*

——————————————— **Name of God** ———————————————

Many terms were used to describe the God of Abraham, Isaac, and Jacob. Jeremiah observed that our God's name was going to be called, "The Lord our Righteousness." *(Jeremiah 23:6)* Holy is His name. *(Luke 1:49)* Unlike the pagans, who named their gods according to their presumed delineated powers, children of God knew that there was only one God *(Mark 12:29; 1 Timothy 2:5)*, and He possessed all power. "And Jesus came and spake unto them, saying, All power is given unto me in heaven and in earth." *(Matthew 28:18)* All power signifies that Jesus was supreme, and to be supreme means to be God. Hence, when Jesus commanded to baptize in the name of the Father, and of the Son, and of the Holy Ghost, the apostles—those who had been taught and sent by Him—readily understood that the name of the Father, Son, and Holy Ghost was Jesus Christ.

In fact, although Paul was not an apostle when Jesus taught His disciples how to baptize, James, Peter, and John, who walked with Jesus, gave Paul the right hand of fellowship to demonstrate that Paul correctly understood the gospel. *(Galatians 2:9; John 1:42)*

Mystery of Godliness

There is no dispute that understanding godliness is a mystery; however, it is given unto the children of God to understand the mystery. *(Matthew 13:11)* Those who walk in the spirit are able to understand the things of the spirit. "And without controversy great is the mystery of godliness: God was manifest in the flesh, justified in the spirit, seen of angels, preached unto the Gentiles, believed on in the world, received up into glory." *(1 Timothy 3:16)* Individuals who have read the scriptures should immediately perceive that Jesus walked in the world as a man (manifest in the flesh), possessed power over all demons (justified in the spirit), preached to the multitudes (preached unto the Gentiles), had disciples (believed on in the world), and ascended back into heaven (received up into glory). The mystery of godliness is not controversial because it is open to different interpretations; it is controversial because the Holy Ghost has opened the understanding of them that believe, while Satan has blinded the minds of them that believe not. *(Matthew 13:11; 2 Corinthians 4:3)*

Jesus Christ commanded the apostles, including Peter and Paul, to teach the people. Those who do not teach what the apostles taught are false teachers, which is why Jesus used the terms Father, Son, and Holy Ghost. He spoke in parables to expose messengers of Satan. According to the false prophets, there is a triune god—a God the Father, a God the Son, and a God the Holy Ghost—three separate and distinct persons in the godhead—commonly referred to as the Trinity.

Jesus – the Son of God

Most people will readily understand that when Jesus spoke of the Father, He was speaking of the One who created the Heaven and earth. "For God so loved the world, that He gave his only begotten Son, that whosoever believeth in him should not perish, but have everlasting life." *(John 3:16)* The Father created the world and sacrificed His Son to save those that believed. Everyone should understand that the Father created the world, and He is the Father of the Son, Jesus Christ. "And Simon Peter answered and said, Thou art the Christ, the Son of the living God." *(Matthew 16:16)*

Remember: The baby born to Mary, Jesus Christ, was God's only begotten Son. *(John 3:16)* God did not have another Son other than the baby born to Mary. Thus, Mary, a virgin, conceived (created) the child in collaboration with the Father. The Son of God did not exist before. God's only begotten Son was born of a woman, the virgin Mary. *(Isaiah 7:14; Isaiah 9:6; Matthew 1:21; Matthew 1:23)*

The Holy Ghost is the Father

The scripture observes that "the birth of Jesus Christ was on this wise: When as his **mother** Mary was espoused to Joseph, before they came together, **she was found with child of the Holy Ghost**." *(Matthew 1:18)* Further, the scripture observes, an angel appeared unto Joseph in a dream and told him, "fear not to take unto thee Mary thy wife: **for that which is conceived in her is of the Holy Ghost**." *(Matthew 1:20)* Mary, a virgin, *conceived* a child. "Therefore the Lord himself shall give you a sign; Behold a virgin

shall conceive, and bear a son, and shall call his name Immanuel."
(Isaiah 7:14; Luke 1:30-32; Matthew 1:23) Mary was found with
child **conceived** of the Holy Ghost. Conceived means created.
Mary was found with child conceived of the Holy Ghost. The Holy
Ghost and Mary conceived the child. The Holy Ghost was Jesus'
Father; Mary was Jesus' mother.

Father is not a name. Father simply describes Creator. Holy
Ghost is not a name. It simply describes God as a Holy Spirit. "In
the beginning God created the heaven and the earth. And the earth
was without form, and void; and darkness was upon the deep. And
the Spirit of God moved upon the face of the waters." *(Genesis
1:1-2)* Hence, the Spirit of God (Holy Ghost) created (Father) the
heaven and earth. Son is not a name. Son simply describes the
child conceived (created) by the father and mother. The Holy Ghost
created (fathered) the Heaven and earth. The Holy Ghost created
(fathered) the Son. Jesus was conceived of the Holy Ghost (spirit)
and conceived of Mary (flesh-and-blood). Jesus was born of the
spirit (Son of Spirit) and born of a woman (Son of flesh). He was
spirit and natural. He was the Son of God *(1 John 4:15)* and the
Son of Man. *(Matthew 20:28)* When we are born again, we are
Sons of God—children who have been born of the Spirit. *(John
1:12; Galatians 4:7; Romans 8:17)* We are Sons of God and Sons of
men. We were conceived (fathered) by the spirit (Sons of God) and
conceived (fathered) of the flesh (sons of men).

(Daughters, do not allow the term Son trouble you. There
are no males and females in Heaven. Fathers, mothers, sons and
daughters are natural terms; spirits are neither male nor female.
The term Father simply means Creator. The terms Father and Son
are used because natural men create natural life. In biology, the
sperm fertilizes (creates life within) the egg; the male chromosome
determines the child's gender, etc. Consider: the angel told Mary
that, "The Holy Ghost shall come upon thee, and the power of the
Highest shall overshadow thee: therefore also that holy **thing** which
shall be born of thee shall be called the Son of God." *(Luke 1:35)* The
angel called Jesus a thing because, since Jesus was conceived of the

Holy Ghost, He was not considered flesh. Jesus' Father was Spirit; Jesus was conceived of the Spirit; and Jesus walked in the Spirit; hence, Jesus, who did not walk after the flesh, was not considered in the flesh. He was manifested in the flesh, yet He crucified the flesh to walk in the Spirit. "But ye are not in the flesh, but in the Spirit, if so be that the Spirit of God dwell in you." *(Romans 8:9)* Since Jesus was conceived of the Spirit and walked in the Spirit, He was not characterized by the angel as flesh. The angel, who knew that God (Spirit) was in Christ (flesh), called Him a thing—a holy sacrifice.)

The Holy Ghost, the Spirit of God, is the power that overshadowed Mary; the Holy Ghost is the power that came upon Peter and the other disciples in the upper room; the Holy Ghost descended like a dove upon Jesus; and the Holy Ghost is the power we receive when we are born again. *(Acts 1:8; Luke 3:22; John 1:12; Joel 2:28; Acts 2:17)* The Holy Ghost transmutes us from the children of Satan (children of a pagan god; children of corruption; flesh-and-blood creatures) into the children of God (children of truth; spiritual beings).

Jesus was called the Son of God because God (Holy Spirit) fathered (created) the flesh-and-blood child within Mary's womb. "That which is born of the {Holy} spirit is spirit." *(John 3:6)* The Holy Ghost was Jesus' Father. Jesus' spirit came from God. Jesus was called the Son of man because He was conceived of the flesh. "That which is born of the flesh is flesh." *(John 3:6)* Jesus was not naturally the son of a man; Son of man implies that Jesus was a child of flesh and blood. Adam is the father of all flesh, which is why in Adam all died. Eve is the mother of all the living; all flesh-and-blood beings come out of the womb of a woman. All flesh comes out of the womb of a woman, and the woman came out of the womb of a man. Since the life of the flesh is in the blood, as a flesh-and-blood being, Jesus was called the Son of Man.

In human terms, father describes the man who, along with the woman, created the child. There are no men in Heaven. There are no women in Heaven. There are no children in Heaven. Everyone in Heaven is spirit. They are neither male nor female. God is not a natural father with a penis and sperms. God is a Holy Spirit. *(John 4:24; 1 Peter 1:15-16)* Father simply means that the Holy Spirit created flesh-and-blood beings on the earth. Son of God simply means Son of Spirit (born of the spirit). Son of Man simply means Son of flesh (born of flesh-and-blood). The Holy Ghost overshawdowed Mary and created a child within her womb. The Spirit of the Father was within the flesh-and-blood child inside of the mother—God in Christ. Ergo, the child had two lives: the life of the Father (spirit) and life of the mother (flesh and blood)—Son of God and Son of Man. No man was involved in the creation of Jesus Christ; no sperm was needed. He needed the spirit of the Father and the blood of the mother. When Jesus was on the cross, the spirit (eternal life) came out of the body. The blood flowed out of the body and died. The Holy Ghost (Father), who had manifested Himself in the flesh and likewise taken on flesh-and-blood like His children, sacrificed its natural life of flesh-and-blood to redeem His creation from death. *(Hebrews 2:14-15)*

The Holy Ghost is the Father. "In the beginning God created (Father) the heaven and earth. And the earth was without form, and void; and darkness was upon the face of the deep. And the Spirit of God moved upon the face of the waters." *(Genesis 1:1-2)* God is a spirit. *(John 4:24)* God is holy. *(Psalm 99:5)* He is the Holy Spirit (Holy Ghost) who created the heaven and earth. He is the Holy Spirit who overshadowed Mary and conceived Jesus Christ. *(Matthew 1:18-20)*

——————— **The Father, Son, and Holy Ghost Are One** ———————

It should be clear that the name of the Son is Jesus Christ. It should also be clear that the Holy Ghost and Mary conceived Jesus Christ; thus, the Holy Ghost was the Father and Mary the mother of the Son of God. The Holy Ghost is the Father; the spirit created humans. The next section will explain how the Son of God is the Father. The scripture tells us plainly that in Christ all shall be made alive, which implies that Jesus Christ is the Father of those who are born again. Nonetheless, I will further explain the mystery since many readers do not have the Holy Ghost and have been raised on the doctrine of Trinity—the concept that there are three different and separate people that comprise the godhead. According to such false teaching, there is a Father God, a Son God and a Holy Ghost God. Because the carnal mind cannot understand the things of the spirit, I will preface my continuation of the mystery with the use of a natural analogy.

A student poured water in a glass. The water was liquid. The student took the glass and placed it in a freezer. The water froze. The frozen water (ice) was solid. The student subsequently took the ice (solid water) and placed it in a pot on the stove. The heat caused the ice to thaw and converted the solid back into a liquid. The student turned the temperature up, which caused some of the water to steam. The steam was a gas. The initial glass of water was converted into three different forms: liquid, solid, and gas. There was not three separate and distinct glasses of water; it was one glass of water.

Jesus Christ, a Spirit *(Philippians 1:19)*, created a flesh-and-blood body within the womb of a woman and filled the body with His spirit *(God in Christ; Creator within the sacrifice; 1 John 4:2)* and redeemed the world back to Himself *(2 Corinthians 5:19)* Jesus formed us from the womb and redeemed us from corruption. He stretched forth the heavens alone and spreadeth abroad the earth by Himself. *(Isaiah 44:24)* Jesus, a spirit, had simply made Himself a body in the likeness of men. *(Philippians 2:7)*

———————— **Abraham Rejoiced to See My Day** ————————

Jesus told some Jews that Abraham had rejoiced to see Him. How in the world, the unbelieving Jews asked, could Jesus have met Abraham? Abraham had been dead for nearly 2,000 years. Jesus was not 50 years old. Jesus told them that He existed before Abraham. They saw Jesus as a liar and picked up stones intending to kill Him. *(John 8:56-59)* Carnal-minded people, disconnected from the Spirit of God, could not understand how Jesus existed nearly 2,000 years before. They were comparable to the ignorant Nicodemus, who did not understand how a man could be born again.

Jesus is the Alpha and Omega, the first and the last, the beginning and the ending. *(Revelation 22:13)* John wrote, in the beginning was the Word, and the Word was with God, and the Word was God. *(John 1:1)* John added, "He was in the world, the world was made by Him, and the world knew Him not." *(John 1:10)* God created the world and subsequently came into the world, yet the world did not know Him. How did the world not know the Father who created the world? Because they saw Him as the only begotten of the Father. *(John 1:14)* They saw Him as the Son of the Father. He was the Father but they saw Him as the Son, because the Father was spirit but had manifested Himself in the flesh. *(1 Timothy 3:16)* The Holy Spirit within the Son of God (God in Christ) was the Holy Spirit that created the world (the Spirit of Jesus Christ). When they saw Him as the Son, they saw flesh-and-blood; they did not know that He had two lives: a life conceived of everlasting spirit and a life conceived of flesh-and blood. They did not know that the Invisible Spirit had made Itself visible—God manifested in the flesh. *(1 Timothy 3:16)* They did not know that the Creator (Holy Spirit) had likewise taken on the flesh-and-blood form of His creation. *(Hebrews 2:14-15)*

Isaiah announced that the child that was born, the son that was given was the mighty God and the everlasting Father. *(Isaiah 9:6)* Jesus was the Father, which is why He told Philip that those who saw Him saw the Father. *(John 14:9)* Jesus was the Father who had made the world, but the people did not know Him. The people saw flesh-and-blood, so they saw Him as the Son. *(John 1:1; John 1:10; John 1:14)* They did not understand that within the Son (flesh and blood) was the Spirit of God, who had made the world.

The Holy Ghost overshadowed Mary and created Jesus, yet Jesus existed before Mary. Jesus existed thousands of years before Mary. Abraham had rejoiced to see His day. *(John 8:56-59)* Jesus had followed the children of Israel out of Egypt. *(1 Corinthians 10:4)* As a spirit, Jesus had created the world; as a man, He died and redeemed the world from corruption. "Thus saith the Lord, thy redeemer, and he that formed thee from the womb, I am the Lord that maketh all things; that stretcheth forth the heavens alone; that spreadeth abroad the earth by myself." *(Isaiah 45:24)* "Thus saith the Lord, thy Redeemer, the Holy One of Israel; I am the Lord thy God which teacheth thee to profit, which leadeth thee by the way that thou shouldest go." *(Isaiah 48:17)* Jesus came to teach us of His ways, so that we could walk in His path. *(Isaiah 2:2-3)* He was our example. *(John 13:15; 1 Peter 2:21)* Jesus was our shepherd; He was also our lamb. *(John 10:11; John 1:29)* He was the savior; He was also the sacrifice. *(1 John 4:14; John 3:16)* He was the Father and the Son.

──────── **Eat of My Flesh; Drink of My Blood** ────────

God broke the power of Egypt over the children of Israel. The people went through the sea, where they were baptized. As the people journeyed through the sea, the angel of God stood as a pillar of fire between the children of Israel and the pursuing Egyptians. It gave light to the people of God, yet it created darkness for their enemies. *(Exodus 14:19-24)* God saved His people and destroyed the Egyptians. *(Exodus 14:30-13)* During their journey to the Promised Land, the people of God ate the same meat and drank the same drink; they drank of Christ, who had followed them. *(1 Corinthians 10:4)* Christ existed before He was born. Mary's son was God in Christ (spirit inside flesh-and-blood) redeeming the world back to spirit. Mary's son was the Lamb of God (redeemer) who had formed the people from the womb (Creator). *(Isaiah 44:24)* In fact, Jesus is our Father. He is the Father of all that are born again of the spirit and have their soul restored. "For as in Adam all die, even so in Christ shall all be made alive." *(1 Corinthians 15:22)* Jesus breathed into His disciples (mighty rushing wind; *Acts 2:2*) and restored our soul. *(John 20:22)*

Jesus came into the earth and entered into a new covenant

with the human family. He would deliver us from the hands of our enemies, whereby we would serve Him in holiness and righteousness all the days of our lives. *(Luke 1:67-75)* He drank out of the cup of sacrifice, and we drink out of the cup of sacrifice. We ate of His flesh and drank of His blood. His flesh was meat. Through His knowledge, we escaped from captivity (pollution of this world). His blood was drink. Having learned how Satan exploited our corruption, we exercised self-discipline and denied ourselves. We refrained from indulging in the lust and corruption inherent within our blood. He shed His life, and, following His example, we shed our life. We were buried with Christ in baptism. We renounced the life of the flesh within our blood, and chose to walk in the life of the spirit. Through His knowledge, Jesus destroyed the works of Satan in our lives and set us free from sin.

The same Christ that saved the children of Israel out of the bondage of Egypt is the same Christ that saved us out of the bondage of sin. Jesus was a spirit when He saved the children of Israel; He was a spirit when He saved us. Christ was a spirit who dwelled in Heaven, even as He walked as a man in the earth. "And no man hath ascended up to heaven, but he that came down from heaven, even the Son of Man which is in heaven." *(John 3:13)* Flesh-and-blood cannot enter Heaven, because flesh-and-blood is corrupt, which is why Jesus had to shed His blood. He was nonetheless in Heaven as the Son, because the spirit within Him (God in Christ) was also in Heaven. The Son that was born was the Son that was given as sacrifice. The Son that was sacrificed was the everlasting Father. *(Isaiah 9:6)* He was God and man; spirit and flesh; the everlasting Father and the sacrificial Son. On the cross, the Holy Spirit (everlasting Father) came out of the body and allowed the Son (flesh-and-blood) to die. Jesus sacrificed the life of His flesh to pay the ransom for those whom He had allowed to be taken into the captivity of sin.

Understand: When the scripture tells us that God so loved the world, that He gave His only begotten Son, we should readily understand that a God of integrity would not sacrifice His child to atone for something He created. We should also understand that if God had a child, the child would have to be a spirit, because that born of the spirit is spirit. The scripture plainly tells us that the Son of God was born of a virgin, and that He was the only child God begat. Hence, God did not have a child who came down from Heaven. The Son of God was flesh-and blood. Jesus existed before Abraham, and Jesus followed the children of Israel out of Egypt. Jesus was the Father of the universe; He was the alpha. Jesus, the Son of God, was the flesh-and-blood body that Jesus, the Holy Ghost, created and used to reconcile the world unto Himself. The life of the flesh in the body was shed on the cross. The life of the Spirit in the body came from God and went back to God. The spiritual life in the body was the Father, the Holy Ghost, which was why God was in the world, the world was made by Him, but they saw Him as the Son. *(John 1:1; John 1:10; John 1:14)*

—— **I Am the Alpha; I Am the First; I am the Beginning** ——

Jesus was the Alpha; Jesus was the beginning; Jesus was first. *(Revelation 22:13)* The Alpha is the Father. Why did the people see Him as the Son if He was the Alpha? Jesus, the Son of God, did not have a natural father. He was His own Father. Jesus, the Holy Spirit, fathered (created) a body for Himself *(Forasmuch then as the children are partakers of flesh-and-blood; He also Himself likewise took part of the same: Hebrew 2:14).* The flesh-and-blood body conceived by God with Mary allowed God to have the blood necessary to offer up as sacrifice for the sins of the people. Thus, Jesus (Father/Creator) made the world, took on a body like the children (creation) and died for His creation's sins. He made the world; He was in the world; but they saw Him as the Son (flesh), because He was in the form of a Holy Spirit when when He created the world. The Son was the flesh-and-blood body created to die for the sins of the people; the Holy Spirit was the Father "who himself likewise took part of the same" as His flesh-and-blood children. *(John 1:1; John 1:10; John 1:14)* The term Father simply connotes that the Son (flesh-and-blood body) was conceived by the Holy Ghost in collaboration with the mother, Mary. Father also references the Creator, who was Jesus. *(Revelation 22:13)*

The Jews thought Jesus was lying when He said Abraham rejoiced to see His day, because they saw a flesh-and-blood body. However, Jesus told the truth. Abraham had rejoiced to see Jesus. He and Jesus had celebrated Abraham's slaughter of the kings. *(Genesis 14:17-21)* Abraham was thankful that Jesus had given him victory over the kings, and gave Him ten percent of what he had taken from them. Jesus, Melchizedek, was God. He had no Father or Mother. He had neither beginning of life nor end of days. *(Hebrews 7:1-4)* So when Jesus said that He was the Alpha and the Omega, He was telling the truth. When Jesus said He was the first and the last, the beginning and the end, He was telling the truth. When He said Abraham rejoiced to see His day, He was telling the truth. Jesus Christ created the Heaven and earth. Jesus, Melchizedek, with no beginning of life or end of days, was an everlasting spirit. Jesus was the mighty God, the everlasting Father. *(Isaiah 9:6; Isaiah 7:14)* So, when the people saw Jesus as the Son of God, they also saw the one who made the world in the beginning. They did not see the eternal spirit (Father); they saw the flesh-and-blood sacrifice (Son). The Holy Spirit was the Father manifested in the flesh of His Son, i.e., God in Christ—Creator manifested in His creation. Those who saw the Father also saw the Son. *(John 14:9)* They were one and the same. *(John 10:30)* Jesus was God and the Son of God; He was the everlasting Father within the flesh-and-blood sacrifice reconciling the world unto Himself.

God in Christ

The wages of sin is death, yet it was God who caused us to go into sin. God allowed Adam to die; God brought us back to life. *(1 Corinthians 15:22)* The Lord took on a body and served as a mediator between Himself and the human family—"God was in Christ reconciling the world unto himself." *(2 Corinthians 5:19)*

God so loved the world that He gave His only begotten Son; the Holy Ghost sacrificed His own flesh-and-blood life. *(John 3:16; Hebrews 2:14-15)* The Son that was given was the everlasting Father. *(Isaiah 9:6)* The Holy Ghost (everlasting Father) came out of the body on the cross and allowed the Son (flesh-and-blood) to die. The life of the flesh was in the blood, and Jesus shed His blood. Jesus renounced the life of corruption and ransomed His people from the grave of sin. He redeemed us from corruption and gave us new life. Jesus Christ is our Father. He created Adam, who sinned and caused all to die; Jesus manifested Himself in the flesh, shed His blood for the remissions of sin, and redeemed the world back to Himself.

Just as He had tested Job to see if he would obey, just as he had tested Abraham to see if he would obey, God tests all of us to see if we will obey. He placed us in sin to see what was in our hearts, whether we would obey or not. *(Judges 3:4)* He delivered those who wanted to serve Him out of bondage. Further, He set an example for us to follow. Although He was the Almighty, being found in the form of a servant, He became obedient unto death, even the death of the cross. Since Jesus tested us and placed us in the bondage of sin, He died that we might receive remission of sins. He will not impute our sins to us, but will forgive us, because we were conceived in sin. When given an opportunity to overcome sin, we obeyed. We are justified in receiving His mercy and will inherit eternal life.

The Holy Ghost created (Father) human beings, redeemed us from corruption (Son), and breathed into us a new life (Holy Ghost). In Christ was all the fullness of the godhead bodily *(Colossians 2:9)*: when we saw the Son (redeemer), we saw the Father (creator) *(John 14:9)*; the Holy Ghost (spirit) which created the Heaven and earth (Father) was in the Son (flesh-and-blood) reconciling the world unto Himself. *(2 Corinthians 5:19)* God (spirit) was in Christ (flesh-and-blood). The spirit came out on the cross and allowed the flesh to die. After the flesh died, the spirit raised the body out of the grave. The blood had been shed; hence, the life of the flesh

(Son) was not in the body; the life in the body was the Holy Spirit. Remember: Jesus told the people that if they destroyed the temple, He would raise it up within three days. He spoke of the temple of His body. Jesus' body is the Holy Spirit (celestial). After three days and three nights, He raised up the temple of His body (the flesh-and-blood body) out of the grave which had housed His spirit. When we are filled with the Holy Ghost, we are now a part of the body of Christ, filled with the Spirit of Jesus Christ. *(Philippians 1:19)* We have a flesh-and-blood body, but we are not humans; we are spirits. *(Romans 8:9)*

Of course, when the spirit raised Jesus' body out of the grave, the spirit was building His church. Christ was delivering His servants out of the grave of sin. Those who made a covenant with Him by sacrifice and turned from their wickedness were forgiveness. Those who made the choice to shed their blood and crucify the sin in their lives to walk in the Spirit of Jesus Christ (body of Christ; lively stones; church) have been resurrected from the grave of sin and have been integrated with God. We acknowledged Jesus was Lord and refused to rebel against Him. Jesus poured His spirit upon us; we received the Holy Ghost and became Sons of God.

Just as Jesus Christ (spirit) was within the flesh-and-blood body born to the Virgin Mary, Jesus Christ lives within us when we are born again of the spirit. *(2 Corinthians 13:5)* We have His spirit, the Holy Ghost, within our soul, which is why the Son is also our Father. He died and ransomed us from the grave. In Christ, we have been made alive. Jesus created within us a new life; He is our Father. He poured out His spirit upon us. "That which is born of the spirit is spirit." We have become new creatures, spiritual creatures, Sons of God.

The Holy Ghost is the spirit that God breathed into Adam and made him a living soul. The Holy Ghost is the spirit that Christ breathed upon His disciples. *(John 20:22)* The Holy Ghost was the breath of life that came upon those in the upper room on the day of Pentecost. *(Acts 2:1-4)* The Holy Ghost was the breath of God that restored life to the dry bones. *(Ezekiel 1:14)* The Holy Ghost was the breath of God that parted the sea and allowed the children of Israel to pass over on dry land. *(Exodus 15:8)* Jesus created all of our lives. He created the earth (Father), took on a body of flesh-and-blood (Son) and died for the sins of the people. After He delivered the people out of captivity, then gave He (Father) them power (Holy Ghost) to become His Sons. Our Father, Jesus Christ, redeemed us from the grave and gave us a new life.

Jesus Lived Before His Mother Was Born

Jesus led the children of Israel out of Egypt more than a thousand years before Mary was born. *(1 Corinthians 10:4)* Jesus told the Jews that Abraham rejoiced to see His day; Abraham lived nearly two thousand years before Mary had her Son. John said Jesus made the world, although the people saw Him as the Son of God. *(John 1:10, 14)* Jesus Christ was simply God (Spirit) manifested in the flesh. *(1 Timothy 3:16)* In other words, God, the Holy Spirit, fathered a flesh-and-blood body for Himself. He had created Adam and Eve—the father and mother of all the flesh—and the Holy Spirit likewise took on the same type of flesh-and-blood. Although the Spirit of God continued to fill Heaven and earth, the Holy Spirit dwelled within a flesh-and-blood body (God in Christ) and offered up His natural life as sacrifice. *(Hebrews 2:14-15)* Thus, those who saw the Son also saw the Father. *(John 14:9)*

Remember, the prophet Isaiah told us that a child was born, and a son was given. Jesus was born in the flesh, and Jesus died in the flesh. However, Jesus had another life inside of Him. He was both spirit and human. He gave His flesh-and-blood life as sacrifice, but His Spirit lived from everlasting to everlasting. That child that was born (Jesus Christ) was God with us. *(Isaiah 7:14; Matthew 1:23)* The child that was born, the Son that was given to redeem the people from their sin, was Jesus Christ—the mighty God, the everlasting Father. *(Isaiah 9:6)*

Recapitulate: Since the Father was spirit, the Son was spirit.

Jesus was also called the Son of Man. In spiritual parlance, Father does not mean male; Father means creator. Son does not imply male; Son implies flesh-and-blood body created by the Father. God created woman (Eve) out of the womb of a man (Adam), and created mankind out of the womb of a woman (Eve was the mother of all the living). *(Genesis 2:22; Genesis 3:20)* Hence, when the scripture says that those who overcome will be His son, it is referring to all of mankind; it is referring to the flesh-and-blood creatures that were fathered (created) by the spirit. "He that overcometh shall inherit all things; and I will be his God, and he shall be my son." *(Revelation 21:7)* Just as Jesus was born of the Spirit (Son), those who overcome corruption and are born again of the spirit are Sons (spiritual children) of God.

-------- **If They Had Known** --------

Isaiah told the people that their God was going to come and save them. *(Isaiah 35:4)* Jesus Christ was God with us; He had come to save us from our sins. *(Matthew 1:23)* The people, however, did not know He was the Creator (Spirit; Father), because they saw Him as a created being (flesh-and-blood; Son). *(John 1:14)* Moses asked God what was His name, so He could tell the children of Israel when they asked. God told Moses to tell the people, I Am that I Am; tell the people that I exist. *(Exodus 3:14)* Jesus could not reveal His name, because had he revealed His name and the people learned who He was, they would not have crucified Him. *(1 Corinthians 2:8)* Without His sacrifice, there would not have been remission of sin. *(Hebrews 9:22)* Jesus concealed His name until He had completed His works in the earth, then He sent His apostles to teach the people. They declared His name: At the name of Jesus, every knee shall bow and every tongue shall confess that He is Lord. *(Philippians 2:10; Revelation 17:14)* There is only one Lord, and the Lord is God. *(Ephesians 4:5; Psalm 100:3)*

———————— **Understand the Mystery of Christ** ————————

God used parables in the scriptures to help people differentiate between those who were led of the Spirit and those who were not. For example, two adjacent scriptures tell us that God made man in "our" likeness and in "his" image. *(Genesis 1:26-27)* Therefore, one scripture gives the idea that man was made in the likeness of more than one person, whereas another scripture tells us that man was made in the image of one person. The Holy Ghost is the Father. That is one person. The child born to the Virgin Mary was God's only begotten Son. Hence, there was no Son in Heaven. Further, the Son was not born until thousands of years had passed from the creation of the earth, so the Son was not there when the earth was created. In fact, the Son could not have been in Heaven. The Son was flesh-and-blood, and flesh-and-blood cannot inhabit Heaven. *(1 Corinithians 15:50)* The Holy Ghost created the Heavens alone and spreaded abroad the earth by Himself. *(Nehemiah 9:6; Job 9:8; Isaiah 44:24)* Why did God say "us" and "our" if He created man alone?

In the beginning, God created man and woman to carry out His purpose. Who would obey Him? Who would rebel against Him? He allowed Satan to overtake the human family. In due time, God manifested Himself in the flesh (Jesus was God with us; *Matthew 1:23*) and redeemed the people. God, as Spirit, could create man. However, as Spirit, Jesus could not redeem man. Redemption required blood. Thus, in order to fulfill His purpose, He counseled with His own will. *(Ephesians 1:11)* Jesus took on a different form (made in the likeness of man; *Philippians 2:7*) to redeem man. Of course, man was made in His likeness. *(Genesis 1:26)* "Forasmuch then as the children are partakers of flesh and blood, he also himself likewise took part of the same; that through death he might destroy him that had the power of death, that is, the devil;" *(Hebrews 2:14)* He took on the form of a servant—flesh-and blood. As a result of His power, Jesus was both Lord and Christ— He was Holy Spirit (the King of kings and Lord of lord) and flesh and blood (human sacrifice offered to redeem man from sin); He was both the Father and the Son. He formed us from the womb and redeemed us from corruption. He sacrificed His flesh-and-blood body to reconcile us unto Himself—Spirit.

Remember: the pillar of fire separated the children of Israel from their enemies. The fire was light to the people of God but darkness to the Egptians. *(Exodus 14:19-20)* Remember: Judas, not Iscariot, asked the Lord, "how is it that thou wilt manifest thyself unto us, and not unto the world?" *(John 14:22)* Jesus answered, the Holy Ghost "shall teach you all things." *(John 14:26)* God answers by fire. *(1 King 18:24)* Jesus spoke in parables and moved in mysterious ways. *(Mark 4:11; Roman 16:25; Revelation 10:7)* Those who walked in the presence of God walked in the light. It was given unto them to understand the mystery. *(Luke 8:10)* The Holy Ghost is light to them. Those who were separated from the Holy Ghost but walked after the flesh were "none of his." *(Romans 8:9)* The Holy Ghost was darkness to them. The gospel was hidden to them.

If the people had been taught by men of God, they would easily understand the mystery of Christ. Who shed His blood to redeem the people from their sins? Jesus Christ. "Take heed therefore unto yourselves, and to all the flock, over the which the Holy Ghost hath made you overseers, to feed the church of God, which he hath purchased with his own blood." *(Acts 20:28)* The Holy Ghost is a spirit and does not have blood. However, the Holy Ghost took on a body (God in Christ) and shed His blood to reconcile the world to Himself.

If the people had been taught by men of God, they would easily understand the mystery of Christ. How did the human family receive prophecy? "For the prophecy came not in old time by the will of man: but holy men of God spake as they were moved by the Holy Ghost." *(2 Peter 1:21)* The Holy Ghost moved on holy men to prophesy. What is the spirit of prophecy? "For the testimony of Jesus is the spirit of prophecy." *(Revelation 19:10)* Jesus, the Holy Ghost, spoke to the holy men of old and moved on them to prophesy. Remember: Jesus made the world in the beginning.

(Revelation 22:13; John 1:10) He was the word. *(John 1:1)* Thus, He told the holy men of old what to prophecy. When He came in the flesh, He was the word made flesh. The people did not know who He was, because they saw Him as the Son (flesh and blood). *(John 1:14)* Jesus, the everlasting Father, was the Holy Ghost (spirit) manifested in the flesh (Son of God). *(Isaiah 9:6; 1 Timothy 3:16; Matthew 1:23; Hebrews 2:14-15)*

The Spirit of Jesus Christ is the Spirit of God. Jesus Christ breathed upon the waters and brought the children of Israel out of the graves of Egypt; Jesus breathed upon the dry bones and brought them out of the grave; and Jesus breathed upon believers and gave us the Holy Ghost. *(Exodus 15:8; Ezekiel 37:9-14; John 20:22; Acts 2:1-4)* Jesus Christ existed before He was born of a woman; He was the everlasting Father *(Isaiah 9:6)* in the flesh-and-blood sacrifice (God in Christ) reconciling the world back to Himself. *(2 Corinthians 5:19)* He created us (Father); He redeemed us (Son), and He saves us (Holy Ghost) from our sins.

– Name of the Father, and of the Son, and of the Holy Ghost –

Those who cannot see Jesus as the Father are like those who could not believe He existed before Abraham—their carnal minds refuse to allow them to see Him other than as the child born to Mary. *(John 8:56-58)* Those who cannot see Jesus as the Father are like those whom John wrote about, when he observed that, He was in the world, the world was made by Him, and the world knew Him not. *(John 1:1; John 1:10)* They saw Him as simply a man. *(John 1:14; the Son)* The Father was the Holy Ghost (Spirit) who created the world; the Son was simply the Holy Ghost (Spirit) made flesh. The name of the Father was Jesus Christ. "I am come in my Father's name, and ye receive me not: if another shall come in his own name, him ye will receive." *(John 5:43)* The name of the Son was Jesus Christ. "Behold, a virgin shall be with child, and shall bring forth a son, and they shall call his name, Emmanuel, which being interpreted is, God with us." *(Matthew 1:21-23)* The name of the

Holy Ghost is Jesus Christ. "But the Comforter, which is the Holy Ghost, whom the Father will send in my name, he shall teach you all things, and bring all things to your remembrance, whatsoever I have said unto you." *(John 14:26)* The apostles observed that the name of the Father, and of the Son, and of the Holy Ghost was Jesus Christ, but the carnal-minded people did not understand the scriptures. The apostles understood the scriptures, which is why they baptized in the name of Jesus Christ. We are commanded that whatever we do, in words or deeds, to do all in the name of the Lord Jesus. *(Colossians 3:17)* The power is in the name of Jesus Christ. *(Luke 10:17)* Jesus has all power. *(Matthew 28:18)* Jesus Christ, the Almighty God, is the King of kings and Lord of lord. *(Revelation 19:16)*

─────── **Be Baptized in the Name of Jesus Christ** ───────

For the purpose of this chapter, the paramount issue is that Jesus commanded the apostles to baptize the people in the name of the Father, and of the Son, and of the Holy Ghost—and the apostles baptized the people in the **name** of Jesus Christ. Jesus opened the apostles' understanding *(Luke 24:45)* and commanded them to teach the people. *(Matthew 28:19)* Whether the people understand the mystery or not, they should admit that the apostles, Jesus' messengers in the earth, understood the scriptures. Further, Peter, James, and John gave Paul the right hand of fellowship, which indicated that Paul also had the right understanding of the word of God. If an angel preaches anything different than what the apostles taught, the angel is going to hell. *(Galatians 1:8)* Those who reject the apostles' teachings will be destroyed. (Hosea 4:6)

CHAPTER NINETEEN
CONCLUSION

In writing this book, one of my principal objectives has been to impress upon the reader that Master means male teacher, and Jesus came to teach us of His ways, so that we could walk in His path. If we learned of His ways and walked in His path, we would walk as He walked—perfect. Jesus exhorted the people to return back to spirit. He did not want the people to remain bewitched by Satan and lust for their own destruction. He came to open the eyes of the people and set them free from the bondage of sin.

As a visionary, Jesus foresaw that false prophets would rise up and deceive almost everyone—only a few would inherit eternal life. Because He did not want any to perish, He warned the people to beware of false prophets. Satan would use false prophets to keep the people in darkness, which would allow him to maintain power over them and keep them separated from the spirit. *(Acts 26:18)*

Since the fear of the Lord is the beginning of wisdom, the devil's principal method of deception, as Eve learned to her detriment, is to disarm the people by appealing to their vanity. As a spirit, Satan cannot talk directly to flesh-and-blood beings; accordingly, he has sent blind false prophets to speak for him. The false prophets teach the people that God loves them unconditionally. According to Satan's messengers, God will love them regardless of their wickedness and disobedience.

When we love someone, we value the person. The scripture

repeatedly denotes that God will cast sinners out of His sight; God hates sinners and will give sinners over into the hands of their enemies. Jesus told the people that He was going to separate the wheat from the tare. The wheat would be placed in His barn, whereas the tare would be burned. In other words, the wheat had value and could be used in the Kingdom of God; the tare was worthless and would be destroyed. *(Matthew 13:24-30)*

Satan is subtle. His blind false teachers will not explicitly tell the people to rebel against God; however, like the children of Israel, most people do not want to give up the only life they know (life of the flesh). Through fear of death, they do not want to confront enemies that they do not believe they can overcome. Satan has sent false prophets to teach the people that they are saved by grace, not by obedience to God's words. The people do not understand that God's grace is His word. *(Acts 20:32)* "He sent his word, and healed them, and delivered them from destructions." *(Psalm 107:20)* Those who wanted to be delivered will obey all of His commandments. *(Matthew 28:20)* God gets His glory when we do the work He has commanded. *(Matthew 5:16)* It is through the word of His grace that He is able to build us up and give us an inheritance among them that are sanctified. *(Acts 20:32)* Hence, grace is the knowledge and power of Jesus Christ. When we obey Him, we escape from the pollution of this world. When the enemy attempts to overtake us, Jesus, the Almighty God, uses His power to save us from death.

Jesus' knowledge is the glorious light that leads us out of darkness and saves us from the enemy. However, those who reject the word of God are going to be destroyed. *(Hosea 4:6)* God has commanded us to live holy. Those who turn from their wickedness and do the works of God are workers of righteousness (children of God); they will be saved from destruction. Those who rebel against God and refuse to turn from their wickedness are workers of iniquity (children of Satan); they will be destroyed. We are going to be judged according to our works. *(Revelation 20:12; Romans 2:6)*

Joshua told the children of Israel that, if they forsook the Lord and served other gods, the Lord, after doing them good, would turn and destroy them. *(Joshua 24:20)* The people listened to the false prophets and rebelled. God destroyed them as Joshua had warned. *(Jude 1:5)* God saved others. After the people rebelled, He also gave them over to their enemies. *(Ezekiel 39:23)* Nonetheless, false prophets teach the people that once they are saved, they are always saved. Such witchcraft is contrary to the word of God. *(Matthew 13:19-22; Luke 8:13; 2 Peter 2:20)* No man who chooses to do the work of God and turns back is fit for the Kingdom of God. *(Luke 9:62)* Stubborn individuals, nevertheless, believe the lying vanities of the false prophets and reject the written word of God.

If God were simply a myth created by men, truth would be of little importance. Our short lives would be of little significance. Since God exists, it is critical we understand His purpose in creating us. Satan and the other fallen angels could not accept that Jesus was Lord. Adam and Eve could not accept that Jesus was Lord. Thus, Jesus allowed Satan to deceive everyone—the entire earth went into darkness. All of us feared death and sacrificed our dignity and integrity. We engaged in all manner of wickedness and evil. We knew that we were weak and frail creatures.

Jesus Christ came and defeated Satan. He demonstrated that He was Lord. There is no god above Jesus; therefore, we should not exalt anyone or anything above Him. Jesus commands those who exalt truth to renounce corruption and embrace integrity. Satan wants the people to exalt themselves and rebel against God. Hence, false prophets teach lying vanities and persuade disobedient people that they are children of God, although the people live in sin. Satan is the father of sinners. *(John 8:34:44)* Like the Roman soldiers, many pretend Jesus is their king, and then they spit in His face and despise His commandments. They honor Jesus with their lips but honor Satan with their lives. *(Matthew 15:8)* They reject Jesus Christ, yet they pay lip service to Him so that when He comes they will be saved from His wrath. However, God is not mocked. Sinners will reap what they have sown.

God sent famine into the earth—not for food or drink, but for His word. The people went into captivity because they lacked knowledge. Jesus subsequently sent His word to heal the people. Those who want to be made whole can escape the pollution of this world through the knowledge of Jesus Christ. We can only remain in captivity if we reject His word. Satan has offered false prophets' lying vanities to bewitch the people. Therefore, the people have a choice: they may believe the word of God and reject the lying vanities of the false prophets; or they may believe the lying vanities of the false prophets and reject the word of God.

No one is so foolish to believe Jesus Christ was crucified so we could serve Satan. We were dead in sin. All of our dignity and integrity had been taken away. Christ came to ransom us from the grave and to give us a new life. He paid the ransom for our sins, so we could escape from death and destruction. He broke the power of Satan over our lives and offered us His grace to restore our integrity. He gave us the opportunity to choose for ourselves whom we wanted to serve. We have the choice to choose life or death.

Renounce Your Natural Inheritance

Although Abraham was positioned to inherit from his pagan father, he had integrity and refused to worship false gods. He renounced his natural inheritance to worship in truth. God blessed him with a spiritual inheritance. Do we have integrity, like Abraham, to admit the truth that Jesus is Lord, and the faith to trust in Him? Or are we like the children of Israel, who, through fear of death, chose to renounce their spiritual inheritance to serve false gods?

Jesus performed miracles and displayed His power to demonstrate that the Spirit of God is not subject to the laws of nature. God has commanded us, as He did Abraham, to come out from pagan worship. He has offered us His power to become His sons. When we are born of the spirit, we are spirits and have power over all demons. We have power over our natural bodies. We can serve the Lord without fear in holiness and righteousness all the days of our life. Or we can reject the Spirit of God and walk after the lust of the flesh. We can rebel against God and reject His power. We can allow Satan to keep us subject to him. Unlike the ignorant false teachers who teach that God gave us unmerited favor, the Lord was required to give us the right to redeem ourselves from corruption. He is a just God and allowed us to choose for ourselves whether to obey or disobey His commandments.

Thief in the Night

Jesus Christ is about to return to the earth and execute judgment. He will return as a thief in the night because most people do not believe He is going to come. Many do not believe He exists. It is going to be a dreadful day when damned men and women realize, like Adam and Eve, that they have been deceived and must live throughout eternity in flames of fire. They were corrupt and chose to embrace corruption. They chose to remain in the bondage of sin.

Jesus prayed and asked the spirit to forgive those who hung Him from the cross—"for they know not what they do." *(Luke 23:34)* Jesus offered them forgiveness because if they had known, they would not have crucified Him. *(1 Corinthians 2:8)* They did not know, however, because God had sent famine into the land and allowed darkness to overtake the people. It was His purpose from the foundation of the earth to come and ransom the people from the grave. Jesus was the light that came into the world to teach the people. Now that Jesus has come, we have no cloak for our sins. *(John 15:22)* Through the grace of God, sin should not have dominion over us; we can overcome sin. *(Romans 6:13-14; Revelation 12:11)*

God has set before us life and death. Are we willing to renounce Satan's corruption and the life of the flesh to bear witness to the truth? Jesus is Lord! Or are we willing to observe the lying vanities of the false prophets and walk after the corruption of our flesh? Unless we are redeemed, we will remain corrupt; and Jesus has made it perfectly clear—corruption cannot inherit incorruption.

We have to rise up out of the grave of sin and walk in the newness of life. In other words, we have to be changed. We must be reconciled with His spirit to enter into His spiritual kingdom. *(Romans 14:17)*

In order to change, we have to give up the only life we have ever known. We have to confront fears and demons that have bedeviled us for years. God knows that our enemies are too strong for us; He knows that He has commanded us to live holy; therefore, He knows that He must save us from our enemies, if we are going to serve Him. A God who cannot lie, He has promised to save all those who call upon His name.

In order to receive forgiveness of sin and obtain mercy, we have to repent of our sins, forsake our ways, and return unto the Lord; we have to change. *(Isaiah 55:7)* Satan, to dissuade us from changing, has sent false prophets to teach us lying vanities: We are saved by grace; Jesus already died for our sins—we don't have to change. Once we are saved, we are always saved—we don't have to change. God loves us unconditionally; God loves us just as we are—we don't have to change. Jesus is our personal savior; Jesus has already paid for your sin—we don't have to change. Nobody is perfect; we are human—we don't have to change. The devil wants us to believe, like he persuaded the other demons, that we can exalt ourselves above the Almighty and live. Jesus took pleasure in destroying His own flesh-and-blood body: He exalted the spirit above the flesh; He exalted the Creator above His creation. He hates every false way. He will not exalt servants above their Lord.

Satan wants sinners to believe that nothing will happen to them when the Lord comes. Isaiah said it was vexation just to understand the wrath God would pour out upon the rebellious. *(Isaiah 28:19)* Felix trembled when Paul told him about the judgment of God to come. *(Acts 24:25)* The rich man was tormented in flames of fire. *(Luke 16:23)* He asked God to allow him to go and warn his brothers to obey God; they did not want to experience the torment of hell. The Lord answered that the people had Moses and the prophets. If the people did not listen to them, they would not listen to one who returned from the grave. *(Luke 16:31)*

When the children of Israel came out of the bondage of Egypt and journeyed to the Promised Land, the Amalekites fought against them. The Lord promised to destroy the Amalekites. At the appointed time, God sent Saul to destroy the Amakites. As Saul went to destroy the Amalekites, he met Kenites. He told them to separate from the Amalekites, "lest I destroy you with them." *(1 Samuel 15:2-6)* In His mercy, God warned those who had joined with His enemies to separate themselves. "So the Kenites departed from among the Amalekites." The Kenites saved themselves from God's wrath. The Lord is going to destroy Satan and has shown mercy unto the people. He has warned us to separate from devils, lest He destroys us with them.

God is not a myth. He created us for His glory. He has raised many from the dead. We bear witness to His existence and saving power. The Lord commands the wicked to forsake his ways and the unrighteous man his thoughts and return unto Him; He will have mercy upon him. *(Isaiah 55:7)* However, the wicked has the right to reject the knowledge of God and believe the lying vanities of the false prophets. They can reject Jesus as Lord and exalt Satan as their king. When the Lord pours out His wrath upon His enemies, He will not spare those who chose to remain among them.

Your body may be in a casket one day; your flesh may die; but your soul will last forever. When you die, you are going to be walking in the holiness of Jesus Christ or walking in corruption like Satan. God has warned the people to obey: We can obey the King or we can incur His wrath. Satan has sent false prophets to deceive you and lead you to believe that nothing will happen to you if you disobey. Do not allow your mind to imagine vain things. "They that observe lying vanities forsake their own mercy." *(Jonah 2:8)*

Printed in the United States
By Bookmasters